THE UAW'S SOUTHERN GAMBLE

THE UAW'S SOUTHERN GAMBLE

Organizing Workers at Foreign-Owned Vehicle Plants

Stephen J. Silvia

ILR PRESS

AN IMPRINT OF CORNELL UNIVERSITY PRESS   ITHACA AND LONDON

First published 2023 by Cornell University Press

Librarians: A CIP catalog record for this book is available from the Library of Congress.

ISBN 978-1-5017-6969-6 (hardcover)
ISBN 978-1-5017-6970-2 (pbk)
ISBN 978-1-5017-6971-9 (epub)
ISBN 978-1-5017-6972-6 (pdf)

To my parents, Pauline Therese Senecal Silvia and William Frank Silvia, I am forever grateful for your love and support, which made it possible for me to become a professor and to write this book.

Contents

Like many books, this project did not start as a book. It began as a working paper for the Hans-Böckler-Stiftung (HBS) on the United Auto Workers' (UAW) ongoing organizing efforts at German automobile plants in the United States. The more I worked on the topic, the more interesting it became to me because it shined a light on so many things: the challenges of gaining union recognition in the southern United States, whether transnational business leaders decide to maintain home-country practice or go native, and the possibilities and limits of transnational cooperation among employee representatives in a more interconnected world.

The UAW's Southern Gamble is a contemporary history, what Germans call *Zeitgeschichte*. I used archives, primary material collected on-site and from participants, news articles, and interviews as evidence to trace the process of organizing attempts at vehicle plants in the southeastern United States. This sort of research is dependent on the kindness and generosity of many whom I would like to recognize here. It is my best recollection that the project began during a discussion at a restaurant in Düsseldorf with Nik Simon, who was head of the Hans Böckler Foundation at the time, and his wife, Ulrike Teubner. Nik and Ulrike have always been extraordinarily kind and supportive to me, for which I am most grateful. My great friend Wolfgang Schröder helped me with the grant proposal that I sent to the HBS by providing me with a successful proposal of his own. I also had several subsequent fruitful conversations with Wolfgang while working on the book. When the HBS approved the proposal, I began working with Stefan Lücking as my *Betreuer*. Stefan was extremely flexible, supportive, and understanding.

Soon after I started the project, I got to know the head of international affairs for Industriegewerkschaft Metall (IG Metall), Horst Mund. Horst invested considerable time and effort in helping to advance the organizing efforts at the Mercedes and Volkswagen plants in the United States. Besides being incredibly knowledgeable, he was always very kind and helpful to me. Berthold Huber also provided me with considerable insight regarding the relationship between the UAW and IG Metall while he was heading the latter, for which I wish to thank him.

My longtime friend Mike Fichter lent a hand to me on numerous occasions while I was working on this book. I benefited greatly from Mike's deep understanding and experience concerning transnational trade union relations. Mike and I had many conversations about how things were progressing in the organizing drives, and Mike commented on earlier versions of this research. I would be remiss if I did not mention Hermann Nehls, who was social councilor at the German embassy in Washington, D.C., while I was working on the book. Hermann kept me informed of developments that I otherwise might have missed. In a similar vein, I greatly benefited from my exchanges with Carsten Hübner, who single-handedly ran the Transatlantic Labor Institute in Spring Hill, Tennessee.

I want to thank Michael Brecht and Frank Patta for taking the time to meet with me in Germany. Their insights were most helpful regarding the role that works councils played in several of these cases. I also would like to thank Sebastian Patta for sharing Volkswagen management's perspective with me. I benefited as well from conversations with Jeff Werner of Daimler Truck North America and Alfons Nowak at the Daimler headquarters in Stuttgart. Gary Casteel, Ray Curry, Kristyne Peter, Tracy Romero, and Mitchell Smith from the UAW were a tremendous help to me in explaining circumstances and enabling me to speak with plant employees. I also want to thank Bob King for speaking with me on the sidelines of a conference in Washington, D.C., and over breakfast in Ann Arbor, Michigan.

I also wish to thank the American Political Science Association Centennial Center for awarding me a Second Century Fund Grant, which supported two crucial trips to Detroit to use the UAW archives at Wayne State University's Walter Reuther Library. The UAW archivist Gavin Strassel was extraordinarily friendly and helpful. His suggestions and guidance enabled me to review a tremendous number of records quickly and efficiently. I can't thank Harry Katz enough for great advice and encouragement at several stages in this project. I also had helpful conversations with Gabe Nelson while he was a reporter for *Automotive News*.

I particularly want to extend very special thanks to Andrei Markovits. He has been a most generous, thoughtful, and insightful mentor to me throughout my academic career. No one has supported and encouraged me more since my early days as a grad student than Andy. He has set an example for what a scholar and person can and should be, to which I can only aspire. I should also say that I thoroughly enjoy Andy's company and conversations, be they about German labor and social democratic politics, the latest scholarship, the Grateful Dead, the New York Yankees, the Buffalo Bills, soccer, opera, golden retrievers, or late-night comics. No one tops Andy.

When I started on this book I would periodically check in with Fran Benson, who did an outstanding job editing my previous book at Cornell University Press, to let her know how things were going. She always gave me excellent advice, for which I am grateful. By the time I finished the manuscript, she had just retired. I've worked with Mahinder Kingra on this book, which has been a great pleasure. The book is substantially better because of Mahinder's advice.

I am grateful to the funders that supported my research: the Hans Böckler Foundation and the American Political Science Association. An earlier version of chapter 3 was published as "The United Auto Workers' Attempts to Unionize Volkswagen Chattanooga," *Industrial and Labor Relations Review* 71, no. 3 (May 2018): 600–24.

I would like to acknowledge the support of my children Christopher, Sean, and Peter. They are great kids whom I love and cherish. I don't tell them often enough how much they mean to me. Above all I am forever grateful to my wife, Jennifer Paxton. She gave me sound advice, considerable time, and an extraordinary degree of support. She covered at home when I traveled and endured me trying out innumerable ideas, concepts, phrasings, and titles. I could not have completed this book if it were not for her.

Abbreviations

ACE	American Council of Employees
AFL-CIO	American Federation of Labor–Congress of Industrial Organizations
ALU	Amazon Labor Union
ATR	Americans for Tax Reform
BMW	Bayerische Motoren Werke
CIC	Bureau of Census Industry Code
COE	"Community Organization Engagement"
CUF	Center for Union Facts
CVWF	Center for VW Facts
DTNA	Daimler Truck North America
EDPA	Economic Development Partnership of Alabama
FTZ	foreign-trade zone
GFA	global framework agreement
GM	General Motors
HBS	Hans-Böckler-Stiftung
IAM	International Association of Machinists
IG Metall	Industriegewerkschaft Metall (Industrial Union of Metalworkers)
IMF	International Metalworkers Federation
JAW	Confederation of Japan Automobile Workers' Unions
MAFFAN	Mississippi Alliance for Fairness at Nissan
MBUSI	Mercedes-Benz U.S. International
NAACP	National Association for the Advancement of Colored People
NCP	National Contact Point
NLRA	National Labor Relations Act
NLRB	National Labor Relations Board
NRWLDF	National Right to Work Legal Defense Foundation
NWOC	Nissan Workers Organizing Committee
OECD	Organization for Economic Cooperation and Development
OSHA	Occupational Safety and Health Administration
PTO	personal time off
SUV	sport utility vehicle
TMIC	Team Members Information Committee

UAW   United Auto Workers
VW   Volkswagen
VWAG   Volkswagen Aktiengesellschaft
VWGOA   Volkswagen Group of America
WEC   World Employee Committee (Daimler)

THE UAW'S SOUTHERN GAMBLE

INTRODUCTION

The South has been American labor's Waterloo, the nut that never cracked.

—Peter Applebome, *Dixie Rising*

This book investigates the United Auto Workers' (UAW) attempts to organize foreign-owned vehicle-assembly plants in the southeastern United States. Organizing unfolded in three phases. The first, which began in the mid-1980s and lasted about five years, had mixed results. The UAW failed to organize a Nissan plant in Smyrna, Tennessee, but successfully organized a truck factory in Mount Holly, North Carolina, owned by the German company now known as Daimler Truck. Exploratory attempts during these years at a Toyota plant in Kentucky and a Bayerische Motoren Werke (BMW) factory in South Carolina made little headway. The UAW launched a second organizing push, this one more strategic and successful, from the late 1990s to the mid-2000s, unionizing two additional truck facilities and one bus plant in North Carolina. There were also setbacks. A second campaign at Nissan failed, and the union was unable to gather enough support at a new Mercedes-Benz plant in Alabama to pursue recognition. In the third phase, which ran from 2011 to 2019, the UAW invested many tens of millions of dollars and adopted numerous innovations but failed to organize any additional workplaces, despite a second unionization attempt at the Alabama Mercedes-Benz plant, three drives at a Volkswagen (VW) factory in Tennessee, and a campaign at a Nissan facility in Canton, Mississippi. The principal objective of this book is to explain why these organizing drives turned out the way they did.

This study shows how employees who supported and opposed unionization, union officials, transnational managers, leaders of the local business community, and state and local politicians developed new tactics and strategies in successive

1

campaigns, in some instances invoking the American Civil War and in others the 1960s US civil rights movement, to sway specific groups of workers. The book explores how deeper transnational market integration and changes in information technology resulting from globalization have impelled and facilitated employee representatives from different parts of the world to cooperate more than in the past, particularly when dealing with a common transnational enterprise. Still, substantial cultural, institutional, interpersonal, legal, and resource constraints remain that minimize the effectiveness of transnational employee cooperation.

Success was not a function of the size or sophistication of transnational employee cooperation. The largest and most advanced effort, which the German metalworkers union Industriegewerkschaft Metall (IG Metall) undertook in cooperation with the UAW at Volkswagen Chattanooga, failed. The unwillingness of the head of VW's works council network, who was also a member of its supervisory board, to press the company to recognize the UAW blunted the impact of the joint union effort, which already faced fierce opposition from the local business and political communities.

In some instances interventions by employee representatives on a foreign corporate board made a crucial difference such as occurred at Daimler Truck North America (DTNA). That said, well-placed employee representatives on corporate boards were not always sufficient to achieve organizing breakthroughs. In later years, the head of Daimler's works council, who was also a member of the company's supervisory board, strongly supported recognition of the UAW at the Mercedes-Benz U.S. International (MBUSI) automobile plant in Alabama but failed to change a determined management's unaccommodating position and obtain union recognition.

The book also chronicles the emergence of an increasingly comprehensive and standardized union-avoidance playbook and its diffusion among management at transnational vehicle manufacturers. The playbook is open source; managers learn from one another through observation. They also hire line supervisors from other transplants and engage the same small group of law firms that specialize in union avoidance whenever an organizing drive emerges. The playbook uses old tactics, such as management-required captive-audience speeches, firing unpopular supervisors to curry favor with the workforce, increasing compensation before a union recognition vote, calling a union a third party from elsewhere that is simply interested in dues money, and suggesting that unionization would produce greater uncertainty regarding compensation and employment levels at the workplace without crossing the line of legality by making threats. The playbook also includes new tactics such as reducing hierarchy, allowing access (albeit controlled) to management to voice complaints and suggestions, offering benefits to line workers that only white-collar employees traditionally received at domestic firms (e.g., subsidized auto leasing), building plants in rural small towns to scatter the workforce, paying "near union" compensation in regions with a low cost of living and few other good-paying jobs, dividing the workforce by relying heavily on lower-paid temporary employees who cannot vote in union recognition elections because they technically work for temp agencies, avoiding layoffs of permanent employees, and developing close relations with the local community through donations and staging events. Darker pages of the union-avoidance playbook prescribe illegal actions, such as surveilling employees, directly questioning employees about organizing efforts, promising rewards if employees vote against unionization, threatening retaliation if employees vote to unionize, engaging in blackmail and physical coercion, and firing union activists.

In addition to the coalescence and dissemination of a standardized union-avoidance playbook, a new phenomenon in US labor relations has developed in recent decades that has made union organizing increasingly challenging. For several decades, state and local government officials—especially in the Southeast—have engaged in increasingly extravagant competitions to persuade globally renowned foreign manufacturing firms to build plants in their state. This phenomenon has led to the unprecedented involvement of state and local officeholders in the affairs of these plants. If a unionization attempt emerges at one of these plants, regional officeholders pressure transnational managers to fight it because they fear the impact of unionization on local business and politics. The substantial state and local subsidies give regional officeholders new leverage over transnational managers because subsidies can be curtailed or eliminated if a firm does not meet performance criteria. Transnational managers go to great lengths to stay in the good graces of regional officeholders because they regularly request additional subsidies to support plant expansions. In instances when the local elite judge the response of transnational managers to an organizing effort to be inadequate, they have launched independent anti-union campaigns of their own. This regional elite-transnational manager nexus has altered US labor relations by carving out nonunion regions in sectors that had previously been fully organized, such as vehicle assembly.

Foreign managers have typically downplayed their role in this transformation, claiming they are merely conforming to the labor relations status quo in the United States. In reality, however, they are essential participants in undermining that status quo by collaborating with state and local officials in the creation of new nonunion regions. The corporate leadership of the foreign-owned vehicle plants often hesitated at first to embrace the aggressive anti-union tactics characteristic of firms in the Southeast but, with intense pressure from local political and business leaders, have ultimately adopted them. In other words, the local norms changed transnational managers rather than transnational managers changing local norms. This has been no less true for German managers, despite their country's well-established postwar domestic tradition of labor-management cooperation.[1]

The fragile and incomplete architecture of transnational employment relations proved inadequate when faced with real-world challenges. Global framework agreements between transnational enterprises and global union federations, the United Nations Global Compact (UNGC), and unilateral enterprise commitments to foster environmental, social, and governance principles in most instances failed to dissuade management from resisting unionization at foreign vehicle plants in the southern United States.

When viewed together, the cases show that organizing drives at vehicle transplants in the South do not inevitably fail, but success is difficult. Involving employee representatives from a firm's home country is not a magic key that guarantees success, as some US union leaders had hoped.[2] Organizing foreign transplants now unfolds on three sites: not only the workplace, which is the traditional venue for organizing, but also the corporate boardroom and the political realm. The latter had been limited to the state and local level, but more recently national political actors have also at times intervened. If actors opposing unionization prevail at any of these sites, the organizing drive fails. In other words, union organizing has become difficult because it is now like opening a combination lock. To be successful, everything must align. Opponents, on the other hand, can thwart it by simply prevailing at just one site. Transnational employee cooperation can make a difference, but there is no single factor that guarantees success. Context and the concatenation of actions within and across these sites determines the outcome.

Why does the hollowing out of unionized sectors matter? In recent years, increasing numbers of policymakers and scholars have called for greater unionization to counteract decades of rising inequality in the United States.[3] This analysis shows how difficult it would be to increase unionization, given current labor relations practices in the United States. Even when unions such as the UAW invest considerable time and resources, innovate, act strategically, and engage in transnational cooperation, they fail more often than not to overcome the obstacles and opponents to unionization. Only a radical reconceptualization and restructuring of labor relations in the United States—one that draws on understandings and practices predating the juridico-discursive regime of truth[4] introduced during Franklin Roosevelt's administration—can rekindle workers' power to such a degree that reversing rising inequality and enhancing employees' voice in the workplace can be achieved.

Organization of the Book

This book has six chapters. The first is this introduction, which presents the book's key findings, data, and method. The introduction also details the growth of foreign-owned vehicle assembly plants (commonly called transplants) in the United States, because it is their rise that prompted the UAW to step up organizing efforts in the Southeast starting in the mid-1980s. Chapters 1 through 4 analyze unionization campaigns at DTNA, MBUSI, Volkswagen Chattanooga, and Nissan's facilities in Smyrna, Tennessee, and Canton, Mississippi.[5] Each of these four substantive chapters focuses on a transnational enterprise and is presented as a historical narrative, because this is the clearest way to explain the dynamics, interconnections, and significance of successive organizing campaigns. Some chapters include thumbnail sketches of organizing activities at other plants and before the 1980s to provide a fuller understanding of the cases under investigation. The conclusion synthesizes the findings and discusses their implications.

Cases

The book investigates all sixteen organizing campaigns undertaken at foreign-owned vehicle plants by the UAW in the Southeast since 1984 (table I.1). An individual campaign represents a case.[6] The sixteen organizing campaigns occurred at nine plants owned by the four transnational enterprises mentioned above. (The number of cases exceeds the number of plants because the UAW made multiple attempts at some plants.) Nine of the cases culminated in a recognition election, and three others ended with a card-check procedure. The other four cases were substantial enough to be considered an organizing attempt but never gathered enough employee support for union officials to ask for recognition. A majority of employees chose the UAW as their exclusive bargaining agent in six of the twelve instances when a recognition process took place, three through an election and three via card check. One plant had both a card-check procedure and a recognition election because some employees challenged the legitimacy of the former. The UAW won both. In total, the UAW prevailed at five of the nine plants. The collective bargaining parties agreed to a first contract at four of those five plants but failed at the fifth—Volkswagen Chattanooga—because management used the appeals process to challenge whether the unit, which was a small group of skilled employees, was "appropriate." The UAW ultimately disclaimed interest in the small unit five years later to terminate the appeals process and make way for a second wall-to-wall recognition election in

TABLE I.1   United Auto Worker unionization attempts at solely foreign-owned vehicle plants in the southern United States, 1984–2019

PLANT	YEARS	FORM OF RECOGNITION	RESULT
1. Nissan Smyrna, TN	1984–1989	Election	Loss
2. Freightliner Mount Holly, NC (DTNA)	1989–1990	Election	Win
3. Nissan Smyrna, TN	1997	No attempt	Failure
4. Mercedes-Benz U.S. International, AL	1998–2000	No attempt	Failure
5. Nissan Smyrna, TN	2000–2001	Election	Loss
6. Freightliner Gastonia, NC (DTNA)	1999–2002	Election	Loss
7. Freightliner Gastonia, NC (DTNA)	2003	Card check	Win
8. Freightliner Cleveland, NC (DTNA)	2003	Card check	Win
9. Freightliner Gaffney, SC (DTNA)	2003	No attempt	Failure
10. Thomas Built Buses, NC (DTNA)	2003	Card check	Win*
11. Thomas Built Buses, NC (DTNA)	2005	Election	Win
2011: The UAW begins a multiplant organizing effort.			
12. Mercedes-Benz U.S. International, AL	2011–2014	No attempt	Failure
13. Volkswagen Chattanooga, TN	2011–2014	Election	Loss
14. Volkswagen Chattanooga, TN (skilled-trades unit)	2015	Election	Win**
15. Nissan Canton, MS	2005–2017	Election	Loss
16. Volkswagen Chattanooga, TN	2019	Election	Loss

* The National Right to Work Legal Defense Foundation supported employee challenges to the card-check recognition. The National Labor Relations Board accepted a joint DTNA-UAW proposal to hold a recognition election in 2005 to settle the challenges.

** Volkswagen management challenged the election. The UAW disclaimed the skilled trades unit in 2019 in order to hold a plant-wide recognition election.

that plant. Overall, in sixteen attempts the UAW successfully unionized four of the nine plants under investigation.[7]

Data and Method

The principal data for this investigation are primary documents from the UAW and the companies and other entities involved in the drives (e.g., foreign trade unions, global trade union confederations, works councils, government bodies, politicians in and out of office, and third-party lobbying entities). Interviews, media accounts, and social media postings are also important source material.

The method employed here is comparative historical case study analysis. I use process tracing to analyze each case. Process tracing is a within-case method of causal analysis that is particularly suited to instances such as we have here whereby simply the presence or absence of a causal variable is not predictive of an outcome; context, timing, and concatenation also matter. Scholars using this method undertake an "examination of intermediate steps in a process to make inferences about hypotheses on how that process took place and whether and how it generated the outcome of interest."[8] "Careful description is a foundation of process tracing," combined with "close attention to sequences of independent, dependent, and intervening variables" to analyze trajectories of causation.[9] After analyzing each case, I compare the findings to gain additional inferential leverage to explain why unionization succeeded in some organizing drives but not others.

The Unusual Process of Organizing Trade Unions in the United States: Implications

Understanding the larger context of interactions is crucial for effective process tracing. One important piece of context is the process of unionization in the United States, which shapes the behavior of the actors and determines the likelihood of success. Although (or indeed because) unionization is familiar to US labor and employment experts, acknowledging how unusual it is compared to most other countries and the implications of the system for US workers endeavoring to improve their influence in their workplaces is important. Elsewhere, joining a trade union is not that much different from joining a professional association, political party, or interest group. An individual simply signs up. Not so in the United States. Unionization in the United States means the designation of an organization as the exclusive bargaining agent for employees in a workplace. In most instances, someone can only become a full-fledged union member if a majority of employees in one's workplace express support for unionization through a formal process specified in the 1935 National Labor Relations Act (NLRA), or if one becomes employed at a workplace where that has already taken place.

The NLRA and subsequent jurisprudence interpreting it have established three routes to unionization. The first is a representation election in a workplace. Employees and unions interested in organizing a workplace must run a campaign to persuade a majority of employees to support a union becoming their exclusive bargaining agent, and employers may campaign against it within confines specified in US labor law. The second is a card-check procedure that allows an employer to recognize a union as the employees' exclusive bargaining agent if union officials can show that a majority of the employees in a bargaining unit have signed union authorization cards. The third is when the National Labor Relations Board (NLRB) designates a union as the employees' exclusive bargaining agent in a workplace because the employer has violated labor law to such an extent that it would be impossible to hold an election there under "laboratory conditions."[10]

The unusualness of this construction—particularly for a country with such a deeply individualistic culture—is striking. In all three routes to unionization, either a collective or a quasi-judicial decision regarding unionization for a workplace as a whole is a prerequisite to an individual being able to join a union. This prerequisite has generated a chronic "representation gap," that is, the difference between those who are union members and those who would like to be members but are not because there has never been a majority vote or a card-check procedure to unionize their workplaces. Surveys from the late 1970s and the late 1990s indicate that roughly one-third of nonunionized employees in the United States would have voted to join a union if given a chance.[11] In recent years, this gap has risen to 48 percent.[12]

Despite the growing representation gap, unionization in the United States has declined for decades. Union density has fallen from roughly one-third of the eligible workforce in the middle of the twentieth century to 10.3 percent in 2021. Declining unionization has been a private-sector phenomenon; roughly one-third of the public sector has remained unionized since a burst of organizing in the 1970s. Private-sector union density, in contrast, dropped from a peak of 35 percent in the mid-1950s to 6.1 percent in 2021.[13] Union density and why employees join unions are long-standing topics in the field of labor and employment relations.[14] This book addresses the perspective of individual organizing drives rather than a macroeconomic level, which is more common in the literature.

The Rise of Foreign-Owned Firms in the US Automobile Sector

A second contextual element framing the UAW's organizing campaigns in the Southeast is the construction of numerous foreign-owned vehicle assembly plants in the region starting in the 1980s. Japanese firms were the first to build transplants in the Southeast. The politics of international trade generated the impetus to do so. In 1980, the governments of Japan and the United States agreed to impose a voluntary restraint agreement that limited Japanese automobile exports to the United States to 1.68 million vehicles annually for three years starting in 1981. The two governments extended the agreement, with a higher cap of 1.85 million cars for 1984 and 2.3 million thereafter. The restraint remained until 1994.[15] As a result, if Japanese producers were to expand their sales and market share in the United States, they had to start making cars there.

Honda built the first Japanese transplant in the United States not in the South but rather in Marysville, Ohio. Honda management picked the location because the company already had a motorcycle factory there. The first car rolled off the assembly line in November 1982. By the end of the year, Honda had produced 1,500 cars. Transplant production ramped up quickly thereafter. In 1983 Nissan opened the first southeastern transplant, in Smyrna, Tennessee. That year, the two Japanese companies made close to 100,000 vehicles in the United States. The next year Toyota entered a joint venture with General Motors (GM), and the two companies began manufacturing autos using Toyota designs in a revamped GM plant in Fremont, California. Ford and Mazda jointly opened a factory in Flat Rock, Michigan, in 1987. Toyota began production at a plant of its own in George-town, Kentucky, in 1988. That year, Mitsubishi and Chrysler jointly started up a plant in Normal, Illinois. The next year, Isuzu and Subaru jointly opened a plant in Indiana. By the end of the decade, annual automobile output at Japanese trans-plants and partner plants with US producers surpassed 1 million. Transplant production accelerated thereafter. The joint ventures with US producers gradu-ally closed, but Japanese companies added more facilities, German producers BMW and Daimler-Benz built plants in the 1990s, and South Korean automakers Hyundai and Kia put up factories in the mid-2000s. In 1995 annual output at transplants reached 2 million. Five years later it topped 3 million. By 2005 it ex-ceeded 4 million, which amounted to 34 percent of total US automobile and light truck output. The 2007–2009 financial crisis dropped production at transplants to 3.1 million, but by 2010 it surpassed 4 million again. Since output by domestic firms had fallen, transplant production accounted for just shy of half of total US automobile and light truck output in 2010. In 2011 VW opened a plant in Chat-tanooga, Tennessee, twenty-three years after shuttering one in Westmoreland County, Pennsylvania. By 2017, transplant production surpassed that of the "De-troit Three" (Fiat-Chrysler, Ford, and GM).[16]

The expansion of transplant production meant trouble for the UAW because it had only managed to organize the joint-venture plants, and most of those either closed or were taken over by one of the partners during the 1990s. UAW member-ship peaked in 1979 at 1,527,858 active members, including 150,000 in Canada (figure I.1).[17] Roughly 70 percent of these members worked in the vehicle sector, including parts production. The bulk of the remaining members came from the aerospace and farm implements sectors. Membership declined markedly there-after, falling to slightly more than 1 million in 1983 because of rising numbers of imported vehicles, the surge of production from transplants, and recessions in the late 1970s and early 1980s. Membership briefly rebounded, reaching 1.2 million in 1985, only to drop for eight straight years thereafter. Rising productivity and

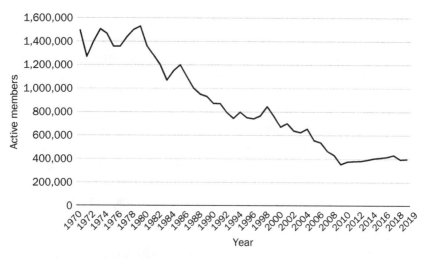

FIGURE I.1. United Auto Workers, active members, 1970–2019. Source: LM-2 Reports, Office of Labor Management Standards, US Department of Labor.

increased competition from foreign manufacturers producing both inside and outside of the United States were the main causes of the decline, along with the departure of 120,000 Canadian members in 1985 to form the independent Canadian Auto Workers. The UAW began to recruit more heavily in service sectors including casinos, education, and state and local governments, which helped somewhat to balance out losses in the vehicle sector. Still, membership dropped below 1 million in 1988 and reached a new low of 745,000 in 1993. Diversification lowered the share of active UAW members working in vehicle production to approximately two-thirds.

Membership again partially recovered, spiking to 846,000 in 1998 in the middle of the dot-com bubble, but then trended downward for eleven years because a fresh wave of transplants opened and imports continued to rise, in particular duty-free parts and vehicles from Mexico under the North American Free Trade Agreement. UAW membership fell to an all-time low of 355,191 in 2009 because of the financial crisis (which triggered the bankruptcies of Fiat-Chrysler and GM); this was just 23 percent of peak union membership from three decades earlier. Membership recovered slowly over the next eight years, reaching 430,871 in 2017 despite Michigan enacting a "right to work" law in 2013 that banned compulsory union membership. Membership edged downward thereafter, settling just below 400,000 again in 2018 and 2019. The share of UAW members in vehicle production in the 2010s averaged 220,000, or 55 percent of active members.[18] About two-thirds of those members worked at a Detroit Three plant.[19]

Raw membership numbers matter because they generate the financial resources and political leverage available to the UAW leadership. Membership
density (i.e., the share of the workforce that is organized) and contract coverage, in contrast, determine economic influence. A common objective of trade
unions is to make it impossible for an individual employer to use lower compensation to gain a competitive advantage over rival firms. Unions do this in
the market by organizing as much of the workforce as possible or through politics by pushing for laws that set minimum and prevailing wages and benefits.

For several decades, the UAW largely succeeded in taking wages out of competition through organizing. From the early 1940s to the early 1980s, union labor
assembled well over 90 percent of all vehicles produced in the United States. Density for the broader category of motor vehicle and motor vehicle equipment manufacturing, which includes parts production, hovered around 70 percent in those
decades (figure I.2). These density levels kept wages out of competition among the
domestic assemblers and obliged parts suppliers wishing to avoid unionization to
provide compensation at or near the union rate. The influx of imported vehicles
and parts in the mid-1970s in the wake of the first oil shock, however, put greater
pressure on domestic compensation. Density shrank in subsequent years. Transplants built during the twentieth century reduced the unionization rate in vehicle
assembly to 86 percent by 1999. The decline in the larger category that included

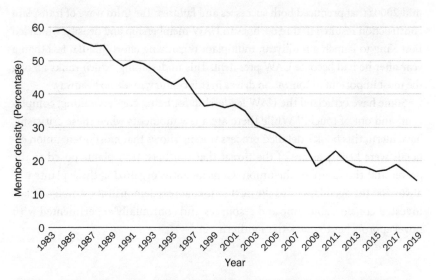

FIGURE I.2. Union membership density, 1983–2019. Motor Vehicles and
Motor Vehicle Equipment Manufacturing (CIC 351, 1983–2002; CIC 3570,
2003–2019). Source: www.unionstats.com.

parts production was much greater because domestic auto producers increasingly sold off parts plants in times of market distress and also because transplants bought parts heavily from either home suppliers or parts transplants that the UAW largely neglected to unionize. Consequently, density for motor vehicles and motor vehicle equipment manufacturing dropped to under 60 percent in the early 1980s and fell below 40 percent in 1998. Density declines accelerated in the twenty-first century as existing transplants increased production and several new transplants opened from an expanding number of countries. Outsourcing parts also picked up pace. Union density in vehicle assembly plummeted to 55 percent by 2009 and dropped to just below 50 percent in 2017. Density in the broader category that includes parts production plunged below 20 percent in 2009 and below 15 percent in 2019.[20]

Taken as a whole, in four decades the growth of transplants transformed vehicle assembly in the United States from a fully unionized sector into a half-unionized one, with nonunion production concentrated in the Southeast. Transplants combined with outsourcing to reduce unionization in the broader motor vehicle and motor vehicle equipment manufacturing category by more than fifty percentage points, turning it into a predominantly nonunion sector.

The first wave of transplant investment in the Southeast starting in the 1980s prompted UAW officials to begin organizing there that yielded one win. The second wave of investment sparked a second round of organizing from the late 1990s to the mid-2000s that produced both successes and failures. The third wave of transplant construction resulted in dire declines in UAW membership and density, which led Bob King to launch a multiyear, multiplant organizing effort in 2011, less than a year after he had become UAW president. This undertaking, which ranks among the most important unionization drives in this century, made no headway.

Some have criticized the UAW leadership for being condescending, complacent, and out of touch.[21] While there are a few moments when these criticisms have merit, this book's detailed process tracing shows that most often, union officials were keenly aware of the threat that southern transplants posed to the power and the future of the union. Consequently, organizing these plants was always on the agenda, and as the next four chapters demonstrate, union officials invested considerable time and resources and continually experimented with novel approaches to crack the southern nut.

DAIMLER TRUCK NORTH AMERICA

Successes and Limits of Transnational Cooperation

> **I'm telling you right now that if there has to be a strike and it's your intention to try to break that strike by using strikebreakers at Freightliner in the USA, then you are going to have trouble with us here in Germany.**
>
> —Karl Feuerstein, chair, Mercedes-Benz general works council

Between 1990 and 2005, the UAW organized three vehicle-assembly plants owned by DTNA in North Carolina.[1] These are the only wholly foreign-owned vehicle-assembly plants that the UAW has ever organized in the US South.[2] The union also organized a DTNA parts plant and two small distribution centers in North Carolina, one of the most hostile states in the country when it comes to unionization. The record in the Carolinas is not one of complete success, however. The UAW failed to organize a DTNA specialty assembly plant in South Carolina.

This chapter analyzes the UAW's organizing efforts at DTNA facilities in the Carolinas, which unfolded in two episodes: first, the drive in the late 1980s and early 1990s to organize Freightliner's Mount Holly factory, and second, the campaigns to unionize several DTNA facilities in North and South Carolina in the late 1990s and early 2000s.

Cooperation between US and German employee representatives and a confidential deal between the UAW and DTNA management played crucial roles in securing organizing success. The chapter also assesses the importance of several other elements that contributed to the successful unionization efforts, including employee mobilization, volatile business cycles, local management missteps, minimal political intervention, and a low volume of subsidies.

Daimler Truck Comes to North America

Commercial truck production in North America has always been a business with relatively low profit margins and sharp demand fluctuations that track business-cycle swings.[3] In the early 1980s, regulatory change produced an additional momentous shock. US president Jimmy Carter began the deregulation of the trucking industry with the Motor Carrier Act of 1980. The act gave haulers autonomy to set prices freely "within a zone of reasonableness," eliminated most restrictions on the commodities that trucks could haul, and deregulated the routes that carriers could use.[4]

Deregulation encouraged new entrants into the shipping industry, which increased demand for trucks and, in turn, the attractiveness of the US truck market to both domestic and foreign producers. In the late 1970s, Daimler-Benz management made expanding production abroad a priority. A 38 percent appreciation in the value of the deutschmark versus the dollar between 1976 and 1980 led to a corresponding rise in the US price of products made in Germany. Daimler-Benz management bought Freightliner Trucks from Consolidated Freight in 1981 in order to eliminate the exchange rate risk.[5]

Consolidated Freight had created Freightliner Trucks in 1942 because the company could not find trucks that would reliably traverse the Rocky Mountains. For decades Freightliner only built plants in the western United States and Canada, with a concentration near the company's Portland, Oregon, headquarters. In the late 1970s, Freightliner built two factories in the Southeast. One was a parts plant in Gastonia, North Carolina, that opened in 1978, and the other was an assembly plant in Mount Holly, North Carolina, that started production a year later. Both towns are just west of Charlotte. Freightliner received no major subsidies or tax breaks from the state or local governments to build these plants. Gaston County was nonetheless attractive because of its easy access to several interstate highways and a large pool of skilled employees. The county had first become a manufacturing hub in the early twentieth century when textile production migrated from the North.[6]

Freightliner management gradually shifted production to North Carolina. By 1988, the Mount Holly plant was producing most Freightliner trucks.[7] In early 1989 after several years of strong growth, Freightliner Trucks bought two more plants in the Carolinas. One had been a bus factory in Cleveland, North Carolina, which is forty miles north of Charlotte. The previous owner was the German heavy vehicle producer M.A.N. The other was a high-end custom truck plant in Gaffney, South Carolina (which is close to the North Carolina border), that Freightliner bought from the Oshkosh Truck Corporation.[8]

The Breakthrough: Mount Holly

Freightliner Trucks ranked among the highest-paying employers in Gaston County. Dean Eason, a Mount Holly employee who eventually became president of the UAW union local, observed that employees found these jobs so valuable that many were willing to take risks to defend them. Nonetheless, there were some disadvantages to working for Freightliner. When there was strong demand for trucks, Freightliner frequently forced employees to work overtime with little advance notice. Some employees complained about arbitrary treatment by supervisors. For example, one reported that supervisors often responded to complaints with the retort "If you can't hack it, get your jacket."[9] Others were concerned about job security. During downturns, Freightliner management fired employees without regard to seniority and at times hired temporary workers, at five dollars an hour, as replacements. Rising health care costs prompted Freightliner management to change the health care benefit in 1989 from full coverage with no deductibles to 80 percent coverage and a $250 deductible.[10] The change led some employees to contact the UAW. The union helped them begin an organizing drive at the plant in June 1989.[11] The UAW faced no competition. The International Association of Machinists (IAM) had unionized Freightliner's flagship plant in Portland four decades earlier, but the IAM had not tried to organize Freightliner's North Carolina facilities.

The US economy had started to slow in the second half of 1989, and demand for trucks quickly softened. Freightliner management responded by shutting down production for three weeks in October. The shutdown suddenly made job security much more important to the 1,350 assembly-line employees working at the Mount Holly factory. It became a central issue in the UAW's organizing drive.[12] Rising interest in unionization led UAW officials to open a full-time office in Mount Holly in October 1989.[13] Despite the shutdown, Mount Holly employees still received a 4 percent raise in October 1989. Plant management asserted that the company based the size of the increase on a regional wage survey and that the unionization drive did not affect it.[14] The increase failed to keep pace with inflation, however, which was running at close to 5 percent.

Persistent sluggish demand for trucks led Freightliner management to lay off indefinitely 114 employees at the Mount Holly and Gastonia plants in mid-January 1990.[15] Some complained that management did not lay off employees using reverse seniority.[16] In mid-February the UAW filed a recognition petition, and the parties agreed to April 6 as the election date.[17] Freightliner management hired a law firm that specializes in union avoidance to help fend off the union.[18] This move came late compared with a typical organizing drive.

The recognition election put Mount Holly management under considerable stress. On March 2, plant manager John Lamey announced that he had asked his superiors to transfer him because he felt that the UAW had attacked him personally. Three days later Ken West, who had been with Freightliner for some time, took over as plant manager. On March 23, Freightliner headquarters in Portland dismissed the Mount Holly plant's personnel manager, Bob Bagerski. The grounds were "irreconcilable differences in management style."[19] Removing local managers is a common corporate tactic to lower the odds that a union will win a recognition election by showing some responsiveness to employee complaints and creating an opportunity for a new manager to offer a fresh start.

On March 28, continuing economic weakness prompted Freightliner management to announce plans for three additional temporary shutdowns for a total of sixteen days around holidays from April to July. The shutdown announcement increased support for the UAW within the workforce.[20]

On April 6, 1990, the NLRB supervised the union recognition election at the Freightliner Mount Holly plant. Employees on both sides judged the campaign to have been "a good, clean fight."[21] The turnout was high, and the results were close: 652 employees voted in favor of recognizing the UAW as their exclusive collective bargaining agent, and 606 voted against it. The results surprised managers in Freightliner's Portland headquarters. The public relations office had prepared a press release in case of a union loss but did not have one ready in the event of a union victory. Chief union organizer Chuck McDonald emphasized that both the union and the employees who voted yes were not anti-Freightliner, "They respect Freightliner. . . . They want to see it grow."[22] Freightliner employees formed UAW local 5285 immediately after the victory in the recognition election.

The drama did not end on April 6, however. Getting a first contract proved to be far more difficult for Freightliner's Mount Holly employees than securing recognition of the UAW as their exclusive bargaining agent. The sequence of events proceeded along a path common to US labor relations. Only 48 percent of units have a completed first contract within a year of certification and 63 percent completed one within two years, typically because of management resistance.[23] Freightliner management made the negotiations painfully slow; the union filed several unfair labor practice petitions while the negotiations were proceeding, and it took a strike to force a resolution. Freightliner's unfair labor practices, which were unforced errors, as well as support from the chair of Daimler's enterprise works council and employee solidarity under pressure proved crucial to the UAW's success.

Freightliner management did not react sharply to the UAW victory. Unions were not a new thing for company officials. Other unions had already organized most of Freightliner's plants west of the Mississippi decades earlier, and management had worked amicably with them. There is also no evidence of Daimler leadership intervening from Germany in any way at this point. Freightliner management slow-walked the negotiations, however. Talks between UAW and company representatives did not start until July 1990, which was the same month the US economy entered a recession. That summer, demand for trucks nationwide dropped by 30 percent. Freightliner's orders only fell by 15 percent because the company heavily discounted truck prices and had just launched a popular new line of "business class" medium-duty trucks after investing $34.5 million in the Mount Holly and Gastonia plants. Still, the company could not avoid shedding jobs. In August 1990 Freightliner management announced immediate layoffs at several plants, including 156 employees at Mount Holly. Employees again complained that management laid off some employees at the top of the wage scale rather than relying on reverse seniority.[24] The company shut down the Mount Holly facility again for one week in October. Freightliner did not pay the employees but permitted them to use vacation time during that week.[25]

By Thanksgiving 1990, UAW and Freightliner negotiators had met twenty-seven times but made little progress. Freightliner management attributed the slow pace to the large number of topics that require negotiation in a first contract. UAW negotiators blamed the company. They complained that Freightliner's negotiators did not have the authority to make decisions without first consulting with the company's Portland headquarters. The UAW negotiators offered to meet daily for as long as it took to reach a settlement, but Freightliner management declined, and the pace of negotiations did not change.[26]

Leadership at Freightliner changed hands in 1991. Dieter Zetsche became president. Zetsche, a German in his late thirties, had just spent the past two years as president of Mercedes-Benz Argentina, where he led a turnaround of the division's troubled operations there. His new assignment was to return Freightliner to profitability.

The relationship between Freightliner and the UAW took a turn for the worse in early 1991. The UAW filed an unfair labor practice action against Freightliner in February. Back in October 1990, Freightliner management gave annual pay raises to the Mount Holly staff employees who were not in the collective bargaining unit but withheld wage increases for 1,300 line employees represented by the UAW. On March 29, 1991, the regional representative of the NLRB concluded that there was sufficient cause to refer the case for consideration to the NLRB in Washington.[27]

UAW negotiators continued to complain about Freightliner management's slow pace in negotiations. On April 13, 1991, exactly one year and one week after the recognition election, the union took a symbolic step in a bid to accelerate the tempo of the talks. UAW Local 5825 held a meeting for all members in a

Charlotte hotel to discuss how to proceed. Ninety-two percent of the approximately 475 present voted to ask the UAW national executive committee to grant the local permission to strike.[28] The vote, however, did not speed up the talks.[29] Rather than strike, UAW officials filed a second unfair labor practice suit against Freightliner after the company dismissed Stanley Roseboro in May. Union officials alleged that the firing was the result of Roseboro's union activities.[30] Pro-union employees also began to report occupational safety and health concerns. The plant quickly accumulated approximately fifty violations.[31]

The atmosphere in the plant was tense in the autumn of 1991. In September, Freightliner management once again gave Mount Holly employees exempt from the bargaining unit a raise but kept frozen the wages of the employees in the bargaining unit. The UAW responded with a new complaint to the NLRB. Negotiations continued, but the list of unresolved items remained long.[32] Sporadic slowdowns and sabotage led plant manager Ken West to post an announcement in October stating that unless production numbers improved he would be forced to take drastic steps, which could include shifting production elsewhere. The threat rang hollow, however, because Freightliner had just invested $20 million in the Mount Holly plant, where the company's hottest-selling truck line was being made. Emotions ran high as rumors of an impending strike grew. Periodically, pro-union workers would break into chants of "contract, contract." A nonfatal poisoning of a manager inside the plant and a mysterious fire outside of it added to the tension.[33]

By November, the UAW negotiators were no longer willing to continue open-ended talks. Large differences remained regarding wages, hours, pensions, insurance benefits, profit sharing, and health and safety. The negotiators set 7:00 p.m. on Friday, November 22, as a deadline "to get all outstanding issues resolved."[34] Talks continued until 3:30 a.m. Saturday, but the parties failed to reach agreement on many items. The UAW negotiators offered to continue to meet over the weekend, but Freightliner management declined. UAW secretary-treasurer Bill Casstevens questioned the sincerity of Freightliner management's interest in reaching an agreement. Casstevens pressed the UAW's demand for compensation parity with Freightliner's Portland employees, who were paid on average a dollar more per hour than those in the Mount Holly plant, asserting, "We refuse to accept second-class status for North Carolina's Freightliner workers. . . . Freightliner charges the same prices for the trucks it produces in North Carolina as the ones it builds in Portland and they should also pay their North Carolina workers the same wages and benefits as Portland workers."[35] The leadership of Local 5285 scheduled meetings of its members at the end of each shift on November 26, two days before Thanksgiving, to see if there was sufficient support for a strike. Within a day of the announcement of the November 26 meetings, Freightliner management presented the UAW bargaining committee with an offer to take to the membership. Approximately 525 members participated in two November 26 meetings. Each meeting discussed the choices: accept the company's offer, keep negotiating, or strike. The membership at both meetings unanimously rejected the company's offer by voice vote. The vote gave the bargaining committee authorization to call a strike.[36]

In the last week of November 1991, UAW representatives personally asked leaders of German employee organizations for help with Freightliner. Bill Casstevens and John Christensen, a staffer from the UAW International Affairs Department, flew to Germany to meet with union, works council, and company leaders to improve the union's leverage in advance of any industrial action at Mount Holly. The German labor relations system gives both unions and works councils roles in representing employees. So, meeting with the leadership of both was important.

Works councils are elected bodies of employee representatives. German law allows workers in any private-sector workplace with five or more employees to form a works council and specifies the responsibilities and rights of such councils. The main concern of works councils is providing a voice for employees in the workplace. The primary focus of unions is collective bargaining over wages and working conditions in addition to representing employees' interests in politics and society. Unions also represent employees in the workplace through networks of local branches and shop stewards. Unions and works councils regularly work together, but the two do not have identical interests, and both are acutely sensitive to preserving autonomy from the other.

Christensen described the trip as "very positive" and "productive" in a memo for his supervisor, UAW international affairs director Don Stillman. The two UAW emissaries experienced firsthand the power of Germany's employee representatives and the system of codetermination.[37] They first met with Franz Steinkühler, chair of the German metalworkers union IG Metall, and Albert Schunk, director of IG Metall's International Affairs Department, at the company's headquarters in Frankfurt am Main. Steinkühler and Schunk were receptive. They had concerns of their own for which the UAW could be helpful. Back in May 1991, Steinkühler had expressed interest in "sound[ing] out in some detail possibilities for further improving our cooperation."[38] He had something specific in mind. Management at the German auto producer BMW had decided to build an assembly plant in the United States and was in the last stage of selecting a site.[39] Establishing a tit-for-tat exchange would therefore benefit both unions.

Casstevens and Christensen explained the circumstances at Freightliner and emphasized the importance of dissuading management from using strikebreakers. Christensen reported that Steinkühler grasped the threat that strikebreakers posed and was willing to use his influence to help the UAW. Steinkühler was a member of Daimler's supervisory board thanks to the board-level component of Germany's codetermination legislation, which allocates half of the seats on the supervisory boards of large companies to employee representatives. Steinkühler said he would raise the matter with the board, and immediately contact Helmut Werner, the managing director of the Daimler-Benz auto and truck division.

Christensen and Casstevens next traveled to Daimler headquarters in Stuttgart. They met with company officials and Karl Feuerstein, who was the powerful head of the Mercedes-Benz general works council. Casstevens explained the situation at Mount Holly and the concern about strikebreakers. Feuerstein turned to the Daimler managers in the room and said, "It is quite clear that the UAW is having problems in reaching an agreement with you at Freightliner in the USA. Before I came to this meeting, I just received a call from Steinkühler who has just spoken to Mr Werner about the situation with Freightliner and the UAW, and he wants you to know we are in cooperation with the UAW." Feuerstein continued, "You know our position on this strikebreaker question. We've told you before when your foreign managers tried in South Africa and Latin America, I really don't need to explain myself again." The works council chief then shook his finger at the lead company official in the room and raised his voice, declaring, "I'm telling you right now that if there has to be a strike and it's your intention to try to break that strike by using strikebreakers at Freightliner in the USA, then you are going to have trouble with us here in Germany." Feuerstein then instructed the company officials to leave the room, and to the amazement of Christensen they did just that. Feuerstein and Robert Steiert from IG Metall's International Affairs Department explained to Casstevens and Christensen that Feuerstein would discuss the UAW's position regarding strikebreakers "at the very top level (Werner) as soon as possible." Christensen remarked that Feuerstein's strong statement "in my opinion was clearly *not* a show put on for our benefit."[40]

Christensen observed that neither Daimler management nor the employee representatives in Germany appeared to have been aware of the unfair labor practice charges or the health and safety violations that had occurred at Freightliner. He concluded, "If this trip did anything, it has now brought the attention of both the Supervisory Board and the works council and IG Metall focused clearly on Mt. Holly, North Carolina," which would make it much less likely that Freightliner management would use permanent replacements in a strike. Don Stillman forwarded his deputy's report to UAW president Owen Bieber.

Once the Thanksgiving holiday had passed, UAW officials accelerated preparations for a strike. A union spokesperson reported that close to 900 of the plant's 1,300 employees had signed union authorization cards, and 700 were "strong members."[41] Freightliner spokesperson Debi Nicholson did not indicate whether Freightliner would try to operate during a strike. Given that many of the employees who had not signed union cards would be unwilling to cross a picket line—at least at first—it was likely that well under half of the employees would be willing to work during a strike.

Hiring permanent replacements to work as strikebreakers was not a viable option for Freightliner management for two reasons. First, the trip to Germany by Casstevens and Christensen made it impossible for upper Daimler management to claim ignorance of the events in Mount Holly and secured the commitment of Daimler's works council leader to take action in Germany if Freightliner management hired workers to break a strike. Second, US Supreme Court decisions have specified that firms may only keep on replacement employees once the strike has ended if the strike is over purely economic issues.[42] If the strike is over an unfair labor practice, an employer must reinstate strikers immediately after the industrial action ends so long as strikers did not commit acts of misconduct during the strike at least as serious as the employer's unfair labor practice.[43] Given the pending unfair labor practice proceedings against Freightliner, the UAW leadership was in a position to declare that a strike was about the unfair labor practices, which would provide added job security for the strikers and less incentive for anyone to become a strikebreaker.

Miscommunication made reaching a settlement harder. UAW spokesperson Reg McGhee claimed that the UAW sent a letter to Freightliner management on November 27 outlining the union's position. The letter urged Freightliner negotiators to return to the bargaining table and requested that personnel head Fred Arterberry participate personally in the negotiations to speed things up. Yet on December 2, Freightliner spokesperson Debi Nicholson said that the company had not yet heard from the UAW regarding "a schedule for when we can resume talks."[44] Later, Nicholson stated that the company had faxed a letter to UAW secretary-treasurer Bill Casstevens on the morning of December 3 inquiring about resuming negotiations. She also said that Scott Evitt from Freightliner's personnel department was flying from Portland to Charlotte to be available for talks on December 4.[45]

This last flurry of activity came too late. On December 3, UAW Local 5285 issued a strike notice. Union workers would walk out on Wednesday, December 4, at 11 a.m. Dan Eason, head of UAW Local 5285, simultaneously released a statement citing four causes of the impending strike:

1. The dismissal of Stanley Roseboro allegedly for engaging in union activities.
2. Withholding of annual raises in 1990 and 1991 for employees in the bargaining unit.

3. Management's refusal to offer compensation equivalent to that of Freightliner's Portland employees.
4. The refusal of the company to bargain after talks broke off early on Nov. 23.

Points 1, 2 and 4 are unfair labor practices. As a result, the UAW leadership declared the action to be a strike over unfair labor practices.[46]

The strike at the Mount Holly plant began as planned on December 4. No one knew how many workers would actually strike. On the first day, eight hundred line employees did not go to work; of those, three hundred to four hundred staffed the picket line. The strike split families. The local newspaper featured a wife on the picket line, whose husband was working in the plant, and two brothers, one working and the other striking.[47] The sentiment on the picket line was determined. A striker, Bobby Fuller, explained: "Nobody wanted this strike, but it was the only thing to prove to the company that we weren't a bunch of rednecks that they can push around."[48]

Freightliner reported that 180 employees, or about one-third of the usual complement, crossed the picket line to work in the first shift; 208, or about 45 percent, went to work on the second shift. The company claimed to have produced 29 trucks on the first strike day, which was down from the usual output of fifty-five. Some of these trucks had already been assembled, in whole or in part, before the strike started.[49] The first shift change during the strike was at 3 p.m. Some picketers yelled "scabs," "leeches," and "don't do it." Others made obscene gestures and spit on vehicles as workers drove in and out of the plant. A group of more collected union members quickly put an end to these confrontational actions. No one was hurt on the first day.[50]

Freightliner strikers found little sympathy in Gaston County. Hostility toward unions was a product of not only a general attitude commonly found in the South but also a specific event in Gaston County's past. In 1929, a two-month strike at the Loray textile mill climaxed with a gunfight on the outskirts of town between the police and the strikers, who were living in tents because Loray mill management threw them out of company-owned housing. The police chief died, and several on both sides were wounded. The 1929 Loray mill strike triggered a decade of labor strife that drew national attention and "fostered a long-lingering distrust of unions" in Gaston County.[51] Most of the local business community and political establishment were critical of the Freightliner strike, but not all. A local franchise of the Hardee's fast-food chain initially offered free coffee to strikers but stopped a few days into the strike after receiving dozens of complaints.[52] That said, neither employers nor politicians waged an organized campaign to influence the outcome of the strike. Some local workers at other firms in the area were also critical. They accused Freightliner employees of greed because Freightliner was already the highest-paying employer in the county.[53]

Freightliner's strike strategy was simple. Management decided to keep operating the Mount Holly plant but not to hire replacements in the hope that increasing numbers of employees would cross the picket line as the strike continued. The number of employees reporting to work increased somewhat after the first day of the strike. It rose by 48 to 436 on Thursday, December 5,[54] the second day of the strike, and reached 451 on December 6. The number of strikers correspondingly fell from 800 to 725. Management claimed that employees crossing the picket line were able to produce twenty trucks on the second strike day and twenty-six on the third, although some strikers hotly contested these numbers, arguing that Freightliner management was including in the count trucks that had been made before the strike. That day, 2 strikers accused a supervisor of intentionally hitting them with her car as she left the plant. There were no other reports of violence.[55]

The two sides deployed strategies to maximize the size of their ranks. Freightliner used a stick, and the UAW used a carrot. On Friday, December 6, Freightliner management gave strikers a deadline of Monday, December 9, to return to work. Despite the jurisprudence regarding reinstatement of employees after an unfair labor practice strike, company officials said that those who missed the Monday deadline might not get their jobs back once the strike had ended. The company would first have to approve their return. UAW Local 5285 president Dean Eason responded by reassuring strikers that US labor law protected their jobs because the strike was over unfair labor practices. Eason also offered to provide strike pay to all who stopped crossing the picket line even if they currently were not UAW members. Local 5285 organized a peaceful rally outside of Freightliner's main entrance at 6 a.m. on December 9, the date the company set for employees to return to work without need of approval. Approximately six hundred strikers held hands in a "show of solidarity." The high attendance at the rally demonstrated that most strikers had chosen to stay out despite the company's deadline. Later that day, Freightliner management stated that the company would operate just one shift with the five hundred employees who were still crossing the picket line. Both sides announced that they would meet to negotiate on December 10. It would be the first talks since the strike began.[56] Negotiations lasted three days, concluding on Thursday, December 12, without making progress. Two days later, Local 5285 held a rally featuring UAW members from a Volvo truck plant in New River Valley, Virginia, and a Mack truck plant in Winnsboro, South Carolina. The visiting UAW members brought words of encouragement and material support in the form of cash and in-kind donations for the strikers.[57]

Talks resumed on Tuesday, December 17. Freightliner spokesperson Debi Nicholson said that the Mount Holly plant produced thirty-six trucks that day, which was eleven more than on the previous Friday. She attributed the rise in output to employees who crossed the picket line putting in voluntary overtime.[58] On the same day, the UAW made its first disbursement of strike pay. The union typically distributes $100 per week to each union member once a strike has lasted ten days. In this instance, the UAW paid not only the $100 but also $100 more in advance for the following week plus a Christmas bonus of $100, for a total of $300. The week's events made clear that the seven hundred striking employees were holding firm. Despite management's decision to consolidate to one shift, the employees crossing the picket line did not have the full range of skills needed to keep the plant operating much longer. The parties reached a tentative agreement on Thursday, December 19, 1991.[59]

The lead negotiators from Freightliner and the UAW, Scott Evitt and Phil Cabreros, released a joint statement that described the contract as an "equitable first agreement,"[60] but it was widely considered a victory for the strikers and the UAW.[61] The collective bargaining agreement included an immediate 8.7 percent wage increase retroactive to October 1991, which resolved the unfair labor practice claims alleging the withholding of wages. The accord also provided for a thirty-five-cent raise in both 1992 and 1993. These pay improvements put Mount Holly employees on par with those at Freightliner's Portland plant. Beside pay increases, the contract added a new 401k program to supplement Freightliner's existing defined benefit pension plan and created two joint labor-management committees: one for health and safety and the other for ergonomics. Both committees included paid positions for union representatives. The contract also contained a full grievance procedure with binding arbitration. The parties settled the outstanding unfair labor practice suit over the dismissal of Stanley Roseboro. Freightliner managers agreed to reinstate him with back pay so long as they could include a two-week disciplinary suspension on his employment record. Union members at the Mount Holly plant voted overwhelmingly to ratify the agreement the next day, ending the strike seventeen days after it had begun.[62]

Beyond material gains, the strike served as a strong bonding experience for the seven hundred employees who struck. Freightliner employee Tommy Elmore captured this well when he said, "We didn't take no Freightliner contract. We took a UAW contract."[63] Freightliner president Dieter Zetsche provided the company's official assessment: "Freightliner believes the agreement is a fair and reasonable settlement of the labor dispute. What is most important now is to restore a unified workforce at the Mount Holly plant and continue producing quality trucks."[64]

Remarkably, animosity between the strikers and the employees who continued to work was relatively low. Victory put most strikers in a charitable frame of mind. The generous contract made it difficult for the employees who crossed the picket line to hold a grudge against their colleagues who struck. The employees who continued working during the strike made a gesture of reconciliation by donating $279 to a charity in memory of Bobby Anderson, who was a striker who was killed near his home during the walkout in a case of mistaken identity unrelated to the strike.[65] Differences remained regarding workers' opinions of unions in general and the UAW in particular. Some would never join the union. From time to time, exchanges between pro- and anti-union employees would appear on the opinion page of the local newspaper.[66] Nonetheless, attitudes toward the UAW were never again a deeply divisive issue in the Mount Holly plant.

Freightliner management's decision not to hire additional employees as strikebreakers was decisive in the union victory, because reliance solely on current employees who were willing to cross the picket line proved insufficient to maintain adequate production levels. The evidence does not definitively establish why Freightliner management made this decision, but there are two plausible explanations: support from German employee representatives and the commission of unfair labor practices by Freightliner management. The trip to Germany by Bill Casstevens and John Christensen to gain the support of German employee representatives, who were in turn able to threaten German management credibly, substantially raised the cost of breaking the strike. The commission of unfair labor practices also raised the cost of breaking the strike, because the company would have to take back all the strikers at the end of the dispute. Management therefore could not promise potential strikebreakers permanent jobs. Either of these scenarios—or both—could explain why Freightliner management did not hire strikebreakers.

Many local business leaders and political figures were dismayed that the UAW prevailed in both the recognition election and the strike, but at no point did they intervene. It is worth noting that the Mount Holly plant was not new when the organizing drive began and that Freightliner had not received large subsidies and abatements from state and local governments to build or to expand it. State and local politicians were therefore far less invested in the plant than were their counterparts in Canton, Chattanooga, and Vance, where substantial sums from the state and local governments subsidized the construction and operation of the plants and where the reputations and political futures of the lawmakers who recruited the foreign firms were on the line.

Consolidation at the Mount Holly Plant, 1992–1997

The Mount Holly plant remained the sole unionized Freightliner facility in North Carolina for more than a decade. UAW representatives made several overtures to the employees at Freightliner's nearby Gastonia parts plant, but they did not receive a sufficiently strong response to proceed further. The UAW's success at Mount Holly also failed to spark successful organizing campaigns at other companies in the region.

Leadership changed at the top of Freightliner shortly after the 1991 Mount Holly strike. Dieter Zetsche moved up at Daimler-Benz. He became deputy chair of the Mercedes-Benz supervisory board. James L. Hebe, a flamboyant American who was Freightliner's executive vice president for sales and marketing, succeeded Zetsche as president.[67] The timing was fortunate for Hebe. Negotiations for the North American Free Trade Agreement finished in October 1992, triggering a boom in truck sales. Freightliner increased truck output by 21.6 percent in 1992 alone.[68] Employment expanded at all of Freightliner's North Carolina plants. To maximize market share, Freightliner adopted many practices pioneered in the automobile sector, including rebates, power train warranties, and leasing.[69] These steps paid off in the short run. Freightliner became the largest truck producer in North America in 1991, which was a first for a foreign-owned company in the sector, and has held that position ever since.[70]

Freightliner acquired several new facilities in the region during the late 1980s and 1990s, including the high-end Oshkosh Custom Chassis plant in Gaffney, South Carolina, and Thomas Built Buses (TBB) in High Point, North Carolina.[71] Freightliner received just under four million dollars in subsidies from the State of North Carolina during the 1990s—which was a small amount even in those days—to improve the Cleveland plant that the company had bought from M.A.N. in 1989 and no subsidies from the State of South Carolina.[72]

Industrial relations at the Mount Holly plant became generally peaceful and positive, occasionally punctuated with moments of tension. Negotiating a second contract in late 1994 is an instance of the latter. The first collective bargaining agreement was set to expire on Friday, December 16. Negotiations had again been difficult. UAW Local 5825 members gathered on December 10 to hear from the bargaining team about the status of the talks. The parties had not reached agreement regarding health insurance and paid sick leave. At Freightliner's Portland plant, management convinced IAM negotiators to accept a premium-sharing arrangement for future retirees. It now wished to implement the same plan at the Mount Holly plant. Freightliner management also pressed to reduce the number of paid union representatives in the plant. The membership meeting included a preliminary strike vote, which was helpful to the union leadership because it would have been difficult to gauge the commitment of the workers to industrial action without one. Even though 1,915 of Mount Holly workers were union members, most had not worked at the plant during the 1991 strike because of turnover and an expansion of employment by roughly 900 to 2,194. The local leadership expressed gratification and relief when 94 percent of those present authorized a strike. Union officials scheduled a second rank-and-file meeting on Sunday, December 18. The leaders would present the results of the final round of negotiations, and the membership would vote whether to accept a tentative contract or go on strike the next day.[73]

The last week of negotiations was difficult. Freightliner management let it be known that if employees went on strike, the company would hire permanent replacements to continue building enough cabs to supply the Cleveland and St. Thomas, Ontario, plants. Since a potential industrial action this time would be over economic matters rather than unfair labor practices, the threat to hire replacements was potent because the company would have no legal obligation to reinstate strikers immediately after a dispute ended. Support from Germany was also less likely this time. The Germans who had helped three years earlier were in no position to assist. Franz Steinkühler had resigned as IG Metall chair in May 1993 after accusations of insider trading surfaced involving Mercedes shares,[74] and Karl Feuerstein was fully occupied with a much bigger problem that was closer to home: the German auto industry suffered a sales downturn that necessitated negotiating the terms of a workforce reduction at Daimler that ultimately topped fifty thousand.[75]

Tension at the Mount Holly plant heightened during the final week of talks. Freightliner management alleged that some disgruntled workers intentionally damaged some trucks, threatened nonunion employees, staged a protest in the management suite, and slowed production down to sixty-two trucks, which was twenty fewer than the daily quota.[76] In the end, however, there was no strike. The bargaining parties reached an agreement on December 16, one hour before the old contract expired. Local 5285 leaders used the December 18 membership meeting to present the details of the contract and to hold a ratification vote. Once again, the contract was generous. Hourly pay would increase by $1 in the first year and 50 cents in each of the next two years, which would bring the top hourly wage rate to $18.30 by the end of the contract. Workers would also receive annual cost of living adjustments and a $350 signing bonus. Overtime pay would become double time after ten hours of work on a single shift. The company added a new health insurance option, and all employees would be covered under a $5,000 life insurance policy. The contract increased the number of annual paid holidays from twelve to thirteen, and workers with twenty-four or more unused sick days could use ten of them as vacation days. Freightliner's contribution to employees' 401k retirement plans would increase from 2 percent to 4 percent of an employee's base wage. The union negotiators made one significant concession; they agreed to premium sharing to cover the cost of future retirees' health care. The agreement created a tax-exempt voluntary employees' beneficiary association trust funded by a payroll deduction of 4 cents an hour to cover the employees' share.[77] Management spokesperson Debi Nicholson said, "We think it's a good contract." The union members agreed. They voted 1,228 to 56 to accept it.[78]

The leadership changed hands at the UAW as Owen Bieber stepped down in June 1995 after serving twelve years as the union's president. Bieber was an easy-going midwesterner who faced difficult times for the auto industry. He did not have the charisma of his predecessor, Douglas Fraser, but at six-foot-four and 265 pounds, he was a presence. The 1995 UAW convention elected Stephen P. Yokich, head of the union's General Motors department, to succeed Bieber. Yokich and Bieber were a study in contrasts. Yokich was gruff and volatile and had a reputation for drinking and gambling. He was often aggressive and always a hard bargainer. Yokich appealed to many in the UAW because they thought that Bieber should have been more confrontational during downsizing in the 1980s. Yokich said that organizing foreign vehicle plants would be a priority.[79]

The good times rolled for a few more years, but the heavy truck sector suffered a short sharp downturn in 1996. Employment at the Mount Holly plant fell by 32 percent to 1,554, and excess inventory prompted Freightliner to idle all but the Gaffney, South Carolina, plant for a week.[80] Freightliner president James Hebe's strategy to overcome the steep cycles in the trucking sector was to diversify within it. Freightliner bought American LeFrance, an ambulance and fire truck manufacturer that was a recognized brand but had just ceased production. The company began producing trucks using that brand name at the Cleveland plant.[81] Demand for heavy trucks recovered rapidly in 1997; sales more than doubled the 1996 totals. Freightliner management quickly rehired most of the laid-off employees.[82] The company also resumed making acquisitions; it bought Ford's heavy truck division, which it renamed Sterling Trucks.[83]

Completing a third collective bargaining agreement for the Mount Holly plant in December 1997 was a much smoother undertaking than the previous two negotiations. The two sides met twenty-five times over two months and expressed positive confidence throughout the talks. The sudden bounce-back in demand put the UAW in a strong position. There were no signs of tension in the plant, and Local 5825 made few preparations for a strike. The talks did go down to the wire; the parties reached an agreement on December 20, three hours before the contract expired. The gains for Freightliner employees were significant. The nominal results were a bit lower than in the previous two agreements, but this was largely a product of the lower inflation rate. The annual wage increases in the three-year contract were 65 cents, 45 cents, and 45 cents, which would increase the top hourly wage to $19.85 in the last year of the agreement. Employees also received a $500 ratification bonus and improvements to the retirement and health insurance plans. Once again, the members ratified the agreement.[84]

Bargaining to Organize: The UAW Expands in North Carolina

In May 1998 Daimler-Benz, Freightliner's parent company, merged with Chrysler to form DaimlerChrysler.[85] The merger had implications for Freightliner. The UAW had organized Chrysler in the 1930s and had a long-standing neutrality and card-check recognition agreement that included a mutual nondisparagement clause. The merger did not include an automatic extension of the neutrality and card-check recognition agreement to Freightliner, but it did mean that most of the North American leadership of Freightliner's new parent company, DaimlerChrysler, was accustomed to working with the UAW. A UAW member, moreover, would now be on the DaimlerChrysler supervisory board (*Aufsichtsrat*). Germany's 1976 codetermination law requires larger companies to allot half of the twenty seats on their supervisory board to employee representatives.[86] DaimlerChrysler management, in consultation with the company's German works council representatives and officials from IG Metall, agreed that a UAW official could hold one of the employee seats on the supervisory board. This decision was also in keeping with the practice at Chrysler. In 1980, Chrysler management had agreed to allow UAW president Doug Fraser to serve on Chrysler's board of directors in exchange for wage concessions. Subsequent UAW presidents had also served on Chrysler's board.

Three weeks after the announcement of the merger, Yokich and UAW vice president Richard Shoemaker met with IG Metall chair Klaus Zwickel. They agreed to three actions. First, IG Metall would cede a seat on the DaimlerChrysler supervisory board to Yokich. Second, Yokich and Zwickel would propose to the DaimlerChrysler board that the company create a world employee committee.[87] Third, the two unions agreed to cooperate in organizing the German auto factories in the United States, including the new Mercedes-Benz plant in Vance, Alabama.[88] The union leaders made no specific commitments regarding Daimler's North American truck unit.

Business was looking up for Freightliner in 1998. Bottlenecks in railroad capacity triggered a new boom in the North American heavy truck market. Freightliner management pounced, expanding plants and adding thousands of employees to ramp up production. The surge in output enabled Freightliner to set a new company sales record. Market analysts nonetheless expressed concern that Freightliner was growing beyond what the market could sustain over the long run.[89] Freightliner continued to add capacity and to diversify the company's product palette. In October 1998, the company purchased TBB of High Point, North Carolina.[90] As a result of the purchase, roughly half of Freightliner's workforce was in North Carolina.

In April 1999, the UAW launched a unionization drive at Freightliner's Gastonia parts plant. On the day before the organizing effort began, Freightliner management announced a $1 per hour pay raise for all nonunion plants and a $1,000 bonus for all employees. Management said it took these steps because 1998 had been such a strong year for the company.[91] The Gastonia unionization campaign lost some steam after the unilateral pay increases. Nonetheless, UAW officials attempted to leverage the union's more robust relationship with DaimlerChrysler to pressure management to extend neutrality and card-check recognition to the Freightliner factories in the Carolinas and the Mercedes plant in Alabama. The union was in a strong position. The North American collective bargaining agreement between the UAW and DaimlerChrysler for the automobile sector would expire that fall, and management wanted to avoid a strike because auto sales were strong. DaimlerChrysler management claimed to accept neutrality in recognition elections but remained opposed to the card-check procedure.[92]

At the May 1999 meeting of the DaimlerChrysler supervisory board, UAW president Stephen Yokich pressed the company to agree to card-check recognition at the Gastonia parts plant and the new Mercedes facility in Vance, Alabama. Jack Laskowski, UAW vice president responsible for DaimlerChrysler and trucks, was upbeat about obtaining card-check recognition for both plants as part of the negotiations of a new contract for Chrysler employees, stating that "there are still a few hiccups to be ironed out," but "the majority of them were worked out."[93] An agreement on card check eluded the UAW, however. Laskowski suffered a fatal heart attack during the negotiations, and Yokich stepped in to complete them. Extending card check to the Mercedes plant or the Freightliner plants was not in the final agreement. Former UAW president Bob King believes that Yokich traded it away for another demand in the final phase of bargaining.[94]

Maintaining the company policy of neutrality at the local level proved difficult at times. For example, in April 1999, Freightliner CEO James Hebe had sent a letter to Gastonia employees urging them to resist the UAW's organizing drive. Thomas P. Stallkamp, who oversaw DaimlerChrysler's Chrysler operations in North America, responded by asking the German management at the top of the company to convey to managers at Freightliner and the Alabama Mercedes-Benz plant "that they're part of a bigger entity." Hebe sent a second letter to employees dated ten days after the first letter that stated, "We will respect our parent company's policy of a neutral position."[95]

The truck market began to cool off in the second half of 1999, despite a frothy economy. The Chinese economic boom and the dot-com bubble in the United States had triggered a worldwide spike in commodity prices. The cost of diesel fuel soared and shortages arose, which led transporters to look for alternatives to heavy trucks. Interest rates had also increased, which put trucks beyond the reach of some customers despite Freightliner's aggressive use of leases and buy-back guarantees. New orders for 1999 fell by 31 percent when compared to the previous year. Production capacity, which several companies including Freightliner boosted during the hot truck market of the previous year, suddenly exceeded demand by 25 percent.

At the February 2000 meeting of the UAW/DaimlerChrysler council, newly named UAW vice president for DaimlerChrysler Nate Gooden announced that German management had agreed to honor a neutrality letter and Freightliner management had agreed to allow UAW representatives in their plants so long as the company received four weeks' notice. The letter did not include card-check recognition.[96]

Economic circumstances worsened with the bursting of the dot-com bubble in March 2000. Demand for shipping fell sharply, prompting companies to thin their truck fleets. The number of trucks coming off leases mushroomed at Freightliner dealerships, which forced dealers to cut prices for used trucks and to reduce orders for new ones. The collapse in demand hit Freightliner's North Carolina operations hard. In August 2000 management announced that it would end the third shift at the Cleveland and Mount Holly plants on October 20, which shrank the workforce by one-third at both facilities (i.e., 1,304 and 825 jobs lost, respectively). The Gastonia parts plant shed relatively fewer jobs—154, or 15 percent—but it was still a substantial blow.[97] Freightliner was not alone. The whole truck sector stepped hard on the brake, cutting production levels in the second half of the year by 40 percent compared to the first half. The job losses came at a difficult time for the region. Even before the layoffs, previous plant closures in the two counties where the factories are located—Gaston and Rowen— had already driven the unemployment rate over 8 percent, which was significantly higher than the 5 percent rate in neighboring counties.[98]

Top management was keen on Daimler projecting an image of a progressive, responsible global enterprise. To that end, Daimler was among the original participants in the UNGC, which the United Nations launched on July 26, 2000. The UNGC "is a voluntary international corporate citizenship network initiated to support the participation of both the private sector and other social actors to advance responsible corporate citizenship and universal social and environmental principles to meet the challenges of globalization." Principle 3 of the compact is "The support of freedom of association and the recognition of the right to collective bargaining."[99] Aggressively combating the fledgling organizing drives at Daimler facilities in the Carolinas would not have been compatible with top management's adherence to the UNGC, and they did not do so.

The slumping truck market made the 2000 negotiations for a fourth collective bargaining agreement at the Mount Holly plant tense. In September, the leaders of UAW Local 5285 kicked things off with a show of force. The union held a rally outside the Mount Holly plant featuring over two thousand union workers from across the South. Top officials from the UAW's Detroit headquarters also took part. Speakers presented the union's opening position for the talks, which included demands for profit sharing, better bonuses, parity with competitors' compensation, supplemental unemployment insurance in cases of layoffs, and improved cost of living allowances and dental insurance for retired workers. The speakers argued that Freightliner could afford these demands despite recent difficulties in the trucking sector because the company made $6 billion in 1999.[100]

On October 31, 2000, labor and management negotiators held the first round of contract talks. The two sides were far apart. The UAW negotiators presented their demands in a twenty-nine-page proposal. Freightliner representatives proposed keeping the existing contract and limiting negotiations to the size of the wage increase. Union negotiators rejected that request. Company officials intensified the tension level by threatening to lock out employees if there were no agreement by December 18, which was three days after the existing contract expired.[101] Huge losses at Chrysler also raised the stakes in the Freightliner negotiations because they intensified DaimlerChrysler management's pursuit of savings in all of Daimler's North American businesses. Chrysler's losses prompted DaimlerChrysler management to replace Chrysler's American CEO, James Holden, with a German, Dieter Zetsche, who had briefly served as Freightliner CEO in the early 1990s.[102]

Initially, the contract talks for the Mount Holly plant made little headway. The pace quickened in December as the deadline neared. Both parties reported progress in the final week, but each also contributed to escalating tensions. On December 10, Freightliner management threatened to move production from Mount Holly to its plant in Santiago Tianguistenco, Mexico, if there were no settlement by December 15. Some employees doubted the credibility of the threat because Freightliner had expanded the Mount Holly plant just a few years earlier; they also argued that a significant number of customers would refuse to buy a truck made in Mexico.[103] The next day, Local 5285 held a raucous standing-room-only rally in the Mount Holly Middle School auditorium in which union members roundly rejected the company's offer to keep the existing contract while increasing wages by $1.15 in the first year and the cost of living in the subsequent two years. The union leadership announced that it would hold another rank-and-file meeting on Sunday, December 18, at which the members would either vote on a tentative agreement or hold a strike vote.[104]

On Friday, December 15, the day the contract expired, parties held a marathon negotiating session that did not end until 4 a.m. the next day. The two sides made considerable progress but had not reached a settlement. They agreed to meet again that evening at 9:30. In the meantime, twenty members of Local 5285 set up a small picket line at the front gate of the Mount Holly plant. The parties finally reached an agreement at 2:30 a.m. on Sunday, December 17.[105]

Once again, the UAW achieved significant gains for Mount Holly employees on several fronts. Wages for employees receiving the top rate would increase by $1.15 in the first year and by 75 cents and 50 cents, respectively, in the second and third years. For employees who had not yet reached the top hourly rate, wages would rise by $1.15 in the first year and by 3 percent in the subsequent two years. They would also receive an additional 50-cent wage increase every six months until they reached the top rate. All employees on the seniority roster, including those who had been laid off recently, received a $2,500 ratification bonus. Workers employed at the plant on October 1, 2001, would receive an additional $500 bonus in December 2001. The new contract also included an annual profit-sharing bonus that would range between $1,000 and $2,000. The amount would never be lower than the general bonus paid to Freightliner employees who were not covered by a collective agreement. Beyond compensation, Mount Holly employees received supplemental unemployment benefits in the form of health, life, and accident/disability insurance for six months after a layoff and would continue to accumulate seniority while laid off or on medical leave. The contract also contained new health and safety measures, including an annual health and safety audit, an ergonomic analysis that included restructuring of poorly designed jobs, and a full-time UAW health and safety representative at the plant at company expense. The UAW flag was added to the others flying outside the plant, and perhaps most important, Freightliner management committed to produce the company's new medium-duty vehicle at Mount Holly unless "compelling economic circumstances" forced it to do otherwise.[106]

Freightliner's financial woes deepened in 2001. Sales of heavy trucks were off by 60 percent from their peak two years earlier, and a flood of trucks coming off lease agreements drove the price of used trucks down by 25–40 percent.[107] Freightliner CEO James Hebe frantically proposed a series of new financing programs designed to expand the number of individuals and firms that could buy trucks and to shore up the used truck market.[108] Freightliner nonetheless lost $100 million in the first quarter of 2001. In May, the leaders at DaimlerChrysler decided to replace Hebe with a German, Rainer Schmückle, just as they had done for Chrysler the year before. Schmückle was familiar with Freightliner. Before serving as a senior vice president at DaimlerChrysler, he had been Freightliner's chief financial officer from 1994 to 1997. Schmückle's assignment as Freightliner CEO was clear but by no means easy: restore Freightliner to profitability.[109] His first step was to cut jobs. Freightliner laid off over 1,000 additional employees worldwide, including 475 at the Mount Holly plant in July and 123 at the Gastonia parts plant in August.[110]

The September 11 attacks on the Pentagon and the World Trade Center sent the US economy into a short, sharp tailspin. A month later, Schmückle announced a three-year $850 million restructuring plan designed to maximize Freightliner's profitability rather than "accumulating market share." The plan included 2,700 additional layoffs, closures of plants in Canada and a parts plant in Portland, a 5 percent pay cut for all nonunion employees, suspension of bonuses, a new monthly employee contribution for health insurance, changes to the company's leasing and truck buy-back programs, and a onetime write-off of $330 million.[111] Freightliner management obtained comparable concessions at the company's unionized Portland assembly plant by threatening to close it if the unions represented there did not agree to the cuts.[112] Mount Holly was the only Freightliner plant where employee compensation did not change. Freightliner management asked the UAW to make concessions, but union officers refused. The plant's three-year collective agreement was less than a year old, and Freightliner management could not credibly threaten to close the Mount Holly facility because it was the only one in the United States producing medium-sized and severe-duty trucks.[113]

The restructuring plan combined with the UAW's success in staving off concessions at the Mount Holly plant sparked new interest in organizing among workers at all of Freightliner's nonunion plants in North Carolina. This was particularly true at the Gastonia parts plant once rumors began to circulate that Freightliner management was considering selling it. When the prospects of unionization began to rise, the Gastonia town elite made their opposition clear. The employees' voluntary organizing committee had difficulty even finding a place to meet in the town. As the drive proceeded, local Freightliner management made plain its hostility toward unionization, despite the DaimlerChrysler policy of neutrality. Elite opposition never expanded beyond the town, however, and elites never mounted a formal campaign against unionization. The UAW collected the target number of authorization cards from Gastonia employees and asked for NLRB-supervised recognition election. On March 18, 2002, two days before the election, Freightliner chief operating officer Roger Nielson held a mandatory captive-audience meeting for all Gastonia employees. At the meeting, Nielson underscored Freightliner's still fragile financial position and threatened workers with reduced pay and benefits as well as job losses if the employees voted for the union. The UAW lost the recognition election by a close margin: 322 to 346.[114]

UAW organizing director Bob King condemned Freightliner management, complaining that it "not only violated both the law and neutrality protections that DaimlerChrysler agreed to and reaffirmed in writing . . . [but] also stole from these workers the union rights and recognition that they deserve."[115] The UAW quickly filed unfair labor practice charges against Freightliner. On July 25,

2002, NLRB regional officer Earl Pfeffer announced that the board's Winston-Salem office would hear the unfair labor practice charges later that year.[116] King also let DaimlerChrysler managers know that "there would be trouble with Chrysler if they did not allow neutrality at Freightliner."[117]

UAW leadership changed hands in June 2002. Stephen Yokich was sixty-six and in failing health. The UAW's thirty-third convention elected Ron Gettelfinger as the union's president. The contrast between Gettelfinger and Yokich was stark. Gettelfinger was a straitlaced and deeply religious Roman Catholic who grew up on a farm in Indiana. He did not drink, gamble, or smoke. Two attributes that Yokich and Gettelfinger shared were that they could at times be abrasive and were hard bargainers.[118] Yokich resigned from DaimlerChrysler's supervisory board when he stepped down as president. Nate Gooden, UAW vice president responsible for the heavy truck sector, took his place.[119]

After three years of at times tense negotiations with DaimlerChrysler management, IG Metall and UAW leaders agreed to create a global works council. The DaimlerChrysler World Employee Committee (WEC) held its constituent meeting in July 2002. The committee had thirteen employees and trade union representatives from four continents. Brazil, Canada, Spain, and South Africa each had a single representative. The UAW had three, and Germany had six. The WEC elected Erich Klemm, chair of the Daimler enterprise works council, as WEC chair, and Nate Gooden as vice chair. It is important to note that the WEC does not have codetermination rights comparable to a German works council. The WEC's scope is limited to information and consultation, which is the norm for global employee committees. The committee meets once a year, which is also the norm.[120]

One of the WEC's first actions was to draft a document jointly with DaimlerChrysler management and the International Metalworkers Federation (IMF), the global union federation in the mechanical engineering sector at the time, based on the UNGC regarding corporate social responsibility, which DaimlerChrysler had already signed. The parties also signed a four-page document titled "Social Responsibility Principles of DaimlerChrysler" in September 2002 at the company's North American headquarters in Auburn Hills, Michigan. The document committed DaimlerChrysler to respect and support compliance with all internationally accepted human rights, including a condemnation of forced labor, a rejection of child labor, equal opportunities and nondiscrimination with respect to employment, and equal pay for equal work. The company acknowledged "the human right to form trade unions," constructive cooperation with employee representatives, and direct, respectful, and fair communication with employees. DaimlerChrysler also "opposed all exploitative working conditions" and supported "protection of health" and "the right to reasonable compensation" in both the firm and its suppliers.[121]

With the NLRB hearing over unfair labor practices at Freightliner pending, Nate Gooden persuaded the DaimlerChrysler supervisory board to ask Freightliner management to negotiate a neutrality and card-check recognition agreement with the UAW like the UAW's existing arrangement for Chrysler facilities. This sort of "leveraging of existing contractual relations with a company in order to make it easier to organize other workers in the company" is known as "bargaining to organize."[122] Codetermination was particularly conducive to facilitating such an exchange because it brought management and trade union representatives together regularly at supervisory board meetings.

In the second half of 2002, Nate Gooden and UAW administrative assistant David McAllister exchanged drafts for the neutrality and card-check recognition agreement as well as a separate confidential "agreement on preconditions" with Rainer Schmückle and Freightliner human resources head Scott Evitt. The union officials made sure that the agreement included card-check recognition as well as neutrality provisions, because corporate verbal declarations of neutrality proved insufficient when the UAW attempted to organize DaimlerChrysler's Mercedes plant in Vance, Alabama, in 1999–2000. The negotiators reached consensus on both the precondition agreement and the neutrality and card-check document in October 2002, and Evitt and Gooden signed final versions in mid-December. The neutrality agreement, which was public, prompted a postponement of the NLRB hearing.[123] The preconditions agreement remained confidential until discovery for an unrelated 2006 lawsuit brought it to light.[124]

The provisions of the Freightliner neutrality and card-check recognition agreement were typical for this sort of arrangement. Freightliner management agreed to send a letter to all employees explaining that the company was taking a neutral position regarding unionization. The union and Freightliner officials would jointly draft the authorization card's language and make a joint presentation at a mandatory information meeting for employees during work hours at which cards would be distributed and collected. During the organizing campaign, UAW representatives would have "reasonable access" to the employees during the workday in nonwork areas, including parking lots, building entrances and exits, break areas, cafeterias, and hallways. The two parties agreed to a nondisparagement clause and to refrain from making media statements unless the text had joint approval in advance. Any organizing campaign would begin on a mutually agreed upon date and end two weeks later. A neutral party would count the authorization cards.[125]

In the separate confidential preconditions agreement, Freightliner management obtained several concessions from the UAW. These included allowance for variation in terms and conditions of employment for each business unit (i.e., buses, chassis, fire and rescue, parts, and trucks) owing to industry differences, no guaranteed employment or transfer rights between units, no severance pay or supplemental unemployment benefits in the event of a layoff or plant closure, no future expectation to meet "the UAW pattern," no subcontracting prohibition provided the economics indicated noncompetitiveness of the unit in question, some burden sharing to cover future increases in benefit costs, and a commitment that "there would be no wage adjustments provided at any newly organized manufacturing plant prior to mid-2003."[126]

An August 20 letter from Evitt to McAllister indicates that wage concessions were not limited to newly organized plants. It stated that "a final agreement is dependent upon receiving some contractual relief at Mount Holly. Specifically, Freightliner expects cancellation of 12/02 wage increase, cancellation of 1/03 profit sharing bonus, benefits cost sharing by employees, and an extension of the current contract with no wage increases."[127]

Once the signatures were on the neutrality and card-check recognition agreement, the UAW acted fast on multiple fronts. The union launched a two-week organizing drive at Freightliner's Cleveland plant on January 17, 2003, and a second drive at the Gastonia plant a day later. A snowstorm on January 16 and 17 produced some initial anxiety among UAW supporters, but it only took one day to achieve a majority at the Cleveland plant and two days at the Gastonia plant.[128] Two months later, UAW president Ron Gettelfinger publicly praised DaimlerChrysler management and Nate Gooden for negotiating the neutrality and card-check recognition agreement at the UAW-DaimlerChrysler joint conference in Detroit.[129] In May 2003, two small Freightliner predelivery inspection facilities in Mount Holly and Cleveland, which employ thirteen and thirty-five respectively, approved UAW representation using the neutrality and card-check recognition agreement.[130]

The UAW made good on its confidential commitment to Freightliner to make concessions at the Mount Holly plant. Freightliner and UAW representatives began negotiations for a new contract for the Mount Holly plant on April 8, 2003, and reached an agreement on June 20, which was a full six months *before* the expiration date of the old contract. The new contract froze wages for three years, as the UAW had promised, and increased the employee contribution to cover the cost of health care. The contract was not wholly concessionary, however. UAW negotiators did manage to retain a profit-sharing bonus and to secure a commitment from Freightliner management to produce a minimum of 70 percent of the company's M-2 medium-duty trucks at Mount Holly, which was significant because Freightliner had also just begun manufacturing M-2 trucks at its Santiago Tianguistenco plant in Mexico.[131] UAW negotiators also made good on their commitment to Freightliner to forgo wage increases at the Cleveland and Gastonia plants until the second half of 2003 by conducting slow-paced negotiations for first contracts. Negotiators completed the contracts and employees ratified them in December 2003. The contract provisions were like those in the Mount Holly contract but did not include profit sharing.[132]

On February 12, twelve days after completing the card-check drive at the Gastonia plant, union sympathizers and UAW representatives began an organizing campaign at the TBB factory in High Point, North Carolina. Wages at TBB were the main issue because they fell short of those at the Freightliner plants in the state. TBB management adhered to the neutrality and card-check recognition agreement, but the UAW's recent success at the Gastonia and Cleveland plants prompted the High Point Chamber of Commerce and the Piedmont Associated Industries to come out publicly against the organizing drive. James Andrews, president of the North Carolina state organization of the American Federation of Labor–Congress of Industrial Organizations (AFL-CIO), which is the peak trade union confederation to which the UAW belongs, responded, stating that the business groups' intervention appalled him. Piedmont Associated Industries president Jim Patterson replied, "All we are trying to do is make sure the employees there hear both sides of the story." By signing a union card, he added, "They are ceding their voice to the union and letting the union represent them and they may not necessarily agree with what the union does." The Piedmont Associated Industries also set up an anti-union website. The small-scale, last-minute local opposition had little impact, but it was a harbinger of things to come elsewhere. On March 15, 2003, the UAW held a rally at a local hotel, and about 250 TBB employees and regional supporters turned out.[133]

The atmosphere in the plant and the community remained tense throughout the organizing drive, which lasted for a little over a year, because opinions differed regarding unionization. The High Point business community continued its campaign against unionization at TBB, expressing concerns that it would bring divisiveness to the community and scare away manufacturing investment from the area.[134] The UAW and TBB management scheduled a two-week period for a card-check procedure from March 4 to 17, 2004, following the process spelled out in the neutrality and card-check recognition agreement. On March 18, Freightliner management and the UAW leadership issued a joint statement announcing that a majority of TBB employees had signed union authorization cards.[135] Gary Casteel, director of UAW Region 8, which covers twelve southeastern and border states from Delaware to Mississippi, said that the margin was not close. Two issues proved to be most salient. First, in recent years TBB management had considered moving production to South Carolina and Mexico, which scared many employees. Second, many longtime employees signed cards because they were concerned about potential cuts to retirement benefits.[136]

The story does not end here, however. On April 14, 2004, Jeff Ward, a TBB employee, filed unfair labor practice charges against the company and the UAW with the support of the National Right to Work Legal Defense Foundation (NRWLDF), an anti-union group based in Springfield, Virginia. NRWLDF assistant Justin Hakes asserted that labor and management conducted a "joint, coercive organizing campaign." Specifically, Hakes claimed that the two compulsory meetings that TBB management and the UAW held as stipulated in the neutrality and card-check recognition agreement "tainted the process" because employees were able to sign union authorization cards at the meeting, which gave "workers the impression that their employer was tacitly endorsing the union." Hakes also complained that management gave UAW personal information about TBB employees and claimed that the UAW ignored employee attempts to revoke union authorization cards. Freightliner personnel head Scott Evitt responded to the unfair labor practice charges by saying that the company "does not have a dog in this fight." UAW Region 8 director Gary Casteel said that NRWLDF had filed similar charges in the past and that the UAW had won every time.[137]

Past performance did not guarantee the same result in this instance, however. The election of Republican George W. Bush to the presidency in 2000 led to appointees to the NLRB who were less accommodating to unions. On June 7, 2004, the NLRB voted 3 to 2 to review the general legality of neutrality and card-check recognition agreements owing to the large number of such cases that had recently come before it. As a result, the Winston-Salem NLRB regional office made a preliminary determination on June 30 that the two compulsory meetings were illegal assistance to the UAW but held back on issuing a formal complaint, given the board's June 7 decision.[138] Successive postponements pushed the case back into 2005. On March 3, TBB management and the UAW proposed a settlement. They asked the NLRB to hold a secret ballot union recognition election at the High Point plant. The NRWLDF dropped its suit a week later, and a week after that an NLRB administrative law judge, George Carlson, approved the settlement, which cleared the way for the election once the settlement had been posted in the plant for sixty days.[139] Gary Casteel said that union officials were "pleased to put this matter behind us, and we're comfortable with this agreement because it will put the decision of whether or not to join a union where it belongs: in the hands of workers at Thomas Built Bus."[140]

The NLRB scheduled a secret ballot union recognition election in the TBB plant for June 29. The mood in the High Point factory was tense in the weeks leading up to the vote. Union supporters wore orange NASCAR T-shirts that read "Go to Victory Lane with UAW." Union opponents wore T-shirts and pins that read "Union Ain't Wanted." In the end, 714 TBB employees voted for the union, which amounted to a 59 percent majority of the votes cast.[141]

On the day that the results of the union recognition election became public, Niels Chapman, leader of the pro-union employees in the plant, said, "We've been working hard for a long time to form our own union, so today's vote is really important for all of us."[142] "It's time for the healing process to begin," he added.[143] Not everyone agreed, however. A week later, the NRWLDF filed a new complaint on behalf of four TBB employees. The complaint alleged that Freightliner management improperly influenced the election by issuing a memo on the day before the vote advising employees that health care costs would rise on September 1. The NLRB dismissed the challenge and certified the election results on July 8. TBB recognized the UAW as the exclusive bargaining agent of the High Point employees on July 11. The NRWLDF continued to pursue actions against Freightliner and the UAW but was unsuccessful.[144] Failure in the initial foray to thwart the UAW from organizing southern vehicle assembly plants did not deter the NRWLDF. The organization continued to intervene in UAW organizing drives throughout the South. In October 2005 TBB reached agreement on a first contract, which the rank and file ratified.[145]

That same year, workers at Freightliner parts depots in Atlanta and Memphis voted to recognize the UAW as their exclusive collective bargaining agent. Altogether in the space of two years, the Freightliner neutrality and card-check agreement facilitated the organization of more than eight thousand employees at eight facilities in the southeastern United States.[146] In this second episode of organizing at Freightliner, the importance of cooperation between American and German employee representatives and German codetermination is unambiguous. The Freightliner neutrality and card-check agreement would not have happened had Nate Gooden not been a member of the DaimlerChrysler supervisory board, but success was also contingent on a favorable environment; local employers and politicians were late to react and had no vested interest in the affairs of the transnational firm.

The UAW's neutrality and card-check recognition agreement with Freightliner management did not result in the unionization of every DTNA plant in the Carolinas. The UAW failed to organize one facility: Freightliner's custom chassis factory in Gaffney, South Carolina. The particularities of the Gaffney plant explain the outcome. Custom chassis production is a high-end niche market that requires a high percentage of skilled, well-compensated employees. Pay was consequently less of a concern at Gaffney than at the other Freightliner facilities. The Gaffney plant was relatively small (it had four hundred employees) and had a young workforce, two attributes that make plants harder to organize.[147] Moreover, custom work was less sensitive to swings in the economy. The Gaffney plant experienced only one round of layoffs under Freightliner management, which was during the brief recession that followed the September 11, 2001, attacks. So, job security was also not an issue that would motivate Gaffney employees to support unionization.[148] This left the UAW little to offer in the organizing drive. Most Gaffney employees judged the cost of unionization to exceed the benefits. By the summer of 2003, more than 70 percent had signed a petition expressing their opposition to the UAW organizing the plant.[149]

On August 11, 2003, two Gaffney employees, with the help of the NRWLDF, filed unfair labor practice charges alleging that the UAW and DaimlerChrysler, as the parent company of Freightliner, were "trying to foist this unwanted 'company union' [the UAW] on the employees."[150] At the heart of the complaint was Freightliner management's decision not to grant scheduled raises to the Gaffney employees because of the UAW organizing campaign. The complaint charged the company and the union with attempting to coerce the Gaffney employees to join a union and unlawful premature bargaining. UAW president Ron Gettelfinger countered that the charges had no merit because it is illegal to alter the terms of employment during an organizing drive.[151]

At regional hearings, NLRB authorities recommended further review of the Gaffney unfair labor practice case. In August 2005, the NLRB general council announced a decision to pursue the case, which prompted Freightliner management and the UAW to negotiate a settlement with the board. The two parties agreed to post "conspicuous notices throughout the Gaffney facility that union officials will not accept unlawful assistance from Freightliner in future unionization attempts, and that no future wage increase will unlawfully be withheld at the behest of union officials."[152]

Why was the UAW able to organize three vehicle assembly plants and a parts plant in North Carolina, a state renowned for hostility to unions? Tracing the process showed several factors that contributed to the UAW's success. First, truck production has a volatile business cycle, which motivated more employees to embrace a union to improve their ability to protect their jobs and compensation in hard times. The two episodes of unionization at DTNA—from 1989 to 1991 and 1998 to 2005—occurred during or immediately after significant recessions. It is notable that the plant with the least economic volatility—Gaffney Custom Chassis—is also the one place where the organizing drive failed.

Second, management heavy-handedness—including the commission of unfair labor practices—contributed to the UAW's victories in both episodes, as is often the case in successful organizing drives.

Third, the comprehensive union-avoidance playbook was just beginning to cohere as managers at Nissan's Smyrna, Tennessee, plant and Toyota's Georgetown, Kentucky, plant began to experiment with new personnel policies, but it had not yet spread during the first round of organizing at DTNA in the late 1980s and early 1990s.

Fourth, the DTNA plants received few subsidies and tax abatements, which helped to keep these organizing drives from becoming statewide political issues.

To be sure, most local business and government leaders did not support these drives, but they never assembled sufficient resources or coordination to thwart them. Since there were few subsidies, tax credits, and abatements granted to DTNA, state and local politicians did not have their reputations as closely tied to the DTNA plants as has been the case in other states where public support was substantial.

Fifth, national anti-union lobbying organizations—in particular the NRWLDF—only became involved late in the second episode of unionization in the Carolinas. They consequently only had limited success.

Sixth, and important for our analysis, the Freightliner cases in the Carolinas show that transnational cooperation between worker representatives can have an impact on the likelihood of obtaining union recognition, but it is not sufficient for success. In these cases, it worked in conjunction with other factors. Two overlapping explanations in the first episode of organizing—transnational cooperation among employee representatives and management mistakes resulting in unfair labor practices—make it impossible to establish with certainty that unionization would not have happened at the Mount Holly plant without transnational cooperation.

In the second episode, however, the evidence suggests that the organizing drives would not have succeeded without the agreement between Freightliner management and the UAW to allow card-check recognition in exchange for economic concessions at the Mount Holly plant. It was advantageous to the organizing drive at DTNA facilities in the Carolinas that the 2000–2003 Mount Holly collective bargaining agreement enabled the employees at that plant to be the only ones in the company who successfully warded off the givebacks that DTNA management very much wanted. This gave national UAW officials a valuable bargaining chip to trade for card-check recognition. After all, the UAW lost the disputed 2002 recognition election at the Gastonia parts plant before it had cut the bargaining-to-organize deal. It was easier for UAW vice president Nate Gooden to persuade Freightliner management and the DaimlerChrysler supervisory board to accept a card-check agreement between the UAW and Freightliner because he was also a supervisory board member. Gooden had the seat because of Germany's codetermination laws and the support of the IG Metall leadership.

The failed Gaffney Custom Chassis organizing drive helps reveal the limits of the power of transnational cooperation between employee representatives to advance an organizing drive. Employee preferences matter. The economic and demographic attributes of the employees and the market segment a plant serves (i.e., young and highly skilled in an economically stable niche) were not conducive to generating interest in unionization. The card-check agreement between

Freightliner and the UAW was not a powerful enough factor to overcome the lack of interest in unionization at the Gaffney plant.

This chapter shows us that under the right circumstances, transnational cooperation between employee representatives can make a difference in organizing drives in the United States. Subsequent chapters help to define with greater precision the forms of cooperation between employee representatives that are (and are not) effective and the impact of different environments and opponents on the efficacy of this form of cooperation.

MERCEDES-BENZ U.S. INTERNATIONAL
Negative Neutrality

> **It's kind of hard to organize a guy driving a Mercedes to work every day.**
>
> —Kenneth "Wa Wa" Walters, president, Local 351, United Steelworkers of America

Mercedes-Benz U.S. International (MBUSI, with each letter pronounced individually) is the official name of the entity incorporated to build and manage a factory that makes Mercedes-Benz cars in Vance, Alabama, which is a small town east of Tuscaloosa.[1] Investigating unionization efforts at MBUSI enables us to refine our tracing of the unionization process at foreign-owned vehicle plants in the South. Specifically, we can assess whether (1) strong employee representation in a parent company's home country leads to union recognition at subsidiary plants abroad when management is resisting unionization; (2) transnational union cooperation, including having a trade union representative from a subsidiary on the parent company supervisory board, results in union recognition at that subsidiary; and (3) transnational agreements requiring respect for employee rights make a difference in organizing efforts. The organizing drives at MBUSI demonstrated that none of these is sufficient to obtain union recognition.

Both the UAW and the IAM failed in multiple attempts to organize the plant. The contrast between DTNA and MBUSI is striking. Although the same individuals made decisions for both units, management accepted the unionization of DTNA but resisted it at MBUSI. Managers claimed that the company was neutral regarding unionization at MBUSI but cast the matter in decidedly negative terms. They maintained that it was up to the employees to decide, but in their view MBUSI did not need a union.

Former UAW secretary-treasurer and Alabama native Gary Casteel stated that he found Daimler management's opposition to unionization at MBUSI "baffling," given "the great relationship" between the union and the company at

DTNA facilities.[2] Daimler management always treated the Vance plant differ-ently. It was a proving ground for new design and production strategies, the first located outside of Germany.[3] Unlike at DTNA, which was an acquisition, MBUSI was built from scratch. This gave management more opportunity to innovate. Managers borrowed from the rapidly evolving union-avoidance playbook by adopting a flexible open-door approach to employee relations pioneered at the Nissan plant in Smyrna, Tennessee, which kept to a minimum incidents that can inflame a workforce and fuel unionization drives.

MBUSI management also added to the union-avoidance playbook by segment-ing the labor force into a core of permanent employees and a substantial periphery of temporaries supplied by outside agencies. The core workers have received high pay and have been insulated from business-cycle swings. The prospect of becom-ing a permanent employee has kept temporaries compliant. Temporaries would never belong to a potential bargaining unit at MBUSI because they do not work directly for the company, which has divided the workforce and made organizing more difficult. Another difference between MBUSI and DTNA is the substantial state and local government financial support that Daimler received to build the Vance plant, which tied Alabama politicians and management closely together. This chapter traces why several organizing drives undertaken by two unions all failed.

The Decision to Build a Mercedes-Benz Plant in Alabama

In the first fifteen years after World War II, Daimler-Benz increased the sales of Mercedes-Benz automobiles in the United States from 1 car in 1948 to 12,225 in 1960. Sales continued to improve in subsequent years as transportation costs and the US tariff on automobiles fell markedly. The company sold 29,108 autos in the United States in 1970 and 53,790 in 1980. The supply-side economic policies of US president Ronald Reagan—which stimulated the economy, trimmed redis-tributive policies, and precipitated a spike in the value of the US dollar—resulted in a surge in Mercedes-Benz purchases in the first half of the 1980s. Sales peaked at 99,314 in 1986 and then dropped abruptly in the subsequent five years, falling to 58,886 by 1991.[4] The main causes of the slump were a change in US tax law that eliminated the deductibility of interest payments from car loans and a sharply appreciating deutschmark. In 1990, management at Daimler-Benz's do-mestic rival, BMW, began to search for a site in the United States to build a plant to cut costs and reduce exchange rate risk. BMW's move prompted Daimler-Benz management to do the same. Daimler-Benz leaders decided to produce a sport utility vehicle (SUV) in the United States, given the growing demand for SUVs in North America.[5]

Many observers thought that Daimler-Benz would build a plant in the Carolinas because the company already had several facilities there engaged in truck and bus production.[6] Daimler-Benz management chose Vance, Alabama, instead because the state and local government leaders offered $253 million in subsidies to build a $300 million dollar plant, which was far more than any other state—including North and South Carolina—had put on the table.[7] Alabama's package included what became known as the Mercedes law, which was a set of changes to the state's tax code including a reduction in employees' personal income tax obligations as well as a twenty-year state income tax exemption and permission to use tax credits to offset construction debt for Daimler-Benz.[8] The plant, which produced its first car—an M-Class SUV—in February 1997, initially employed 1,200 and had an annual capacity of sixty thousand units.[9]

UAW Leadership's Initial Response to the Decision to Build the Mercedes-Benz Plant

In April 1993 shortly after Daimler-Benz management announced that the company would be building a Mercedes-Benz plant somewhere in the United States, UAW officials considered how best to respond. They first drafted a letter that pointed out the good relationship that had developed between Daimler-Benz and the UAW at DTNA's Mount Holly plant and requested "an informal meeting with top Mercedes-Benz management."[10] The UAW leaders did not send that draft, however. They instead wrote a new letter that made a case for locating the plant in Michigan without even mentioning unionization or a meeting. The letter's signatories were the directors of the four UAW regions that cover Michigan rather than UAW president Owen Bieber. The letter was translated into German and sent to Herbert Gzik, head of engineering at Mercedes-Benz, who had an important role in selecting the US plant site.[11]

Press accounts indicate that by August 1993, Daimler-Benz management had winnowed the contending sites down to five, all of which were in the southeastern United States.[12] By September, Daimler-Benz had narrowed the choices to sites in North Carolina and Alabama. On September 27, 1993, UAW officials sent a second letter, this time to the chair of the Mercedes-Benz supervisory board, Helmut Werner. The authors were different: UAW president Owen Bieber, Secretary-Treasurer Bill Casstevens, and the union's four vice presidents. The contents of the letter differed as well. The first and last paragraphs of the letter, which was in English this time, restated the pitch for locating the plant in Michigan, but the middle two paragraphs focused on the UAW:

> The UAW would welcome an opportunity to meet with Mercedes to discuss cooperative labor-management relations which will help your company's new plant be among the most competitive in the world. We understand that innovative manufacturing processes and the most modern technologies require enlightened and innovative labor-management agreements which create a profitable business environment for the company and workers.
>
> The UAW is working in the domestic auto industry in creative ways such as with General Motors at Saturn. We would be pleased to discuss team concepts in manufacturing and limited job classifications which create flexibility to adapt to changing market conditions.[13]

The UAW's second letter arrived too late to affect site selection. On September 30, Daimler-Benz management announced that the company would build a plant in Vance.[14] On the day of the announcement, UAW vice president Stan Marshall sent a memo to Owen Bieber expressing concern that the Allied Industrial Workers of America would try to organize parts suppliers for the Mercedes-Benz plant if the UAW did not do so first.[15] Marshall added, "We also have to watch them in BMW and Mercedes. We need to stake out our rights to these plants—that means on-site action. We should try to get friendly people hired."[16]

Mercedes-Benz president Andreas Renschler sent a belated response dated November 2, 1993, to the UAW's September 28 letter to Helmut Werner. Renschler thanked Bieber for the letter, briefly described the exhaustive nature of the site search, and stated that "we hope to continue our good relationship as future neighbors in the U.S." The letter did not include an offer to meet.[17]

Officials from the powerful German metalworkers union IG Metall had already begun discussing increased cooperation with the UAW in the spring of 1991, soon after it became known that BMW was planning to build an assembly plant in the United States.[18] IG Metall leaders saw the investment as a threat; German labor costs had increasingly outstripped those in most of the world, including the United States.[19] BMW chair Eberhard von Kuenheim confirmed the concerns of German union officials in 1992. Two years before the company opened its plant in Spartanburg, South Carolina, Kuenheim stated that he would prefer to operate the plant without a union and would employ methods that South Carolina firms use to resist unionization, including hiring a law firm that specializes in union avoidance.[20]

IG Metall vice chair Klaus Zwickel, who was a member of the BMW supervisory board, sent a sharply worded letter to Kuenheim in response to his position on unionization in South Carolina. Zwickel wrote that "BMW should explain its decision for the U.S. with justified economic reasons and not combine it with a challenge to the American trade unions." He added that BMW would be "no exception" to the union's policy that workers in German-owned plants abroad should have union representation. Employee representatives on the BMW supervisory board would only approve the construction of a plant in South Carolina "if management . . . does not close its mind to trade union organization of the U.S. workforce."[21]

In practice, however, IG Metall leaders were unable to change the position of BMW management. They had no direct leverage through collective bargaining because the agreements covering BMW were regional contracts for the entire mechanical engineering industry. They also had insufficient clout within the institutions of codetermination. Although employees had ten of twenty seats on BMW's supervisory board, the 1976 Codetermination Act stipulates that one employee representative be an upper-level white-collar employee. That board member regularly voted with management. Union officials were unable to sway the BMW works council leadership to pressure BMW management to recognize the UAW. Company loyalty and paternalism had always characterized the relationship between management and the works council at BMW. Most are also IG Metall members, but primary loyalty is with the firm. So long as management assured works councilors that the South Carolina plant would not cost jobs in Germany, they were willing to go along with it.

IG Metall and UAW officials nonetheless engaged in several years of ad hoc actions to pressure BMW management to engage with the UAW. Owen Bieber met with two top BMW mangers in Munich. Bieber's executive administrative assistant, Dick Shoemaker, exchanged letters with the head of the Spartanburg plant, but BMW management's position remained unchanged regarding unionization.

UAW and IG Metall officials often misunderstood one another and their respective commitments while working together, which hampered their efforts and generated considerable frustration.[22] In a bid to improve interunion cooperation, Klaus Zwickel—who had recently advanced to chair of IG Metall—proposed "a draft for an agreement of orderly cooperation" between his union and the UAW.[23] In a cover letter, Zwickel stated his belief that the draft agreement delineates "a reasonable procedure that we certainly already practice in part." Zwickel added, "We should also show to the media how we defend ourselves against the attempt of multinational concerns to shut out trade unions."

Zwickel's draft agreement began with a brief description of the considerable amount of foreign direct investment between Germany and the United States in recent years, then depicted the relationship between foreign corporations and trade unions as "often extremely difficult" because "workers' representatives and trade unions are frequently under extreme pressure to make concessions for the sake of protecting the company's competitiveness within the corporate group," and "corporations try to avoid any trade union involvement and go to great lengths to obstruct the unions' attempts at organizing the workforce." The draft stated that the decision to "define a system of mutual support for organizing the workforce and come to each other's assistance in any conflict emerging within multinational corporations" was "prompted by a number of negative experiences." [24]

The meat of the draft agreement outlined the actions that would make mutual contributions more effective:

Information on Activities

– The trade union that represents the workers of the corporation will receive timely information about the start, development and results of campaigns organized in a subsidiary company of a multinational corporation.
– Prompt, and, where possible, written information (circulars, posters, flyers, etc.) including an assessment of strategies of the management and the subsidiary company concerned will be made available.

Mutual Coordination of Activities

– Policies vis-à-vis the management of the subsidiary company and the corporate management are to be coordinated and agreed to in time to prevent trade unions from being played off against one another on the strength of alleged demands.
– Unions' statements on the position and strategies of the parent company in the media must be shared in time for affected trade unions to speak with one voice instead of being quoted as having different positions.

Information of the Workforce

– Partner unions will inform the workforce of the parent company and subsidiaries of a corporation about current events (journals, handouts, flyers, etc.). Background information and updates on development of potential conflicts promotes solidarity and support for further action among members.

Information of Officials

– Partner Unions will inform their officials continuously (organizers, union officers, works councilors, board members, etc.) about conflicts of an ongoing campaign (circulars, meetings, seminars, etc.).

Additional Support

– Partner organizations will review and jointly agree on further
  activities and ways of lending support to one another. This
  includes mutual visits and discussions with the respective workforce, organization of events with speakers from the parent
  company and subsidiaries concerned, joint distribution of
  handouts etc.

Establishment of a Working Group

– When necessary, representatives of both organizations will jointly
  prepare a concept and schedule and submit them to the decision-
  making bodies of both organizations.

Publication of the Agreement / Seminar

– Contents and objectives of this agreement will be submitted to trade
  union members and officials. The signatories agree to conduct a
  seminar in the United States where responsible officials of the
  unions in the United States (organizers etc.) will be informed
  about trade unions and labor laws in Germany and equally,
  German officials will be informed about the situation in the U.S.

Review

– At the end of three years, the parties concerned shall review the
  agreement and evaluate its implementation.[25]

In internal correspondence UAW president Owen Bieber stated, "I don't see
any big problem" with the draft except for the clause calling for submitting any
conceptualizations and decisions to cooperate "to the decision-making bodies
of both organizations." The two union leaders signed a version of the agreement
revised to address Bieber's concerns in Chicago on June 21, 1994.[26] In practice,
however, the new agreement proved insufficient to change behavior. The relationship between the two unions remained ad hoc, ineffectual, and often frustrating
for both parties.

The UAW leaders were active on more than one front in their effort to organize MBUSI. They tried unsuccessfully to use local political pressure. Owen
Bieber asked Bobby Lee Thompson, the director of UAW Region 8 (which extends from Maryland to Mississippi), to "put the arm" on Alabama governor Jim
Folsom Jr. to help the UAW with the unionization effort.[27] Folsom, a Democrat,
became Alabama governor in April 1993 when a scandal forced his predecessor
to resign. As a result, it was Folsom who completed the negotiation of the huge

incentives package for Daimler-Benz to bring the plant to Vance and shepherded it through the state legislature.[28]

In the summer of 1994, Folsom was in a very close election campaign. Thompson wrote to Ted Letson, chair of the Alabama UAW Community Action Program Council, to express the union leadership's observation that Governor Folsom's "very tight race in the up-coming General Election" was "a golden opportunity for your CAP [Community Action Program] Executive Board, along with the CAP Representative Jerry McNish and Brother Red Peoples, Organizer, to meet personally with Governor Folsom in regards to his commitment to helping us at the Mercedes Plant." Thompson added, "At the same time, we should also discuss how we could put a little extra effort into the Governor's campaign to making sure that this is another victory we both can chalk up on November 8."[29] Folsom lost in November by 0.7 percentage points. Ironically, the incentive package cost him votes. His opponent, Republican Fob James, attacked it for being exorbitant, and the charges resonated.[30] The transfer of state political leadership to the Republican Party would add obstacles to organizing at MBUSI.

Daimler management saw that IG Metall and UAW officials were unable to force their counterparts at BMW to take an accommodating position regarding unionization. In Alabama, they took a similar approach to BMW. The only difference was one of style rather than substance. Daimler managers asserted that they were neutral when it came to unionization at MBUSI and that it was up to the employees to decide, but the managers would always add that they did not think that a union was necessary.

The UAW got an early toehold in the Vance plant, albeit surreptitiously. In December 1994, director of the UAW's organizing department Ben Perkins reported to UAW vice president Stan Marshall that the UAW was going to hire three interns from the Industrial Union Department of the AFL-CIO, the peak confederation for trade unions in the United States, to work on "the Mercedes, BMW, and Nissan projects."[31] One Industrial Union Department intern, an Alabamian, had done two interviews at MBUSI. He asked Perkins if he should take the job if offered. Perkins wrote to Marshall that he replied "by all means. We would much prefer him in there than out working with us." Ultimately, MBUSI hired the intern in the first group of twenty line employees. The company sent this group to Germany for six months of training. The UAW leadership asked IG Metall representatives, as Ben Perkins put it, to "adopt this group of 20, explaining to them the advantages of unionization, in hopes they will follow this course in the United States, it could help us out tremendously."[32]

In early 1995, the UAW opened an office near the MBUSI plant to have "people on site" during the initial training of employees.[33] The union began posting messages on a billboard near the plant shortly after it opened in 1997 just "to let them know that we're part of the equation," explained UAW regional organizer Chuck McDonald.[34] After failing for a decade to organize any Japanese-owned plants, the UAW leaders hoped for better luck at MBUSI. After all, the UAW had organized a Daimler-owned Freightliner truck plant in Mount Holly, North Carolina, in the early 1990s, and VW management had readily accepted unionization at a plant in Westmoreland County, Pennsylvania, which VW operated from 1978 to 1987. UAW leaders hoped that the failure to organize the BMW plant in South Carolina was the exception.

AFL-CIO leaders created the Organizing Institute under the leadership of Richard Bensinger in 1989 as one of many measures introduced in the 1980s to expand support for organizing and to develop innovative organizing methods for all its member unions. In the mid-1990s, Region 1A director Bob King (who became UAW president in 2010) served as a member of the Organizing Institute Task Force.[35] King's background was unusual for a labor leader. His father had been director of industrial relations at Ford Motor Company. King's early education was at Jesuit institutions. He graduated from University of Detroit Jesuit High School and attended College of the Holy Cross, studying religion and philosophy, before transferring to the University of Michigan, where he earned a bachelor's degree in political science in 1968. During summers while in college, King worked in Chrysler, Ford, and GM plants. After graduation, King served in the US Army for two years in South Korea. When he returned to the United States, he worked for Ford in the company's Detroit parts depot and became a member of UAW Local 600, which represents Ford's River Rouge complex. While at Ford, King apprenticed as an electrician and attended the University of Detroit Law School, where he earned a JD degree in 1973.[36]

King was elected vice president of Local 600 in 1981 and president in 1984. In 1987, the UAW leadership named him chair of the UAW-Ford Negotiating Committee.[37] Industry observers identified King as one of the "bright young hopes for the future"[38] and a "militant . . . up-and-comer."[39] King became director of Region 1A in 1989. The next year he cofounded and later cochaired the Labor/Management Council for Economic Renewal, a nonprofit organization for small businesses and local unions to advance best business practices. In 1994, King ran for a UAW vice president position but lost.[40]

In November 1997, the UAW restructured to enhance the importance of organizing. The union leadership created the National Organizing Department and picked Bob King to head it.[41] Hal Stack, director of the Labor Studies Center at Wayne State University, commented, "You've seen a shift to a more strategic approach to organizing" with this change. Some of King's first steps were to create six regional organizing centers and to intensify organizing vehicle parts suppliers. He also pushed to unionize workers beyond the automobile industry, including public-sector employees, casino workers, and graduate students. More than a third of the sixty thousand workers organized during King's decade-long tenure in the post worked outside of the automotive sector. King relied heavily on the card-check procedure (which recognizes a union as the exclusive bargaining agent in a workplace when the union can show that a majority of employees had signed cards indicating that they authorized the union to be their agent) and employer neutrality agreements in union organizing drives.[42]

In April 1998 Stephen Yokich, who had succeeded Owen Bieber as UAW president three years earlier, said that the UAW would all but stop trying to organize Japanese transplants. Yokich said, "We are working with the unions in Germany to organize the German plants here. . . . It's hard to tell if that will bear fruit, but I don't think it will be as tough as it was with the Japanese plants."[43]

A major development in the automotive world transformed the way UAW officials approached organizing the plant in Vance. On May 7, 1998, Daimler-Benz and Chrysler announced a "merger of equals." The managing chairs of the two companies, Robert Eaton and Jürgen Schrempp, became cochairs of the combined company called DaimlerChrysler.[44]

Many at the outset praised the merger as the formation of the first truly transnational vehicle production company. The merger was actually a takeover; Daimler-Benz spent $38 billion to acquire Chrysler. The hope was "to take Mercedes' dedication to quality, its thorough engineering practices and advanced technology and marry it to Chrysler's low-cost product development, its creative designs and innovative Extended Enterprise."[45] That hope was never realized, however. Instead, "clashes between the mid-market cowboys of Detroit and the high-end knights of Stuttgart" produced a lack of trust that left "the potential synergies that were used to justify the deal . . . unrealized."[46]

The merger produced a complex relationship between management of the new company and the UAW. DaimlerChrysler was legally a German company; it was therefore subject to Germany's 1976 codetermination act that requires ten of the twenty members of the supervisory board to be employee representatives.[47] The UAW had unionized Chrysler's units in the 1930s and 1940s; this did not change for the new company. There was also precedent at Chrysler for union representation on the corporate board. In exchange for concessions in the late 1970s, UAW president Doug Fraser gained a seat on Chrysler's board and served from 1979 to 1983. His successor, Owen Bieber, was a board member from 1983 to 1991.[48]

Fraser, commenting from retirement, viewed the merger optimistically but hedged his assessment with a note of caution: "This is a great opportunity for labor. I think it naturally follows that the two unions will work together more closely. . . . The labor costs in Germany are significantly higher than they are in the US. If Daimler-Benz decides to build in the US rather than Germany it could rub them [i.e., IG Metall's leaders] the wrong way."[49] On the other hand, Daimler-Chrysler general works council chair Karl Feuerstein expressed concern: "I have warned the board of management that we will do everything in our power to prevent DaimlerChrysler from becoming an Americanized business. The American managers don't like our consensus approach. They think it's like having a log strapped to one leg. But they will have to learn to love it."[50]

When Chrysler executives informed UAW president Stephen P. Yokich of the merger on May 5, 1998, his immediate response was "Ah, we get Alabama, huh?," referring to the Mercedes-Benz plant in Vance. "You know they've been turning their backs on us down there," Yokich said. He then added, "They ain't going to do that no more. We're going to become one big, happy family, right!" Dennis Pawley, head of manufacturing at Chrysler, replied, "Hey, Steve, you know how the laws work in this country. You don't force anybody to be in the union, but there won't be anybody standing in their way."[51] The next day, Yokich held a press conference where he announced that the UAW supported the DaimlerChrysler merger and stressed that he was going to make sure that "this merger works for the workers of DaimlerChrysler, not just the stockholders."[52]

Just three weeks after the announcement of the merger, Yokich and UAW vice president Richard Shoemaker met with IG Metall chair Klaus Zwickel. They agreed to three actions. First, IG Metall would cede a seat on the DaimlerChrysler supervisory board to Yokich. Second, Yokich and Zwickel would propose to the DaimlerChrysler supervisory board that the company create a world employee committee.[53] Third, the two unions agreed to cooperate in organizing the German auto factories in the United States. Yokich suggested including the Vance plant in the UAW's Chrysler contract, but company officials rejected the idea, claiming that it would not be permissible under US labor law without a recognition process involving the plant's employees.[54]

Early Organizing Efforts at MBUSI

Daimler management has repeatedly asserted over the years that the company is neutral when it comes to unionization, but neutrality meant something different at MBUSI than at Chrysler. At Chrysler, neutrality meant that management accepted a card-check procedure for union recognition whenever Chrysler opened a new plant, but at MBUSI it did not. DaimlerChrysler chief executive officer Jürgen Schrempp expressed a preference for a union recognition election at MBUSI, declaring it "a very democratic way to solve" the question of unionization. That said, MBUSI spokesperson Trevor Hale made it plain that

DaimlerChrysler management's preference was to operate the Vance plant without a union when he stated, "We don't feel the need for a third party."[55]

DaimlerChrysler management made unionization less appealing to MBUSI employees by adopting inclusive management techniques that grant considerable responsibility to employees and by providing hourly wages between $20 and $25 and generous benefits, which were comparable to what the UAW had obtained from domestic auto producers and about twice the Alabama average for production workers.

Some workers at the Vance plant still had complaints. MBUSI management sped up the assembly line in the fall of 1998 to increase output per shift by 36 percent (i.e., from 138 to 188 vehicles) and made overtime mandatory. Several employees blamed the speedup and overtime for causing occupational injuries and burnout. Many also complained that the mandatory overtime kept them from seeing their families.[56]

In mid-January 1999, the UAW petitioned the NLRB for union recognition elections at the Alabama factories of two auto parts suppliers: Pressac, an electronic components manufacturer, and ZF Industries, a German-owned axle producer. Although these suppliers were independent of MBUSI, observers and participants alike viewed these elections as indicative of the UAW's ability to organize in the South. Winning these elections should have been relatively easy; hourly wages at the suppliers were half those at the Vance plant. Yet, the UAW lost badly at both plants. MBUSI plant managers put the results of the ZF election on the plant's internal TV system and called meetings to inform employees of the results.[57] UAW officials subsequently accused ZF management of engaging in unfair labor practices, specifically intimidating employees and firing five for engaging in union activities.[58]

Despite the losses, the UAW moved forward at MBUSI. In April 1999, the union put a new message on its billboard. It featured a picture of Yokich and a toll-free number—1-800-2-GET-UAW—for workers interested in the union. Half a dozen UAW organizers moved into a hotel a few miles from the plant, and the union rented a small office in Vance. The organizers began holding informal meetings with employees. Within a week, close to 200 out of the 1,300 eligible workers joined the union organizing committee. Some MBUSI workers began to wear pro-UAW stickers.[59] That same month, the UAW held a meeting of several hundred of its officers from across the United States in Birmingham, Alabama, which is thirty minutes from Vance. While in Alabama, Yokich and 9 other UAW officials took time out to tour the Vance factory. Since Yokich was a member of DaimlerChrysler's supervisory board, the company could hardly refuse to let him visit. "He didn't come for a social call," MBUSI president Bill

Taylor observed. "He came to make his intentions known."[60] Jack Laskowski, UAW vice president responsible for relations with DaimlerChrysler, said MBUSI is "doing things that would be considered unfair labor practices," but the UAW had not filed complaints with the NLRB because union leaders would "just as soon try to resolve things in a peaceful manner."[61]

In May 1999, Yokich raised card-check recognition again with DaimlerChrysler management in Germany. Both sides were upbeat that they could soon reach a mutually acceptable compromise on rules of engagement for the Vance plant. That said, DaimlerChrysler's leaders did not budge from their position that they would remain neutral regarding unionization but preferred that the plant remain unorganized and would not accept card-check recognition.[62] Thomas P. Stallkamp, president of DaimlerChrysler's North American operations, explained, "We think it's more in the American tradition to let people in the plant decide, particularly in the state of Alabama, which is a right to work state." Alabama AFL-CIO president Stewart Burkhalter accused the company of "turning their anti-union persons loose on the floor," but MBUSI president Bill Taylor countered, "We manage our operations here in a very open manner. That's the culture we've set up here. . . . I can't imagine that being anti-anything—I think we're very pro-people."[63] By midyear 1999, roughly one quarter of MBUSI employees had signed union authorization cards.[64]

Some workers opposed unionization. Steven H. Merrill, who was one of MBUSI's first employees, formed an anti-union group called the Team Members Information Committee (TMIC). In May the TMIC began holding weekly meetings, produced a newsletter, and maintained a website. Merrill was quick to declare that "the company is doing nothing to support this."[65] The TMIC, which had 325 members, relied on funds from MBUSI employees, small businesses in nearby Tuscaloosa, and the Tuscaloosa County Industrial Development Council.[66] Employee organizations opposed to unionization with connections to the local business community and opaque financing were becoming increasingly commonplace at organizing drives in the South.

The UAW ratcheted up the campaign at MBUSI in July 1999. UAW organizers took two groups of MBUSI employees to the GM Saturn plant in Spring Hill, Tennessee, to show them the benefits of a cooperative labor-management relationship.[67] While in Stuttgart to attend a DaimlerChrysler board meeting, UAW president Stephen Yokich charged that DaimlerChrysler CEO Jürgen Schrempp had allowed MBUSI management to aid covertly the employee anti-union group. UAW officials told reporters that they were considering using their "nuclear bomb," namely a nationwide strike of DaimlerChrysler's seventy-six thousand Chrysler employees to get a card-check agreement for MBUSI.[68] Despite the added pressure, DaimlerChrysler management did not change its preference for a union recognition election over card check at MBUSI. DaimlerChrysler co-chair Robert Eaton explained, "We're trying to be totally and completely unbiased, neutral in this and leave it totally up to our employees."[69]

The collective agreements for the US plants of DaimlerChrysler, Ford, and GM all expired on September 14, 1999, which gave the UAW leadership additional leverage. The UAW leaders traditionally pick one company to be the lead in contract talks. The last time they had picked Chrysler was in 1976, because in subsequent years Chrysler had been too weak to assent to a strong settlement. On August 20, they chose the now more robust DaimlerChrysler to be the lead company. Many anticipated that UAW negotiators would obtain card-check recognition for MBUSI in a side deal while negotiating a new contract.[70]

The Alabama business community feared that DaimlerChrysler would agree to card-check recognition and ultimately unionization at MBUSI because they were a German company with different sensibilities, pressures, and constraints. After all, Daimler management had acquiesced to unionization in North Carolina. The leaders of the Economic Development Partnership of Alabama (EDPA), a private organization that Alabama business leaders founded in 1991 to make the state more attractive to major investors, decided to take matters into their own hands to forestall the UAW from organizing the Vance plant. In 1999 the EDPA created the Alabama Right to Work Foundation, which hired Jay Cole from a Chicago-based law firm that specialized in union avoidance to assist MBUSI employees who opposed unionization.[71] EDPA president Neal Wade, who was a key figure in the effort to persuade Daimler-Benz to build the Mercedes-Benz plant in Alabama, explained, "The reason why we're doing this is because Mercedes has taken a neutral stance. The UAW is supporting those who want a union, but no one was supporting the [employee] committee that wants to stay non-union."[72] Wade also argued that fending off the UAW was in the best interest of the state because a union victory "could make it harder to sell Alabama."[73]

The EDPA's actions were controversial. DaimlerChrysler was a member of the EDPA, which led labor leaders to question whether the company was truly neutral. Observers wondered whether creating the Alabama Right to Work Foundation signaled that the Alabama business community would endeavor to thwart all future unionization efforts throughout the state. On September 3, 1999, the EDPA backpedaled; it dissolved the Alabama Right to Work Foundation and canceled Jay Cole's $10,000-a-month contract. Cole continued to advise the anti-union employees at MBUSI nonetheless; the sources of his compensation subsequently became murky. The Tuscaloosa Industrial Development Agency created the Concerned Citizens Committee to support the work of the TMIC.

Tuscaloosa Industrial Development Agency executive director Dara Longgrear disclosed that the Concerned Citizens Committee had been in contact with Cole but refused to say whether it had hired him.[74]

Word circulated within the UAW leadership that the union's lead negotiator, Jack Laskowski, had tentatively obtained neutrality and card-check recognition at MBUSI in the negotiations with DaimlerChrysler. Laskowski, however, died suddenly of a heart attack in the middle of the talks. UAW president Stephen Yokich took over as lead bargainer. In the run-up to the talks Yokich said, "I think in the near future, you will see more transplants come under the banner of the UAW."[75] But when agreement emerged on September 16, 1999, there was no side agreement—formal or informal—providing for neutrality or a card-check recognition at MBUSI. Yokich had traded away this bargaining-to-organize arrangement for other gains.[76]

The UAW leadership had also asked for a list of MBUSI employee names and addresses during the DaimlerChrysler negotiations. It was common for domestic auto producers to provide this information to the UAW when they opened new plants. At MBUSI, anti-union workers heard about this request and used an internal system for submitting suggestions and complaints to request that MBUSI management not provide the union with that information. When asked how MBUSI would respond to these competing requests, spokesperson Trevor Hale replied, "We are aware that some of our team members have expressed concerns regarding their privacy and we will do our best to protect that privacy." The UAW never received an employee list.[77]

A union pamphlet distributed in late September 1999 indicated that 285 employees, who amounted to 22 percent of the eligible workforce, had signed union authorization cards.[78] The UAW leadership stepped up the organizing drive, sending a dozen additional organizers to Vance in the hope of wrapping up the campaign before Christmas. The UAW leadership softened its approach somewhat and made it local. The union put a new message on billboards that had a picture of children from a daycare center at a unionized Chrysler parts plant in Huntsville, Alabama. The message on the billboard read "UAW/DaimlerChrysler: Building a Better Alabama." References to the company in union literature were respectful. UAW literature described the union's objectives as protecting workers' jobs and health as well as forming "a true partnership with our company." UAW organizers even offered to fly at least one anti-union TMIC leader to Detroit to talk things over, but he declined.[79]

The TMIC opened its own office in Vance in November and rented two billboards with the message "No UAW. Save our Jobs for Alabamians." Union-avoidance expert Jay Cole continued to work with the TMIC. TMIC head Steve Merrill said he did not know who was covering Cole's expenses, but Cole said that the TMIC was reimbursing him. TMIC literature asserted that signing a UAW contract would mean that laid-off UAW workers from elsewhere could get jobs in the Vance plant instead of local workers. UAW literature stated in response that UAW members from elsewhere would not be able to "bump Mercedes workers out of their jobs" if the Vance plant was unionized, but UAW members "would have preferential hiring rights over people off the street."[80]

On November 15, 1999, the TMIC sent a letter to UAW president Stephen Yokich asking the UAW either to file a request with the NLRB for a union recognition election by early January or call off the campaign. The letter accused the UAW of using "divide and conquer" tactics "where[by] team members are turned against each other causing disruption, fear and hate."[81] Yokich raised card-check recognition once again at the December meeting of DaimlerChrysler's supervisory board, but management again declined to change the company's position against it. By the start of 2000, most UAW organizers had returned home. It became increasingly clear even to sympathetic observers that the organizing drive at the Vance plant was falling short. Doug Gulock, president of the UAW local at a DaimlerChrysler parts plant in Huntsville, Alabama, conceded that the UAW is "getting a cold response" from many MBUSI workers. Wade Smith told a *Wall Street Journal* reporter that working plenty of overtime enabled him to earn over $100,000 in 1999. "There are places that need a union," Smith observed, "but not here." Tim Earnest called his job at MBUSI "the hottest ticket in the state." Kenneth "Wa Wa" Walters, president of a United Steelworkers of America Local 351 representing a tire plant in Tuscaloosa, Alabama, remarked, "It's kind of hard to organize a guy driving a Mercedes to work every day."[82]

By mid-February Bob King, the UAW's vice president for organizing, acknowledged that the UAW was no longer "in an active phase" at MBUSI because the company had "made enough improvements that there wasn't an urgency with the workers at this point to go ahead and form a union."[83] Union-avoidance lawyer Jay Cole concluded, "I think they're just worn out." Trevor Bain, labor expert at the University of Alabama, said he was not surprised that the organizing drive was having difficulties because "at the moment, there doesn't seem to be a single issue for them to rally around." Bain concluded, "If the plant is going to get organized, it's going to get organized from the top down—either in Detroit or Germany."[84] Neither IG Metall officials nor DaimlerChrysler works councilors from Germany assisted the UAW during this first organizing effort.

Rising tension at the top of DaimlerChrysler culminated in the announcement of the resignation of cochair Robert Eaton in January 2000, two years earlier than planned, which left Schrempp as the sole chair.[85] A month later at a UAW/DaimlerChrysler council meeting in Las Vegas, newly named UAW vice president for DaimlerChrysler Nate Gooden informed the union council that DaimlerChrysler management agreed to honor a neutrality letter. The letter permitted UAW representatives to enter the plant with four weeks' notice but did not include card-check recognition. Gooden was still pleased, stating "if it takes six months, a year, or two years, . . . the Mercedes-Benz plant in Alabama will be UAW."[86]

The UAW research department produced a fifteen-page comparison of wages and benefits in the DaimlerChrysler master agreement to those at MBUSI. MBUSI had marginally higher wages (hourly wage of $21.90 vs. $21.83 for assemblers and $25.89 vs. $25.62 for tool and die maintenance), a longer lunch break (forty-five vs. thirty minutes), and more vacation time, but in other areas—such as attendance, cost of living adjustments, education and training, employee representation, grievances, health care, health and safety, holidays, job security, legal services, overtime, and pensions—the DaimlerChrysler master agreement was superior.[87] Taken as a whole, however, it was hard to argue that the UAW contracts with domestic producers were better than compensation at MBUSI.

In a bid to rekindle the MBUSI organizing drive, UAW president Stephen Yokich visited the Vance plant for a second time in April 2000. UAW national organizing director Bob King accompanied him. The TMIC distributed antiunion stickers for employees to wear. After the plant tour, Yokich spoke at a rally for union supporters at Vance Elementary School. He asserted that the UAW would push hard again over the next few months to organize MBUSI, but the union dedicated no additional organizers or resources to the drive. The drive slipped into quiescence for three years.[88]

The irascibility, provincialism, and poor health of Yokich hampered transnational union cooperation. DaimlerChrysler general works council chair Eric Klemm wished to assemble an "international automotive working group" of DaimlerChrysler employee representatives in July 2000 with delegates from Brazil, Canada, Germany, South Africa, Spain and the United States. The working group was to be a step toward creating of a world employee committee for DaimlerChrysler, which was one of three objectives that IG Metall and UAW leaders had set out immediately after Daimler-Benz and Chrysler had merged in 1998. Yokich, however, refused to allow any UAW representatives to participate because the proposed dates were during "shutdown," the time when auto plants cease production to retool for the next model year, which is when UAW leaders and members traditionally take vacations.

Doctors diagnosed Yokich as suffering from coronary artery disease,[89] which limited his capacity and desire to travel. Yokich declined to participate in a trip organized by DaimlerChrysler to Austria, the Czech Republic, France, and Germany because he "will be on vacation at this time." He also did not attend a June 2000 meeting in the United Kingdom of the Central Committee of the International Metalworkers' Federation, which was the global union federation for the mechanical engineering sector at the time,[90] that union leaders typically attend. Yokich instead sent the head of the UAW's International Affairs Department, Don Stillman.[91]

On August 28, 2000, DaimlerChrysler announced that it would add a second assembly line at the Vance plant to produce a crossover "GL-Class" vehicle similar to the M-Class SUV. The expansion would create 1,750 additional jobs. The company would receive an additional $115 million in incentives from the state.[92] Alabama committed to launching "Project Triad" as a part of the incentives package, which included $37.5 million worth of job-training benefits for new MBUSI employees and $2.5 million for additions and modifications to MBUSI's training center. In return, state officials secured an explicit commitment from the company to use "its best efforts to hire Alabama residents to the fullest extent possible."[93] The fresh round of incentives and DaimlerChrysler's commitment to hire locally strengthened the ties between MBUSI management and Alabama's political establishment, which was decidedly anti-union.

The Chrysler unit began to run huge losses in 2000. The burst of the dot-com bubble cut into sales, and poor production decisions forced the firm to offer steep cash-back incentives on minivans. In September, Chrysler issued a warning that the company would post a $500 million operating loss in the third quarter of 2000. On November 10, 2000, the head of DaimlerChrysler's general works council, Eric Klemm, called for an extraordinary meeting of the Labor Committee of DaimlerChrysler employee representatives, which the international automotive working group created back in July, for November 16, one day before DaimlerChrysler's supervisory board meeting, because the board intended to make major personnel decisions in response to the problems at Chrysler. Yokich again decided not to travel to Germany.[94] On November 15, two days before the board meeting, DaimlerChrysler CEO Jürgen Schrempp announced the departure of Chrysler unit president James P. Holden and named Holden's replacement: Dieter Zetsche, who had briefly been head of Freightliner. Zetsche's mission was to "mop up the mess" by cutting costs fast.[95] A *Detroit News* article reporting Holden's removal bluntly stated the significance of the leadership change: "The installation of Zetsche effectively dispels any pretense that the Chrysler unit is anything other than the North American Unit of DaimlerChrysler."[96] Numerous reporters asked for comments from Yokich about the shake-up at Chrysler. The UAW president's response to staff was that UAW vice president for DaimlerChrysler "Nate Gooden should do this—if he wishes. I don't."[97]

On November 27, 2000, Yokich, Gooden, and Gooden's administrative assistant David McAllister had an introductory meeting with Dieter Zetsche, chief operating officer Wolfgang Bernhard, and four other managers from the Chrysler Group at Chrysler's headquarters in Auburn Hills, Michigan. *Detroit News* columnist Daniel Howes speculated that Yokich would ask for card-check recognition at MBUSI and Freightliner's unorganized plants in North Carolina in exchange for concessions at Chrysler, but no deal along those lines emerged from the gathering.[98] There was a follow-up meeting on January 26, which Yokich did not attend, that also produced no results.[99]

Ultimately, UAW leaders decided to make no concessions. Nate Gooden stated publicly, "Our contracts with DaimlerChrysler will be fully enforced."[100] That said, UAW leaders also recognized that Chrysler would not survive without layoffs and did not organize opposition to them. Chrysler unveiled its turnaround plan on January 29. It included the elimination of twenty-six thousand, or one out of every five white- and blue-collar positions. The UAW leadership's standoffish position did not endear Zetsche and his colleagues to the union, which had repercussions for future organizing efforts at MBUSI.

In 2001, the UAW did score some organizing successes at MBUSI suppliers in Alabama. Ron Gettelfinger, who was the vice president responsible for the UAW's Ford department, convinced Ford management, who had a separate joint venture with ZF, to persuade ZF managers to dispense with aggressive anti-union tactics at the Tuscaloosa plant. They did, and ZF employees voted overwhelmingly in favor of the UAW as their exclusive bargaining agent.[101] That same year, the UAW also organized the Multicraft plant in Cottonwood, Alabama, which was a unit of Delphi that assembles cockpits for MBUSI.[102] When asked in mid-2001 about UAW organizing priorities, however, Yokich replied that the union was focusing on Japanese transplants, parts suppliers, and workers in nonindustrial settings.[103]

Stephen Yokich was sixty-six when his second four-year term as UAW president ended in June 2002. The dominant Reuther Caucus (aka Administration Caucus) within the UAW, to which Yokich belonged, forbids members who are age sixty-five or older to run for a union office. Even absent this provision, it was unlikely that Yokich would have run because his health was failing. He died of a stroke on August 15, 2002. The UAW elected Ron Gettelfinger as Yokich's successor.[104] Gettelfinger and Yokich were a study in contrasts. Yokich was temperamental and profane. Gettelfinger was a no-nonsense Hoosier and a devout Roman Catholic.[105] Yokich had also stepped down from DaimlerChrysler's supervisory board when his presidency ended. UAW vice president responsible for DaimlerChrysler Nate Gooden succeeded him.[106]

In mid-2000, a collection of DaimlerChrysler's employee representatives from around the world finally achieved the second joint objective that IG Metall chair Klaus Zwickel and UAW president Stephen Yokich set immediately after the DaimlerChrysler merger, namely the creation of a global works council for the company. The DaimlerChrysler WEC held its constituent meeting in July 2002.

The committee had thirteen employee representatives from four continents. Brazil, Canada, Spain, and South Africa each had a single representative. The UAW had three, and Germany had six. The WEC elected Erich Klemm—already chair of the DaimlerChrysler general works council—as WEC chair and UAW vice president Nate Gooden as vice chair. It is important to note that the WEC does not have legally anchored codetermination rights comparable to a German works council. Its scope is limited to voluntary information and consultation, which is the norm for global employee committees. The committee meets once a year, which is also the norm.[107]

One of the WEC's first actions was to draft a document jointly with Daimler-Chrysler management and the IMF based on the UNGC on corporate social responsibility.[108] (DaimlerChrysler had already signed on to the UNGC unilaterally on July 26, 2000; the UNGC obliges firms to promote human rights, fair labor practices, environmental protection, and anticorruption measures.) The parties also signed a four-page document titled "Social Responsibility Principles of DaimlerChrysler" in September 2002 at the company's North American headquarters in Auburn Hills, Michigan. The document committed DaimlerChrysler to respect and support compliance with all internationally accepted human rights, including a condemnation of forced labor, a rejection of child labor, equal opportunities and nondiscrimination with respect to employment, and equal pay for equal work. The company also acknowledged "the human right to form trade unions," constructive cooperation with employee representatives, and direct, respectful, and fair communication with employees. In addition, DaimlerChrysler "opposed all exploitative working conditions" and supported "protection of health" and "the right to reasonable compensation" in both the firm and its suppliers.[109] DaimlerChrysler's embrace of the new social responsibility principles altered nothing in Vance, however. The company did not change its position defining neutrality narrowly and negatively to exclude card-check recognition and to include an expressed preference that MBUSI employees do not organize.

By 2003, the Vance plant had 2,400 employees. The 1993 incentive package had an unintended deleterious impact on Alabama's state finances, however. Other companies took advantage of the Mercedes law tax changes, which cost Alabama $3 billion in lost revenue and produced a fiscal crisis for the state. Alabama governor Bob Riley proposed a $1.2 billion tax increase, but Alabama voters rejected it by a two-thirds majority.[110]

The four-year contract covering employees at Chrysler plants throughout the United States was due to expire in September 2003. The company's financial position was dramatically worse compared to the previous round of negotiations. DaimlerChrysler lost $1.1 billion in the second quarter of 2003. The red ink was coming principally from Chrysler. Management proposed closing seven Chrysler plants to stanch the losses.[111] Once again, there was considerable talk within the UAW of securing card-check recognition and preferential hiring of laid-off UAW members at MBUSI in exchange for accepting the plant closures. In July, UAW vice president for DaimlerChrysler Nate Gooden confidently predicted, "I will say that Vance, Alabama, will be organized very, very soon.... I would say less than a year. Before these talks are over with they will agree to a card check."[112]

Despite Gooden's inside position on Daimler's supervisory board and success at securing card check for the North Carolina plants of DTNA, his prediction proved false. On September 14, 2003, the UAW and DaimlerChrysler reached agreement on a new contract for Chrysler workers in the United States. The contract contained no language about the Vance plant. Rumors continued to swirl even after the negotiations ended about a swap of card-check recognition at Vance for the closure of seven plants. UAW vice president Nate Gooden repeated his claim that MBUSI would soon be unionized and asserted, "Under my watch, the Mercedes-Benz plant will have a UAW flag on it."[113] Speculation was particularly rife regarding Chrysler's Huntsville, Alabama, parts plant, which was one of the seven unionized plants on Chrysler management's closure list. Many anticipated at least a hiring preference for Huntsville UAW members to fill out the new MBUSI assembly line in exchange for allowing the Huntsville plant to close, but they were wrong.

The Alabama business and political establishment mobilized against such a move and used state subsidies as leverage. David Azbell, spokesperson for Republican governor Bob Riley, said, "The state provided incentives for Mercedes to hire Alabama workers and not import workers to Alabama from Michigan. Communities surrounding the plant also promised incentives with the belief that workers would come from along the Interstate 20/59 corridor." The Huntsville plant was two hours from Vance and on a different interstate. Abzell maintained, "The decision whether to unionize that plant shouldn't be forced on the Mercedes workers." He would not say if a clause requiring a preference for laid-off UAW members would cause the state to withdraw some of the $370 million in incentives it had provided to MBUSI since 1995. He only said, "We certainly hope it wouldn't get to that point. This matter is certainly showing up on the governor's radar screen." President of the Alabama AFL-CIO Stewart Burkhalter argued that hatred of unions was the source of Governor Riley's animus. "He's just afraid that Mercedes will hire UAW members who will organize the whole plant."[114]

Dara Longgrear, executive director of the Tuscaloosa County Industrial Development Authority, pointed out that the local communities agreed to substantial incentives for MBUSI with the understanding that their citizens would get the jobs at the plant and stressed, "That's the cornerstone of these agreements." He added, "I think any kind of backroom deal that would cut out Alabama workers, or in any other way harmfully affect the operations of the Mercedes plant, is totally unacceptable. The UAW's concern is only for itself. How dare they try to steal positions away from local Alabama employees." Threatening to withdraw incentives appeared to work. Plant spokesperson Linda Sewell responded sympathetically. "In our agreement with the state, we made a commitment to hire Alabama workers and with preference given to local applicants. The commitment from local communities has been very strong."[115] No deal ever materialized between the UAW and DaimlerChrysler to exchange card-check recognition at Vance for plant closures elsewhere, and talk of unionization died out for a few years. Back in Germany, shareholder dissatisfaction led the supervisory board to terminate Jürgen Schrempp as DaimlerChrysler's CEO effective January 1, 2006, and replace him with Chrysler head Dieter Zetsche.[116]

By 2006, the Vance plant had increased output to 160,000 vehicles per year and was exporting them to 135 countries. The *Birmingham News* named MBUSI chief William Taylor Alabama's 2006 CEO of the year.[117] MBUSI's success stood out as an exception in the North American car market. Gasoline prices had almost doubled between 2002 and 2006. Increasing numbers of consumers purchased more economical vehicles, which tended to be imports rather than domestically produced gas guzzlers. This change in consumer preference triggered a wave of layoffs at US-owned auto manufacturers and parts suppliers that hit the UAW hard. In 2006 alone, UAW membership fell by over 10 percent to less than six hundred thousand. *Business Week* ran an article by David Welch reporting on the union's troubles titled "Twilight of the UAW."[118]

IG Metall leaders had become disdainful of their American counterparts owing to the complacency and lack of strategic thinking that dominated the UAW during the Bieber and Yokich years.[119] The two unions also differed over some policies such as trade liberalization.[120] The relationship took a turn for the worse in the mid-2000s. The norm for German employee representatives on supervisory boards is to reach a common position on items before the board and to vote as a bloc. Nate Gooden, the UAW representative on DaimlerChrysler's supervisory board, did not adhere to this norm, to the considerable aggravation of his German employee colleagues. He had developed a close relationship with Dieter Zetsche, which contributed to Gooden's decision not to side with IG Metall members of the board on a vote in 2004 regarding the appointment of a top manager. IG Metall officials had had enough in late 2005 when Gooden supported a management proposal to institute company-wide layoffs that German union officials opposed. Gettelfinger, Gooden, and other UAW officials met with a delegation of IG Metall representatives, including Thomas Klebe, who was the director of IG Metall's Department for General Shop Floor Policy and Codetermination and a DaimlerChrysler board member, in Washington, D.C., on February 13, 2006 to find a new modus vivendi.[121] They crafted a joint statement on UAW stationery signed by Gooden and Klebe that affirmed the following:

> UAW and IGM are convinced that the employee representatives within the supervisory board of Daimler-Chrysler in the spirit of international solidarity have to speak with one voice and vote unanimously.
>
> To ensure this there is a pre-meeting of the employee representatives before each meeting of the supervisory board. In this meeting the necessary decisions are discussed. In this discussion the members who are most affected by the upcoming decision give a recommendation which usually will be followed by the other members. But in the end the majority of the employee representatives is decisive.
>
> UAW and IGM believe that this procedure is an indisputable basis for a close cooperation of the employee representatives in international solidarity.[122]

The leadership of the two unions also agreed that Gooden, who was sixty-seven years old, would step down from the DaimlerChrysler supervisory board; Ron Gettelfinger replaced him.[123] Gooden passed away on November 7, 2006. Despite the settlement, Gooden's dissonant votes left a residue of distrust between the leaderships of the two unions that took a few years and changed circumstances to dissipate. Gettelfinger made other changes in the UAW's leadership. He named Vice President Bob King as head of the Ford department and named newly elected vice president Terry Thurman to replace King as director of the National Organizing Department.[124]

Unionization at MBUSI became an issue again at the Vance plant in 2006. At the behest of a group of MBUSI workers, the IAM launched a new organizing effort in late February. "We want a union and one of us has got to go first to give the rest of these boys an opportunity. Somebody's got to get these dominoes falling," explained Bobby Ray Thomas, a forty-nine-year-old MBUSI employee.[125] The IAM sent a dozen organizers who stayed in a hotel across from the plant and opened an office in Woodstock, seven miles away. The campaign included billboard advertising, television and radio ads, a newsletter titled *The Trend Setter*, a web page, and outreach to community leaders.[126]

Since MBUSI wages were still comparable to those at the Big Three domestic auto producers (i.e., between $26 and $30 an hour), the IAM made "a voice at work" and job security the centerpiece issues of its organizing drive.[127] Some employees felt that their say at the plant had diminished in recent years.[128] Other issues included excessive overtime, cuts in health benefits for retirees, the absence of seniority rights, and heavy use of outside contractors to supply temporary employees. One-quarter of MBUSI's four thousand workers were actually employees of temporary employment agencies. They were paid significantly less than the MBUSI employees and were not in the bargaining unit because they worked for temporary employment agencies, not DaimlerChrysler.[129] Don Barker, a Texas-based IAM official leading the organizing effort, also raised as an issue the falloff in sales in the auto industry owing to a spike in gasoline prices, arguing that "if there was ever a time for workers to have professional representation and a voice at work, this is it."[130] Barker explained, "Big companies are outsourcing more and more work. That's something we've dealt with in the aerospace industry with good contracts."[131]

MBUSI spokesperson Linda Sewell said that the company would again remain neutral during the organizing drive. The group of MBUSI employees who had been adamantly opposed to earlier unionization efforts revived the Mercedes TMIC and rehired Jay Cole, the anti-union consultant they had used earlier. Cole observed, "What we learned the last time with the UAW, these folks with Mercedes are making the best money and benefits they could possibly get anywhere. They beat any union contract that's out there. All the union can do is pose problems and possibly cause that to change."[132] The TMIC again held meetings with employees. The fear remained powerful among many employees that any union would give new jobs at the Vance plant to laid-off workers from elsewhere instead of hiring Alabamians.

The IAM also faced a challenge from within the labor movement. The UAW leadership did not take kindly to the IAM organizing campaign. A furious Ron Gettelfinger went to the AFL-CIO to challenge the IAM's organizing drive at the Vance plant. The UAW asserted that all automobile plants are under its jurisdiction. To bolster this claim, UAW representatives reopened the union's office in Vance and began doing home visits of MBUSI employees again. IAM president Tom Buffenbarger responded that his union started the organizing drive because "the Mercedes workers came to us."[133]

IAM lead organizer Don Barker said that the unionization drive at MBUSI was the IAM's top priority. In May and August 2006, the union submitted unfair labor practice charges against MBUSI to the Birmingham office of the NLRB alleging that supervisors harassed pro-union employees.[134] In September, the NLRB's Atlanta office sided with the machinists union regarding one count; it found that supervisors illegally monitored conversations of pro-union employees. MBUSI management filed an appeal.[135] In November the IAM and MBUSI reached a "non-board settlement." The IAM dropped all charges in exchange for the company taking certain actions, which remain confidential.[136] The IAM organizers were unable to leverage the unfair labor practice charge into greater support for the union. Don Barker tried to rekindle the organizing drive at MBUSI from April to August 2007 but got nowhere. The IAM shed staff over the course of the year and closed the local office. The AFL-CIO ultimately ruled on the jurisdictional dispute in favor of the UAW.[137]

German managers and shareholders lost patience when Chrysler lost close to $1.5 billion in 2006. Top management decided to put Chrysler up for sale in early 2007.[138] On August 3 Cerberus Capital Management, a US hedge fund, acquired an 80.1 percent stake in Chrysler for a sticker price of $7.4 billion. A close analysis revealed that Cerberus actually received $650 million in exchange for taking responsibility for Chrysler's liabilities.[139] DaimlerChrysler management shortened the company's name to Daimler AG. MBUSI remained part of Daimler's Mercedes-Benz division. Ron Gettelfinger lost his seat on the supervisory board once the sale went through, even though DTNA, which had eight facilities in North America with UAW representation, remained a part of the company.

At the start of 2008 the head of the UAW's National Organizing Department, Vice President Terry Thurman, committed in an officers meeting to holding a recognition election at one transplant by midyear, but nothing materialized.[140] Berthold Huber, who had become chair of IG Metall in 2007, toured the MBUSI plant in April 2008, but there was little forward progress in Vance or at any other transplant. Consequently, Gettelfinger made a change of leadership of the UAW's National Organizing Department in June. He had no choice but to keep Thurman on as a vice president because the UAW convention elected him to that position, but Gettelfinger asked up-and-coming officer Cindy Estrada to run the organizing department. Gettelfinger expressed concern about burnout among organizers, emphasized the need to increase the UAW's presence in the South, and stressed the need to be more strategic.[141]

Ron Gettelfinger increased the focus on structural innovations within the UAW and new resources for organizing at a time when membership was shrinking. For example, he suggested to Marcello Malentacchi, general secretary of the IMF, that the IMF ask affiliates to contribute to a special fund designated to support organizing. Malentacchi deftly deflected the request by suggesting that he was open to a reorientation of the federation's existing "Program of Activities towards incorporating some explicit organizing-related and workers' rights objectives" and that "the priority of organizing, union building and workers' rights . . . should be reflected in the next Action Programme." Malentacchi added, "This latter two-fold approach may well be equivalent to your proposal in effect while requiring less administrative inputs."[142] Malentacchi's failure to take up Gettelfinger's suggestion to create a special fund meant that the IMF would not be a source of additional material resources for the UAW.

The 2007–2009 financial crisis triggered change on multiple fronts. Mercedes-Benz sales in the United States for October 2008 fell by 25 percent compared to October 2007, prompting MBUSI management to offer buyouts and early retirement packages for the first time to any employee willing to resign. There were no layoffs, but significant numbers of temporary employees lost their jobs. It is worth noting the contrast between MBUSI and DTNA, where few temporary employees and sharp swings in demand resulted in mass layoffs that stoked organizing efforts in the North Carolina plants.

Ron Gettelfinger spent most of late 2008 and early 2009 negotiating bailouts for Chrysler and GM. Gettelfinger made both enduring friends and enemies for the UAW in the process. The administration of President George W. Bush and congressional Democrats reached agreement on a stop-gap bailout for Chrysler and GM. Conservative Senate Republicans, including Bob Corker (a former mayor of Chattanooga, Tennessee) and Richard Shelby of Alabama, demanded that the package include deep cuts in wages, benefits, and pensions. Gettelfinger refused, arguing that the UAW had already made major concessions in recent collective bargaining agreements. Gettelfinger accused Corker and the others of singling out "workers and retirees for different treatment and . . . mak[ing] them shoulder the entire burden of any restructuring."[143] The Republican Senators attempted to block the bailout. Shelby called it "a bridge-loan to nowhere."[144] The Bush administration provided bridge loans to the companies anyway.

In the first half of 2009, GM executives explored a variety of restructuring plans. Several options included the sale of GM's European subsidiary, Opel. Ultimately, however, GM went bankrupt on June 1, 2009, without selling Opel. The US government bought GM's assets and led the restructuring of the company. That same month, the Italian automaker FIAT bought Chrysler.[145]

One by-product of the financial crisis was a repair of the ties between IG Metall and the UAW. IG Metall chair Berthold Huber, unlike his predecessors, had a good command of English. Huber got on well with Gettelfinger, who was much easier to work with than the irascible Stephen Yokich. The relationship between Huber and Gettelfinger deepened during the discussions of the future of GM.[146]

During the financial crisis, Gettelfinger continued to work on internal structural innovations to improve organizing. Notes from a March 3, 2009, meeting captured his enormous dissatisfaction with the status quo. At the top of his notes he wrote, "Current structure vs *change* Pres[ent], Director & 3 A.D.'s Past— coordinators." He then listed thirty-eight "Issues with both":

1) Staff selection
2) Regional politics / difficult to blend together
3) Local politics /
4) Staff locations
5) Potential to pit regions and departments against each other
6) Lack of focus

7) Two reports = no reports
8) Lack of training—no structure or basis—thin on-going training
9) Involvement of other departments—adds to confusion
10) Amount of time off
11) Staff Lack of self esteem
12) Lack of respect for superiors
13) Ineffective
14) Too many excuses—con game for some—probing
15) Limited success / no success
16) Time discipline lacking
17) Beat down—staff feel unappreciated
18) Constant movement—org to serving
19) Staff unhappy with being away from home—time on road
20) Constant negotiating over schedule & work hours
21) Lack of commitment—do only what we're told
22) Expert in staff meeting—flounder on a drive
23) Difficulty in relating to workers—dwell on personal experiences
24) Feel like "macho" is good—but underneath it's different story
25) Inexperience in workers' place of employment
26) Hard work—vs— . . .
27) On the ground—no one is in charge—everyone is in charge
28) Staff flow back and forth between drives—no ownership / no responsibility
29) Chimneys—way too many
30) Nat'l vs. TOP [technical, office, professional]—where the same / different
31) Too much bureaucracy
32) Institutional commitment
33) Lack of organization in drive / meeting agenda / planning & etc.
34) Little regard for effectiveness of anti-union campaign
35) targeting strategy
36) Research
37) Morale—
38) Reliability of information from org

In the left margin, Gettelfinger wrote:

Structure
Structure
Structure

———

Training
Ownership
_____
Implement Plan

Most of the issues (twenty-one out of thirty-eight) involve personnel shortcomings of various sorts. Twelve issues are structural. The remainder of the notes sketch out seven alternative institutional structures for organizing. There is no evidence of meaningful follow-through from the March 3 meeting. Gettelfinger's dissatisfaction with the status quo was in part a product of the state of the campaign at MBUSI, which he summarized in mid-2009 as "starting from scratch."[147]

Across the ocean, IG Metall leaders had a concrete reason to reach out to UAW officials. The prospect of Daimler playing off workforces in Germany and the United States suddenly became real. Word got out to employee representatives in late 2009 that Daimler was considering shifting production of C-Class cars for the North American market to Vance. In late November 2009, IG Metall and UAW officials discussed strategy at an IMF meeting in Frankfurt. IG Metall International department head Horst Mund committed to helping the UAW in its organizing efforts. Eric Klemm, who chaired Daimler's general works council and WEC, also said that if the UAW needed support, it would get it.[148] Looking back, however, Bob King—Gettelfinger's successor as UAW president—said that Klemm "never went to bat" for the UAW.[149]

Once workers heard of Daimler management's plans to make C-Class cars in Vance, twelve thousand of them protested at the Sindelfingen factory where Daimler made that model. A picture of a protester wearing an IG Metall hat and carrying a sign with a crudely drawn American flag and the words "C-Klasse, NO NO—AMERIKA" quickly made it across the Atlantic.[150]

On June 15, 2010, Ron Gettelfinger retired, and Bob King became UAW president. King was sixty-three years old. Since King was a member of the Reuther Caucus, he could only serve one term. UAW grassroots dissident Gary Walkowicz ran against King, making the race the first contested UAW presidential election since 1992. Walkowicz criticized King for accepting concessions in recent contracts with Ford management. King nonetheless won handily at the UAW convention, garnering 2,115 votes to Walkowicz's 74. Observers described King as "cerebral," "unconventional," "a fiery free thinker," and a strategist, which distinguished him from his predecessors, who could best be described as tacticians.[151]

King set as his primary objective the revitalization of the UAW by organizing transplants.[152] There was certainly a pressing need for this. The union represented a shrinking share of automobile-sector employment. In 2010 UAW membership was 386,677, which was one-quarter of its peak in 1979. The share of the automobile workforce that was unionized also had fallen, principally because of the expansion of foreign-owned producers in the United States. Between 1980 and 2010 Japanese, German, and Korean firms built more than twenty automobile manufacturing plants, mostly in the Southeast. These plants produced 43.6 percent of the vehicles made domestically in 2010 and employed more than 100,000 people. The UAW had been unable to organize any auto plants owned wholly by foreign firms.[153]

Both Ron Gettelfinger and Bob King had concluded that revitalizing organizing was necessary to rejuvenate the UAW, but their ideas for accomplishing it differed. Gettelfinger focused on internal restructuring, although he did work increasingly closely with German employee representatives in the final years of his presidency. King, in contrast, concentrated on a cognitive reframing of the UAW both internally and externally as a prerequisite to reaching top-down agreements with foreign employee representatives and managers that would facilitate unionization.

At the 2010 UAW convention that elected Bob King president, the new UAW leader argued that to revitalize the union, "the UAW of the twenty-first century must be fundamentally and radically different from the UAW of the twentieth century." The union must abandon an adversarial approach to industrial relations and embrace management "as partners in innovation and quality." King also directly addressed executives from foreign-owned firms in the speech. "The best way to deliver shareholder value, is to partner with the UAW on quality, productivity, attendance, employee morale, and the overall goal of providing the best product at the best price to the customer." He added, "I guarantee that employers with UAW partnerships are going to outperform nonunion employers in every key measurable!"[154] King persuaded the delegates. They approved spending $60 million on organizing.[155]

In December 2010, the UAW's seventeen-member International Executive Board authorized a statement designed to buttress Bob King's new approach to organizing titled "UAW Principles for Fair Union Elections."[156] The UAW released the document on January 3, 2011, a week before Detroit's annual North American International Auto Show, to maximize media attention. The statement, which took the form of a preamble and eleven principles, was innovative for the UAW in several respects. The preamble explicitly rejected adversarialism:

> In order to promote the success of our employers, the UAW is committed to innovation, flexibility, lean manufacturing, world best quality and continuous cost improvement. We are moving on a path that no longer presumes an adversarial work environment with strict work rules, narrow job classifications or complicated contract rules.

The subsequent principles outlined the details of the UAW's new postadversarial approach. The first principle declared that unionization is a human right. The UAW had previously portrayed unionization as a human right in passing, but stating it first placed greater emphasis on this conceptualization, which would resonate in particular with foreign producers and their trade unions. German producers, for example, had all signed accords with IG Metall and the IMF and its successor organization, IndustriALL. The German producers as well as Japan's Mitsubishi Motors and Nissan had joined the UNGC, which aims to mobilize a global movement of sustainable companies through adherence to ten principles, one of which describes joining a union as a human right. Framing unionization in human rights terms also enables UAW officials to label any company resisting unionization as a human rights violator.

The next three principles covered employees' right to decide on unionization free from interference. Principle 2 stressed that "employees must be free to exercise the right to join a union or refrain from joining a union in an atmosphere free of fear, coercion, intimidation or threats." Principle 3 stated that employees would suffer "no repercussions from management or the union" from choosing to support or not support unionization and that any negotiations between the union and management would be in good faith. Principle 4 forbade both the union and management from making any wage or benefit promises contingent on employees' decision whether to unionize. Principle 5 required equal access to employees for both management and the UAW and also prohibited mandatory meetings about unionization unless UAW representatives also participated.

Principles 6 through 9 covered the conduct of union recognition processes. Principle 6 aimed to neutralize "threats from community allies," which had become increasingly prevalent in the South. It asked management to "explicitly disavow, reject and discourage messages from corporate and community groups that send the message that a union would jeopardize jobs." The UAW pledged to do the same if "community groups . . . send the message that the company is not operating in a socially responsible way." Principle 7 called for "no disparaging of the other party." Principle 8 required the "immediate Resolution . . . of any disagreements between the UAW and management about the conduct of the organizing campaign." Principle 9 marked a cautious departure from the UAW leadership's long-standing preference for the card-check procedure to determine union recognition and stated that "a secret ballot election incorporating these principles was an acceptable method of determining union representation . . . if there is no history of anti-union activities."

Principles 10 and 11 are distinctive because they commit the UAW to assisting corporations achieving their business goals in exchange for according respect to employees. Principle 10 states that the collective bargaining parties will bargain to reach "an agreement that takes into account the employer's need to remain competitive; the dignity, respect, and value of every employee; the importance and value of full employee engagement and creative problem solving; and that provides a fair compensation system." The principle adds that "if no agreement is reached within six months of recognition, the parties may mutually agree to mediation and/or interest arbitration to resolve any outstanding issues. Principle 11 was the most conspicuous. It stated that if the UAW won a union recognition election, the union "will be committed to the success of the employer and will encourage . . . members to engage in the employer's successful achievement of its mission," embracing "a performance-based and participatory culture where the union contributes to continual improvement of processes and shared responsibility for quality, innovation, flexibility and value." The purpose of this principle was to make it clear that Bob King was offering a sharp break from the oppositional grievance culture that still existed in some domestic plants with UAW representation.

In interviews over the course of 2011, King described the new drive to organize foreign-owned plants as "unlike anything that's been seen in the UAW in many, many years." At times he framed his objective beyond his union and even the United States: "Our goal is not just rebuilding the UAW but rebuilding the American middle class and building a global middle class."[157]

King was explicit that the UAW's approach would have both carrots and sticks. He stressed that the union's default position was to focus on helping companies to become more competitive, but if they refused or used anti-union tactics, he threatened to wage a global campaign to "rebrand" them as contemptuous of human rights.[158] King underscored the urgency of organizing transplants for the UAW using a poker analogy. He said that the upcoming organizing effort at foreign-owned firms was "an all-in hand. If we lose, we'll die quicker. If we win, we rebuild the UAW."[159] King acknowledged in a subsequent interview that more than membership numbers was at stake. "Ford, GM, and Chrysler are willing to have decent wages and benefits, but if they keep getting undermined by the transnationals, then that puts competitive pressure on them."[160]

Bob King acknowledged that to succeed, the UAW would have to change the minds of managers at the foreign-owned firms; he asserted, "We just have to convince them that we're not the evil empire that they think we are."[161] He disclosed that the UAW had already held "informal and confidential discussions with company representatives" but did not say which.[162] King said the union would decide in three months which companies to target. The UAW's goal was to have at least one foreign-owned plant organized by the end of 2011.[163]

For the German automakers, King's strategy can be boiled down to a heavily top-down attempt to secure a commitment from IG Metall and the works councils

at Daimler and VW to pressure management in Germany to allow UAW representatives to make the case for unionization directly to the employees in the companies' American plants without inside or outside interference. (Under King, the
UAW undertook no efforts to organize BMW's Spartanburg, North Carolina,
plant.) King and his colleagues were convinced that a majority of employees would
vote in favor of UAW representation under such conditions, even in the South.[164]

Ties between IG Metall and the UAW became closer under King. He and IG
Metall chair Berthold Huber had similar personalities, and the two got on well.
They were both analytical and somewhat introverted. They shared a deep interest
in long-term strategy. King visited Germany in February 2011 to meet with the
IG Metall leadership and the chair of the Daimler general works council, Erich
Klemm, to discuss his strategy and enlist help. King did not return home empty-
handed. Both Klemm and Huber decided to support King's effort to organize
German plants operating in the United States and dedicate an unprecedented
amount of time and resources to these efforts.[165] The local business community in
Alabama took notice. For example, Henry Hagood Jr., CEO of Alabama Associated General Contractors, described the UAW's plan as an aggressive attack that
if successful would be "at the expense of our state's economy."[166]

Officials from the Daimler works council, IG Metall, and UAW began exchanges of American and German Mercedes-Benz employees. In August 2011,
a group of German works council members and staff met with MBUSI employees in Alabama. IG Metall and UAW representatives met again in November 2011
at a union summit in India.[167] Helmut Lense, IMF automotive director, made
the case for assisting the UAW's organizing drive at MBUSI in the Daimler works
council magazine *Brennpunkt*:

> If we in Germany limit temporary work, but it is an option without
> limit in America, then more production will just go to America. Or, if
> dislocations or working time changes in Germany are a mandatory
> topic of codetermination, but in America management has a free
> hand, why then should decisions about new production be made just
> to the benefit of German sites? And if wages in America can be uni-
> laterally set by management, everybody can figure out that German
> works councils will be hampered at every negotiation.
>
> Therefore we must not leave this confrontation just to our Ameri-
> can colleagues, but also confront management in Germany.[168]

In February 2012, Daimler management and employee representatives reaffirmed social responsibility principles, which they wrote and signed in 2002
when the company was DaimlerChrysler. The document had a new title, but
there were no changes to the text. Daimler management again acknowledged

"the human right to form trade unions," pledged to maintain "constructive" relations with employee representatives, and committed the company and its executives to remain neutral during organization campaigns.[169] Daimler CEO Dieter Zetsche and personnel head Wilfried Porth signed the document for management. Daimler works council chief Erich Klemm and Bob King, who were chair and vice chair, respectively, of Daimler's WEC, signed it for the employees. Reaffirmation of the principles of social responsibility did not alter the position or behavior of Daimler management when it came to organizing the Vance plant. The company held fast to a policy of negative neutrality.

Bob King joined the supervisory board of GM's European subsidiary, Opel, in February 2012, which meant that he traveled regularly to Germany. When in Germany, King conferred with the leadership of IG Metall. In the same month Kirk Garner, an MBUSI employee, attended the annual meeting of the Daimler WEC as an observer. In the spring of 2012, the UAW and the German works council staff held workshops in Alabama for MBUSI employees interested in learning more about works councils and German industrial relations. In August 2012, a group of thirteen Mercedes-Benz employees from the Gaggenau and Sindelfingen plants visited Vance. All the Germans were IG Metall members; some also had roles on works councils.[170]

The 2012 German employee delegation brought with them a flyer that included a group picture and a letter of introduction. As the flyer explained,

> We are here because we want to meet with you. **Vance is the only unrepresented plant in the Mercedes Car Group.** We look forward to the day when Vance is among the represented plants and you can join us in the important global discussion about the future of our company that we as Daimler employees have through our global union network and by electing representatives to the Daimler World Employee Committee.
>
> We are here in Vance because we want to meet with you to tell you that we support you if you choose to be represented by the United Auto Workers union. And, **we think that it is in the interest of all employees to have input in our company's future through union representation**.

The German employee delegation also brought with them a slick magazine for MBUSI employees titled *Spark*, which the Daimler works council produced in Germany. The issue opens with a one-page article titled "The 21st Century UAW," which explains the union's new embrace of "innovation, flexibility and continuous improvement," followed by a letter from Bob King and an interview with the chair of Daimler's general works council and the Daimler WEC, Erich Klemm. The biggest pieces in the issue are a detailed five-page illustrated explanation of German industrial relations and six pages of questions and answers about union organizing drives, the UAW, works councils, and labor relations at Mercedes-Benz. A professional-looking logo appears throughout the publication. It is a stylized depiction of a bird with the colors of the US flag on its right wing and the German flag on its left wing. The bird hovers over the logos of the UAW, IG Metall, and the Daimler works councils. The last item in the issue is a telephone number, an email address, and a website: www.togetherforabetterlife.com. The logo appears again on the back cover along with the slogan "*Gemeinsam für ein gutes Leben*," which IG Metall had begun using a few years earlier, and "Together for a better life," which although not a literal translation captures the message of the German slogan. MBUSI management did not allow the German delegation to enter the Vance plant. Instead, the Germans accompanied UAW representatives and pro-union employees on "house calls" to Vance employees. The Germans reported that many employees hesitated to speak to the group because they feared the consequences of aggravating MBUSI management.[171]

Recognition election victories in 2012 at two auto parts producers in Tuscaloosa County—the French-owned Faurecia and Johnson Controls—buoyed the hopes of UAW organizers and supporters that they could win at MBUSI. The union had previously organized the German-owned ZF Industries, JCIM, and Inteva. All these plants supply parts to MBUSI.[172]

In late January 2013, twelve MBUSI employees who were members of the organizing leadership council went to Sindelfingen for a week to meet with Daimler works council and IG Metall representatives and to see how German industrial relations worked in practice at Daimler. A month later, Daimler labor relations director Wilfried Porth reiterated that the company maintained a neutral stance on unionization but added that the UAW would find no open door at MBUSI. Porth's assessment was that the UAW faced an uphill battle in Vance because wages and benefits were competitive and MBUSI management had maintained an open relationship with the employees and also because of the history of the Big Three, in particular the contraction of the domestic producers over the last forty years.[173]

A second issue of *Spark*—again produced by the Daimler works council in Germany—came out in February 2013. It opened with short notes from Bob King and Erich Klemm. King expressed his "admiration and support for your impressive progress in building a union at MBUSI" and added, "Much has been learned from past efforts to build a union at Vance. This time, the unprecedented support and involvement of the German union IG Metall and the Daimler Works Council have made all the difference. Team members are learning that under the Daimler model of co-determination, management and union are not adversaries." Klemm, assuming a more critical posture, stated that "we are irritated by the attitude of the Daimler management against the efforts of the UAW to organize workers at MBUSI. The management should, in our view, not hide behind the cloak of neutrality. Rather, we expect compliance with the newly adopted Integrity Code, which assures all workforces in the Daimler Group freedom of coalition." The remainder of the issue contained letters from four MBUSI employees attesting to "Why I want a Union at MBUSI," three letters from German colleagues detailing "German Support for Union Effort at MBUSI," and an article titled "The Basics of Bargaining." In June 2013, MBUSI employee and UAW supporter David Gilbert went as an observer to the annual Daimler WEC and reported back on his experience. The UAW also produced a video with testimonials in support of organizing from David Gilbert, UAW Region 8 director Gary Casteel, Eric Klemm, Helmut Lense, deputy head of the Daimler general works council Michael Brecht, head of the Baden-Württemberg branch of IG Metall Jörg Hofmann, and employee representatives from Brazil, Hungary, Italy, Japan, South Africa, and the United Kingdom.[174]

In mid-2013, the UAW moved into a larger office near the plant. Organizers put the flags of the UAW and IG Metall side by side on the wall. The union also created a new website: www.uawvance.org. The organizing drive focused on six issues: three years of wage adjustments in the form of onetime lump-sum payments rather than increases to base pay, the large number of temporary employees in the plant, the need for improvements in the pension plan, more control over shift scheduling, better ergonomics, and ending a "buddy-buddy" system that favors employees who have ingratiated themselves with management. Union adherents also claimed that in recent years management had increasingly emphasized the bottom line over the concerns of employees, which damaged morale in the plant. The timing of the organizing drive was relatively good. The plant was running at full capacity, output was at a record high, and MBUSI was looking to hire one thousand new employees to produce the C-Class sedan.[175]

As the organizing drive gained momentum, it again attracted opposition. Anti-union employees launched a new website: www.uawno.org. This group questioned the motives of IG Metall, asserting, "We know the German union IG Metall is not here to make a better life for us, they are here to make sure we do not get more jobs in Alabama and to take the ones we do have away from us and back to Germany."[176] Some employees interviewed by local reporters said that they did not support unionization because the pay and benefits at MBUSI already matched those at domestic producers. Others asserted that the UAW was only interested in dues money. Dara Longgrear, executive director of the Tuscaloosa County Economic Development Authority, once again said that unionization would damage the local economy by making it harder to persuade investors to build plants in Alabama. The regional newspaper ran editorials against unionization.[177] Many who opposed the UAW assert that the union was at least partly responsible for the 2009 bankruptcies of Chrysler and GM and the woes of the city of Detroit. Alabama governor Robert Bentley visited the Vance plant in June 2013 to send off MBUSI chief executive Markus Schaefer, who was returning to Germany. At the event Bentley said, "I really don't believe they have any need for unionization and an intermediary between them and management. I don't think it's going to happen."[178]

The unionization drive continued over the summer of 2013. German Daimler employees once again traveled to Alabama, including some who had done so previously. Denise Rumpeltes, an IG Metall member and works councilor at the Sindelfingen plant, explained the motivation behind helping the MBUSI employees organize. She noted that MBUSI was Daimler's only nonunionized plant. It was also the only one without representation on Daimler's WEC. "It's necessary that we have somebody we can talk to, to ensure the company doesn't play us off against each other."[179]

Daimler's neutrally came increasingly into question as the unionization drive progressed. Speaking at the Frankfurt Auto Show, Andreas Renschler, production chief for the Mercedes-Benz brand, observed, "The governor of Alabama said himself that he doesn't want factories oriented towards trade unions. Workers are happy because they have direct access to management." Daimler chief financial officer Bodo Uebber repeated that the company maintained a neutral position regarding unionization but was "happy" with the status quo. When asked about creating a works council at MBUSI, Renschler replied, "We just don't need it." This position differed starkly from that of VW management at the time, which was actively promoting the creation of a works council at its Chattanooga plant.[180]

Both sides ratcheted things up in the late summer of 2013. Management agreed to let both pro- and anti-union employees distribute literature at the plant gates, the central atrium inside the plant, and the employee cafeteria and team centers, which are break areas near the assembly line. Employees could only pass out literature in team centers when the assembly line was down. Union opponents rented space on two billboards on the main highway near the plant. One read "Just say NO to the UAW. Because Alabama is the home of winners, not losers," and the message on the other was "Don't let the UAW turn Alabama into the next Detroit." Sonny Hawthorne, a leader of the anti-union forces, told local media that donations from employees opposed to unionization paid for the billboards. Hawthorne added that he thought that the UAW organizing drive "has hit a wall"; he estimated that it was falling well short of having authorization cards from the minimum 30 percent of the employees required by law to call a union recognition election.[181] Some anti-union workers hired Thomas Scroggins, a Tuscaloosa attorney, to represent them. Scroggins was critical of the support that IG Metall was providing to the pro-union workers.: "Here, people value independence and they value having their own voice. These unions in other places in the world are not the UAW and they're not in Alabama."[182]

On September 3, 2013, the UAW filed unfair labor practice claims with the NLRB against MBUSI, accusing management of using harassment and intimidation to stop union supporters from talking about the union with other employees. One charge arose out of an incident when management stopped pro-union employees from distributing literature in the atrium of the plant. A second was the result of a manager preventing a pro-union employee from making critical remarks about Archie Craft, MBUSI's vice president for human resources. Pro-union employees also complained that the company applied restrictions on soliciting in team areas unevenly; management allowed employees to engage in nonwork activities, such as selling Girl Scout cookies, but did not allow employees to advocate for a union in the same spaces.[183] Union proponents claimed that the company's actions violated Daimler's own principles of social responsibility.[184] Management representatives countered that they had given pro-union employees opportunities to talk to coworkers about unionization in other areas of the plant. The restrictions were to ensure safety and to maintain timely and high-quality production. Union opponents asserted that the UAW proponents were "grasping at every straw they can" because the unionization "efforts have been stalled for six months." In late January 2014, the NLRB issued a complaint and announced that an administrative law judge would hold a hearing about the case in Birmingham starting on April 7, 2014.[185]

Momentum began to slip away from the pro-union employees in 2014. The UAW loss in the February union recognition election at Volkswagen Chattanooga dealt a severe psychological blow to pro-union employees at Vance because the union was much stronger at VW than at MBUSI, and VW management was far more accommodating toward unionization than its Daimler counterparts. Matt Patterson, head of the Center for Worker Freedom, an organization with ties to Washington-based antitax advocate Grover Norquist, fresh off the anti-union campaign at VW, announced that the Center for Worker Freedom would set up shop in Alabama to help defeat the organizing effort at MBUSI.[186] That same month, US senator Richard Shelby, a Tuscaloosa resident, visited the Mercedes-Benz plant. He said he saw no benefit to unionization and claimed that the auto industry expanded in Alabama because of the union-free environment.[187] While touring a Honda plant in Alabama a few days later, Shelby said he believed that most Republican leaders in Alabama would speak out against any intensification of organizing drives at automobile plants. "If we didn't, we would be failing our people," he asserted.[188]

In late May 2014 a group of pro-union employees, including Kirk Garner, who had gone to the Daimler WEC as an observer in 2012, publicly asked the UAW to halt the organizing campaign. "This has gone on for two-and-a-half years, and people are burnt out," Garner explained. Garner and Jim Spitzley, another MBUSI employee, said that at one point the UAW had authorization cards from more than 30 percent of Vance employees, which is enough to trigger a representation election, but that the union's goal was 65 percent, which the two men judged to be too high. As a result, many of the cards, which are valid for a year, had expired. Both men complained about a lack of advertising, the use of rookie organizers, and UAW officials who were preoccupied by "a master plan" that prioritized the campaign at VW over MBUSI. Spitzley said that the UAW officials were "in denial right now, and they're wanting to keep it going" even though the core group of pro-union employees at MBUSI had dwindled from 180 to about 50. "It's all about the image with the UAW, and it's not about the workers," Spitzley added. Garner and Spitzley said that they were among a group of employees who had spoken with the IAM; they would now prefer to work with the IAM. "There's a lot of people that will not sign a card with the UAW. They're tired of it. They've done it before and nothing has come of it," Spitzley explained. UAW Region 8 director Gary Casteel issued an immediate response in writing, stating that the union intended to continue the organizing effort at MBUSI. Casteel also pointed out that the AFL-CIO had given the UAW exclusive jurisdiction over MBUSI in the wake of the IAM's failed attempt to organize the plant in 2006. A week later, UAW officials announced at the union's quadrennial convention in the first week of June that they would soon unveil a new plan for organizing MBUSI and VW.[189]

King's strategy to revive the UAW by organizing foreign-owned vehicle assembly plants proved to be far more arduous an undertaking than he had anticipated. King was not able to achieve the goal of organizing at least one foreign-owned plant during his presidency, which he later described as "a great frustration and disappointment."[190] As a report to the UAW's 2014 convention on organizing noted,

> Members of the Daimler Works Council in Germany have spent a considerable amount of time on the ground in Alabama to talk to workers at the Mercedes facility. This level of solidarity has been critical in breathing new energy into the Mercedes organizing campaign and will be critical in assisting the U.S. Mercedes workers in successfully organizing their own UAW local union.
>
> IG Metall, the UAW and the various works councils are committed to this approach to co-determination and international union building in the years ahead.[191]

The convention elected King's deputy, Secretary-Treasurer Dennis Williams, as the new UAW president and Gary Casteel as the new secretary-treasurer.

Williams was a veteran organizer who led two strikes against the Caterpillar construction vehicle manufacturer in the 1990s. Casteel—a native of Florence, Alabama—had been heading UAW Region 8, which covers the Southeast from Maryland to Mississippi. Casteel had thus been the UAW officer directly responsible for organizing both MBUSI and Volkswagen Chattanooga. Williams was not as driven as King to organize foreign-owned automobile assembly plants, but he was willing to let Casteel continue the effort.

In early July, the new UAW leadership announced that the union was making "a historic move." It would embrace a "German-style strategy" that departed from the "all-or-nothing NLRB process." The UAW intended to form locals in Chattanooga and Vance without first having secured recognition of the union as the sole bargaining agent of the employees. In Vance, union representatives distributed a flyer with *Spark Extra* on the masthead and the headline "It's Time to Form Our UAW Local Union at MBUSI!" The subtitle read "the UAW, IG Metall, & the Daimler World Employee Committee (WEC) have pledged ultimate support in the immediate formation of a union local at MBUSI." Under the header "What this Means," the flyer stated, "We will have our own UAW local union," "We will have global influence. . . . [T]he Daimler World Employee Committee (WEC) will grant a permanent seat to an elected delegate from the MBUSI local union," and "We can start signing up members now." The backside of the flyer was titled "Questions: Answered." One question was "Has this ever been done before?" The answer was "This is unique . . . nowadays in the U.S. In the early days of the UAW, many workplaces were organized in a similar fashion. . . . It is still very typical today in Germany and in much of the rest of the world. . . . This UAW local will be built in an innovative German-American style, pulling the best practices of American & German labor organizing together and tailoring a union that fits the unique culture and needs of MBUSI Team Members."

Another question was "How is establishing this UAW local union different from what we were doing before with authorization cards?" The answer explained that employees could join the local immediately. The members would then elect officers and work together to address issues of concern in the plant. The flyer added, "This does not depend on MBUSI, the NLRB, or anyone but Team Members ourselves." MBUSI, however, had no legal obligation to bargain with a local that the federal government had not certified as the exclusive agent of the employees. The flyer made it clear that members of the new local need not pay dues until thirty days after a collective bargaining agreement is signed.

The over-the-top language of the July 2014 flyer could not disguise the reality that the decision to create a local for MBUSI employees was an experiment born out of desperation. It was a second-best solution designed to placate the pro-union employees who were frustrated by the lack of progress and to repli-

cate a parallel effort at Volkswagen Chattanooga. The organizing drive had pla-
teaued well short of the numbers needed to pursue a representation election with
any confidence. There was nothing to lose by forming a local to see if that attracted additional employees to the union. The new approach was enough of a
step forward to bring back into the fold some union supporters, such as Kirk
Garner and Jim Spitzley, who had expressed doubts earlier in the year.[192]

Back in April, Daimler's general works council vice chair Michael Brecht was
elected chair of that body, succeeding the retiring Eric Klemm. In late July, Daimler's WEC met and elected Brecht to be its chair and Casteel its vice chair.
Brecht expressed unflagging commitment to organizing the Mercedes-Benz
plant in Alabama.[193]

Days later, NLRB administrative law judge Keltner W. Locke ruled on the
pending unfair labor practice charges against MBUSI. Locke dismissed charges of
management threats and intimidation but found that MBUSI maintained an
"overly broad solicitation and distribution rule" and ordered management to bring
it into conformance with federal law. He also ordered management to post a notice
advising employees that the company had violated the labor law and acknowledging that employees not on work time could distribute literature, which is standard
practice in these sorts of cases. Locke declined to impose a fine, however. Daimler
management declared the ruling a victory for its neutrality policy because there
was no fine. Gary Casteel used the ruling to denounce Daimler. "It is clear that
Daimler has acted with hostility and in direct contempt of its neutrality policy in
its dealings with pro-union workers at its Alabama plant in Tuscaloosa. It's deplor-
able that Mercedes was found in violation of US law and then publicly claimed it as
a victory and an example of its neutral pledge."[194] The unfair labor practice ruling
had no impact on organizing at MBUSI, however.

On September 5, 2014, Daimler managing board chair Dieter Zetsche gave a
speech at the Vance plant to mark the start of production of the C-Class sedan.
Zetsche used the occasion to announce that Mercedes-Benz was going to build
an additional model, the ML Coupe, at the Alabama plant as part of the company's five-year $2.4 billion expansion plan. When complete, the investment
would permit the company to employ seven thousand and produce three hundred thousand vehicles annually. Mercedes-Benz management wished to expand
production in Alabama because the United States had become the company's
biggest market. In 2013, Mercedes-Benz sold over three hundred thousand cars
in the United States. Recent declines in the value of the dollar, which increased
the dollar price of vehicles made in Germany, was another motivation for expanding production in the United States.[195]

When asked about the unionization effort, Zetsche told reporters "we will
maintain our position of neutrality" and also said that unionization was "up to

our employees to make their call." Zetsche added, "The team here in Tuscaloosa has decided for the last twenty years not to organize with the UAW or any other union. . . . As long as a company does what they should do with their workers—treat them with respect and treat them correctly—they are never going to unionize." Alabama governor Robert Bentley, who attended the event, again said that if the UAW succeeded organizing the Vance plant, it would hurt his ability to attract foreign firms to his state. He added, "I am not anti-union. I really am not. However, I have to look at it from a recruiting standpoint. . . . . A company like Mercedes, if they were to unionize, would it hurt my ability to recruit companies to Alabama? Absolutely it would."[196]

The UAW formally chartered the Vance local, giving it the number 112, on October 3, 2014. Before the chartering ceremony, IG Metall vice chair Jörg Hofmann and Daimler enterprise works council and WEC chair Michael Brecht toured the MBUSI plant in their capacities as Daimler supervisory board members and conversed with plant managers and employees. At the ceremony, Brecht praised MBUSI employees and declared, "We lend our support to all workers at Daimler so they can make their voices heard and be represented by a strong union." Hoffmann affirmed, "We expect management to work constructively with the UAW local. Codetermination and trade union rights must be self-evident on the worldwide locations of German firms. We want to see effective worker representation at MBUSI. We believe now is the time to fulfill the promise of codetermination in Alabama and we believe that the UAW is the right partner to assist the workers." Hofmann also emphasized, in light of negotiations to establish free trade between the United States and the European Union, that "we expect German firms to signal clearly that free trade is not a Trojan horse to limit participation and collective bargaining. This can be established through the practical question of recognition of union representation in their own transplants."[197]

Brecht, Hofmann, and UAW president Dennis Williams used the chartering ceremony to sign a letter of intent that made more formal the cooperation among IG Metall, the Daimler WEC, and the UAW to organize MBUSI employees. The letter was meant to make it clear to both employees and management that IG Metall and the WEC would remain steadfast in their support. The next day, IG Metall issued a statement demanding "genuine codetermination and effective employee representation for the employees of the American Mercedes plant."[198]

All the speakers at the chartering ceremony stressed that it was unacceptable that MBUSI was the only Daimler-owned assembly plant without a union. MBUSI employee Rodney Bowens said, "We are asking Daimler to respect our right to representation and give the same opportunities to Alabama's working families that have been extended to our counterparts elsewhere in the US and around the world." Dennis Williams asserted, "What happens here is important to the future of the labor movement. . . . It's time for the committed and hard-working employees at MBUSI to have the same representation that Daimler employees enjoy around the world. It's the right thing to do. Plus, it will improve productivity and quality, ensuring success for both the company and the workforce." Williams pointed out that the UAW already represented seven thousand Daimler employees at DTNA facilities. He added, "Our hope is that management will recognize the importance of today's announcement and welcome our new local union into the Daimler family."[199]

UAW officials said that more than 750 of the 2,500 permanent employees had joined Local 112. Local 112 members said they hoped to attract more members by focusing on advancing plant safety, improving workplace ergonomics, and creating a way for the 1,000 temporary workers at MBUSI to become permanent employees. They also pledged that they would get involved in the community by supporting charitable causes, youth programs, and other local efforts.[200] Gary Casteel indicated that the UAW did not intend to pursue a recognition election at MBUSI. "Why would we go down that road again?," he said, with the recent recognition election loss at Volkswagen Chattanooga in mind. "I don't think the political atmosphere in Alabama is any different than it is in Tennessee."[201] The union would instead press for a card-check procedure, despite Daimler management's repeated insistence that it would only accept a recognition election.[202]

Daimler management issued a statement in response to the formation of UAW local 112. "This does not change our position on neutrality or how our teams work together within our organization. We are committed to providing our Team Members with a safe and professional workplace where they can have an open, continuous dialogue with their colleagues and supervisors on all matters related to their job. We believe the culture we have established is our best path forward for a successful future."[203] UAW officials barred anti-union MBUSI employee Sonny Hawthorne from attending the chartering ceremony, but he spoke to the media outside the hotel where the event took place. Hawthorne denounced the formation of Local 112 as "just another backdoor tactic that the UAW's trying to use to gain entry into our plant. It's a way of getting around having an election, because they will never win an election at Mercedes."[204] NRWLDF president Mark Mix also issued a statement. "Again and again the UAW hierarchy cut backroom deals with outside groups, and even companies, that are designed to push workers into union ranks whether the employees like it or not."[205]

The creation of Local 112 temporarily boosted the morale of union sympathizers at MBUSI, but it did not move the Vance employees further down the path to union recognition. Local 112 continued the tactic of filing unfair labor practice complaints against MBUSI in an effort to gin up membership and lay the groundwork for an unfair labor practice strike if need be, which would provide greater protections to strikers. The union won some of these complaints, but this did not translate into more employees signing union authorization cards.[206] One factor that continued to make organizing at MBUSI challenging was the generous compensation. A Center for Automotive Research study found that in 2013 the average hourly labor cost of $65 at MBUSI was the highest in the United States. GM's hourly cost was $58, Ford's was $57, Honda's was $49, Chrysler's and Toyota's were $48, Nissan's was $42, Hyundai and Kia's were $41, BMW's was $39, and VW's was $38.[207]

Despite setbacks, the UAW did not give up on German-style codetermination as a means to advance the union. A resolution at the union's March 2015 Special Convention on Collective Bargaining identified codetermination in the form of works councils, global employee committees, and worker representation on corporate boards as "another successful model to guide our efforts."[208]

The May 2015 gathering of the Daimler WEC brought home the uncertain position of Local 112. The WEC elected Local 112 president George Jones to serve as one of three US representatives on the WEC. Yet when Jones made his travel plans, MBUSI management stipulated that he use vacation time to attend the meeting because the company did not recognize Local 112. The company relented only after WEC and Daimler enterprise works council chair Michael Brecht insisted. At the May meeting, Daimler employees expanded the size of the WEC from thirteen members from six countries to twenty-three members from fifteen countries. The enlargement corresponded to Daimler's global expansion. The WEC reelected Gary Casteel as deputy chair.[209]

The balance of forces has changed little at the MBUSI plant since the formation of Local 112. Roughly a quarter of the eligible permanent workforce supports unionization. The UAW continues to provide financial assistance to Local 112. Gary Casteel retired as UAW secretary-treasurer in 2018.[210] The UAW convention elected Region 8 director Ray Curry to succeed him. Curry was familiar with Daimler. He had worked at Freightliner, which is a part of DTNA, in Mount Holly, North Carolina, from 1992 to 2004 before working full-time for the UAW. With the support of IG Metall, Curry was elected to an employee seat of the Daimler supervisory board in 2018. Continuing cooperation between IG Metall and the UAW has helped to maintain a floor of support to the unionization effort at MBUSI. For example, in September 2018 Michael Brecht and Ray Curry toured the Vance plant and spoke to plant management and employees in their capacity as members of the Daimler supervisory board. While they were there, they also were guest speakers at a Labor Day rally sponsored by Local 112.[211] This floor of support, however, has not been sufficiently robust to facilitate movement off the status quo.

The efforts to organize MBUSI failed. Failure was by no means inevitable, as the successful organizing drives within the same company at DTNA and the details of the Daimler cases make clear. Explaining the failure is a complex undertaking for these cases, given the numerous twists and turns during the multiple attempts by two unions to organize the plant over two decades.

First, the missed opportunities stand out from 1999 and 2003 to secure card-check recognition for the Vance plant as a side deal during negotiations of Chrysler's collective bargaining agreement. The evidence presented above suggests that during the DaimlerChrysler years, management was willing to move off a policy of negative neutrality regarding unionization at MBUSI and accept card check if the price were right. It was UAW leaders who chose other priorities over a card-check deal at Vance.

Second, Daimler management was unique among foreign vehicle assemblers in taking a high road strategy for permanent employees when it came to compensation. Hourly compensation at MBUSI has consistently been the highest in the United States, even higher than compensation at the domestic vehicle assemblers with UAW contracts. This tactic from the union-avoidance playbook is effective but expensive, which is why no other firms have copied it. MBUSI management compensated for the cost by hiring large numbers of temporary employees at a much lower rate, a practice that became standard fare at most transplants. Temporaries also served as a buffer, enhancing employment security for permanent employees and reducing the appeal of unionization. MBUSI's employment relations were thus much like those at DTNA's Gaffney, South Carolina, specialty truck plant, which the UAW also failed to organize. Since Daimler's high road strategy eliminated the material advantage of unionization for permanent employees, organizers stressed safety and voice in the workplace as selling points, but only about a quarter of the permanent labor force at MBUSI ever found these important enough to warrant signing a union authorization card. It is worth noting that MBUSI management never needed to implement a plan designed by a law firm specializing in union avoidance because the company's high-compensation strategy and two-tier workforce obviated the need to do much more.

Third, substantial state subsidies made unionization more difficult because they drew regional politicians deeply into the affairs of the plant and greatly increased the vulnerability of Daimler management to regional political pressure. The contrast with DTNA is stark. DTNA received few subsidies, and regional pressure to resist unionization was sporadic and largely confined to local business communities.

The relationship between the leaders of the UAW and IG Metall changed considerably in the years after Daimler-Benz management decided to build a

Mercedes-Benz plant in the United States. In the mid-1990s, the two unions signed an agreement to cooperate that neither side ever really used. The practical steps taken in 1998 in the wake of the Daimler-Chrysler merger—namely IG Metall leaders ceding a seat on the DaimlerChrysler supervisory board to a UAW official and endeavoring to create a world employee committee for the company—proved more effective, but subsequent relations between IG Metall and the UAW were not always smooth. The mid-2000s were particularly difficult when UAW president Stephen Yokich, in failing health, lost interest and Nate Gooden failed to maintain employee solidarity on some important decisions before the supervisory board. Daimler management's decision to build C-Class cars in Vance, the global financial crisis, and the election of UAW presidents with more strategic vision triggered a turnaround in relations between the two unions. IG Metall and the Daimler works councils (especially under the leadership of Michael Brecht) spent significant amounts of time and money to help the UAW in the effort to organize MBUSI. That said, there was no "Feuerstein moment" like there had been in 1991 for the Mount Holly Freightliner plant when the head of the Mercedes-Benz general works council, Karl Feuerstein, flexed his muscles with top Daimler management to the benefit of the UAW. In other words, greater transnational union cooperation alone was not sufficient for success in union organizing in these cases.

It is worth noting that neither UAW nor IAM officers looked for allies in the labor movement or in civil society to help with their unionization efforts. There are no civil society organizations in Vance itself because it is a small town, but there are civil rights, church-based, and other organizations in cities nearby, such as Tuscaloosa, and at the state level. Union organizers never tried to bring them in to strengthen their efforts, however. They opted instead for a largely top-down approach.

The Daimler cases make it clear that the mere existence in the home firm of an extensive set of participatory institutions from the plant to the international level, a strong trade union, a tradition of cooperative labor-management relations, a framework agreement with a global union federation, and corporate commitments to codes of conduct are not sufficient to ensure success in unionization drives at subsidiaries in the South. Daimler management's position of negative neutrality made organizing at MBUSI difficult, and policies such as high compensation and job security for core employees and close cooperation with regional politicians kept the UAW at bay. Would management taking a more accommodating stance toward unionization be sufficient to achieve organizing success? Chapter 3, on the UAW's attempts to organize Volkswagen Chattanooga, provides some answers.

VOLKSWAGEN

From Unionized Company
to Anti-union Stalwart

We know if we go for a traditional election where outside organizations campaign against us, we'd probably lose.

—Gary Casteel, director, UAW Region 8

Volkswagen Chattanooga is the most exasperating of all the recent attempts to organize a foreign-owned plant in the southern United States from the perspective of the UAW because, as former UAW president Bob King said, "VW was our best chance."[1] Indeed it was, given VW management's professed commitment to corporate social responsibility and social partnership as well as the strong position of German employee representatives in the firm. The UAW actually won one of three recognition elections held at the Chattanooga plant between 2014 and 2019, but in the end the union was unable to obtain a collective bargaining agreement out of any of the three attempts. UAW officials were not static in the three-act Chattanooga drama. They were innovative in each effort and changed both the strategy and the tactics in response to the previous experiences. Yet innovation also caused problems, because it precipitated VW management's move from positive neutrality (i.e., an instrumental acceptance of unionization) in 2014, to negative neutrality in the 2015 election for a small skilled trades unit, to adopting an unadulterated union-avoidance campaign in 2019.

Like elsewhere, workers were at the center of the drives. Strategies and errors mattered. The three VW cases best illustrate the scope of influence that parties beyond the employees, management, and the union have to affect the outcome of organizing drives. Concerns that global expansion of production would enable transnational firms to reduce compensation throughout the firm by playing off workers in different parts of the world led German employee representatives to assist the UAW to an unprecedented degree in the organizing drives. Massive subsides to attract foreign firms to build factories in the South have given state and local anti-union economic and political elites leverage to insert themselves into organizing drives, especially when they conclude that the company has taken an insufficiently firm line against unionization.

The story of VW in America is like a set of Russian dolls. It is important to start at the beginning to understand subsequent outcomes, because each episode is explicable only with a grasp of what had previously transpired. This chapter therefore starts with VW's entry into the US car market after World War II and the construction of the company's first factory in the United States three decades later, which was in Westmoreland County, Pennsylvania. The use and misuse of the history of the Westmoreland plant continues to this day. Thereafter, the chapter traces three union recognition elections in Chattanooga.

Volkswagen Goes to America

VW entered the US market in 1949; the company sold two vehicles. Sales steadily improved to 28,907 in 1955, which led VW management to briefly explore producing in the United States. The company purchased a factory from Studebaker-Packard in North Brunswick Township, New Jersey, and created a subsidiary of Volkswagen AG (VWAG): Volkswagen of America.[2] When a feasibility study found production costs in New Jersey to be excessively high, VW management abandoned the plan to build a plant in the United States and instead used the new subsidiary to improve service to a growing network of dealerships.[3]

VW's simple, reliable, and inexpensive cars proved attractive particularly to younger consumers. Pioneering iconoclastic advertising campaigns solidified VW's image as the 1960s counterculture's car of choice. By 1970, VW had become the leading auto exporter to the United States. Its US sales reached a high of 569,696 cars, which amounted to 6.8 percent of the US market. That same year, VW began to export cars from its upscale Audi division to the United States.[4]

Market conditions began to shift against VW in the 1970s. VW was unable to capitalize on the 1973–1974 energy shock—despite its lineup of fuel-efficient cars—for three reasons. First, the German mark had appreciated sharply, increasing by 50 percent against the US dollar between 1968 and 1973 and then by an additional 24.5 percent between 1973 and 1978. The mark's rise pushed up the dollar value of VW's home hourly labor cost to $13.60, which far exceeded US labor costs and forced the company to raise prices. Second, VW had not kept up technologically. The company was still relying mostly on models first designed in the 1950s, the 1940s, and, in the case of the iconic Beetle, the 1930s. New emissions and safety requirements in the United States made it impossible to continue selling many of them. Third, Japanese competitors increasingly exported cars to the US market that were superior to VWs in terms of price and quality. By 1978, VW's US market share had fallen to 2.5 percent.[5]

VW's leadership decided to improve the company's position in the US market by upgrading its offerings and producing some cars in the United States. VW already had considerable experience operating facilities in Brazil, South Africa, and Mexico. VW's management expected fewer challenges operating in the United States than in low-income countries. Gaining approval from the supervisory board for the investment would not be pro forma because of Germany's codetermination laws, which allocate ten of twenty seats on the supervisory boards (*Aufsichtsräte*) of companies with more than two thousand employees to employee representatives, and VW's unique corporate governance and ownership structure.

The West German federal government sold its shares of VW to the public in 1960 as a part of a partial privatization law, but the state of Lower Saxony—where VW is headquartered and has its flagship Wolfsburg plant—retained an ownership stake in the company, two seats on VW's supervisory board, and 20.2 percent of the shareholder votes. VW company statutes require a four-fifths majority vote of the supervisory board for approval of any major decision, such as building an assembly plant abroad. So, management would have to persuade both the employee members of the supervisory board and the two board members representing the state government of Lower Saxony to support building an assembly plant in the United States for the investment to move forward.[6]

VW's supervisory board voted in favor of building a plant in the United States in April 1976 only after management gave employee representatives from the powerful German mechanical engineering union IG Metall, the firm's works council network, and the two board members appointed by the state of Lower Saxony "strong guarantees" that the US production would not cost German jobs.[7] In October 1976, VW signed a thirty-year lease with the government of Pennsylvania at a price of $40 million for the use of an assembly plant that Chrysler built but never put into operation in Westmoreland County, Pennsylvania, thirty-five miles southeast of Pittsburgh. VW received what was seen at the time as the princely sum of $70 million in incentives from the state and local governments in the form of infrastructure improvements and tax abatements to invest $250 million to outfit the plant.[8] The plant was a novelty. The only other foreign-owned producer to have manufactured automobiles in the United States was the British firm Rolls Royce, which operated a plant in Springfield, Massachusetts, from 1921 to 1931. The first car, a white VW Rabbit hatchback,[9] rolled off the assembly line on April 10, 1978. VW had developed this model to replace the Beetle as an entry-level economy car. At the plant opening VW chief executive officer Toni Schmücker said, "This may be one small step for America, but it is a giant leap for Volkswagen."[10]

Once the plant had a workforce, VW management recognized the UAW as their employees' collective bargaining agent, using the card-check procedure rather than a representation election to determine the employees' preference for two reasons. First, all automobile assembly plants in the United States at the time had unionized labor. VW management had no intention of departing from that practice. Second, pressure from IG Metall contributed to VW management readily accepting unionization. IG Metall chair Eugen Loderer was also vice chair of VW's supervisory board. Loderer's family friend Karl-Heinz Briam was VW's personnel director.[11] Briam maintained cordial and accommodating relationships with union officials even after he moved into a career in personnel management. VW's Wolfsburg headquarters leadership made its preference clear to the plant managers in Pennsylvania. An American executive who had worked in the plant recalled, "The word came over, 'We want you to look favorably on the UAW organizing the plant.' The fact was that IG Metall put a big threat on Volkswagen in Germany—'Help them organize, or else.'"[12]

VW management's decision and timing to invest in the United States initially appeared fortuitous. The second oil shock of 1979–1980 drove up gasoline prices to record highs, which helped to boost sales of economy cars such as the Rabbit. Reviewers initially praised the Rabbit for its handling and mechanical systems, which included a diesel motor as an option. The construction and start-up went smoothly. General manufacturing manager Richard Dauch remembers, "In that period, every single goal set by the board of directors was met or exceeded. We launched on time and early. We were staying within budgets. We were actually making profits."[13] In 1980, the Westmoreland plant was operating at capacity; it produced 246,111 cars and employed more than 5,700 workers;[14] the company's US market share rose to 3 percent.[15] The early success made management so hopeful that VW purchased from Chrysler an old missile plant in Sterling Heights, Michigan, and began converting it to make the sportier Jetta. Schmücker's objective was "eventually to make the North American operation 90 percent self-sufficient, with only transmissions supplied from German plants."[16]

Labor relations at the Westmoreland facility were initially bad. Most workers came from the greater Pittsburgh area, which had a strong labor tradition. Only 20 percent had ever worked for an automobile firm. The average age was twenty-five, and most workers were male, which made for an "independent and militant" workforce.[17] VW hired mostly castoff managers from US domestic auto firms to run the plant. They, in turn, hired line managers who also came from US plants "where conflict with the union was a normal part of the workday."[18]

Industrial strife first broke out at the Westmoreland plant six months after it opened. Workers staged wildcat strikes to bring their compensation on par with the domestic automobile firms. A memorable chant from the picket line, playing off the model's name—Rabbit—was "No money, no bunny!" By twenty months, the workers had struck six times for a variety of reasons. Minorities also picketed the plant, asserting that the company had discriminated in hiring. A lawsuit ensued. VW ultimately reached a settlement a decade later.[19]

Industrial relations quickly settled down, however, once differences regarding the initial collective bargaining agreement were ironed out. After March 1981, the plant did not lose a single hour of production due to any labor-management differences.[20] Relations between the UAW leadership and local management were friendly. For example, plant manager Donn Viola sent UAW president Owen Bieber a kind note on November 22, 1985, thanking him for visiting the Westmoreland plant for the celebration of the one millionth vehicle to come off the assembly line.[21]

VW's fortunes reversed quickly in the 1980s for several reasons. The price of oil fell by 25 percent from a peak of $40 per barrel in 1980, which substantially reduced demand for economy cars such as the Rabbit. Complaints about the Rabbit as a vehicle began to accumulate. Some criticized the "Americanization" of the Rabbit. VW used a softer suspension and less expensive interior materials in the US version that some critics called "downright tacky."[22] Others criticized the Rabbit for not being American enough, calling it "a vehicle designed in Europe for Europeans. . . . It was just another plain Jane econobox" that had no cupholders or other accessories that Americans had come to expect.[23] In stark contrast to the Beetle and the VW Bus, the Rabbit was not reliable. It had "a worse than average maintenance record, including an oil burning problem" that led to engine fires.[24] Rabbit sales quickly fell.

VW management responded to consumer complaints by having designers make over 1,300 changes to the Rabbit for the 1983 model year, including stiffening the suspension and upgrading the interior.[25] VW management hoped that "the new Rabbit can win back some of the market share that they once enjoyed,"[26] but sales did not improve. Despite the numerous modifications, VW management stuck to an eight- to ten-year life cycle for the Rabbit, a decision that proved disastrous. VW's competitors had increasingly adopted four- to six-year product life cycles, so car styles changed swiftly in the mid-1980s. Curved "jelly mold" cars such as the Ford Taurus became the new fashion. Boxy hatchbacks such as the Rabbit were quickly out. Besides design, some attributed VW's falling sales to a loss of marketing touch, which had been so instrumental to the company's success in the 1960s.[27] So, in the end "the Japanese grabbed their market away from them."[28]

Other foreign firms intensified competition in the North American car market by relocating production there. In 1982, Honda became the first Japanese automobile company to open a plant in the United States. Nissan followed suit in 1983. Toyota established a joint venture with GM in 1984, and Mazda opened a plant in cooperation with Ford in 1987. The Japanese producers used the latest robotics in their US plants. The Westmoreland factory, in contrast, was "virtually outdated by the day it opened."[29] A comparable Chrysler plant that began production at the same time could make 50 percent more vehicles than VW's factory. To make matters worse, the Westmoreland facility had to run at 85 percent capacity to break even, which is high for an automobile plant.

When VW's sales fell by half in the early 1980s, the Westmoreland plant began to run significant losses. German upper management and the US plant managers feuded frequently over a range of issues, many grounded in cultural differences, which generated considerable dysfunction.[30] As part of a retrenchment plan, VW management sold the Sterling Heights plant back to Chrysler in 1983 without ever producing a car there. Despite the sale, VW personnel director Karl-Heinz Briam assured UAW president Owen Bieber that "Volkswagen had no intention of abandoning the operation" in the United States.[31]

By 1987, the Westmoreland plant had been operating for five years at less than half capacity and losing over $100 million annually. VW's US market share had fallen to 1.5 percent, and more Japanese-owned plants were scheduled to open in the next few years. The UAW leadership offered the company substantial concessions including a wage cut in a bid to keep the plant open, but compensation reductions would have been insufficient to make up for the large losses. Westmoreland closed on July 14, 1988, eliminating 2,500 jobs. A handful of the remaining workers boxed up much of the plant's machinery to ship it to China.[32]

Consensus opinion at the time pointed to management shortcomings as the principal reason behind VW's failure at the Westmoreland plant. Shortly before the plant closed, Chester B. Bahn, Volkswagen of America public relations manager, stated that the plant was "falling victim to a volume-related illness."[33] Gerald Myers, management professor at University of Michigan who had been an executive at Ford and Chrysler and CEO of American Motors, observed, "They could have done it there, but they didn't. They had the resources. They had the funds. They had the talent to do it, but they didn't do it because of a lack of dedication to the market."[34]

UAW president Owen Bieber and Vice President Bill Casstevens, head of the union's VW division, concurred but used much less tact. They attributed the plant closing to "poor performance by a VW management team that failed to give the Pennsylvania plant a new model line that would appeal to the American consumer in sufficient volume to sustain the facility. It shows a shortsighted, bottom-line mentality."[35]

Regarding employment relations, Bahn's letter to the *Pittsburgh Post-Gazette* in April 1988 dismissed "the perception among so many people that organized labor somehow has played a part in our plant's forthcoming closing." "Nothing could be further from the truth," he asserted. "VW Westmoreland had an exemplary labor-management relationship" once the difficulties with the first contract had been resolved.[36]

It is important to note that Volkswagen Westmoreland is the only automobile assembly plant wholly owned by a foreign firm that the UAW has ever successfully organized. (The UAW would subsequently organize some automobile assembly plants jointly owned by a foreign and domestic producer and DTNA assembly plants in North Carolina.) Yet success was not due to the resources, strategy, or tactics of the UAW. It was organized because VW management did not want to be the first company in four decades to attempt to operate a nonunion automobile assembly plant in the United States, and German employee representatives applied considerable pressure on VW management to recognize the UAW. Although VW received subsidies, the business and political establishment in western Pennsylvania did not use them to press VW management to keep the UAW out of the plant because it was in the northeastern United States in a region with a strong union tradition.

Westmoreland entered VW company lore as a costly and traumatic experience that the company never wished to repeat. In subsequent years, VW management turned its attention toward expanding elsewhere in the world, and VW all but disappeared in the United States. By 1993 sales had fallen to 49,533 units,[37] and VW's market share slipped to 0.43 percent.[38]

VW has become one of the world's leading companies in corporate social responsibility in large part because of the firm's unique relationships with its stakeholders. Lower Saxony's significant ownership stake disqualifies VW from joining an employers association because the bylaws of these associations forbid firms with significant public ownership from being members. VW's isolation has left the firm more vulnerable to union pressure. The company has a single-firm collective agreement with IG Metall that is much more generous than the region-wide agreements the union has for the mechanical engineering sector, which cover the other German carmakers. VW's isolation has also led corporate leadership to integrate the company's works councils far more deeply into the process of firm decision-making than is the case at BMW and Daimler.[39] VW's unique position also benefits the firm. It secures employee buy-in, which is particularly helpful for contentious decisions such as layoffs and selecting new sites for plants.

The presence of two representatives from the state government of Lower Saxony on VW's supervisory board has also contributed to the company's commitment to more accommodating labor and social policies than has been the case for other German automobile companies, particularly when the left-of-center Social Democratic Party of Germany has been the leading party in state-government coalitions, which has been the case for more than 60 percent of the time since 1945.[40]

Germany's postwar codetermination laws have ensured that employees have a voice in the workplace through works councils elected by employees in each workplace and employee representation on corporate supervisory boards for large firms such as VW. VW is a complex company with multiple overlapping sets of works councils. Each VW plant in Germany has a works council. These councils send representatives to a group works council (*Konzernbetriebsrat*) for the German plants that make VW models. The firm also has an enterprise works council (*Gesamtbetriebsrat*) that includes subsidiaries in Germany (e.g., Audi) that are a part of the VWAG.

Over the last three decades, VW's network of works councils has expanded. In 1990, VW employees unilaterally created a European Works Council, which management recognized two years later. In 1998, VW management and employee representatives agreed to create the Volkswagen Global Works Council (which has antecedents in meetings of VW employee representatives that date back to the late 1960s). The Global Works Council meets once a year and has information and consultation privileges rather than the stronger set of codetermination rights that German works councils have.[41]

The next expansion of corporate social responsibility in employment relations was a global framework agreement titled "Declaration on Social Rights and Industrial Relationships at Volkswagen."[42] VW management and employee representatives (i.e., the VW Global Works Council and the IMF global trade union federation) signed the global framework agreement in Bratislava, Slovakia, on June 6, 2002. VW management committed to respect the core standards of the International Labor Organization, specifically: the right to organize, nondiscrimination, rejection of forced and child labor, compensation at least corresponding to local laws and standards, work hours that at least match national legal requirements, and occupational safety and health protection.

That same year, VW management unilaterally joined the UNGC on corporate social responsibility, which is a voluntary, nonbinding agreement for enterprises launched two years earlier by United Nations secretary-general Kofi Annan to encourage firms to commit to sustainable and socially responsible business practices, including respect for labor rights, and to report regularly on their implementation.[43]

In subsequent years, VW management signed several international agreements on occupational safety and health as well as cooperative information exchange with worker representatives. On October 29, 2009, VW went a step further by signing the "Charter on Labour Relations within the Volkswagen Group," otherwise known as the "social charter," with the firm's European Works Council, VW Global Works Council, and the IMF.[44] The social charter's language is far more expansive than analogous agreements at BMW and Daimler. The charter committed the firm to provide for "the in-house participation rights of democratically elected employee representatives" through a works council, a trade union, or something equivalent that conforms to national law and practice at all the company's facilities worldwide, including facilities built after the agreement came into force, such as the Chattanooga plant.[45]

The German labor relations system gives both unions and works councils roles in representing employees. The primary focus of unions is collective bargaining. The main concern of works councils is representing employees' interests in the workplace.[46] Unions and works councils regularly work together, but the two do not have identical interests, and each is acutely sensitive to preserving autonomy from the other. At VW, the works council network is generally more influential than is IG Metall because of the great lengths to which VW management has gone to embed the works councils into the decision-making process of the company.

The Transformation of Volkswagen into a Global Company

Starting in the 1980s, VW management executed a series of acquisitions and expansions that transformed the company into one of the largest automobile producers in the world. Between 1982 and 1990, VW gradually gained control over the Spanish automobile company SEAT, which became its first non-German subsidiary. In 1984, VW company began producing in China. Once the Cold War came to an end, VW engaged in a major eastward expansion. It acquired majority control over the Czech auto firm Škoda in stages during the first half of the 1990s and added production capacity throughout much of central and Eastern Europe. VW expanded its luxury offerings in 1998 by buying Bentley, Bugatti, and Lamborghini and spent much of the early to mid-2000s restructuring these acquisitions and consolidating the upscale marques into the Audi group and the mass-market makes into the VWAG.

In 2008 Martin Winterkorn, newly named CEO of VW, opened a new chapter for VW by launching the ambitious "Strategy 2018," which included a new corporate goal: becoming "the world's most profitable, fascinating and sustainable automobile manufacturer" by 2018.[47] Strategy 2018 quickly became intertwined with an additional objective: becoming the world's largest car company in terms of sales. To achieve that goal, VW could no longer neglect the US market. Strategy 2018 set the objective of tripling US sales in ten years. In 2007, the company sold 330,000 VWs and 93,500 Audis in the United States, which amounted to a market share of 2.5 percent. Although this performance was an improvement on VW's 1993 ebb, the company trailed far behind most Japanese manufacturers and lost money in the United States more often than not. As early as 2005, VW executives talked about building a new plant in the United States as a part of Project Moonraker, which included sending twenty-two VW engineers to the United States to learn about American car preferences, but there was no follow-through.[48] Now, as a part of Strategy 2018, the new VW leadership committed to building a production plant in the United States to bring down the cost of the company's Passat sedan there. Bernd Osterloh, who was the leading figure in VW's works council network as chair of the enterprise and group works councils and a member of VW's supervisory board, embraced the idea, observing, "Winterkorn presented a persuasive US strategy. . . . If we want to pass Toyota and want to advance our growth strategy, then we must win market share in the USA."[49]

VW management considered sites in Alabama and Michigan for building a US plant but ultimately announced in July 2008 that the billion-dollar plant would be built in Chattanooga, Tennessee, because the local and state governments offered the company an unprecedented $577 million incentive package. Chattanooga also offers easy access to several interstate highways and is thirty minutes from an intermodal transfer center with an excellent rail connection to the Port of Savannah on the Atlantic Ocean.[50]

VW management appointed Frank Fischer, a German national with an engineering degree from the University of Washington who had worked for the company since 1991, to head the project team starting on October 1, 2008.[51] He would become the plant's first CEO once operations began. Construction would begin on March 2, 2009, and take two years. With the investment decision in place, VW management set new corporate goals for the US market: increase sales to eight hundred thousand VWs and two hundred thousand Audis by 2018, which would more than double the company's market share to 6 percent.[52]

Bob Corker, Republican US senator from Tennessee and former mayor of Chattanooga, played an important role in persuading VW management to invest in the city.[53] Leading Tennessee politicians who were also members of the Republican Party secured private assurances from VW management that the company had no interest in associating with the UAW and would resist any UAW efforts to organize the plant.[54] This promise greatly complicated subsequent labor relations at the plant.

The UAW's Effort to Organize Volkswagen Chattanooga

Although UAW leaders hoped to cooperate with VW management regarding unionization, the first action the union took regarding VW's Chattanooga plant was hostile. In July 2009, the Chattanooga Chamber Foundation applied on behalf of VW to designate Chattanooga a foreign-trade zone (FTZ) on both an interim and permanent basis.[55] FTZ status permits firms to defer or reduce tariffs on imported production equipment and imported components used in products that are subsequently exported. VW management estimated annual savings to be $1.9 million. The Foreign Trade Zones Board of the US Department of Commerce approves temporary/interim authority within three months only if no party objects, but the UAW objected.

UAW deputy director of international and governmental affairs Douglas S. Meyer wrote in an August 17, 2009, letter to Foreign Trade Zones Board executive secretary Andrew McGilvray that "the UAW welcomes Volkswagen's investment in Chattanooga, TN, and the employment contribution this facility will make to the American economy," but argued against granting VW temporary/interim FTZ authority because it "would unfairly place domestic automobile manufacturers and suppliers at a competitive disadvantage" by "effectively provid[ing] duty-free trade status to German-produced automotive products entering into the FTZ, without providing a reciprocal benefit to US products exported to Germany," and "could potentially result in a net loss of US employment and income, as disadvantaged suppliers to GM, Ford and Chrysler were forced to further reduce employment and benefits to their existing workers." The UAW's objection pushed back VW receiving FTZ authority to February 2011.[56]

On the other side of the Atlantic, IG Metall leaders had become increasingly concerned that German automakers were diverting production to the United States to take advantage of the lower labor costs. They hoped that assisting the UAW to organize German plants would reduce the wage disparity.[57] UAW and IG Metall officials had already been working together for many years because of the Daimler-Chrysler merger (which lasted from 1998 to 2007) and the unionized plants of DTNA in North Carolina. In late November 2009, UAW president Ron Gettelfinger, UAW vice president responsible for organizing Cindy Estrada, and Gary Casteel, director of UAW Region 8 (which includes Tennessee) flew to Frankfurt am Main, Germany, to represent the UAW at a gathering of the IMF.

Casteel's background was an asset for organizing in Chattanooga. He is a native of Florence, Alabama, which is just ten miles south of the Alabama-Tennessee border, and played football for the University of Tennessee.

On the side, the UAW delegation met with representatives of IG Metall and VW's European and Global Works Councils. The meeting had two purposes: to explain the IG Metall leadership's perspective to the UAW delegation and to prepare the UAW representatives for a follow-up meeting with VW's personnel director Horst Neumann, personnel director for the Chattanooga plant Hans-Herbert Jagla, and leader of the VW works council network Bernd Osterloh.

In the first meeting, IG Metall officials expressed distress about developments in the United States. Both BMW and Daimler management had built assembly plants in states with low union density that prohibit compulsory union membership and claimed to be neutral when it came to unionization but resisted it in practice. Both were expanding output and the range of models produced in their US plants, which potentially put employment at German plants at risk. VW was due to begin hiring line employees in the first quarter of 2010 and start production in April 2011. IG Metall officials said that VW management also decided to invest in the South, and the company's position on unionization "would be watched very closely." They cautioned, however, that UAW officials should not "overtax" Neumann regarding union recognition at the next meeting. Even though Neumann was sympathetic to organized labor—he had worked in IG Metall's Economic Research Department from 1978 to 1994 before switching to a career in management—he was just one of five members of VW's managing board (*Vorstand*). He could not act unilaterally, they explained. They recommended patience, suggesting that management turnover may improve prospects.[58]

Representatives from VW's European and Global Works Councils offered the UAW "cooperation and trust." They explained that VW management was looking for a "reliable partner who knew the business," a single "point of contact" to make communication efficient, and a "partner that the corporation can count on to support co[mpany] targets." They suggested "co-planning rounds" among employee representatives from both countries to develop a road map for coordinated action. IG Metall officials assured the UAW delegation that they were committed to helping the UAW organize the Chattanooga plant. Representatives from the two unions discussed moving beyond the conceptual stage by forming a bilateral working group to develop contract language. UAW leaders described the hostility toward unionization in not only the Tennessee political establishment but also VW's newly hired local management.[59] VW management had named Don Jackson as head of manufacturing for the Chattanooga plant in 2008. Jackson was attractive to the company because he had twenty years of experience working in Japanese transplants. He was avowedly anti-union, however, and hired a cadre of like-minded supervisors.[60]

At the follow-up meeting, VW personnel managers Neumann and Jagla gave an overview of the company's recent performance and plans for the Chattanooga plant. Gettelfinger, following the advice he received in the previous meeting, expressed the union's interest in VW's success, stated that the UAW intended to be a reliable partner, and addressed "prejudices" about the UAW. He discussed drafting a memorandum of understanding that would provide the company with flexibility and a sound mechanism for conflict resolution. Gettelfinger also emphasized the importance of localizing representation. Neumann said that VW wanted "people represented properly" and "to be seen as a good company." VW management wanted "to gain trust and have [the] confidence of [the] UAW," akin to the relationship in recent years between the union and Ford.[61] Neumann suggested coordinating VW press statements and said that the company and the union would "come to agreement—step by step." Osterloh suggested that someone would be assigned to the United States for further discussions. The meeting concluded with a commitment to exchange documents and to arrange a meeting between Gary Casteel and Hans-Herbert Jagla.[62]

UAW and IG Metall officials were satisfied with the meeting, but Bernd Osterloh felt slighted because the UAW representatives focused on unionization rather than a works council and spent most of their time speaking to Neumann and Jagla. Osterloh's umbrage was just the first of many misunderstandings that strained relations between UAW and VW works council leaders, which made finding a viable accommodation between the company and the union over Chattanooga so elusive.

VW management began hiring in 2010. VW management decided not to copy the high-wage strategy that Daimler management used at its Alabama Mercedes plant because the principal objective of having a plant in the United States was to lower the cost of the Passat. Starting pay was set at $14.50 an hour, or about $30,000 per year, which was better than wage rates at most other employers in southeastern Tennessee but well below the typical $28 an hour wage for autoworkers at domestic producers. The benefits package also exceeded the local market but did not match a union contract. The compensation was good enough for VW to attract over eighty-five thousand applications for two thousand jobs. VW management hired mostly local workers for assembly-line jobs.[63]

On June 4, the Volkswagen Academy opened to train new employees.[64] On April 18, 2011, the first Passat rolled off the assembly line at VW's new Chattanooga plant. The company set the car's base price at $20,000, which was roughly 25 percent lower than the price of the imported version of the vehicle. UAW organizers had been active in Chattanooga the year before. Transatlantic exchanges and video conferences involving employees and employee representatives began in late 2011. Chattanooga employee Justin King participated as an observer at the VW Global Works Council in November 2011. Over the next three years, IG Metall officials provided advice and material support and sponsored employee exchange visits in both directions.[65]

The union's principal reasons for sending Chattanooga employees to Germany were to develop transnational contacts and enable the American employees to see both the constructive relationship with VW management that is commonplace in Germany and the considerable influence that German employee representatives have. The larger message to American employees was that they could have a similar degree of influence in Chattanooga if they unionized and formed a works council. German employees traveling to the United States also helped to build transnational connections and allowed Germans to see firsthand the challenges of organizing unions in the US South.

Self-interest was certainly an important motivation behind IG Metall leaders' decision to help the UAW. Horst Mund, head of the union's international affairs department, explained, "If we allow union-free zones elsewhere, that will sooner or later fall back on us."[66] Günther Scherelis, head of communications for Volkswagen Chattanooga, did not criticize employee exchanges. He said that the right of employees to have a voice in the company was one of VW's core values.[67]

The leaders of IG Metall and VW's works council network did not see eye to eye regarding the specifics of employee representation in VW's Chattanooga plant, which complicated working with German employee representatives. Four months after the Chattanooga plant opened, Bernd Osterloh stated that creating a works council there—with or without the UAW—was the priority. Osterloh said that as an IG Metall member, he supported Chattanooga employees joining a union, but he would not try to persuade VW management to recognize the UAW. It was up to UAW representatives to make the case for union representation and for plant employees to decide.[68] Nine months later, Osterloh reiterated this position. "Of course," he said, "we will support the UAW; we've said that all along. But there's one thing we cannot do. We can't take workers at VW Chattanooga by the hand when it comes to voting. One has to be in favor if one wants union representation." He then observed that "sentiment in the southern U.S. isn't exactly in favor of unions," and he speculated that if the Chattanooga workers rejected the UAW, "we would make efforts to bring about some sort of interest lobby. . . . It's important that this site has a voice on the global works council."[69] Frank Patta, general secretary of the Global Works Council, traveled to Chattanooga in June 2012 to deliver a message in person: Employees would benefit from having a works council.[70]

It is clear that at this point the leaders of VW's works councils were unaware of American jurisprudence regarding such bodies. Nothing like a works council had been established in the United States since the 1930s. The reason is US labor law. When trade unions in the United States began growing rapidly in the 1930s, some firms started to create company-dominated "workplace committees" to stave off unionization. The rising popularity of workplace committees as a union-avoidance tool led lawmakers to ban them in the 1935 NLRA.[71]

NLRA section 8(a)(2) declares it "an unfair labor practice for an employer . . . to dominate or interfere with the formation or administration of any labor organization or contribute financial or other support to it." This clause became salient again decades later when US firms began to create Japanese-style joint employee-employer quality circles to discuss ways to increase competitiveness. In 1992 and 1993, the NLRB found quality circles at the nonunion plants of the DuPont and Electromation corporations to be in violation of section 8(a)(2) because the circles appeared to be "dealing," that is, negotiating about compensation and working conditions. They were also dependent on company financial support. The NLRB's decision clarified that it was permissible for a collective agreement to create a joint employee-employer body such as a quality circle at a unionized workplace because the presence of a union precluded an employer from using such an entity as a company union.[72]

German works councils would not pass the independence test set out in the DuPont and Electromation rulings. Works councils are independent of unions, and firms in Germany finance works councils and routinely reach agreements with them over working conditions. So, if the Volkswagen Chattanooga plant were to have a works council, it would first have to be unionized. The works council, moreover, would have to be derivative of rather than independent from a union. When Bob King became UAW president in June 2010, he embraced the idea of the union negotiating to create a works council in Chattanooga should the UAW be recognized as the employees' exclusive bargaining agent.

Once the leaders of VW's works council network learned about the jurisprudence regarding worker committees, they became instrumentally supportive of unionization because it was the only way to get a works council. The challenge from the perspective of the German works council leadership became finding a means to construct a works council in Chattanooga that would be in conformance with NLRB jurisprudence but not be dominated by the UAW. UAW officials saw things quite differently. They mistakenly imagined works councils to be akin to "jointness committees," which are the labor-management bodies that the UAW and domestic auto producers had established starting in the latter half of the 1980s to deal with issues such as workplace safety and scheduling. Equating jointness committees with works councils overlooked big differences between the two. For example, unions select the worker participants on jointness committees. In contrast, German employees elect works councilors in a process that has no formal role for trade unions. Leaders of the VW works council network and the UAW never came to a common understanding on the powers and position of a works council in Chattanooga, which eroded trust and hindered cooperation between them.

UAW leaders initially hoped for a "low key, low budget" drive that would not come to the attention of the state and local political elite or ruffle VW management. By mid-2012, however, labor relations at the Chattanooga plant had already become contentious. VW management dismissed the controversial head of manufacturing, Don Jackson, in June because he insisted on using "the Toyota way," which included opposition to unions, rather than "the Volkswagen way," which did not. Dismissing Jackson did not solve the problem, however. Many of his subordinates who had been with him at Toyota, whom he hired into line managerial positions, remained at VW.[73]

In January 2013, Sebastian Patta became head of human resources at the Chattanooga plant. He was previously head of personnel at VW's Braunschweig plant. Patta came from a VW family. His father was an Italian immigrant to Germany who worked on the line in a VW factory. His brother, Frank, held several prominent roles in IG Metall in Wolfsburg and on VW works councils. Sebastian Patta's approach to industrial relations was very much in keeping with the German postwar tradition of "social partnership" between labor and management.[74] Regarding the question of unionization at the Chattanooga plant, Patta's view was that it was up to the Chattanooga workers to decide, but his approach can best be characterized as positive neutrality rather than the negative neutrality practiced by Daimler.[75]

In March 2013, the UAW stepped up its unionization drive. UAW leaders assigned four full-time organizers to Chattanooga and produced a joint brochure with IG Metall titled "Co-determining the Future: A New Labor Model."[76] The brochure opened with an article titled "The 21st Century UAW," describing the union's new embrace of "innovation, flexibility and continuous improvement." It was the same article the UAW used a year earlier in a brochure for the organizing drive at the Alabama Mercedes plant. A brief introduction to IG Metall was next, followed by a letter from the IG Metall chair Berthold Huber urging VW employees to join the UAW. The brochure also contained excerpts from VW's "Declaration on Social Rights and Industrial Relations" and the "Charter on Labour Relations within the Volkswagen Group," an article from IG Metall international affairs department head Horst Mund praising codetermination, and brief statements from seven Chattanooga employees in support of unionization. Huber's message was also sent separately as a letter to all Volkswagen Chattanooga employees.

A works council became a much bigger selling point at Volkswagen Chattanooga than it had been at the Mercedes plant in Alabama because a works council was wanted by not only the German employee representatives but also VW management. The UAW leadership was happy to use VW management's wish to have a works council at the Chattanooga plant as a fulcrum to increase the leverage of the unionization drive. From this side of the Atlantic "the works council was a Trojan horse to get the UAW in," a pro-union employee observed in retrospect. The UAW leadership was "trying to have a soft-serve variation of a union, something that they thought would be easier for Southern workers to swallow. And the union had management to help sell it."[77]

In March 2013, VW human resources director Horst Neumann revealed to the public that managers from the company's headquarters had been talking with UAW officials about employee representation at the Chattanooga factory. Neumann said that the UAW was a "natural partner" because its officials knew the industry and had ties to IG Metall.[78] Neumann reiterated that the company's objective was to create a works council in Chattanooga. He said it was unclear to him whether the UAW leadership really wanted a works council or simply expressed support for creating one as a tactic to unionize VW. UAW president Bob King quickly responded that the UAW "is very interested in, and has great respect for, the system of codetermination where the company has strong collaboration with management, unions and works councils."[79]

Neumann's announcement intensified opposition in the Tennessee establishment to the UAW organizing drive. Ron Harr, chair of the Chattanooga Area Chamber of Commerce, led a business delegation to meet with VW management in Wolfsburg. Harr said, "We really don't understand any need for having a union. . . . One of the great advantages that Chattanooga has enjoyed is being in a right-to-work state without the major presence of unions."[80] Republican Tennessee governor Bill Haslam also issued a statement criticizing VW management cooperating with the UAW: "I would hate for anything to happen that would hurt the productivity of the plant or to deter investment in Chattanooga."[81]

Meanwhile, VW Chattanooga management made a surprise announcement. The company planned to lay off five hundred temporary-contract employees because Passat sales were below expectations. The announcement came as a shock, because workers and the public had previously only heard glowing reports from VW management. Job security became a new theme in the organizing drive.[82]

In April 2013, UAW leaders traveled to Wolfsburg to meet again with VW management and works council officials. UAW leaders continued to compliment the company. Region 8 director Gary Casteel said, "We have great admiration for VW's integrity, and their business model and philosophy as it pertains to their workforce."[83] Bob King stated, "One of the reasons Volkswagen is arguably the most successful company in the world is that in every single one of their facilities, with the exception of Chattanooga to this point, they have employee representation."[84]

Neumann's disclosure of meetings between UAW and VW officials also stirred anti-union political forces outside of Tennessee. Mark Mix, president of the NRWLDF, said he was concerned that the UAW was pressuring VW management to "cut backroom deals" that would lead to union recognition at VW Chattanooga without consulting employees. Mix offered free legal assistance to any employee who felt intimidated by UAW organizers.[85] Mark West, a local right-wing Tea Party leader, held a public forum titled "Chattanooga, UAW and Free Markets" in mid-July at a local hotel. The objective, West said, was "to inform and educate the community on the dangers of the UAW and the threats they would represent to Volkswagen [and] also to our community and state."[86]

Political entrepreneurship was an important catalyst for outside anti-union actions. For example, Matt Patterson, senior fellow at the Competitive Enterprise Institute, a right-wing lobbying organization based in Washington, D.C., launched an "educational campaign" called the "Keep Tennessee Free Project." The project began with a modest budget of $4,000. Patterson placed anti-union opinion pieces in local and national media outlets in which he equated the UAW with the Union Army, which the Confederate Army of Tennessee fought twelve miles southwest of Chattanooga in the Battle of Chickamauga (September 19–20, 1863) during the American Civil War. He brought together local anti-union activists, including Tea Party representatives, through information sessions and rented a billboard a few miles from the plant with the message "Auto Unions ATE Detroit. Next Meal Chattanooga?" The message aimed to "other" the UAW in the eyes of Chattanooga employees and generate fears of plant closures and social decay. In August 2013, Patterson's political entrepreneurship paid off. He found a lucrative backer: Grover Norquist, the right-wing antitax advocate and president of the Washington-based Americans for Tax Reform (ATR). Norquist made Patterson the executive director of the Center for Worker Freedom, a special project within ATR tasked to work against unionization at VW.[87]

Bob King kept up the positive talk about a works council in Chattanooga as the organizing drive continued. He insisted that a works council "would absolutely work" in Chattanooga, adding, "What's really interesting is that everybody is represented in the works council—union members, nonunion members, blue-collar and white-collar workers." But he was short on specifics. When asked how a contract would differ at a US workplace with codetermination, King replied, "That gets to areas that we'd eventually have to do with the company. . . . We'll have to see." Gary Casteel added, "It's kind of a fluid question."[88]

In June 2013, IG Metall international affairs director Horst Mund participated in some pro-union events in Tennessee, arguing that Chattanooga employees did not want to be the "odd man out" at VW by not unionizing. Gary Casteel told VW employees, "We're very, very close"; the question would soon be how, not if VW would recognize the UAW. [89] King and Casteel continued their praise of VW as "an extremely honorable company." When asked about the actions of Tennessee politicians, Casteel replied, "I would hope that Governor Haslam and Senator Corker understand the Volkswagen system, and really work together with the IG Metall, works council, to make this a great facility, and get new product" but said that this has not happened. Casteel added, "I've reached out to Corker, and talked to his staff about the possibility of a meeting to discuss how we work together. He has not responded, twice. . . . I don't think that there's one politician that has commented on the Chattanooga situation, from the Governor to the Senator, that has taken the time to understand Volkswagen's culture and philosophy and success factors." King answered a question about whether he thought the UAW would be the collective bargaining agent of the Chattanooga VW employees within a year by saying, "I'm an optimist." Casteel added, "There's factually no reason it can't." [90]

Interested parties on both sides continued to advance arguments for and against unionization. Stephan Wolf, who was Osterloh's deputy on VW's works council and a member of the company's supervisory board, told reporters that German employee representatives on the board would only agree to an expansion of the Chattanooga plant if there was a works council in place. UAW president Bob King used Wolf's remarks to make the case for unionization. "If I was a worker, if I was a member of the Chattanooga community, and I wanted to have the best chance of getting new investment and new product, I would want a voice on the world employee council. I would want somebody there representing the interests of Chattanooga. I wouldn't want a decision made where every other plant in the world has representation there, and I don't have somebody speaking up for me." [91]

Senator Bob Corker rejected Wolf's assertion as "totally and absolutely false," adding, "I know for a fact that at the highest levels of VW, they're aware that if the UAW became involved in the plant, it would be a negative for the future economic growth of our state. . . . It has already created some obstacles to us." Regarding the UAW organizing drive, Corker complained, "I don't know how they can say they're the new UAW when the same people . . . are in leadership," but he added, "I'm not trying to influence what the employees do." [92]

The organizing drive continued apace. UAW leaders announced in July 2013 that the union had authorization cards from a majority of the Chattanooga plant's employees. (Well after the drive had ended, Casteel said that the highest share of cards they had from the eligible workforce was 56–57 percent.) [93] UAW representatives traveled to Wolfsburg again in late August to ask VW management to accept card-check recognition. VW management refused the request because they were "concerned about antagonizing Republican politicians in Tennessee."[94] These concerns were well founded. A confidential Tennessee state document dated August 23, 2013, that surfaced several months later itemized $300 million in additional subsidies that VW would receive if the firm added a second line to produce an SUV at the Chattanooga plant that would expand employment by at least 1,350. The document included a proviso at the top: "The incentives described below are subject to works council discussions between the State of Tennessee and VW being concluded to the satisfaction of the State of Tennessee."[95] When asked about the documents and accompanying emails, Haslam replied, "It's no secret at all that we had an opinion about what should happen there."[96]

On September 6, 2013, the UAW issued a press release confirming a meeting on August 30 in Wolfsburg with VW management that "focused on appropriate paths, consistent with American law, for arriving at both Volkswagen recognition of UAW representation at its Chattanooga facility and establishment of a German-style works council." The union statement stressed, "Ultimately, however, it's the workers in Chattanooga who will make the decision on representation and a works council." The press release concluded by pointing out that "VW workers in Chattanooga have the unique opportunity to introduce this new model of labor relations to the United States, in partnership with the UAW."[97]

On the same day, plant CEO Frank Fischer and plant vice president for human resources Sebastian Patta sent a letter to all Volkswagen Chattanooga employees to explain the company's position:

> Dear Team Members:
> The Volkswagen Group respects the employees' right for an employee representation on plant level at all locations worldwide. This certainly also applies to the Chattanooga plant.
> In the U.S. a works council can only be realized together with a trade union. This is the reason why Volkswagen has started a dialogue with the UAW in order to check the possibility of implementing an innovative model of employee representation for all employees.
> By now there is a very lively discussion in the Chattanooga plant regarding a labor representation. In respect to this please allow us, the plant management, to give one important note: Every single team member takes his or her own decision and this will be respected by us.
> Furthermore we jointly want to prevent any attempt of influence from outside driving a wedge into our great team. We are a strong team. And only as a strong team we achieve top performance and top quality which make our cars in the U.S. successful. This we have proven so far and we jointly want to prove so as well in the future.[98]

VW managers hoped that rejecting the UAW's request for card-check recognition in favor of a union recognition election would allow the company to occupy a middle-ground compromise position that both UAW officials and the Tennessee business and political establishment would accept. They were wrong. Senator Corker denounced the meeting between VW managers and UAW officials with expressions of betrayal and disbelief. He asserted that VW leaders "agreed on the front end" when they chose Chattanooga that "they would have nothing to do with the UAW."[99] He then lamented,

> For management to invite the UAW in is almost beyond belief. . . . I'm a little worried Volkswagen could become a laughingstock in many ways. . . . We've talked to management, and to me it's beyond belief that they've allowed this to go that far and displayed this kind of naivety that the UAW is somehow different than they were years ago. . . . I'm discouraged and I do hope that they will pull back from this.[100]

Casteel responded to Corker's comments, saying they were "spoken from a position of ignorance. It's ludicrous to think that Chattanooga benefits from being the only outlier in this system."[101] Osterloh also rejected Corker's remarks, declaring that "VW has only acquired its global strength because workers are tied into corporate decisions. We will continue the talks in the US to set up a German-style works council with the UAW."[102] It is noteworthy that the UAW leadership also did not support VW management's proposed compromise, which was to hold a recognition election. Gary Casteel prophetically observed, "We know if we go for a traditional election where outside organizations campaign against us, we'd probably lose."[103]

VWAG's personnel director Horst Neumann lamented, "I find it very depressing how deeply divided the country is on the issue of labor unions. Had they [i.e., Tennessee business leaders and politicians] been here to listen to the roundtable discussion [between German automobile industry executives and senior IG Metall officials], they would have seen that we work together—it's a model for success."[104]

Corker and senior US senator from Tennessee Lamar Alexander attempted to shut down the discussions between the VW and UAW leaders by intervening at the top. They sent a one-page letter dated September 19, 2013, to VW CEO Martin Winterkorn. The letter, which became public months later, stated,

> During your negotiations to bring Volkswagen to Tennessee, your recruitment team made clear commitments to Senator Corker that the company did not have any interest in associating with the United Auto Workers and would resist efforts they might make to organize the plant. Despite that understanding, we have been very disappointed to learn

that there are active conversations going on between Volkswagen and the UAW.

While we know you are aware of our views on this subject, we want to reiterate how concerned we are about the damage we believe will be caused to Chattanooga, the state of Tennessee and over time possibly the entire southeastern United States if you invite the UAW to organize the plant. . . .

Our most significant concern is the way that some members of the Volkswagen management team have opened their arms to the UAW, sending very confusing signals to employees about where the company stands on this issue. We hope that you will clarify your position with your employees and with the Chattanooga community in the very near future.

This is a critical issue for our state, and, as always, we would be glad to discuss it with you or your staff at any time.[105]

The exchanges of the late summer of 2013 made one thing clear: it would be impossible for VW management to accommodate everyone.

The UAW pressed onward. In mid-September, Bob King expressed the UAW's position. "We have a majority of VW workers who have signed union authorization cards saying they want to be represented. The United Auto Workers would like Volkswagen AG to voluntarily recognize the U.S. union. Doing so would eliminate the need for a more formal and divisive vote. . . . An election process is more divisive. I don't think that's in Volkswagen's best interests. I don't think that's in the best interests of Tennessee." A week later, Gary Casteel restated the UAW's case. "We've got a majority. The company is not disputing that. We want to keep things positive."[106] The UAW leaders' arguments had no effect, however. Volkswagen management's position remained unchanged: unionization could only happen with a recognition election.

Anti-union forces responded to the UAW's progress with more vitriol. Corker said that success for the UAW in Chattanooga would damage the area "for generations to come. . . . It's not that I'm anti-union. I am very, very anti-UAW. The UAW's been a very destructive force in our country. I can't imagine a company in America, left to their own accord, voluntarily associating themselves with the UAW."[107] Anti-UAW employees circulated an anti-union petition, gathering over six hundred signatures, which amounted to about 40 percent of the permanent workforce of 1,500. Opponents grew in number and focused their criticism on the card-check process. Former head of manufacturing at VW Don Jackson opined, "The only true way to find out where the [workers] lie is a secret ballot. . . .

I see them in the community, at church, and people tell me all the time they don't want the union."[108]

In September 2013, the NRWLDF sent two lawyers to Chattanooga to help employees who opposed unionization to write up press releases. They also filed an unfair labor practice complaint with the regional office of the NLRB in Atlanta on behalf of eight Chattanooga employees against both VW and the UAW on September 25. The complaint alleged that UAW organizers misled employees into thinking that the union authorization cards would only be used to call for a secret ballot election. It also asserted that some cards were no longer legally valid because they were signed over a year earlier and that the UAW made it excessively difficult for workers who wanted their cards returned to them by requiring the workers to retrieve the cards at the union office.[109] The complaint was eventually dismissed, but filing it created an opportunity for the NRWLDF to suggest improprieties regarding the organizing drive.

Mike Burton, a paint shop employee, began to bring together workers who opposed unionization. Burton produced anti-UAW flyers, built a website (http://www.no2uaw.org), and set up a Facebook page. On October 4, Burton announced that he had collected 563 employee signatures opposing unionization.[110] Union opponents shared a fear that UAW representation could lead to management closing the plant. They perceived the UAW as an outside organization from the North that was responsible for Detroit's decline. The NRWLDF assisted four additional VW employees in filing a second unfair labor practice charge alleging that Stephan Wolf's June statement amounted to illegal coercion of employees to support UAW representation.[111]

Efforts to find a compromise continued throughout the fall. In October and November, leading VW officials, including works councilors, engaged with Tennessee business leaders, politicians, and their staff to see if a compromise could be reached. The first meetings were preparatory. On October 28, VW's head of government relations, Thomas Steg, newly elected head of the VW Global Works Council Frank Patta, and VW government relations specialist Ariane Kilian met in Chattanooga with Governor Haslam's chief of staff, Claude Ramsey, and the city's Chamber of Commerce president Ron Harr. The Germans then flew to Washington to meet Todd Womack, Senator Corker's chief of staff.[112]

On November 15, Bernd Osterloh met with Bill Haslam and Bob Corker. Corker's spokesperson called the meeting "candid." Haslam's spokesperson described the discussion as "frank" and "a very good conversation." Osterloh made three points. First, he said, "It's important to note that the issue for us is works councils, not unions." However, he continued, it is US law that requires unionization as a prerequisite to forming a works council, which is why works councilors support unionization at Chattanooga as necessary. Second, Osterloh said that VW's works councilors agreed with management's rejection of card-check recognition and support of a union recognition election. Third, contradicting Stephan Wolf, Osterloh made it clear that the decision about producing a second vehicle in Chattanooga "will always be made along economic and employment lines. It has absolutely nothing to do with the whole topic about whether there is a union there or not."[113] Governor Haslam responded that VW management had stressed maintaining competitive labor costs and the need to attract a greater number of suppliers to the Chattanooga region. He continued, "Well, it's hard to imagine a scenario in which labor costs are helped by the UAW coming in, and I know that bringing suppliers close would be more difficult."[114] Haslam concluded, arguing that successful organization of VW's Chattanooga plant would create a "beachhead that would grow from there."[115]

VW's global works council members went along with the preference of Osterloh and VW management to reject the card-check procedure against the wishes of the UAW. Former global works council member Jürgen Stumpf conceded in retrospect that they did not appreciate the ferocity of the anti-union campaigns that often accompany union recognition elections in the United States: "We thought we had a majority" in favor of unionization in the Chattanooga plant. "We never thought it could be turned around. . . . We never realized that it would be a problem in the land of democracy."[116]

The closing months of 2013 brought turnover in some key positions. Detlef Wetzel became the new chair of IG Metall in November 2013, succeeding Huber. Wetzel quickly made it clear that IG Metall remained committed to organizing German-owned plants in the United States. "Low wages and union-free areas; that's not a business model that the IG Metall would support. . . . If companies—from VW to ThyssenKrupp—entered those states in order to be free of unions, meaning not to acknowledge a fundamental pillar of any democracy, then we're in North Korea. That cannot be accepted."[117]

As 2013 ended, Jonathan Browning stepped down as head of Volkswagen Group of America (VWGOA) after a disappointing sales year.[118] Michael Horn replaced Brown. Berthold Huber, who remained president of IndustriALL (the successor global union federation to the IMF), sent a letter dated December 18 to the employees at VW's Chattanooga plant advocating once again for the UAW and a works council. It read:

> You will soon have an opportunity to decide about collective representation for your interests at the Volkswagen plant in Chattanooga. I recommend that you choose to have a democratic voice in your workplace and vote for union representation by the UAW. . . .

If you vote for union representation, you will establish your own local in Chattanooga. In the next step you can then elect a works council. . . .

Through the works council you will become a part of the [VW] Group World Works Council. . . . In Group World Works Council you will receive first-hand information about the company's global strategy and development and can suggest ways to build on the company's success.

Dear colleagues, union representation is a necessary precondition for the election of a works council according to US labor law. Therefore, IG Metall recommends that you vote for union representation through the UAW. . . .

IG Metall has developed excellent relations with the UAW. On behalf of IG Metall I would like to assure you of our support and cooperation.

As president of IndustriALL Global Union, the world wide federation of manufacturing industry unions representing almost 50 million workers worldwide, I wish you much success in building a democratic voice for workers in Chattanooga and gaining more influence over your working and living conditions and the directions of your plant.[119]

The timing and contents of Huber's letter implicitly indicated that UAW leaders recognized they had failed to persuade VW management to accept a card-check procedure. The letter also signaled that an agreement was at hand regarding the details of a recognition election and the relationship between a union local and a works council were the union to win. Further confirmation that an election was near came on January 15, 2014. The UAW released a document titled "Media Background Sheet on Codetermination" that announced a representation election would be held on February 12–14.

On January 27, VWGOA and the UAW signed and released the "Agreement for a Representation Election."[120] This neutrality agreement specified the procedure for a union recognition election. In addition, it delineated the structure and roles of a union local and a works council were the UAW to win. The unstated goal was for the UAW and VW to present a compelling common document designed to persuade employees to vote in favor of unionization.

The agreement, which has fifteen pages of single-spaced text plus two exhibits, starts with a list of the commitments of both parties. Among these are confirmation that VWGOA "recognizes, supports and has adopted the principles affirmed in VWAG's Global Labour Charter on Labour Relations . . . and Declaration on Social Rights and Industrial Relations at Volkswagen Group" (1–2). The UAW, for its part,

acknowledges, supports and shares VWGOA's commitment to the development of an innovative model of labor relations at the Chattanooga
Plant, including the establishment of a works council, in which a law-
fully recognized or certified bargaining representative would delegate
functions and responsibilities ordinarily belonging to a union to a plant
works council that engages in co-determination with the employer. (3)

The agreement uses the German name "the Dual Model" for this division of labor
between a union and a works council.

The accord then sets out the specifics for the recognition election and codi-
fies a bargain that the UAW and VW had reached when the organizing drive
began. The UAW agreed to forgo picketing and organizer visits to employees'
residences (aka house calls), which are a key component of most organizing
drives in the United States but are unheard of in Germany (7). In return, the
company would provide the names and home addresses of the employees and
would permit UAW representatives to speak to employees in the plant at a voluntary gathering (6, 9). VWGOA also agreed to give the UAW a room at the plant
in which to meet with employees and space in nonwork areas to distribute literature (9). VWGOA committed to train supervisors and managers, "with respect
to the election and VWGOA's position concerning the election, the Dual Model
and . . . neutrality and the right of Employees to decide whether they wish to be
represented by the Union" (9). UAW leaders hoped this step would constrain
anti-union line managers, who were still a matter of contention. In practice, it
did not.

The agreement also set out "Post-Election Obligations" should the UAW win.
The UAW and VWGOA "shall establish the timing and details for the establishment and functioning of the Dual Model" (9). The UAW shall "delegate to a
Works Council to be established by VWGOA at the Chattanooga Plant certain
issues, functions and responsibilities that would otherwise be subject to collective bargaining" (9). Were the UAW to win the recognition election, union officials agreed not to engage in "picketing, strikes, boycotts, or work slowdowns"
during contract negotiations, and management agreed not to lock out employees (12). If they proved unable to agree to a first contract, the parties would select
a mutually acceptable mediator, who may use interest arbitration. (First contract
arbitration is a long-standing policy reform for which US trade unionists have
advocated.)

The five-page Exhibit B, titled "Dual Model, Including Works Council,"
spelled out the details for a works council and the local union's relationship to
it. The language in Exhibit B was extremely important. In Germany, a federal
law—namely the Works Constitution Act (Betriebsverfassungsgesetz)—anchors

the parameters and duties of works councils. The United States has nothing like it. Consequently, the authors of the agreement envisioned that Exhibit B and the first collective bargaining agreement between the UAW and VW would serve as the functional equivalent of the Works Constitution Act. Exhibit B made clear that

> The Dual model is based on the Volkswagen Culture of cooperative labor relations, which is practiced by companies in the Volkswagen Group all over the world. The Dual Model is intended to adopt the practices of the Volkswagen Group culture to the fullest extent possible, in a manner consistent with all applicable US labor and employment laws. (Exhibit B, 2)

Exhibit B then details the division of labor between the works council and the union under the Dual Model after providing a general description:

> Under the Dual Model employees are represented by a union for collective bargaining with their employer. They also participate in and receive representation by a Works Council that plays an important role in the day to day operation of the plant. In the Dual Model, the respective roles and responsibilities of the union and the Works Council would be established through collective bargaining between the Company and a Union. . . .
>
> The Dual Model is conceived as a model of labor relations that would allow for development and establishment of a robust Works Council through collective bargaining between the Company and a legally recognized/certified labor union that represents a unit of employees. Under this model, the Union and the Works Council would each have defined roles and responsibilities, which would be established and defined through collective bargaining. . . .
>
> A Works Council is intended to offer a voice for all plant employees (except employees employed in supervisory and/or managerial capacities as those terms are defined under the National Labor Relations Act). All employees (other than supervisors and managers) (including both hourly and salary employees) would have the right to participate in Works Council elections regardless of whether they are represented by or belong to a union. (Exhibit B, 2)

The exhibit also describes the authority and role of the works council. It would "operate on the basis of authority delegated to it by the Union and Employer and in compliance with U.S. labor and employment laws to carry out assigned roles" (Exhibit B, 2). Specifically, the works council would

- Represent the interests of employees in the day to day running of the plant, including dealing with complaints and suggestions and cases where there is a need of individual support and advice.
- Serve as a contact for management for all intra-company issues concerning the topics and tasks assigned to the Works Council under the collective bargaining agreement.
- Communicate to employees concerning the Works Council's activities and conveying information given by the Employer to it.
- Initiate discuss and/or negotiate ideas and other intra-company needs with management.
- Act in a respectful and non-discriminatory manner in the interests of all employees.
- Conduct its activities in a manner that ensures compliance with regulations and the adherence to the applicable laws.
- Carry out operational management and guideline setting with respect to designated matters, in accordance with the direction of the parties. (Exhibit B, 3).

Exhibit B states that the collective agreement would "provide for delegation of specific responsibilities to the Works Council" (Exhibit B, 3). It then follows the German model by stating that "each delegated topic would be assigned to the Works Council with a particular 'participation right,' either Information, Consultation or Co-Determination" (Exhibit B, 4).

Exhibit B ends with a concession to the fact that codetermination would be new to the United States. It states that the works council would start with a smaller range of topics and then gradually expand the scope. To start, the works council would focus on

a. Topics where a high need for involvement is readily apparent; these include work organization, especially agreements on shift calendars and scheduling of overtime;
b. "social issues," such as health and safety; and
c. participation in the implementation of a grievance procedure (Exhibit B, 4).

Exhibit B suggested that the same approach be taken when it comes to participation rights. At first, the works council would only be permitted the rights on information and consultation. Codetermination would come later (Exhibit B, 5).

The election agreement included two more items worth noting. First, the UAW and VWGOA agreed to "advise one another of their planned communication activities and shall seek, as appropriate, to align messages and communications" (6). Second, the agreement addressed the question of competitiveness:

The parties recognize and agree that any such negotiations for an initial collective bargaining agreement and any future agreements shall be guided by the following considerations: (a) maintaining the highest standards of quality and productivity, (b) maintaining and where possible enhancing the cost advantages and other competitive advantages that VWGOA enjoys relative to its competitors in the United States and North America, including but not limited to legacy automobile manufacturers. (11)

This language on competitiveness was consistent with comments that Bob King had made since he was elected in 2010 about the twenty-first-century UAW, but it proved particularly problematic in the recognition election because the language could be read as committing the UAW leadership up front to keep compensation at Volkswagen Chattanooga lower than compensation at other automobile assemblers in the United States.

Steve Early, longtime national organizer for the Communication Workers of America, accurately characterized the UAW-VWGOA election agreement as an example of "bargaining to organize," which is a controversial strategy within the labor movement of exchanging concessions to secure a favorable process for union recognition.[121] Although the UAW-VWGOA deal differs in detail from the 2002 agreement between Daimler management and the UAW, which exchanged concessions at Daimler's Mount Holly truck assembly plant for a neutrality agreement covering the unorganized North Carolina plants of DTNA, both are top-down neutrality agreements between an employer and union leaders that did not involve consultation with the employees at the workplaces that were the organizing target. Bargaining to organize can be effective at neutralizing employer opposition, but a by-product of this strategy is weaker engagement with grass-roots members.

That said, the neutrality agreement between VWGOA and the UAW was unique when compared to other neutrality agreements in that the language to create a works council would have placed much of what a local union does in the United States (e.g., contract implementation and grievances) under an elected body with some autonomy from the UAW whose voting constituency would extend beyond those eligible to vote in a union recognition election and be members of the local. In this case, white-collar employees would also be eligible to vote in works council elections and serve as works councilors. Although Bob King and Gary Casteel thought it worth the risk to agree to this language to secure VW management taking a neutral stance in the recognition election, there were skeptics within the UAW leadership who worried about the union setting a precedent of ceding its monopoly over local representation of employees to an autonomous body with a membership extending beyond that of a local.

The agreement between the UAW and VWGOA also incensed anti-union employees. Burton complained, "There are going to be two team meetings of 500 to 600 workers each and we won't even be able to take the podium for equal time. That's wrong."[122] Burton immediately sent letters to VWGOA management asking for speaking opportunities and access to the employee contact list equal to that of the UAW.[123] Management refused on the grounds that the anti-union employees were not an "entity." In response, Burton, with the help of Maury Nicely, a Chattanooga-based lawyer for Evans Harrison Hackett PLC, filed papers to form a nonprofit organization called Southern Momentum. Nicely led fundraising for the group, which amassed funds "in the low six figures" from Chattanooga area businesses and individuals.[124] Southern Momentum repeated the request for access, but VWGOA management refused again. Governor Haslam sent a letter dated February 4 to plant CEO Frank Fischer expressing his concern regarding equal access:

> It is our understanding . . . that the Company is allowing the UAW to use Company facilities to advise and attempt to influence employees to vote in favor of union representation, while at the same time denying similar facilities to Volkswagen employees and groups in opposition to UAW representation. This distinction favoring the UAW at the expense of employees opposed to unionization is of concern to us. We expected the Company to assume a position of neutrality that would provide an "even playing field," if you will. It is of such concern that I felt it necessary to speak on behalf of those Tennessee citizens who are employees at the Chattanooga facility. While many will choose to differ on the advisability of union representation, there should be a general consensus that the manner in which the Company administers and oversees this process is critical not only to the Company, but also to the general perception and acceptance of any result by the employees and the community in which they live and work.[125]

Fischer did not change the policy.

On February 3, VWGOA filed a petition with the NLRB asking for a union recognition election beginning just nine days later on February 12 and closing on February 14. Burton's response was "this is the shortest campaigning period that we've ever heard of. . . . We're looking into whether this is legal."[126] It was legal, albeit unusual. The default and maximum length for a union recognition campaign is forty days. It can be shorter if union and company representatives agree, but employers typically prefer forty days to maximize the time available to get across their message to employees. As a result, most campaigns are forty days long.

VW management allowed twenty UAW organizers access to breakrooms and lunch areas. Union supporters could also post campaign literature on bulletin boards. On February 4, Casteel gave the first UAW presentation at the plant to VW employees. When he started to speak, approximately one hundred anti-union employees left the room. Those who stayed for the hour-long presentation were not permitted to ask questions. When reporters asked Casteel why he did not allow questions, he replied, "The UAW is the only one up for election."[127] On February 7, Governor Haslam criticized VW again at a breakfast sponsored by the Knoxville Chamber of Commerce, repeating that auto suppliers had told him that they would not come to the Chattanooga area if the UAW organized the plant. He added, "The state of Tennessee put a whole lot of money in that plant."[128] Senator Corker, in contrast to the governor, said, "During the next week and a half, while the decision is in the hands of the employees, I do not think it is appropriate for me to make additional public comment."[129] Southern Momentum leaders held their own informational meeting off-site on February 8.[130]

The UAW-VW agreement dismayed other union opponents. Don Jackson, even though he no longer worked for VW, complained that "Volkswagen wants the works council so badly they don't care how they get it."[131] NRWLDF president Mix expressed concern about "backroom deals" between the UAW and VW.[132] Patterson, the anti-union activist working under antitax advocate Norquist, wrote, "Unions are a big driver of government. Unions are very political, the UAW is one of the most political. If they help elect politicians who pass huge government programs, that requires taxes."[133] Mike Cantrell, a Volkswagen Chattanooga employee who had taken a lead in the organizing drive, objected especially to Patterson's role. "He's making money by coming into our community from Washington and telling me and my co-workers what's best for us. What does he know about the auto industry?"[134]

With the election imminent, additional voices joined the fray. The *Wall Street Journal* editorial board penned a scathing editorial accusing IG Metall chair Wetzel of backing the Chattanooga unionization drive to "reduce the competitiveness of US plants."[135] Norquist's ATR began direct attacks on the UAW for making political contributions. Returning to a familiar tactic, the ATR's Center for Worker Freedom rented eleven additional billboards around Chattanooga to post anti-UAW messages. Some played into the cultural divide in the United States. One read "UNITED AUTO OBAMA WORKERS. The UAW spends millions to elect liberal politicans [*sic*] including BARACK OBAMA."[136]

The anti-Obama pitch was likely to resonate in this southern city of 170,000; 9 out of 10 employees were white, and the vast majority were male. Another billboard proclaimed, "The UAW wants Your Guns," justifying the claim by pointing out that the union had endorsed candidates who supported gun control.[137] A third continued the effort to define the UAW as an alien, northern, destructive force. It had a picture of abandoned factory ruins. The caption read "Detroit. Brought to you by the UAW." They also bought anti-union newspaper and radio ads.[138] Casteel responded, "Never have we seen this much activity from outside, third-party groups." He added, "From my experience, billboards are a waste of money."[139]

Southern Momentum ran radio and newspaper ads, organized a forum for VW employees that featured Don Jackson and Maury Nicely, and hired the Union Proof Team from Projections, a prominent union-avoidance consultancy, to produce three anti-union videos, which were shown at two public meetings, put on the no2uaw website, and placed on flash drives that were distributed to employees.[140] One video featured a former VW worker at the company's shuttered Westmoreland plant. Another stressed the UAW's support for liberal political groups that fight gun control.[141]

There was considerable coordination among the anti-union forces. A series of emails unearthed by reporters from a Nashville television station, NewsChannel 5, revealed that top staffers of Corker and Haslam worked with Don Jackson, Maury Nicely, Chattanooga Area Chamber of Commerce head Ron Harr, and Chattanooga Regional Manufacturers' Association chief Tim Spires to maximize the number of VW employees who saw the videos.[142] The pro-UAW employees issued a statement calling on the ATR to stop its campaign against the UAW.[143]

Days before the vote, both sides stepped up their campaigns. Members of VW's group works council and the Global Works Council[144]—Gunnar Kilian and Frank Patta, respectively—talked with Chattanooga employees about the benefits of being a part of VW's works council network. The interaction between UAW officials and representatives of VW's works council network again proved difficult. Patta was committed to helping the UAW, but Kilian had doubts that UAW officials would be sufficiently attentive to the specific concerns of VW because they represented many more workers at Ford, GM, and Chrysler.

Opponents attacked the UAW on several fronts. They made much of the union's decision in 2013 to increase dues from 2 to 2.5 hours worth of wages per month. Don Jackson alleged that voting for the UAW would make it less likely that Volkswagen Chattanooga would get a second vehicle to produce, but he added, "I don't know that for a fact, but it's just economics."[145] Southern Momentum's leader, Mike Jarvis, zeroed in on the UAW's promise of "maintaining and where possible enhancing the cost advantages and other competitive advantages that VWGOA enjoys relative to its competitors," calling it evidence that "the UAW has already sold us out."[146] Similarly, Sean Moss, another Southern Momentum member, protested, "We're not even unionized and the UAW is already starting to bargain away our rights behind closed doors. How many more backroom deals have they done behind our backs?"[147] Prominent Tennessee state Republicans criticized the agreement between VWGOA and the UAW and made explicit threats to withhold further subsidies should VW employees vote to recognize the UAW as their exclusive bargaining agent. Speaker pro tempore Bo Watson said,

> Volkswagen has promoted a campaign that has been unfair, unbalanced and, quite frankly, un-American in the traditions of American labor campaigns. . . . I do not see the members of the [Tennessee] Senate having a positive view of Volkswagen because of the manner in which this campaign has been conducted. The workers that will be voting, need to know all of the potential consequences, intended and unintended. . . . Should the workers at Volkswagen choose to be represented by the United Auto Workers, any additional incentives from the citizens of the state of Tennessee for expansion or otherwise will have a very tough time passing the Tennessee Senate.[148]

Tennessee House Speaker Beth Harwell agreed. "It would definitely put those (incentives) in jeopardy. . . . That would jeopardize a very good arrangement for Volkswagen to locate here. And I hate that, because I want Volkswagen here, we're so proud and honored to have them here, but unionization is a huge setback for our state economically."[149] House majority leader Gerald McCormick also issued a statement:

> I encourage the employees of Volkswagen to reject bringing the United Auto Workers Union into the Plant and into our community. As you consider your vote, ask yourself this question—Will I be better off with the UAW? When you consider that question, I believe the answer will be NO! I wish the UAW had been willing to have an open and fair debate within the workplace. The fact that the UAW refused to allow all points of view to be heard and discussed demonstrates how they are unwilling to have an open, honest representation to ALL employees. The taxpayers of Tennessee reached out to Volkswagen and welcomed them to our state and our community. We are glad they are here. But that is not a green light to help force a union into the workplace. That was not part of the deal. To the employees of Volkswagen: You are leaders, and you are setting the course for the future of our community and our region. You have performed well. You have built the Car-of-the-Year.
>
> You have good wages and benefits. All of this happened without the heavy hand of the United Auto Workers. I urge you to keep your voice and vote NO.[150]

Tennessee state representative Mike Sparks provided a political explanation for Republican opposition. "The UAW does not donate to Republicans. . . . That's one fear, let's just call it like we see it."[151]

VWGOA personnel head Sebastian Patta responded to criticisms of the company, asserting that VW was acting fairly. "Volkswagen America is committed to defending our employees' legal right to make a free choice. . . . Outside political groups won't divert us from the work at hand: innovating, creating jobs, growing, and producing great automobiles. Volkswagen of America is committed to defending our employees' legal right to make a free choice."[152]

Democratic Tennessee House minority leader Craig Fitzhugh responded with outrage to the statements of the Tennessee Republican leadership. "In my 20 years on the hill, I've never seen such a massive intrusion into the affairs of a private company. When management and workers agree—as they do at Volkswagen—the state has no business interfering. Words have consequences and these types of threats could have a ruinous effect on our state's relationships with not just Volkswagen, but all employers." House Democratic Caucus chairman Mike Turner was also dismayed. "This is an outrageous and unprecedented effort by state officials to violate the rights of employers and workers. Republicans are basically threatening to kill jobs if workers exercise their federally protected rights to organize. When the company says they don't have a problem with it, what right does the state have to come in and say they can't do it?"[153]

Casteel invoked the words of Bob Corker in attempting to silence the Tennessee state Republicans, observing, "Other politicians should follow the lead of Senator Corker and respect these workers' right to make up their own minds."[154] Casteel's move backfired. Corker issued a statement the next day with a new position on the VW recognition election:

> I am very disappointed the UAW is misusing my comments to try to stifle others from weighing in on an issue that is so important to our community. While I had not planned to make additional public remarks in advance of this week's vote, after comments the UAW made this weekend, I feel strongly that it is important to return home and ensure my position is clear.[155]

Casteel replied, "It's unfortunate that Bob Corker has been swayed by special interests from outside Tennessee to flip-flop on his position on what's best for Chattanooga's working families."[156]

Once voting had begun, Corker released a carefully crafted statement. "I've had conversations today and based on those am assured that should the workers vote against the UAW, Volkswagen will announce in the coming weeks that it will manufacture its new mid-size SUV here in Chattanooga."[157] The statement implied that VW would be more likely to invest in Chattanooga if the workers voted against union recognition, but the statement would also be accurate if VW intended to invest in Chattanooga regardless of the vote's outcome, which is precisely what VW management had said months earlier. Corker followed up his statement with multiple interviews. He accused the UAW of being interested in dues money only. He also echoed Governor Haslam's statements, saying "there's no question that the UAW organizing there will have an effect on our community's ability to continue to recruit businesses."[158] Corker's assertions received widespread coverage. Plant CEO Fischer released a response asserting that there was "no connection between our Chattanooga employees' decision about whether to be represented by a union and the decision about where to build a new product for the US market."[159]

US president Barack Obama also injected himself into the election. He said that everyone was in favor of the UAW representing VW employees except for local politicians who "are more concerned about German shareholders than American workers."[160] Obama's statement was not particularly helpful, because few believed that local opposition to unionization was rooted in concern for German shareholders. Corker reiterated his claim about future investment in the Chattanooga plant, adding, "After all these years and my involvement with Volkswagen, I would not have made the statement I made yesterday without being confident it was true and factual."[161] Despite efforts by Volkswagen Chattanooga's top management to enforce neutrality, many of the line supervisors remained anti-union. Some supervisors harassed and targeted pro-union employees for discipline. Many wore anti-union T-shirts and distributed anti-union literature during the campaign.[162]

The atmosphere was tense when retired circuit court judge Sam Payne announced the results of the union recognition vote on the evening of February 14 as VW's Fischer and the UAW's Casteel looked on. Eighty-nine percent of the employees voted: 712 were against the UAW, and 626 were in favor. In other words, 46.8 percent voted for unionization. Shortly after the announcement, Fischer and Casteel spoke to the media. Fischer tried to salvage what he could from the company's perspective in his prepared statement:

> They have spoken, and Volkswagen will respect the majority. . . . Our employees have not made a decision that they are against a works council. Throughout this process, we found great enthusiasm for the idea of an American-style works council both inside and outside our plant. Our goal continues to be to determine the best method for establishing a works council in accordance with the requirements of US labor law to meet VW America's production needs and serve our employees' interests.[163]

Casteel thanked the company. "We commend Volkswagen for its commitment to global human rights, to worker rights and trying to provide an atmosphere of freedom to make a decision." He went on to denounce the outside interventions. "Unfortunately, politically motivated third parties threatened the economic future of this facility and the opportunity for workers to create a successful operating model that would grow jobs in Tennessee."[164] In Detroit, King conceded,

> To lose by such a close margin is very difficult. . . . We're obviously deeply disappointed. . . . While we certainly would have liked a victory for workers here, we deeply respect the Volkswagen Global Group Works Council, Volkswagen management and IG Metall for doing their best to create a free and open atmosphere for workers to exercise their basic human right to form a union.[165]

King also looked to the future with a note of optimism. "One great thing about the UAW, one great thing about workers: We don't quit. We're going to fight for what's right. We take setbacks. We get up and fight another day to make sure that workers have a real voice." VW works council official Gunnar Kilian expressed resolve. "The outcome of the vote . . . does not change our goal of setting up a works council in Chattanooga."[166]

Senator Corker was elated with the results of the recognition election. "I'm thrilled for the employees and thrilled for our community. I'm sincerely overwhelmed. . . . The UAW had all the advantages. Everybody but the UAW had both hands tied behind their backs."[167] A spokesperson for Bill Haslam related, "The Governor is pleased with the outcome and looks forward to working with the company on future growth in Tennessee."[168]

Why did the UAW lose? Several factors contributed. First, the impact of interventions from the Tennessee establishment and Washington special interest lobbyists on the recognition election cannot be overstated. Volkswagen Chattanooga employee and union supporter Steve Cochran observed, "Whenever you have a politician who is supposed to be in the know on these things saying that if you vote no, I can guarantee you'll get that, of course it's going to change some people's minds. Their words carry a lot of weight."[169] Other Chattanooga employees reported that coworkers said that the statements from leading Tennessee politicians led them to vote no when they had intended to vote yes. UAW president Bob King expressed outrage over "the outside interference in this election. It's never happened before that a US senator, a governor and a leader of the State House of Representatives threatened the company and threatened the workers."[170]

Second, subsidies made VW management vulnerable to political pressure. Fear of losing them was an important consideration in VW management's decision to rule out card-check recognition as an option, which greatly reduced the odds that the UAW would succeed in the organizing effort.

Third, the UAW leadership used a top-down approach in the organizing drive, which proved highly problematic because it disempowered union supporters in the plant. Union organizers often kept plant employees in the dark, and the organizers themselves were also often out of the loop. Union leaders justified this approach as the best way to keep union strategy and tactics from leaking. The drawback to the top-down approach was that it did not leave room for plant employees "to start acting like a working union."[171] This approach ran counter to a key finding of Bronfenbrenner and Juravich, namely that "union success in certification election and first-contract campaigns depends on using an aggressive grassroots rank-and-file strategy focused on building a union and acting like a union from the very beginning of the campaign."[172]

Fourth and related, the top-down strategy resulted in not placing the concerns of the Chattanooga employees at the forefront of the organizing drive. The centerpiece of the UAW's top-down campaign was a promise to create a works council if employees recognized the union. The UAW leadership did this to entice German employee and management representatives to facilitate unionization at the plant. In other words, this is another example of bargaining to organize except that it involved far more parties than was the case at DTNA and that this portion of the union-employer exchange was public rather than secret, which may help explain why the UAW was successful at DTNA but not at VW. There are other reasons as well. Prominent among them is the focus on getting a works council. Analyst Chris Brooks observed, "A works council is an abstraction that most VW workers cannot relate to, are not passionate about, and has no direct connection to the everyday problems they face on the job."[173] Interviews that I and others conducted with VW employees indicated that the workers' biggest concerns were inadequate training, workplace injuries, an unhealthy fourteen-day rotation between working the day and the night shift, and arbitrary treatment by supervisors.[174] UAW officials and German employee representatives saw a works council as a tool to address these problems, but most workers did not connect the dots.[175]

Chattanooga activists identified a fifth cause, which was also a product of the UAW's top-down strategy: the UAW's failure to engage with the community. Most organizers were not from the Chattanooga area. Union representatives did not build relationships with civil rights, church-based, or other civil society groups in Chattanooga. Activists from Chattanooga for Workers, a community group established to build local support for organizing drives, complained about the insularity of the UAW's approach. Gloria Jean Sweet-Love, president of the Tennessee State Conference of the National Association for the Advancement of

Colored People (NAACP), stated that UAW officials contacted her for the first time just three days before the recognition election. As a result, the union had no buttress of community support to help it withstand the attacks of the anti-union forces.[176] UAW president Bob King conceded that this was a "huge mistake."[177]

Southern Momentum's Jarvis offered a sixth explanation. He said that pointing out the paragraph in the UAW-VWGOA agreement committing the UAW to "maintaining and where possible enhancing the cost advantages and other competitive advantages that VWGOA enjoys" was his group's most effective tactic. "We got people to realize they had already negotiated a deal behind their backs."[178] This clause mattered because VW offered the lowest compensation in the US automobile industry. Labor costs for 2014 at VW averaged $38 an hour, which compared poorly to $41 at Hyundai and Kia, $42 at Nissan, $48 at Toyota and Chrysler, $49 at Honda, $57 at Ford, $58 at GM, and $65 at Mercedes.[179] The clause would have locked in VW at the bottom of the table. Union supporters in the plant "were caught off guard" because the UAW leadership and organizers did not inform them of the clause in advance. They had trouble defending it once it became public.[180]

Seventh, despite VW's bottom position when it comes to compensation in the automobile sector, for a large portion of the permanent production employees their job at VW provided the best wages and benefits they ever hoped to earn in a region that lost much of its manufacturing base over the past half century. The alternative was low-paid precarious employment in the service sector; VW employees knew there were plenty of people who would take their jobs in an instant. Some employees reasoned that they would work at VW for about a decade while they were still young. Once their bodies could no longer take the brutal assembly-line work, they would move on. From such a perspective, getting a greater say at work was less important. A possible strike down the road would simply waste the precious time when they were still physically capable of working at an auto plant.[181]

Eighth, Timothy Minchin pointed out that the UAW's critics effectively linked the union with Detroit and the domestic automakers, arguing that the union held some responsibility for the decline of both and that voting for the union would bring a similar decline to Chattanooga.[182] The repeated labeling of the UAW as a "Detroit-based union" by opponents was also a rhetorical tactic intended to "other" the union in the eyes of the Chattanooga workforce.[183]

These eight explanations are not mutually exclusive and vary regarding the intensity of their impact. Several concatenate (i.e., one and two, three through six, and seven and eight). The lead causes in those concatenations are external interventions by union opponents, large subsidies that require political approval thereby enhancing politicians' political leverage over firms, the top-down nature of the organizing drive, and retention of a rare well-paying blue-collar job.

Beyond the causal question, the February 2014 recognition election at Volkswagen Chattanooga illustrates how extraordinarily difficult it is to organize unions in the United States. Even when management is amenable to unionization and a union embraces cooperation, the American industrial relations system allows third parties to intervene in the organizing drive, which can affect the outcome.

The failed election had consequences. The positive relationship between the UAW and VW did not last much beyond it.

The Wake of the 2014 Recognition Election

On February 21, 2014, the UAW filed for an appeal regarding the recognition election on the grounds of the outside interference of an unprecedented scale and intensity. Six weeks later, UAW lawyers issued subpoenas to twenty individuals, including Bob Corker, Bill Haslam, Todd Womack, Beth Harwell, Gerald McCormick, Bo Watson, Grover Norquist, and Matt Patterson.[184] The US Congress opened an investigation into Haslam's August 23, 2013, "Project Trinity" email.[185] In mid-April, Womack announced that he and Corker would ignore their subpoenas.[186] Haslam and his aides soon followed suit.

On April 21 the union abruptly dropped the appeal, including the subpoenas, citing concern that anti-union forces could use it to delay the final certification of the vote, which would push back the start date for the twelve-month pause before another recognition election can be held as specified in NLRA Section 9(e)(2).[187] An additional cause for the UAW leadership's about-face only became known more than two years later.[188] On March 21, 2014, the UAW and VW had reached a confidential ten-point agreement in German titled "Weiteres Vorgehen Chattanooga" (Further Action in Chattanooga), which Horst Neumann and Bob King signed at the bottom under the phrase "As discussed with each other."[189] The one-page document had ten points:

1. Cooperation in the workplace, "one team," <u>bring along 700 + 600</u>
2. B-SUV in consensus—Democrats + Republicans, UAW + VW employee representatives—bring to Chattanooga. No prejudice for further plant location decisions.
3. Recognition of the UAW as 'Members Union.' Make it possible to access the workplace pragmatically and legally. No support for company unions.

4. End challenge to the election result. No petition for a new election within two years by VW or UAW. Premise: no serious organizing attempt by another union.

5. Management-employee cooperation bodies / Start precursor of a works council. Qualified build team. Goal: build up competent employee representatives, resolve technical topics (working time, CIP [i.e., continuous improvement process], health and safety).

6. Explore interest of the white-collar unit in the union.

7. Communicate in the USA dual codetermination/works council as part of the worldwide successful Volkswagen business model.

8. Improve the political and legal framework conditions for innovative forms of employment relations in the USA.

9. Reactivate positive and objective local political relations.

10. Personnel topics: BoM [Board of Management] VWGoA/Plant management Chattanooga.

The one-page document offered considerable opportunity for progress, but UAW leaders also found themselves in a difficult position. More than six hundred Volkswagen Chattanooga employees had voted in favor of unionization, but union leaders had committed privately not to hold a second recognition election for at least another two years. How would they keep employees engaged? After weighing the options, they decided that the best action was to establish a local for VW Chattanooga employees despite the loss in the recognition election. "The election was so close, we don't feel it's right to turn our backs on these workers," explained Gary Casteel.[190]

On July 10, 2014, at a public ceremony, fifteen Chattanooga employees signed a charter to form Local 42. The action was novel. The UAW had not formed a local without prior certification as the exclusive bargaining agent in eight decades (i.e., since the NLRA became law). The local would elect its own officers, draft its own bylaws, and provide "representation for employees," albeit not exclusive representation. The local's members would have the same rights as other UAW members, but they would not have to pay dues unless the UAW signed a collective bargaining agreement with VW. Local 42 membership cards contain the same language as the recognition cards authorizing the UAW to represent the signatory for the purposes of collective bargaining. They thus could be used in a card-check procedure or for calling a new recognition election.[191]

UAW officials and the new Local 42 members hoped that establishing a local would provide an opportunity to dispel the perception that the pro-union forces were a group of outsiders from Detroit. It would also give union members the chance to be active participants as UAW Local 42 in the community. Casteel, who had just been elected UAW secretary-treasurer, said that UAW officials did not anticipate the local getting formal recognition from VW, but he "would fully expect that Volkswagen would deal with this local union if it represents a substantial portion of its employees."[192]

Union opponent Mike Jarvis said he was "mad"; the union was trying to bully its way into the plant despite having lost a recognition election. Mike Burton declared, "They chose to ignore the no-fly zone." When union supporters started handing out membership applications, anti-union employees first distributed a flyer critical of the union and later handed out de-authorization cards.[193]

On July 14, 2014, VW announced that the Chattanooga plant would produce an SUV called Atlas alongside the Passat sedan. Several who voted against unionization felt that the announcement vindicated their position.[194] The State of Tennessee agreed to provide an additional $262 million in support of VW's $600 million investment. The decision was welcome news, not least because sales of the Passat, which thus far had been the only car manufactured in Chattanooga, had continued to disappoint. In 2013, sales had fallen by 6.3 percent to 109,652 units; VW's US market share slipped from three to 2.6 percent.[195]

In August 2014, Casteel announced that Local 42 had signed up "substantially more than 700 members," which constituted a majority of the eligible employees. Local 42's recruiting success prompted anti-UAW employees to form (with the help of labor lawyer Maury Nicely) their own organization, which they called the American Council of Employees (ACE). Burton, who spearheaded the anti-UAW movement, said that he had already collected more than one hundred signatures. When told about the plans to form ACE, Casteel responded portentously, "What does an anti-union union offer?"[196] Sean Moss served briefly as ACE president but then stepped down "in order to attend to personal matters." David Reed succeeded him.[197]

Anticipation in Chattanooga ran high in November 2014. Cantrell, the newly elected Local 42 president, sent a letter to his members:

> We are writing to update you on our progress toward being recognized as Volkswagen's bargaining partner. It is our understanding that Volkswagen this week will announce a new policy in Chattanooga that will lead to recognition of Local 42. . . . Our expectation that Volkswagen will recognize Local 42 is based on discussions that took place in Germany last spring, between representatives of the UAW and Volkswagen.[198]

VW's action was not quite what UAW and Local 42 leaders had hoped. The company issued policy HR-C20 titled "Community Organization Engagement" (COE).[199] Its purpose was to "allow eligible organizations the opportunity to engage in constructive dialogue with Volkswagen and its employees" (1). The document set three levels of engagement based on the share of employees who belong to an organization.

Level 1 was for organizations with membership greater than 15 percent of the workforce. Such organizations "are free to reserve and use space in the Conference Center for internal employee meetings on nonwork time once per month, post announcements in company-designated locations, and meet monthly with Volkswagen human resources staff to present topics of interest to their membership" (2).

Level 2 was for organizations with a membership share greater than 30 percent. In addition to the opportunities available to level 1 organizations, level 2 organizations may use the plant's conference center for meetings once a week, invite external representatives of their organization to such a meeting once per month, post materials on a dedicated bulletin board, and meet quarterly with a member of the Volkswagen Chattanooga management executive committee.

Level 3 was for organizations with a membership share of greater than 45 percent of the workforce. In addition to the level 2 opportunities, organizations qualifying for level 3 may use on-site locations for meetings on nonwork time with staff or employees "as reasonably needed" (3), meet biweekly with VW human resources staff and monthly with the Volkswagen Chattanooga Executive Committee. The COE document makes clear that "this policy may not be used by any group or organization to claim or request recognition as the exclusive representative of any group of employees for the purposes of collective bargaining" (3–4).

The COE fell far short of achieving VW's principal objective: instituting German-style codetermination in Chattanooga. It also fell short of the UAW's principal objective: a collective bargaining agreement. Volkswagen Chattanooga human resources executive vice president Sebastian Patta explained the motivation behind the policy. "We recognize and accept that many of our employees are interested in external representation, and we are putting this policy in place so that a constructive dialogue is possible and available for everyone."[200] The policy did not violate NLRA section 8(a)(2) because there would be no "dealing"; employees could raise topics and make suggestions but not bargain. Management would not provide funds to the participating organizations. VW management saw the COE as fulfilling its commitment in the March 21 ten-point agreement to recognize the UAW and to allow it access to the workplace, but UAW leaders disagreed politely, as Casteel's response indicates:

> We appreciate Volkswagen's effort to articulate a policy for how it will engage with UAW Local 42 and its members in Chattanooga. We have questions about this policy, which we'll work through in discussions with management, but this is a step forward. . . . In the first conversa-

tions that occur, we will remind them of the mutually agreed-upon commitments that were made by Volkswagen and the UAW last spring in Germany. Among those commitments: Volkswagen will recognize the UAW as the representatives of our members.[201]

The VW Global Works Council, which VW employees run, did permit Local 42 president Mike Cantrell and Vice President Steve Cochran to attend meetings in the hope that this move would put additional pressure on VW management to recognize the UAW as the Chattanooga employees' bargaining agent as a prerequisite to creating a genuine works council. Pro-union employees did not take full advantage of the COE to establish a greater union presence on the shop floor, however.[202]

ACE representatives judged the COE positively because it left an opening for their organization.[203] Governor Haslam downplayed it. "I don't think there's really any new news in this beyond what they said before."[204] IG Metall chair Wetzel praised the COE for "creating the precondition for the recognition of trade union representation," but he was the most critical. He said, "We expect VW to show its true colors and recognize the UAW as its collective bargaining partner, once it proves that it represents the majority of workers." Wetzel explained that IG Metall had supported the organizing efforts of the UAW and other American trade unions for many years to guarantee trade union rights and to make codetermination possible even in difficult political environments to prevent "social dumping" between production sites at the expense of plant employees. Wetzel added, "There must not be any cooperation between Volkswagen and anti-union groupings and company unions."[205]

The COE triggered a race between the UAW and ACE to become the first organization recognized for engagement with VW management. In mid-December 2014, VW announced that the independent auditor had verified that the UAW had signatures of more than 45 percent of the Volkswagen Chattanooga workforce, which meant that Local 42 qualified as a level 3 organization.[206] Local 42 head Cantrell said that the local's next objective was gaining recognition from VW as the employees' exclusive bargaining agent.[207] The recognition of Local 42 under the COE led King's successor, UAW president Dennis Williams, to conclude, "We think we have the right strategy. We believe we have the kind of relationships in the South that can succeed."[208] In mid-February 2015, VW management announced that the independent auditor's report verified that ACE had a membership of at least 15 percent of the labor force. It therefore qualified as a level 1 organization.[209]

It is important to note that neither Dennis Williams nor UAW organizing director Mark Haasis was committed to Bob King's strategy to trade assistance from VW management to organize the Chattanooga plant in exchange for the creation of a works council. Gary Casteel, in contrast, did continue to pursue King's approach but no longer had the same degree of support that he had enjoyed earlier.

A leadership challenge within VW briefly shook up the company. VW supervisory board chair Ferdinand Piëch attempted to remove CEO Martin Winterkorn in April 2015. The attempt failed, in part because the works councilors and IG Metall officials on the supervisory board sided with Winterkorn. Piëch resigned from the board, and former IG Metall Chair Berthold Huber, who was board vice chair, became acting chair. The failed coup stirred hopes at the UAW that the rise of Huber might allow for reconsideration of the policy rejecting card-check recognition. The UAW acted quickly. On May 7, 2015, the UAW leadership made a new push to get exclusive recognition at the Volkswagen Chattanooga plant. Casteel presented the "Vision Statement for a Collectively Bargained Works Council in Volkswagen." The statement resurrected the Dual Model of union recognition from the January 27, 2014, election agreement between the UAW and VWGOA, including the blueprint for a works council. Not to be outdone, ACE leaders produced their own works council proposal.[210] Neither proposal went anywhere.

Casteel claimed that Local 42 had 816 members, which was a majority of the employees in the bargaining unit. He offered to work with VW to implement the Dual Model in exchange for exclusive recognition using the card-check procedure. Casteel's hopes were quickly dashed. Huber declined to change company policy to preserve the reputation of employee representatives on supervisory boards as responsible consensual actors. VWGOA spokesperson Carsten Krebs responded that the COE "has been a very effective way to start a dialog with each of the groups and we intend to continue with the community organization engagement policy."[211] In August 2015 UAW leaders asked again for card-check recognition, and the company refused.[212]

In Dubious Battle: The 2015 Skilled Trades Micro-Unit Recognition Election

Since VW management would not budge regarding card-check recognition, the UAW leadership took a new approach. On August 6, 2015, Local 42 leaders informed VW that a majority of 164 skilled trades employees who repair the plant's equipment had signed an authorization card and asked the company to recognize this smaller unit using a card-check procedure. Management refused. So, on October 23, 2015, Local 42 leaders petitioned the NLRB for a recognition election for this "micro unit." Local 42 president Cantrell explained the decision. "A key objective of our local union always has been, and still is, moving toward collective bargaining for the purpose of reaching a multi-year contract between Volkswagen and employees in Chattanooga."[213] Casteel put the decision in context from the perspective of the UAW's headquarters:

> Volkswagen's [COE] policy in Chattanooga was a gesture and our local union has engaged accordingly. At the end of the day, the policy cannot be a substitute for meaningful employee representation and co-determination with management. The international union will provide ongoing technical assistance to the local union as it strives toward collective bargaining and its rightful seat on the Global Group Works Council.[214]

Volkswagen Chattanooga managers made known their displeasure with the Local 42 petition, but they did not challenge it at first. Plant CEO Christian Koch and personnel head Sebastian Patta sent a letter to all employees explaining that the company found "the timing of this development unfortunate, given the challenges we are facing as a plant, Brand, and Group" (i.e., the VW emissions scandal had emerged the month before).[215] They noted, "The petition for election was submitted by the UAW, not the company"; there was no election agreement this time between the UAW and VW, and "there was no clear path to form a works council for the whole plant from a bargaining unit representing only the maintenance team." Nonetheless, they stated that they would "respect our employees' right to petition and vote and will remain neutral in the process."[216] Both Casteel and Cantrell asserted that the decision was unrelated to the VW diesel emissions scandal. Casteel said that the union was "fine with and unfazed by Volkswagen's language" in the letter.[217]

ACE president David Reed was critical of the decision. "This is a time of great stress and uncertainty for VW-Chattanooga employees and the Volkswagen organization as a whole. It is unfortunate, however, that the UAW would try to take advantage of the current situation by demanding an immediate election. This is an obvious attempt to use fear to further divide VW-Chattanooga employees."[218]

Within two weeks, Volkswagen Chattanooga management reconsidered. At a November 3 hearing, the company asked the NLRB to reject Local 42's petition for a union recognition election. VW management's grounds were that "the maintenance-only unit requested in the petition is not consistent with our 'one team' approach at Volkswagen Chattanooga, our production system and organization design."[219] A micro unit not only runs counter to the postwar German practice of "unitary unionism," which is to have one union with jurisdiction for all the employees in a plant,[220] but also was too small to serve as a vehicle for creating a works council for the whole plant. In fact, forming the micro unit could make creating a plant-wide works council more difficult. UAW representatives responded that the skilled trades employees were an appropriate bargaining unit consistent with US labor law and jurisprudence. VW's challenge led to a postponement of the recognition election to give the NLRB regional director time to decide. The challenge furthermore suggests that management's earlier cooperation with the UAW was instrumental. The company's objective was always to create a works council or something equivalent. VW management was increasingly comfortable with the COE policy as the way to hear from employees and saw no reason to do more.

On November 18, 2015, the NLRB regional director ruled in favor of the UAW and set December 3 and 4 as new election dates. On December 1 VW filed an appeal, but the NLRB decided to proceed with the vote.[221] The recognition campaign for the maintenance employees proceeded with far less drama than was involved with the February 2014 election. Far fewer outside actors intervened. IndustriALL president Huber and IG Metall federal executive committee member Wolfgang Lemb sent letters of support. Lemb explained to the media that "it is becoming increasingly clear to our colleagues in Germany that if we continue to have a pronounced low-wage sector here [in the United States], it will increase pressure on employees in German companies."[222] Senator Corker had no comment. Governor Haslam expressed concerns about the timing of the vote, given the emissions scandal. ACE posted a critical letter in the plant that asked the skilled employees to vote "no." Others stayed out of the election.[223]

Just before the vote, Volkswagen Chattanooga plant managers met with UAW Local 42 officers in a vain attempt to persuade them to call off the recognition election.[224] The UAW won the election for the skilled employees decisively, 108 to 44 (i.e., a 71 percent majority), the only time the UAW had won at a wholly foreign-owned automobile manufacturer in the American South. Most maintenance employees, in contrast to production-line workers, were skilled electricians and machinists. Most had seen firsthand the benefits of unionization, and many had been union members in previous jobs. As a result, they were the union stronghold in the Chattanooga plant. Ray Curry, Casteel's successor as UAW Region 8 director, praised the workers. "Volkswagen employees in Chattanooga have had a long journey in the face of intense political opposition, and they have made steady progress. We're proud of their courage and persistence."[225] Curry urged VW to accept the election results. Casteel set the accomplishment in context. "To the overall grand plan of the UAW it's probably not monumental, but to those workers, it's a big deal."[226] The statement from VW Chattanooga management was not conciliatory:

> As has always been the case, Volkswagen respects the right of our employees to decide the question of union representation. Nevertheless, we believe that a union of only maintenance employees fractures our workforce and does not take into account the overwhelming community of interest shared between our maintenance and production employees.[227]

On December 21, seventeen days after the recognition election, the UAW filed an unfair labor practice charge against VW for refusal to bargain.[228] At year's end, VW filed an appeal to the NLRB to have the vote set aside. Local business groups expressed support for VW management's action.[229] In January 2016 VW's new CEO, Matthias Müller, traveled to Chattanooga. Müller told reporters that he had not made up his mind about labor issues at the plant. "Surely we must take a few weeks to understand and relate to this very complex topic." Casteel hoped that new leadership "will provide an opportunity, soon, to reset the dialogue. We're hopeful Volkswagen will recommit to core principles like codetermination, adhere to federal law and begin collective bargaining."[230]

The UAW continued to apply pressure on VW to bargain. In February 2016, the UAW filed a new unfair labor practice petition alleging that a fired African American employee, James Robinson, was the victim of discrimination. Gary Casteel did not hide the strategy behind filing the unfair labor practice. "If Volkswagen maintains this position, more and more charges will accumulate, and the company will further damage its relations with employees. We remain hopeful that Volkswagen will comply with the law and move forward soon, in good faith."[231] On February 23, 2016, the executive council of the AFL-CIO, the peak confederation of trade unions in the United States, issued a statement denouncing VW for refusal to bargain with the UAW and demanding that the company "make corporate social responsibility more than just a slogan and public relations strategy."[232]

On April 13, 2016, a two-to-one decision of an NLRB panel denied VW's request to review the December election. Casteel issued a statement:

> We hope Volkswagen's new management team will accept the government's decision and refocus on the core values that made it a successful brand—environmental sustainability and meaningful employee representation. We call on Volkswagen to immediately move forward with UAW Local 42, in the German spirit of codetermination.[233]

A week later, VW announced that it would appeal the decision in federal court. VW management retained Littler Mendelson, one of the country's most aggressive law firms specializing in "union avoidance," to represent the company.[234] Casteel responded caustically, reflecting the adversarial turn in the relationship:

> We reject the company's claim that recognizing and bargaining with the skilled-trades employees would somehow splinter the workforce in Chattanooga. Recognizing clearly identifiable employee units is common in the US. Furthermore, Volkswagen plants all over the world—including in countries such as Italy, Russia and Spain—recognize multiple unions that represent portions of a workforce. So the company's current argument against the National Labor Relations Board rings hollow. At a time when Volkswagen already has run afoul of the federal and state governments in the emissions-cheating scandal, we're disappointed that the company now is choosing to thumb its nose at the federal government over US labor law. At the end of the day, the employees are the ones being cheated by Volkswagen's actions.[235]

An external party once again weighed in on events at the VW plant in Chattanooga. In early May, US presidential candidate Hillary Clinton expressed her support of the UAW by retweeting Gary Casteel's tweet, "By choosing to fight the NLRB, @Volkswagen is in clear violation of federal law," and later tweeting "Volkswagen workers in TN are raising their voices for rights they deserve. VW should meet them at the table. -H."[236]

VW's new human resources director, Karlheinz Blessing, agreed to meet with Casteel in Stuttgart on May 11 to try to salvage the relationship. Blessing had been an IG Metall official decades earlier before switching to a management career in the steel sector. He made it clear before the meeting that VW's position had not changed. "We can accept a vote of the entire workforce, but we cannot accept fragmentation."[237] Casteel agreed to meet with Blessing nonetheless, because "the UAW would like to re-establish a trusting relationship with Volkswagen." Casteel added, "The company's contradictory statements and refusals to abide by US labor law make this difficult. . . . When I meet with Dr. Blessing, I'll present him with the documentation of that agreement that was signed by his predecessor Dr. Neumann" in March 2014.[238] Blessing and Casteel met for fifty minutes. Afterward Blessing had no comment, but Casteel said that Blessing "offered no indication that he was seeking a solution, but just kept saying, 'I have no mandate.' Now, we're considering legal action. They committed to recognizing us and now they're thumbing their noses at the NLRB."[239]

The UAW leadership tried again to increase pressure on VW, this time from an international angle. IG Metall chair Jörg Hofmann, who had become vice chair of

VW's supervisory board, criticized VW management's actions. "It is not acceptable that companies abide by the law in Germany but disregard it in other countries. Workers' rights should be respected worldwide—particularly by companies headquartered in Germany."[240] In late May 2016 at the UAW's request, the IndustriALL executive committee unanimously passed a resolution calling on VW "to cease all of its attempts to invalidate the vote of Chattanooga skilled trades workers for collective bargaining, and immediately to begin negotiations," and for IndustriALL to take steps that "could lead to the eventual revocation of the Global Framework Agreement between IndustriALL and Volkswagen" if the company had not agreed by June 22 to begin collective bargaining with the UAW.[241] Conspicuously absent, however, was the voice of works council head Bernd Osterloh, whose support of unionization in Chattanooga had always been tepid. Disunity among German employee representatives made it easier for VW management to maintain a position opposing the creation of the skilled trades unit.

On June 21, 2016, the UAW made public the March 21, 2014, 10-point agreement between King and Neumann that included the commitment to recognize the UAW as a "members union." On a conference call Casteel said, "Volkswagen never fulfilled its commitments to recognize the union as a representative of its members. The unfulfilled commitment is at the heart of the ongoing disagreement between the company and the union." Casteel added that the "common thread" between VW's diesel emissions scandal and the labor dispute with the UAW "is a disregard for its corporate commitment and in our case a disregard for US law. We believe the company is better than this."[242]

Blessing's cutting response came a day later at the 2016 VW shareholders meeting. "If the UAW wants to organize the American auto workers at our plant in Chattanooga it has to do so by itself, like the IG Metall does it in Germany. The VW management board or the IG Metall cannot handle this for the UAW."[243] With that remark, the faint hope of a revival of a cooperative relationship disappeared.

The UAW leadership continued to apply pressure through any available means to persuade VW management to begin negotiations. In July, sixty-three members of Congress sent a letter to plant CEO Christian Koch and personnel head Sebastian Patta imploring them to "respect the rights of the skilled trades employees," explain their actions, and begin bargaining with UAW representatives.[244] Seven weeks later, VWGOA senior executive vice president for public affairs David Geanacopoulos replied. His letter reiterated VW's position "that union representation of only the maintenance employees would divide our workforce and ignore the overwhelming community of interest shared by our maintenance *and* production employees." He added, "Because the NLRB itself is divided on this question based on NLRB Member Miscimarra's pointed dissent, Volkswagen is taking the necessary steps to have this issue reviewed by the appropriate United States Circuit Court of Appeals. . . . For these reasons, we don't believe it is appropriate, nor is it required, to begin the bargaining process while the legal review of this issue is ongoing."[245] Dissatisfied with the NLRB ruling, VW management took the case to the US Court of Appeals in Washington, D.C. Most labor law experts considered VW management's action quixotic, given the preponderance of jurisprudence did not support it.[246]

Gary Casteel responded to VW's decision on the same day:

> We're disappointed that Volkswagen is continuing to thumb its nose at the federal government. . . . Volkswagen's refusal to comply with the law is especially troubling when IG Metall President Jörg Hofmann and other top German labor leaders have said it is not acceptable for the company to abide by the law at home but disregard it elsewhere in the world. Volkswagen's ill-advised appeal is nothing more than a stall tactic to try to delay the inevitable. It's overdue time for the company to meet the local union at the bargaining table.[247]

Criticism of VW management from US political circles continued. This time it came from the executive branch. On September 11, 2016, US secretary of labor Tom Perez expressed his disapproval of VW management's behavior in an interview in the German newspaper *Die Welt*:

> I am very irritated with Volkswagen. . . . I think VW shouldn't only listen to its lawyers, but also apply its common sense. . . . . I am truly disappointed that Volkswagen is refusing to negotiate with the UAW in Chattanooga. I was hoping that they would abide by the NLRB ruling. . . . It's a real shame Volkswagen has been that VW appears to be so badly advised and appears to be so scared.[248]

In late September 2016, the UAW's workplace rival was relegated. VW's annual membership audit under the COE policy revealed that fewer than 15 percent of the eligible workforce belonged to ACE, which meant that ACE did not even qualify as a level 1 organization. ACE leaders attempted to put a brave face on the downgrade. They asserted that falling out of the COE would enable the organization to make a "strategic shift" to focus more broadly on employee concerns, but soon thereafter ACE collapsed and disappeared. In contrast, the audit showed that Local 42 remained a level 3 organization; a majority of eligible VW employees belong to it.[249]

The Second Global Congress of IndustriALL met in Rio de Janeiro from October 3 to 7, 2016. The congress passed a resolution titled "Holding Volkswagen Accountable" that identified "a disturbing trend where employers who previously agreed to conduct themselves in a socially responsible manner, have abandoned these promises." The text then specifically denounced VW management's refusal to bargain with the skilled trades employees in the Chattanooga plant, characterizing it as a violation of the company's Global Framework Agreement. The resolution noted the statement from the May meeting of the IndustriALL executive committee that "called on Volkswagen to get in line or face further actions, including the possibility of revoking the GFA," but then observed, "Yet Volkswagen continues to ignore the choice of its Chattanooga workers and defy U.S. labor law." The resolution concluded:

> Now it is time for IndustriALL to act. To hold Volkswagen accountable and to give life to our Charter of Solidarity in Confronting Corporate Violations of Fundamental Rights, IndustriALL shall:
>
> - Arrange an immediate meeting between Volkswagen, IndustriALL, IG Metall, UAW and key affiliates to seek a settlement of this matter;
> - As quickly as possible, convene a meeting of all affiliates with members employed by Volkswagen, to exchange information and produce a detailed report of the company's labor relations practices and establish common ground for collective action;
> - This meeting shall decide on a near-term date for a Day of Action at Volkswagen plants around the world, and decide on specific activities—including industrial actions and demonstrations—to hold the company accountable;
> - Prepare a plan for media activity in countries with Volkswagen plants, calling attention to Volkswagen's behavior and its denial of workers' rights in Chattanooga; and
> - If Volkswagen doesn't respect workers' rights, initiate action to revoke our Global Framework Agreement with the company.[250]

The 1,500 delegates from over one hundred countries passed the resolution unanimously.

UAW Local 42 acting president Steve Cochran traveled to Wolfsburg to represent the Chattanooga plant at the December 2016 meeting of the Volkswagen Global Works Council. Cochran took aim at the COE policy. "We don't have codetermination. Some people wanted to believe that the COE policy is a workable substitute, but I pointed out how limited and unreliable that policy is. And Volkswagen's failure to recognize Local 42 as our representative—as they promised two years ago—means the COE has no teeth." Cochran told the gathering that poor treatment of employees had generated high turnover, and management "did not take seriously" employee input about job design or product processes. Cochran reported to his colleagues, "The presentation was very well received, and many people came up to me and thanked me for the information."[251]

The unexpected election of Donald Trump to the US presidency disrupted the status quo on many fronts, including employment relations jurisprudence. All parties anticipated that the new president would appoint individuals to fill two vacancies on the NLRB who would reverse numerous NLRB rulings. The NRWLDF jumped on the opportunity, assisting a Volkswagen Chattanooga employee in February 2017 with filing an amicus curiae brief supporting VW's position in the DC circuit of the US Court of Appeals. NRWF head Mark Mix commented in a prepared statement that "the gerrymandering scheme that union bosses used to gain a foothold in the Chattanooga Volkswagen plant is unfair to the workers who voted against union representation only to have the ground rules changed and are now forced into a monopoly union."[252] Steve Cochran responded, "Special interests from Washington have no business meddling in the affairs of workers in Chattanooga. . . . [F]ederal courts have consistently upheld the rights of employees to organize in distinct units within a workforce."[253]

In the spring of 2017, UAW leaders working with IG Metall and IndustriALL rolled out a multipronged, multinational, multimedia pressure campaign in advance of VW's annual shareholder meeting on May 10 to end management's refusal to bargain with the Chattanooga plant's skilled trades employees. IndustriALL officials placed a poster on their website with the slogan "Volkswagen's Empty Promises! Union-busting in Chattanooga." Depicted on it was a gasoline gauge with the VW logo in the middle and the needle indicating that the tank was close to empty.[254] The web page asked people to print out the poster, take a selfie with it, and upload the picture on IndustriALL's website.

On April 12 and 13, union representatives from Germany, Brazil, Mexico, Poland, South Africa, Switzerland, and the United Kingdom traveled to Chattanooga to hear from employees. The group issued a joint statement at the end of their visit:

> We have been appalled to learn about VW Chattanooga's ongoing mistreatment of workers and refusal to bargain with the United Autoworkers (UAW) Local 42. . . . VW not recognizing UAW in this case is illegal, violates workers' fundamental rights, and violates the Global Framework Agreement VW signed with us in 2002. Many of us have raised concern with VW about this, but the company's bad behavior continues. Because of this, we have unanimously committed to the following:
>
> • We will educate our members about VW's union-busting in Chattanooga.
> • We will approach our VW plant managers about VW's behavior in Chattanooga and demand they raise our concerns with higher management.

- We will again discuss this matter at IndustriALL's Executive Committee meeting on 27–28 April in Geneva and seek continued support for Local 42's struggle.
- We will continue to encourage our members to support this struggle in line with the "Holding Volkswagen Accountable" resolution.
- We will forcefully raise the matter of VW's union-busting in Chattanooga at the August meeting of the VW Global Works Council.
- We will continue to seek dialog with VW at all levels in an attempt to get the company to end its union-busting in Chattanooga and enter into negotiations for a first collective bargaining agreement with UAW Local 42.
- Depending on VW's response, we will escalate support for the struggle.[255]

The next day, IndustriALL general secretary Valter Sanches reiterated his organization's position in front of the VW Chattanooga plant.[256]

Employee representatives took additional actions in the two weeks before VW's annual shareholders meeting. The AFL-CIO released a report titled *At What Cost? Workers Report Concerns about Volkswagen's New Manufacturing Jobs in Tennessee* detailing the hazardous health and safety conditions and the anti-union climate at the Chattanooga plant.[257] IndustriALL uploaded onto its YouTube channel selections from the interviews with Volkswagen Chattanooga employees that provided much of the information in the AFL-CIO report.[258] Gary Casteel sent an email to one million active and retired UAW members nationwide asking them to sign a petition imploring VW to "stop union-busting." By the end of May, over sixty-three thousand had signed it.[259] Casteel was still careful not to depict VW management in a completely negative light. He said that he believed VW management is "not opposed to unionization per se. We're still talking to them. They've told me they still are interested in a plant-wide election. But we have to resolve this [NLRB issue] first. We can't unscramble a broken egg."[260]

The 2017 annual general meeting of VW's shareholders held on May 10 included a motion calling on VW management to negotiate with the skilled trades unit in Chattanooga. UAW Local 42 president Steve Cochran spoke at the meeting in Hannover, asserting that by refusing to bargain, "VW management is disregarding fundamental labor rights, U.S. labor law and its own code of conduct."[261] The Association of Ethical Shareholders Germany supported the motion,[262] and the German media reported about it.[263] Still, the motion failed to pass because the Piëch and Porsche families controlled a majority of VW's voting shares.

The next week the NLRB filed a complaint against VW, alleging that the company increased health insurance costs and changed the work hours of the skilled trades employees unilaterally. A Volkswagen Chattanooga spokesperson replied that the company acted unilaterally because pending litigation precluded it from negotiating.[264] In late May 2017, Bob Corker and eleven other senators introduced legislation to reverse the 2011 NLRB decision that allowed micro units.[265]

In the summer of 2017, federal authorities accused Fiat Chrysler Automobiles executives of making illegal payments to UAW officials and engaging in financial improprieties to cover them up. Over subsequent years the investigation implicated over a dozen individuals, including two UAW presidents: Dennis Williams and his successor, Gary Jones. Jones stepped down in November 2019 in the wake of federal accusations against him and ultimately pleaded guilty to embezzlement and racketeering charges.[266] The scandal gave union opponents a powerful new argument against the UAW, which they used repeatedly and to great effect as the scandal got worse.[267]

Antonio Pinto replaced Christian Koch as head of the Chattanooga plant in August 2017. Pinto, a Portuguese national, had thirty years of experience with VW, including stints in South Africa and Mexico.[268] Pinto, unlike his German predecessors, did not mix with the employees, which made him unpopular.

The action returned to the courtroom toward the end of 2017. The US Court of Appeals for the District of Columbia heard oral arguments on the company's challenge to the NLRB ruling upholding the legality of the skilled trades bargaining unit. The lawyer representing VW made a new argument that was an about-face. He claimed that the NLRB erred when it approved the combination of three separate departments—body, paint, and assembly—that do not work together and have no history of maintenance employees moving between them into a single skilled trades bargaining unit. When a judge asked whether separate bargaining units for each of these departments would be appropriate, VW's lawyer said it would.[269]

On December 19 in an unrelated case, the new Republican majority on the NLRB reversed the board's 2011 decision that permitted micro units.[270] Days later, the NLRB asked the Court of Appeals to return the VW case to the Board. VW attorney Arthur Carter filed papers supporting the NLRB request "in light of the controlling case law." Steve Cochran, who had become UAW Local 42 president, denounced the request, vowing that the union "cannot and will not go backward and undo the results of a free and fair election." He expressed hope that the Court of Appeals would "uphold the rights of the hard-working men and women of Chattanooga."[271] UAW president Dennis Williams commented, "That rises to a different level of how we feel about the NLRB. . . . Because we may have to go back to striking to get recognition if that's how they're gonna act."[272] A week later, the Court of Appeals sent the case back to the NRLB.[273]

New vacancies opened on the NLRB as members' terms expired, which the Trump administration was slow to fill and the US Senate was slow to confirm, and this stalled progress on the case for many months. After years of employee complaints, plant management finally agreed in 2018 to poll employees regarding their preference for organizing shifts at the plant. The result led management to switch from the two-week rotation between the day and night shifts for individual employees to a fixed day or night shift.[274]

VW management's decision to challenge the skilled trades unit soured the relationship with employee representatives worldwide. IndutriALL general secretary Valter Sanches sent a letter dated December 4, 2018, to new VW CEO Herbert Diess and management board member responsible for human resources Gunnar Kilian, who had formerly headed VW's group works council, informing them of a resolution that the IndustriALL executive committee approved at its Mexico City meeting on November 30, 2018. The unanimous resolution once again expressed regret that VW continued to refuse to recognize the results of the December 4, 2015, recognition election and asked VW management to withdraw the legal challenge to the election, recognize the UAW as the bargaining agent of the skilled trades employees, and begin collective bargaining. Otherwise, IndustriALL would suspend the Declaration on Social Rights and Industrial Relations at VW effective January 21, 2019, and convene a meeting of VW affiliates to determine "further actions including a media campaign in countries with VW plants, industrial actions and demonstrations, and other necessary actions to be continued until VW shall have withdrawn its legal challenge and entered into good faith collective bargaining negotiations with the UAW."[275] Sanches concluded the letter with the observation that "we would deeply regret such a step, because . . . the very good regulations at Volkswagen in the area of employment relations and the social dialog are basically highly valued by us and have for us in many instances exemplary character."[276]

On December 6, VW's group works council passed a resolution that stated, "We protest against the fact that Volkswagen has still not accepted the election of the maintenance workers and has not complied with related bargaining rights and thereby tries to use the anti-union legal environment in the USA to avoid entering into collective bargaining."[277]

Gunnar Kilian sent a reply to Valter Sanches dated January 15, 2019, expressly regretting IndustriALL's intension to terminate the Declaration on Social Rights and Industrial Relations at Volkswagen. He declared, "Volkswagen is clearly committed to recognizing and implementing these rights anchored throughout the world. That also applies to Volkswagen Chattanooga." Kilian invoked the original justification for challenging the skills trade unit, namely "Volkswagen has always believed that employee representation in Chattanooga should be consistent for all employees." He stated that "the Board of Management of the Volkswagen Group has repeatedly made it clear that it will accept the upcoming decisions and not take any further legal action" once the NLRB ruled again on the case. "In light of US legislation," he continued, "we offer the employee representation a unique opportunity of involvement in the US," namely the COE policy. The letter concluded with a statement of what IndustriALL would lose if it suspended the Declaration on Social Rights and Industrial Relations at Volkswagen: "I would also like to point out that we are currently consulting the World Group Works Council on a possible extension of this social charter, for example on supplier relations. It would be unfortunate if this important process would stall due to the termination of the Social Charter by IndustriALL."[278]

Valter Sanches replied on January 21, 2019, with a letter addressed to Gunnar Kilian titled "Suspension of the 'Declaration on Social Rights and Industrial Relations at Volkswagen'":

> We very much regret that Volkswagen is not prepared to comply with our main demand, namely to acknowledge the result of the election in the skilled workers area at the plant in Chattanooga form December 4, 2015 and to immediately discontinue the legal steps associated with it.
>
> Based on the unanimous decision of the Executive Committee of IndustriALL Global Union of 30.11.2018, we would like to inform you that we consider the "Declaration on Social Rights and Industrial Relations at Volkswagen" of 2002 suspended as of today. This is therefore not a cancellation of the agreement but a suspension until the issue at hand has been clarified.
>
> The right to freedom of association and collective bargaining is of such central importance to us that we cannot tolerate even the slightest disregard. . . .
>
> Let me stress once again that we are extremely sorry to have to take this step, as there is no doubt at all that employee rights and social dialogue at Volkswagen are generally far-reaching and positively developed and that the company is a very important partner for us.[279]

Volkswagen announced in early 2019 that the company would spend $800 million to build a second plant in Chattanooga that would produce electric vehicles. The Tennessee state government committed $50 million in state infrastructure upgrades, which helped to replenish the economic leverage of Tennessee political leaders over VW management.[280]

By January 2019, the UAW leadership's micro-unit strategy was on the verge of failure. International pressure had failed to change VW management's decision not to bargain with the skilled trades unit. It appeared to be simply a matter of time before the NLRB, which Trump administration appointees had come to dominate, declared the micro unit at Volkswagen Chattanooga as impermissible. Union proponents therefore began to consider new strategies.

The 2019 Recognition Election: Third Time Unlucky

The decision to ask for another recognition election for the entire Chattanooga plant arose out of the UAW's search for an alternative to VW management's success in impeding the establishment of a skilled mechanics unit and local management mistakes. Plant CEO Antonio Pinto did not engage with employees the way his predecessors had, which frustrated many, made the community organization engagement policy less effective, and reinvigorated interest in unionization among the production employees.

Things came to a head in mid-December 2018 when plant management announced in the plant newsletter the 2019 calendar for plant shutdowns and a new policy for personal time off (PTO).[281] In addition to the normally scheduled shutdowns from Christmas Eve to New Year's Day and during the week that includes the Fourth of July, management added December 23, 2018, and January 2–4, 2019, as shutdown days because of the preparations to start up the second assembly line that would make the Atlas SUV. Besides adding four shutdown days, management ended the "no pay, no penalty option," which allowed employees to take time off without pay during a shutdown to preserve vacation days, to mitigate the impact on production of employees taking off days; replacing it with a more restrictive policy requiring employees to take PTO days only during company-designated PTO periods.

Approximately forty-five employees led by UAW Local 42 members responded to the announcement by shutting down the assembly line and going to plant management to demand that it rescind the new PTO policy. After the impromptu meeting work resumed, and plant managers decided not to implement the changes to PTO. Volkswagen spokesperson Amanda Plecas put the best face on things by saying management realized that the changes had been communicated too late, and "We listened to them this morning."[282] That day, Local 42 leaders wrote up and distributed a flyer with the UAW logo on top:

> Today, several dozen of us marched to HR and demanded that they rescind their new forced PTO policy that was announced in the Jump-Start newsletter. This is time off that we have earned through our hard

work and countless hours in the shop, but the company has the nerve to tell us when we can take our own earned time? Right before Christmas, VW once again shows what we already knew: That they care more about making money than they do about us.

As a direct result of our actions, the Company has agreed that on January 2nd, 3rd, and 4th we will have the choice to use PTO or take no pay, no penalty. This action did gain positive changes, but the only real way to negotiate these terms and make the company accountable is a legally binding contract! Only when we come together as a group and rally around our common issues will our voices be heard.

Are you ready to stand together and have our voices be heard?

For more information please contact a member of your Local 42 Executive Board.[283]

The spontaneous challenge to the December 14 PTO announcement demonstrated that many employees had reached their limit when it came to management acting unilaterally, that they were willing to act, and that action could succeed. An employee observed in retrospect, "Volkswagen had done such a good job screwing up so many areas of the plant that there was a lot of reluctant momentum for a union, . . . not because they love the UAW, but because they think a union is the only means to change things for the better."[284]

The successful spontaneous action persuaded Local 42 officers and the UAW leadership in Detroit that it was time to begin laying the groundwork for a new recognition election. This drive would differ from the 2011–2014 effort in several respects. The focus of the campaign would be on the actual problems in the plant rather than on the creation of a works council. A works council was at best an abstraction for most employees, and the shortcomings of the community organization engagement policy diminished the value of a works council as a selling point for unionization. Without underlying legislation such as the German Works Constitution Act, it was difficult to see how creating a works council would be much of an improvement on the status quo. That said, UAW supporters would frequently point out that the Chattanooga plant was the only wholly owned VW facility worldwide that had no independent employee representation, which meant it could not engage with VW management from an autonomous position or participate as full members on the company's global works council.

The strategy for this recognition election was to do an "ambush drive," that is, to act quickly to leave VW management and external forces little time to mount opposition. The specifics of the drive followed from that choice. UAW leaders did not use "bargaining to organize" this time. There was no attempt to negotiate a neutrality agreement with VW management, and there was no request for a card-check procedure. As a result, there would be no waiting for VW management to grant card-check recognition, which proved debilitating in the 2011–2014 organizing drive. A quick campaign would not make foreign support a priority. Since foreign support did not produce success in the 2011–2014 organizing effort or at Nissan Canton in 2017, the impact of dropping it was judged to be minimal. Third, the UAW leadership in Detroit assigned a single seasoned staff member, Brian Rothenberg, to serve as an information point person who would respond rapidly to anything involving the drive.

The union dispatched organizers to Chattanooga in early 2019. On February 10, 2019, UAW president Gary Jones and organizing director Tracy Romero spoke in Chattanooga with about fifty employees, most of whom were hard-core union supporters. Romero laid out the challenge and the stakes:

> So, Gary [Jones] talked about the signing of the cards and the 65 percent. You know, we have benchmarks at the organizing department. All the organizers you met, they all know what those benchmarks are. There's a reason that those benchmarks are set. You know, there's a VOC [voluntary organizing committee] commitment that has to take place, there's a signing of a card; but it's not just me talking to my coworker and getting them to sign a card, right? Especially here; this has been going on for a long time. You guys have asked them to sign cards several times, right? It's not about that, it's about the commitment; that they're going to vote, "yes."
>
> When that right-to-work comes in town; you know, trust me, when I start flying back to Detroit, I'll be sharing a seat right next to them. They're coming in from DC; the politicians, they're coming in. The billboards, they're going up. The radio ads, they're coming after us. So, it's not just about signing that card. It's about knowing that they're willing to take action and to stand up and fight inside of that facility.[285]

The UAW officials took several actions to "remove the face" of the 2011–2014 drive to make it clear that this campaign would be different. This included giving the campaign its own slogan (It's Time) and logo (a stylized clock) as well as changing the location of the office in Chattanooga. UAW organizers created and posted several short videos on Local 42's Facebook page that addressed various employee concerns, such as forced overtime, the pension plan, and plant safety.[286]

As soon as word spread about a revival of organizing activities, plant management began to take actions to address long-standing employee criticisms. On

March 20, Volkswagen Chattanooga announced that production workers at all levels would receive a 50-cent wage increase per hour effective July 1, which would bring up the minimum by 3 percent to $16 and the maximum by two percent up to $23.50. A statement from plant CEO Antonio Pinto accompanied the announcement (which had not happened previously). Pinto said, "We want to motivate people in our workforce because we are very proud of them."[287] Pinto did not mention the nascent unionization drive. Plant management made several other changes that the Local 42 leadership had suggested in previous COE meetings, including lowering the temperature in the plant to 72 degrees, letting employees wear shorts, and going back to four ten-hour shifts per week rather than five eight-hour shifts.[288] These actions proved insufficient to slow the organizing drive, however.

On April 9, 2020, Local 42 president Steve Cochran used a press release and a video posted on the local's Facebook page to inform the public that the UAW had filed a petition for a new recognition election that day. Cochran, standing next to a highway outside of the plant, said,

> Greetings, sisters and brothers of the Chattanooga Volkswagen plant. Today, we have filed for an election for the workers to be represented by the United Auto Workers. You have worked hard. You've created this. You drove this. We've done it. You've done it. Now it's time. This is it. This is where we make our future. This is how we protect ourselves forever. Congratulations, and thank you! And thank everyone. We got this.[289]

The picture then faded to a light-blue background with the campaign slogan "It's Time" in simple white letters in the middle of the frame, followed by the UAW logo. The video post received over thirty comments, including several from other UAW locals, one from Germany, and one from the United Kingdom. The petition indicated that the UAW sought to hold the election on April 29 and 30. UAW officials stated that at least 65 percent of the employees had signed cards.[290]

In a press release, Cochran emphasized the unequal treatment of Chattanooga workers:

> Why are Chattanooga workers treated differently than even other auto assembly workers at plants like GM Spring Hill [Tennessee]? . . . Why are we in Chattanooga not treated like other VW employees around the world? Why in Chattanooga do we have to make suggestions, not sit down and bargain like every other VW plant?
>
> This isn't about politicians. It isn't about outsiders. It's about Chattanooga workers. We deserve the same rights as Spring Hill workers and every other VW worker in the world.[291]

The statement also provided a quote from Annette Stallion, a VW production worker, with a justification for a plant-wide vote. "Our maintenance workers voted to form a union and VW still refused to bargain. They said they would bargain if production and maintenance workers voted—so let's vote." Local 42 also launched a website for the campaign that included an authorization card and six areas where the UAW would focus: improving health insurance, raising health and safety standards, tightening seniority provisions, stopping favoritism, getting temporary workers hired as permanents sooner, and shortening the time it takes to get to the top of the wage scale.[292]

In a press conference the same day, Cochran said that "pressure from the workers" led Local 42 and the UAW leadership in Detroit to push for a second recognition election.[293] Cochran emphasized, "It's not about money. It's not about greed. . . . It's going to be respect and consistency. That's the two big things we want."[294] Ten new short videos of employees discussing a range of concerns were posted on the Local 42 Facebook page.[295] Cochran also expressed hope that there would be no repeat of the outside interference that was so prominent in the 2014 recognition election. Union leaders asked for the vote to take place only twenty days after the filing, which would help to minimize outside interventions. UAW spokesperson Brian Rothenberg said that the election should be "about Chattanooga workers and nobody else."[296]

The quick-election strategy was a credible choice, particularly considering the bad experience with the first organizing drive at the plant, but it did have shortcomings. The breadth and depth of support in the plant was shallow by some measures. The UAW organizing department typically requires at least 10 percent of the employees in the plant to belong to a voluntary organizing committee before proceeding. Only 60 out of 1,700 eligible workers were members of the Volkswagen Chattanooga voluntary organizing committee, however, which is 3.5 percent. Organizers also prefer to have more time to assess the firmness of the support of employees who have signed cards than they had in this instance. Moreover, the decision to act fast to preserve surprise did not leave UAW leaders sufficient time to "disclaim" interest in the skilled trades bargaining unit (i.e., formally withdraw the claim to represent the skilled trades unit and drop the unfair labor practice actions over VW's refusal to bargain with that unit), which would prove problematic because the skilled trades employees were also included in the wall-to-wall unit proposed in the petition.

The quick filing for a recognition election did succeed in catching VW management by surprise. Management's initial reaction was to "remain neutral on this topic," which was what it did in the first two organizing drives.[297] VW spokesperson Amanda Plecas said that management was reviewing the petition, but it was too soon to comment further.

Outside union opponents, in contrast, did not hesitant to opine. Patrick Semmens, vice president of the NRWLDF, expressed surprise that the UAW went forward with the petition, "given that so much of the union hierarchy is wrapped up in the ongoing union corruption prosecution in Detroit." NRWLDF attorney John Radabaugh, who had been a member of the NLRB, used the same argument that outside groups used in the first organizing drive to justify getting involved; that is, VW management's neutral position meant that "one major source of information is essentially silent—the employer. Who's going to provide information to employees?"[298]

Emails with the subject line "UAW and Unions" began circulating among aides of Governor Bill Lee on the day Local 42 leaders filed for a recognition election. On April 12, VW management reached out to the governor's office. VWGOA vice president David Geanacopoulos emailed Governor Lee's chief of staff, Blake Harris, to brief him on "how we are handling the recently announced UAW petition."[299]

On April 16, an NLRB administrative law judge held a hearing in Chattanooga on Local 42's petition. The day before the hearing, UAW lawyers announced that Local 42 had held a vote among the skilled trades employees and that they approved disclaiming their unit, but the union had not dropped the pending unfair labor practice charges against VW for refusing to bargain.[300]

In the hearing, Littler Mendelson lawyers representing VW management used the late disclaimer (which the NLRB had yet to accept) and the still-pending unfair labor practice charges to the company's advantage. Research has shown that employees are less likely to vote for union representation when an election is delayed.[301] The lawyers filed documents asking the NLRB to stay the recognition election because the one-year ban on new elections specified in the NLRA was still in effect for the skilled trades unit, since an administrative law judge had not yet accepted the disclaimer and the unfair labor practice cases had not been withdrawn. Michael Schoenfeld, an Atlanta-based attorney the UAW had hired, objected to the request for a stay. "Volkswagen has concocted a captious last-minute challenge. . . . Its desperation is evident, as there is no well-founded reason to not proceed to election in the wall-to-wall unit."[302] The administrative law judge did not dismiss out of hand VW's argument but instead gave the attorneys from both sides a week to submit briefs. It was clear at that point that a recognition election would not happen at the end of April, as UAW leaders had first proposed.[303]

A day later, VW rolled out a new aggressively anti-union strategy, which plant management had developed with the assistance of Littler Mendelson consultants. VWGOA president and CEO Scott Keogh and plant head Antonio Pinto issued a "Special Communication" that supervisors read at the start-up meeting for each shift. The company also sent it to employees and posted it around the plant.[304]

Colleagues,

The National Labor Relations Board (NLRB) has notified the company that the United Auto Workers (UAW) has petitioned for a secret-ballot election of eligible hourly production and maintenance employees.

We were surprised by the timing of the filing, considering our recent announcements and continued investments in Chattanooga and Tennessee. We've heard the concerns that our workers have raised in an open dialogue and we've responded with improvements in working conditions: we've adjusted shift work, we've reduced overtime to have more predictability, and we've raised wages.

We intend to continue that open dialogue but we believe we can achieve more for us all by continuing that open dialogue directly.

We will respect our employees' right to petition and vote and will remain neutral throughout this process. We hope everyone will take the time to inform themselves about the relevant facts before casting a vote.

Please note that there are a few differences between this election and the ones in 2014 and 2015:

- The petition for the election was submitted by the UAW, not the company.
- There is no Election Agreement between the UAW and Volkswagen.
- The election will be for *both* production and maintenance employees.

The UAW has requested the NLRB hold the election as soon as possible with a target of April 29 and 30, though this has not yet been confirmed by the NLRB and may still change.

The company *will* hold special information sessions and provide additional communication in the coming weeks. In the meantime, we have attached a summary of our expectations as we move through this process. Please take time to review it in full. As always, if you have any questions, please feel free to contact Human Resources.

The UAW's official response was resolute. "Volkswagen might think that if they stall and delay, we will give up. But we will continue to work for a seat at the table, the same as every other Volkswagen worker around the world. . . . After all these years, we know the issues and have all the information we need to make a decision." Local 42's website accused management of "stall tactics," "game playing," and "double speak." It included the demand that VW "Let Chattanooga Workers vote!" An employee reacted to the VW Special Communication scathingly. "Passive aggressive is their style. . . . 'Why would you unionize? We are family. Boo hoo.' . . . [It's a] very abusive family, where they play the victim when called out."[305] That said, the delay was a setback for the UAW. It gave plant management more time to develop a countercampaign and created more doubt among workers about the ability of the UAW to prevail.

Outside intervention escalated immediately after the UAW filed the petition. Richard Berman, a former labor lawyer for the US Chamber of Commerce who resided in New York, established the Center for Union Facts (CUF) in Washington, D.C., to undertake a media campaign against the UAW. Berman had the nickname "Dr. Evil" because of his previous lobbying efforts against groups such as Mothers Against Drunk Driving. The CUF's first action was to take out a full-page advertisement in the Chattanooga *Times Free Press*, the *Detroit Free Press*, and the *Detroit News* that read "Think the UAW has workers' best interests in mind? Think again. Multiple union officials pleaded guilty in a scheme to enrich themselves with worker training funds. The union has paid more than $1.5 million of members' dues to defend itself in the investigation."[306] CUF spokesperson Charlyce Bozzello announced the launch of a new website, www.UAWInvestigation.com, to publicize corruption allegations. CUF also rented billboards to post anti-union messages.

Marsha Blackburn, Bob Corker's successor in the US Senate, also criticized the recognition election using language that continued the othering of the UAW. "We don't need union bosses in Detroit telling Tennessee what's best for our workers." Brian Rothenberg was quick to respond. "Where was Senator Blackburn when Chattanooga workers had to scramble to arrange child care because of last-minute overtime notifications? . . . Why would any politician not want Chattanooga workers to be treated the same and be able to bargain as every VW worker in the world and even Tennesseans in Spring Hill do? Why, Senator?"[307]

US representative Chuck Fleischmann, a Republican who represented the district where the VW plant was located, told the Chattanooga Rotary Club "I really think Volkswagen is better served and the suppliers are better served with the employers and employees working that out on their own. . . . I just think that some of the labor union tactics have been very disadvantageous to industries in other parts of the world. That's why they're here."[308]

Political intervention intensified when the new Tennessee governor, Bill Lee, visited VW's Chattanooga factory on April 29. Lee was a Republican who owned a construction company. Plant management did not invite media, nor did it give them access during Lee's visit. The governor described the visit as on his "own time."[309] Spokesperson Amanda Plecas said that the governor decided to visit on his one hundredth day in office and that it "was not union related."[310] The visit quickly became controversial, however, when the governor expressed his opinion regarding the unionization drive. At the twelve-minute mark Lee said,

> I know you all have an important vote that is coming up; that there is [*sic*] differences of opinion around that. I do believe, based on my personal experience working with hundreds of skilled-trades people over 35 years of working, that every workplace has challenges. I also believe that your voice, and your representing your challenges and the things that you want to see improved in your workplace—my experience is that when I have a direct relationship with you, the worker, and you're working for me, that's when the relationship works best.[311]

At that point, some workers booed the governor while others cheered him. One shouted, "What's the difference between Spring Hill and here?" Lee's response to the growing agitation was "I respect your differences of opinion but just felt compelled to share my opinion."[312]

That day, a statement from Local 42 appeared on Facebook topped by a picture of the governor at the Spring Hill GM plant shaking hands with the head of the plant's UAW local:

> Governor Lee visited our plant today on his 100th day in office and addressed the day shift. He started off great, sharing his vision of how to move Tennessee forward. But then he tried to influence our votes by suggesting it would be best to have direct communication instead of voting yes for a binding contract with the company. His message was not well received. We know what direct communication means to Volkswagen. It means "I'll get back to you."
>
> One question the Governor ignored was why Spring Hill GM workers can have their union, but Chattanooga VW workers should not. After all, the state of Tennessee has supported the Spring Hill plant with millions of dollars of assistance over the years.
>
> LET CHATTANOOGA VW WORKERS DECIDE. VOLKSWAGEN MUST STOP STALLING. WE DEMAND A VOTE![313]

A lively and lengthy online discussion followed, with close to forty participants. One asked, "Who was the idiot that was shouting at the governor? We don't need his type." Some agreed, arguing that disrespect was counterproductive. Others replied that the governor disrespected Chattanooga employees by taking a side.

The day after Governor Lee spoke at the plant, a press release declared the revival of the anti-union organization Southern Momentum and announced a campaign called "No Way UAW" that included a website (https://noway.uaw.com/)

and featured statements from plant employees. The site quoted VW employee Jeremy Metzger: "Like the governor shared with us this week, there are things in every workplace that employees wish were different. But the UAW is not the answer." VW employee Brian Dyke's statement was that "the UAW continues to peddle 'fake news' inside our plant, but the facts speak for themselves. We are working hard to educate our colleagues about the damage it would cause if we invite such a corrupt Detroit-based union into our workplace, and we have been encouraged by the response we have received so far." VW employee Keri Menendez said, "The UAW is promising the sun, moon and stars but their track record shows that many of the plants they represent go out of business, particularly foreign-owned companies. We do not want them here and are working to educate our fellow members on the real UAW, not the false narrative the union is peddling." The release also had a quote from Southern Momentum's éminence grise, local labor lawyer Maury Nicely: "The UAW and its track record of corruption and discord was a bad fit for Chattanooga and Volkswagen in 2014 and it is a bad fit now."[314] Nicely was a close friend of VW's counsel in Chattanooga, Ian Leavy. Questions again arose regarding Southern Momentum's funding. Nicely said funds came from VW workers and Chattanooga residents. Critics charged that east Tennessee business owners bankrolled the organization. That same day, the CUF posted a new anti-UAW video on YouTube.[315]

The absence of a neutrality agreement and the reliance on Littler Mendelson led VW management to take a sharply different approach to this organizing drive compared to the first unionization effort. In the first organizing drive, management did endeavor to make it clear to line supervisors that the company's position was neutrality, although it did not always succeed in enforcing compliance. This time, line supervisors read prepared anti-union statements to employees at shift start-up meetings and passed out anti-union flyers. One listed four recent closings at facilities that the UAW had organized. The second suggested that employees could lose bonuses and benefits—in particular the popular below-market auto leasing program—at the bargaining table if the employees voted in favor of the UAW. (Nissan, which also employed Littler Mendelson consultants, used the auto lease claim effectively to dampen support for unionization.)

Plant management added a section to "JumpStart" called "Sidewall." It contained arguments against unionization. Assistant managers whom the employees had not seen previously began to appear on the shop floor to monitor employee interactions. Employees suspected that they were from Littler Mendelson.[316] UAW organizers (who now numbered forty) and pro-union plant employees made house calls, which upset some employees. Disagreements over the tactic led Antonio Pinto to include a statement in the May 1 edition of "Jump-

Start" in an attempt to referee between pro- and anti-union employees, but Pin-to's statement included criticism of house calls:

> Dear Colleagues:
>
> People have very strong feelings about the UAW and the future of our plant. Everyone is entitled to his or her own opinion, and everyone is entitled to state it. Period.
>
> It has come to my attention that some of our employees have been victim of extremely distasteful bullying regarding this issue. I have also heard that employees are being followed to their homes and confronted about their views. I am tremendously disappointed.
>
> Let us agree or disagree, but let us agree or disagree respectfully.
>
> This is our future. There is a lot at stake. Everyone is entitled to his or her voice without threat or fear of harassment.
>
> Thank you.

On May 3, the NLRB granted VW management's request for a stay to the rec-ognition election in a two-to-one vote.[317] The single-sentence opinion—"The Em-ployer's request to stay all proceedings is granted."—provided no justification for the decision and set no expiration date.[318] A determined reaction appeared on Lo-cal 42's website. "Despite VW's legal maneuvers, we will not give up and will con-tinue to fight for our dignity and respectful treatment on the job. Why is VW so scared of us voting to form our union?"[319]

VW management released a reserved statement:

> We respect our colleagues' right to decide on representation. Any elec-tion for the Chattanooga plant should include both production and maintenance employees. This is why we appealed the UAW's petition for an election for only the maintenance employees in December 2015. Before we proceed, we asked the National Labor Relations Board to en-sure that the pending NLRB decision is properly resolved first.[320]

Southern Momentum, in contrast, issued a triumphant press release that quoted Volkswagen Chattanooga employee Tom Haney: "This is a victory for Volkswagen workers. . . . We will continue to educate our colleagues on the neg-ative impact the UAW would have on our factory and remain confident that if another election occurs in the future, workers will vote no and soundly reject the UAW." The statement concluded with a quote from Maury Nicely:

> We could not be more pleased with this decision and are glad the regional director halted the UAW's attempt to push through a quick election before

workers had the opportunity to mobilize and make their voices heard. . . .
Clearly the UAW's attempt to disavow its own supporters in a dues-
and-membership grabbing ploy backfired. If I have said it once, I'll say
it a thousand times: the UAW was wrong for Chattanooga and Volkswagen in 2014 and it is wrong for us today.[321]

On the following Monday, May 6, the Detroit headquarters of the UAW released
an additional statement on behalf of Local 42:

> Let Chattanooga workers vote. After insisting for the last four years that
> they would only agree to a vote of all production and maintenance
> workers, Volkswagen has now blocked just such a vote. VW's manipula-
> tion of the NLRB process to halt a vote of its workers is a travesty.
>
> Free, democratic election are a cornerstone of American life, whether
> it's the PTA or President of the United States. After all these years, why in
> the world is it okay to deny Chattanooga workers their vote of yes or no?
>
> Volkswagen's actions in this matter are the definition of duplicity.
> In the wake of the recent dieselgate scandal, it is shocking that Volks-
> wagen continues to employ such a strategy.
>
> Chattanooga workers have a simple message to the politicians and
> political appointees in Washington, D.C., and the Volkswagen cor-
> porate brass—Let us vote![322]

Maury Nicely fired off a response on behalf of Southern Momentum on the same
day:

> Federal labor law clearly states that a new election cannot be held at a
> plant with an unresolved election pending before the National Labor Re-
> lations Board. . . . The UAW either knew this fact before filing a petition
> for a new election and is intentionally misleading workers or is wholly
> incompetent. The UAW is again showing its true self in a sad attempt to
> collect dues to be sent to Detroit. The choice is clear: the UAW was wrong
> for Volkswagen in 2014 and it is wrong for our workers today.[323]

Also on that day, Bob Rolfe, commissioner of the Tennessee Department of
Economic and Community Development, weighed in on the recognition election
via an opinion piece in the Chattanooga *Times Free Press*:

> As the UAW seeks yet another vote at the same facility, I believe it is
> part of my job as the state's chief recruiting officer to share with you
> how this could negatively affect our state's recruitment efforts. . . .
> I truly believe that allowing unionization to occur at Volkswagen could
> negatively impact the livelihoods of thousands more Tennesseans. It is

my hope that the employees will once again strongly reject the union so that, together, we can ensure Chattanooga continues to be the city that you are proud to call home.[324]

Rolfe's piece was unusual because his predecessors had avoided commenting on contentious matters in general and the two previous union recognition elections in particular.

In response to the stay on the election, Local 42 leaders asked for a hearing in order to withdraw the allegations of unfair labor practices against VW. An NLRB Region 10 panel accepted the withdrawal on May 9, which cleared the way for the local to file a petition to ask the NLRB to lift the stay on an election.[325] In response, Littler Mendelson lawyers representing VW management filed a new brief with the NLRB. It repeated the argument that there should be no election in the Chattanooga plant until the NLRB had resolved all issues involving the skilled trades unit.[326] On May 13, AFL-CIO general counsel Craig Becker sent a letter to Roxanne Rothschild, NLRB executive secretary, and sent copies to the ranking members of the House and Senate committees that handle labor affairs. The letter argued that maintaining the stay on an election at the Chattanooga plant "clearly suggests that the Board is not acting as a neutral decision maker." The AFL-CIO also sponsored a petition on the Action Network—an open platform supported by progressive organizations, including the AFL-CIO, to promote progressive causes—calling on VW management to "treat your workers in Tennessee with respect!" VW management's legal strategy had effectively thwarted the UAW plan to hold a quick election. UAW spokesperson Brian Rothenberg denounced actions of the company. "It's sad how Volkswagen's strategy of using high-priced legal games can stand in the way of the right to vote for Chattanooga workers. Chattanooga workers deserve to know from VW, how much money have you spent on these lawyers to try to stop us from having a voice?"[327]

The delay expanded the opportunity for a range of actors to attempt to influence the organizing effort. US representative Chuck Fleischmann weighed in again:

> Tennessee has a proud tradition of being a right to work state. I think one of the reasons it is one of the greatest economic magnets for business in the country is that we do not have a major labor union presence in Tennessee. This is going to be something though that the men and women who work there will have to make that decision. I do hope that they do not select to be a part of the UAW. I think that's rather disadvantageous.[328]

The 2019 election included a negative campaign against VW for the first time. Joe DiSano, a Michigan Democratic political consultant, established the Center for VW Facts (CVWF) in mid-May. DiSano had a tarnished past. He once had been forced to issue public apologies as part of the settlement of a defamation suit in a Michigan statehouse election. The CVWF's Facebook page described the organization as "a nonpartisan group of concerned citizens fighting corruption with the truth and transparency,"[329] but the intent behind creating the CVWF was to counterbalance the CUF and other anti-UAW organizations with information critical of VW management. The CVWF had a web page and released newspaper, radio, and television ads. The CVWF focused on the diesel scandal and accusations that "Volkswagen has engaged in a deceptive campaign to discourage employees at Volkswagen's Chattanooga factory from joining the United Auto Workers."[330] Some Chattanooga employees reacted negatively to the CVWF's criticisms of VW as unnecessarily running down the company's reputation.[331]

The CVWF website stated that it was "not affiliated with the United Auto Workers or any labor organization." In fact, UAW president Gary Jones and his chief of staff Mike Stone—who had previously served as director of the UAW's Michigan Community Action Program, the political-legislative arm of the union—hired DiSano without informing anyone else in the union. Jim Schmitz, a lead UAW organizer in Chattanooga, was livid on the day that NLRB representatives counted the ballots when he found out what Jones and Stone had done because organizers and union supporters had repeatedly denied that the UAW had anything to do with the CVWF, and DiSano's ham-fisted tactics did more harm than good in the campaign.

Critics of the UAW point to a failure to engage with the local community as a flaw in both plant-wide organizing drives.[332] A prime example of this occurred on May 20. The Chattanooga Area Central Labor Council hosted a rally in support of the UAW's organizing drive at Miller Park in downtown Chattanooga. Representatives from seventeen area local unions and the Chattanooga AFL-CIO sponsored the event. A flyer advertising the rally was on the Local 42 Facebook page, but UAW organizers did little else to promote it. The turnout was disappointing as a result. Just seventy people showed up in total, and only a handful of those were VW workers. Local 42 recording secretary Billy Quigg tried to explain away the low participation by saying that many of his colleagues had to be at work, but the excuse rang hollow.[333] Among the seventy, however, were a few unwanted attendees. A small group from the CUF attended with a sign that read "It's time for the UAW to fix its culture of corruption."[334] Other criticisms of the UAW's effort included organizers not mapping the plant's supply chain to find vulnerabilities and failing to produce a complete and reliable assessment of which employees backed the union and the firmness of that support.[335]

UAW leaders made one attempt to use countervailing political pressure to influence VW management. US senators Gary Peters (Michigan), Debbie Stabenow (Michigan), and Sherrod Brown (Ohio)—all Democrats—sent a letter dated May 21, 2019, to VWGOA CEO Scott Keogh to urge him "to immediately drop any efforts to oppose or postpone the election" at the Chattanooga plant. The letter questioned the sincerity of VW management's professed commitment to neutrality and asked Keogh to respond to eleven detailed questions within seven days. VW spokesperson Mark Clothier confirmed that the company received the letter and would reply,[336] but the letter failed to change VW's position and practices. Maury Nicely's reaction to the letter was a caustic non sequitur: "Maybe Senator Brown should focus on Ohio, where the UAW has driven many auto plants out of business and put thousands of his constituents out of work."[337]

On May 22, 2019, in a two-to-one decision, the NLRB accepted VW's legal argument and dismissed the petition for a recognition election because unfair labor practice cases had still been pending for the skilled trades unit when the union filed it. The decision explicitly blamed solely the UAW for causing the delay in holding the recognition election because the union "filed its petition during the certification year" for the skilled trades unit. Board member Lauren McFerran dissented, writing that the majority's decision "is inconsistent with Board precedent, undermines the policies of the National Labor Relations Act, and defies common sense. . . . 'Heads, the employer wins; tails, the union loses' cannot be the Board's new motto."[338]

The ruling did contain some relatively good news for the UAW. Since in the interim the union leadership had disclaimed the skilled trades unit and the NLRB Region 10 panel had accepted the local's withdrawal of the unfair labor practice allegations against VW, the legal issues were now resolved. Hence, the NLRB made clear in the majority decision that the "dismissal of the petition is without prejudice to the Petitioner's right to immediately file a new petition."[339]

Maury Nicely used the decision to denounce the UAW again on behalf of Southern Momentum. "Workers should not put their faith in a union that refuses to follow the law, blames others for their mistakes, repeatedly attacks an employer who has meant so much to this community, and has a track record of failure and divisiveness." The Southern Momentum statement quoted VW employee Tony Walker: "This is yet further proof that the UAW is dishonest, does not care about us and is only interested in lining its own pockets." The UAW issued a statement criticizing Volkswagen again for continuing "to use legal games to aggressively deny its workers the right to vote for years." But, the statement continued, "We will be on the NLRB's doorstep immediately to file again and demand a speedy election."[340] UAW spokesperson Brian Rothenberg went on offense and said, "Chattanooga workers deserve to know from VW, how much money have you spent on these lawyers to try to stop us from having a voice?"[341] The new petition, which UAW officials filed within hours of the NLRB decision, asked for a recognition election on June 12, 13, and 14. VW management accepted these dates at an NLRB hearing nine days later.[342]

Once UAW representatives filed the second petition for an election, plant management rolled out its now well-prepared campaign against the union. The company opened a well-crafted website that included not only the logistics of the vote but also VW's position, video testimonials about the advantages of the status quo, and a resources site.[343] On a page titled "Volkswagen's Position," management made clear its preference that employees not vote for UAW representation, which is a sharp departure from the 2014 election agreement with the UAW. The key sentence was "We have accomplished many great things working directly together and we prefer to continue our direct relationship with you, working together as one team."[344] "One team" was management's slogan for the anti-union effort. The page included the company's definition of neutrality, which also differed markedly from the 2014 and even the 2015 election agreement:

> To be clear, neutrality does not mean that Volkswagen must be silent in the face of attacks on the Company. Neutrality also does not mean the Company is prohibited from responding to misrepresentations and promises made to our employees. Volkswagen has a right and an obligation to provide balanced factual information relating to the important decision employees face in the upcoming vote.

The "Working at Volkswagen" page included a section titled "Listening" where VW management took credit for eleven actions—such as the move to fixed shifts, change of the start time for night shifts, hourly and salary round tables, inclusion of temporary workers in all team meetings, self-nomination as an option for team leaders' selection process, and preservation of "no pay, no penalty" for shutdowns—even though most of these actions originated as Local 42 suggestions under the COE policy. The page also praised the COE process as a reason not to support unionization, asserting that "Volkswagen is perhaps the only major employer in the United States to implement such an inclusive and open policy for its employees."[345]

The website also had a page titled "About the UAW" that highlighted dues and described membership as an enforceable contract that subjects members to an internal trial and punishment if they violate it.[346] Other pages stated that "it is hard to decertify a union,"[347] "the actual law about how collective bargaining works states that employees could just as likely end up with the same or less than they have now,"[348] and "We do know that a European style works council is unlawful under US labor law, and if the UAW wins the election, there cannot be a European style works council at the Chattanooga plant."[349] All of these assertions were technically accurate but were cast in the worst possible light in order to dissuade employees from voting for union representation.

On May 24, Volkswagen announced in a letter to all employees a major action in the union-avoidance effort: the departure of the unpopular plant CEO Antonio Pinto. Frank Fischer, the Chattanooga plant's first CEO, would come back to replace him. VW spokesperson Amanda Plecas said that the change had nothing to do with the recognition election,[350] but replacing an unpopular plant CEO right before an election is an action that union-avoidance consultancies frequently recommend.[351] VW management also removed three of the most belligerent line managers, which is another common union-avoidance tactic. It later surfaced that the company did not fire the three but instead placed them on medical leave, which meant they were eligible to return.

Many Volkswagen Chattanooga workers, including union activists, liked and respected Fischer because of his open demeanor and record of adhering to the neutrality agreement during the 2014 recognition election despite protestations from anti-union forces. A Local 42 flyer hailed Fischer's return while making the case that a change in personnel was not enough to improve things at Volkswagen Chattanooga:

> A SINCERE "WELCOME BACK TO CHATTANOOGA" TO FRANK FISCHER AS OUR NEW PRESIDENT AND CEO. Many of us know Frank and have chatted with him on the floor. He's a good man.
>
> Volkswagen managers come and go. Some are effective; some are not. But those of us who build the cars and maintain the plant are here for the long haul. We come to work day in and day out, year in and year out, and hope to retire from this plant with our health and with a secure future.
>
> SO NO MATTER HOW SKILLED OR POPULAR ANY ONE INDIVIDUAL IS, WE NEED AN ONGOING AGREEMENT WITH VOLKSWAGEN THAT INSURES RESPECTFUL TREATMENT OF EMPLOYEES, AND HAS CLEAR PROCEDURES FOR THINGS LIKE SWITCHING SHIFTS OR SEEKING A DIFFERENT JOB IN THE PLANT. It's not about giving Volkswagen another chance, it's about finally fixing the problems.
>
> After all, we never know who or what tomorrow will bring.
>
> FOR A SAY IN OUR FUTURE
> VOTE YES[352]

Fischer held two all-plant captive-audience speeches on May 28. He received a standing ovation when he greeted the first shift. Fischer once again toed the company line. This time, however, the line had changed to opposition to unionization at the Chattanooga plant. Fischer acknowledged that morale at the plant had fallen over the years and promised to make changes, for example, ending last-minute impositions of mandatory overtime. He then attacked the UAW, blaming labor unrest for the 1988 closure of VW's Westmoreland plant despite the consensus at the time of closure that management mistakes rather than employment relations were to blame. He also linked the unionization effort with Joe DiSano's anti-VW campaign, saying "people that would attack Volkswagen, they attack each of us. They hurt our brand. In the end, they also hurt our sales. This happened also at Westmoreland and it is not supposed to happen again in Chattanooga."[353]

Fischer posted a letter personally apologizing for the treatment of employees under previous management and promised to fix things. Plant management followed up Fischer's speech with daily anti-union sessions at each shift start-up. Line managers distributed flyers highlighting recent closures of UAW-organized plants and the UAW corruption scandal as it continued to unfold.[354] Supervisors pressured workers who wore pro-union stickers or UAW-branded safety glasses to remove them. Some responded by wearing UAW temporary tattoos and turning their backs when supervisors attacked the union in the start-up briefing. Security guards at times harassed pro-union employees distributing flyers in the parking lot.[355]

At the end of May, the UAW started running a professionally produced sixty-second television ad with actual Volkswagen Chattanooga employees speaking in succession as they focused on the problems in the plant:

> My frustration has grown. Schedules change. Families in a bind. Our time's disrespected. We have no say. No say. No say at all. For Chattanooga VW workers, it's time for a change. We local Chattanooga workers deserve better. We deserve a voice in our future. It's time for a say over our schedules. It's time for fair and simple bonuses. It's time for respect in the workplace. It's time [repeated five times]. It's time to put Chattanooga workers first.[356]

In the end, Local 42 posted another series of videos on YouTube and Facebook of Chattanooga employees making the case for voting "yes."[357] Some ads featured employees who voted "no" in 2014 explaining why they would be voting "yes" this time.[358] These ads ran repeatedly during the National Basketball Association championship and on screens at gas station pumps near the plant.

Southern Momentum responded with its own radio and television ads. The first TV spot was a statement from VW employee Carol Gruber that played off the UAW's "it's time" slogan of the organizing drive:

> If it wasn't for Volkswagen, I wouldn't have what I have today. My children wouldn't have what they have today. I can't risk losing all of

that. My kids can't risk losing all of that. I've got three fixin' to go to college. Am I going to go flip burgers for $24 an hour? After eight years? No, no I'm not. It's time for the attacks to stop. It's time to build that quality car that gives us a paycheck in our bank account every two weeks. It's time to stop so we can move forward and build the quality car that we know we can build. I am Volkswagen. And when you're attacking Volkswagen, you're attacking me, my friends, my family."[359]

Another video posted on YouTube claimed that the UAW was "attacking VW and trying to strong arm workers" because "as UAW plants close across the country, they're desperate for new members. Now they're coming to Chattanooga to take money out of your paycheck." The video ended with the admonition "Send a message to this out-of-state special interest: this is our plant, our community, and we're proud of it. Vote no on UAW."[360] Southern Momentum also ran radio ads with a similar message.[361] One Southern Momentum ad included a worker saying "You continuously are badgered every day. You can't even pump gas anymore without hearing the commercials. Just back off."[362]

Facebook's imperative to earn profits brought the third-party anti-union effort to a new level of sophistication. Jeremy B. Merrill, a news apps developer at ProPublica, discovered that Facebook was data-mining Chattanoogans' activity to discover who was interested in the UAW and then sold access to those individuals to the CUF. The CUF then pushed out ads on Facebook to them with negative stories about the individual behind CVWF, Joe DiSano.[363]

The VW recognition election continued to attract the attention of numerous local politicians. On May 30, Governor Lee again weighed in against the UAW. In an interview at a Chattanooga television station Lee said, "Reality is that it's more difficult to recruit companies to states that have higher levels of organized activity.... I think it's in the best interest of Volkswagen—and really for the economics of our state—that the Volkswagen plant stays a merit shop."[364] A week later, Republican state senator Bo Watson and state representative Robin Smith both said it would be harder to get state subsidies for the Chattanooga plant if the UAW were to win the recognition election. UAW spokesperson Brian Rothenberg challenged the Republican legislators' claim, pointing out that the unionized Spring Hill GM plant had received significant amounts of state aid.[365] Chattanooga mayor Andy Berke, a Democrat, expressed his support for the UAW,[366] but Hamilton County mayor Jim Coppinger, a Republican, urged VW employees to reject the union.[367]

The original UAW strategy was to focus on problems in the plant and have a quick recognition election. This left little room for international cooperation. VW management's counterstrategy of delaying the election changed the calculus. It gave employee representatives in Germany a reason and an opportunity to engage, and they used it. IG Metall chair Jürgen Hofmann wrote a letter of support to Volkswagen Chattanooga employees dated June 4, which was posted on Local 42's Facebook page. The letter was in English. Unlike the letters from 2011–2014, however, which UAW officials routinely reviewed and edited, this letter appeared to have been composed and translated without the assistance of a native English speaker:

> IG Metall stands on your side in your continued efforts to get a voice and a say on your working conditions in VW plant Chattanooga.
>
> You have been trying to organize for many years now. You have stayed strong and you have grown stronger despite many obstacles. You have our full respect!
>
> Now is the time for the final decision if you as a team join the hundreds of thousands organized workers all over the world, whether in Germany or in the UK, in Hungary or in Slovakia, in South Africa or in Brazil. . . .
>
> By joining hands and forces with your teammates in the US and abroad your voice and influence becomes more relevant.
>
> In the globalized economy that Volkswagen is a part of you need access to information about VW's activities and plans in its worldwide operations. You need to be organized to get this information.
>
> A binding collective agreement is a condition for job security. By voting to organize you vote for security!
>
> We support you in your efforts to get a collective voice in the company's dealings.
>
> On behalf of IG Metall I wish you success and a fair election.[368]

On June 6, Bernd Osterloh and Johan Järvklo sent a letter to Volkswagen Chattanooga employees as chair and general secretary of VW's European and Global Works Councils with even more dodgy prose:

> We write this letter on behalf of the European and Global Group Works Council of the Volkswagen Group.
>
> We were happy to hear about the decision to go for an election of an employee-representation at the Volkswagen-plant in Chattanooga from 12th of June–14th of June 2019.
>
> We all are aware of the long prehistory of this election and we all know about the partial [sic] intensive legal and political disputes in the run-up to it.
>
> Now it is up to us! Let's look ahead and get a mandate of the workforce by achieving a convincing election result for the UAW.

As in the past we will continue to fight for this side by side with you.

Therefore we want to use this opportunity to express our solidarity to you. We strongly support you in building up and establish [*sic*] a strong employee-representation for our colleagues at Volkswagen in Chattanooga. In our eyes, the UAW is the natural partner to achieve this common goal.

We know about the big challenges directly linked to this election and we are aware of the legal situation on-site, which makes it always hard to build up a union-based employee-representation in a company. That is why we all will have to ensure, that everybody is playing by democratic rules.

This means to ensure a neutral behavior of the company-side. In the past we often had to acknowledge a lack of objectivity and neutrality in this matter by the company and that there have been different attempts of influence. The European and Global Group Works Council of the Volkswagen Group has got a clear expectation in this matter to the company itself as well as to the responsible members of the management. We will strongly have a look, that any attacks of [*sic*] democratic rights of the workforce to influence the election will not take place again.

All together we will do everything possible to give a voice to our colleagues in Chattanooga and to be part of the European and Global Group Works Council of the Volkswagen Group: Against any resistance and as an integral part of the Volkswagen Family with all its union-based identity.

Over 600,000 employees out of the Volkswagen Group are looking to Chattanooga at the moment and they are all looking forward to welcome [*sic*] their colleagues in the European and Global Group Works Council of the Volkswagen Group as soon as possible.

Brothers and sisters, we wish you all the best for the upcoming elections: For the employees and workers at Volkswagen in Chattanooga, for Volkswagen and the whole Volkswagen-Family![369]

These letters—written in international trade union bureaucratese and sounding like they came straight out of google translate—elicited little more than head-scratching from most Chattanooga employees and had no discernible impact on the campaign. The letter from Osterloh and Järvklo vowed that there would be no further attacks on democratic rights but failed to identify specific consequences that would result if attacks continued.

German employee representatives did go beyond letters in their effort to help the UAW. IG Metall officials offered to send organizers again, but the UAW leaders declined because they "were just so gun shy because of what happened in 2014," and they "wanted the conversations in the plant to be about the issues inside Chattanooga and not about the German organizer that was in town."[370] VW Global Works Council general secretary Johan Järvklo made a support video for Local 42. Osterloh and Hofmann, as members of the Volkswagen supervisory board, put the Chattanooga union recognition election on the agenda. At the meeting they made four requests, which the board formally adopted, but none stopped the company from continuing to use union-avoidance practices to thwart a UAW victory in the recognition election. For example, the supervisory board gave Chattanooga "the clear directive . . . to stay neutral in the election," but plant managers claimed that all their actions were neutral because they did not violate US labor law. Hofmann and Osterloh also persuaded the board to require that plant management stop working directly with Littler Mendelson consultants. The plant management's response was to have the consultants move out of the factory and into a nearby hotel but to otherwise continue the relationship.[371]

Local 42 received more than fifty messages expressing support from twenty countries.[372] IG Metall members from Berlin-Brandenburg, Emden, and Hannover in Germany and autoworkers and their organizations at Volkswagen plants in Germany, Brazil, Hungary, and Mexico posted messages of encouragement on Local 42's Facebook page.[373] Several locals of the UAW and other domestic unions expressed their support. The messages raised the spirits of some union supporters, but none changed management behavior.

The delay extending the length of the organizing drive to nine weeks worked out fortuitously for VW management. Family Day at the plant, which was on Sunday, June 9, came three days before the election period began. Over five thousand people went to the factory grounds for free musical entertainment, food, games, blue "One Team: I Am Volkswagen" T-shirts, and other giveaways. The occasion boosted a positive image of the company and plant management. Many employees wore their One Team T-shirts to work after Family Day to signal that they were not voting for the union.

On June 10, two days before the start of the election period, Frank Fischer held a captive-audience speech at the start of each shift. Any worker who left before the speech ended received an attendance demerit, which figured in quarterly bonus calculations. On their way into the meetings, workers each received a free Chick-fil-A sandwich. As workers left the meeting, Southern Momentum supporters gave them water bottles with anti-union stickers on them and handed out additional anti-union stickers.[374]

Fischer admitted to the workers that "I am over here because of the election" in order to emphasize the importance that VW management placed on the vote, even though the admission contradicted Amanda Plecas's earlier statement. Fischer maintained that Volkswagen was neutral but added "we also want you to know the facts." He then attacked the UAW, again blaming the union for the closure of the Westmoreland VW plant. He pointed out that UAW membership fell in 2018 but neglected to say that the drop was largely the result of the State of Michigan adopting "right to work" legislation that banned involuntary membership in unions. Fischer used an othering tactic by asking, with his heavy German accent and syntax, "Would you rather have someone from a 313 area code represent you, or someone from a 423 area code represent you? . . . Do you think that a union based [in] and running commercials with a 313 area code is really caring about what is happening with us here in the South?"[375]

Fischer also asserted that the Chattanooga plant was "the most democratic one I know of in the Volkswagen world and maybe even more worldwide because union plants don't vote, nonunion plants also don't vote, but you are allowed to vote." In reality, workers in the Volkswagen plants in Germany and most other locations around the world have far more rights. Most European plants have extensive codetermination rights anchored in law that require employers to obtain approval from works councils before they can introduce new technologies or implement mass layoffs. Volkswagen Chattanooga, in contrast, simply had the COE policy, which management created unilaterally (and could also revoke at any time), that served solely as a forum for periodic nonbinding discussions between management and qualifying employee organizations, and union recognition elections as specified in the NLRA. Employees had no role in determining the timing and wording of the occasional question that management submitted to employees for a nonbinding vote.[376]

The return of Frank Fischer put union advocates in a difficult position. His new anti-union rhetoric hurt the organizing drive, but attacking him directly could easily backfire, given his popularity among employees. So, UAW supporters put out a flyer right before the election that expressed empathy toward Fischer while remaining critical of Volkswagen. It said that Fischer was "in a tough spot." His task was to convince employees that "Chattanooga management is really going to change" after years of ignoring employee concerns. The statement questioned Fischer's assertions that the Westmoreland plant closed because of labor unrest and that union representation was antithetical to VW's "one team" message. It also argued that many proposed improvements—such as protection from last-minute overtime and control over PTO—were at management's discretion without collective bargaining.[377]

Unlike in 2014, VW management did not give UAW representatives an opportunity to speak to employees on plant grounds, and there was no UAW-VW preelection agreement. So, the Local 42 leadership instead put the union's closing argument in many places, including on the back of the flyer about Frank Fischer:

> This election isn't about Union Facts or "Southern Momentum" or VW Facts or politicians or outside lawyers. *It's about US!* Amidst all the noise and outside interference, let's remember why we started.

- It's about *control over our PTO.*
- It's about *forced overtime* and *predictable schedules.*
- It's about treating us as adults, with *respect and dignity.*
- It's about respecting our *family time.*
- It's about taking our *safety* seriously.
- It's about having some *sick days* for unexpected illnesses.
- It's about recognizing our contribution with *fair bonuses.*

> REMEMBER, AND VOTE YES![378]

By June 12, both sides had made their cases. All that was left was the election itself, which had one dramatic moment.

German employee representatives were stunned on the first day of the voting when plant management denied entry to Johan Järvklo—who was both VW Global Works Council general secretary and a supervisory board member—to observe the election. Järvklo was shocked and furious. Works council chair and VW supervisory board member Bernd Osterloh issued an angry statement: "I cannot understand why our neutral election observer Johan Järvklo was denied access to the Chattanooga plant. . . . He is . . . quite experienced with workplace elections, and is therefore a valuable adviser. I urge the company to finally act neutrally in these democratic elections, as has been promised."[379] The head of IG Metall's Wolfsburg local, Hartwig Erb, also denounced the move:

> I am horrified and outraged by the behavior of VW management in Chattanooga. Denying a Volkswagen supervisory board member access to a VW plant is a really blatant action. I demand strict neutrality from the company and more respect for employee representatives in the Volkswagen group. The company seems to be showing its true face here, and absolutely wants to set an example. We will definitely oppose that. Our solidarity lies with the representatives of our sister union, the UAW.[380]

IG Metall chair Jörg Hofmann criticized the behavior of VW management more broadly:

IG Metall supports the efforts of the United Auto Workers. . . . Volkswagen has committed to behave neutrally in the run-up to the election in accordance with American labor law. But, according to our information, this has been circumvented many times in the past. Anti-union leaflets were distributed at the plant, and supervisors have asked to give management a chance to solve problems without the union. We have made the company aware of these violations of the rules of compliance and the company has committed to eliminating them. We want fair behavior and wish our UAW colleagues much success in the upcoming election.[381]

The statements from German employee representatives had no impact on management behavior. Johan Järvklo was never able to enter the plant, which served as a message to Volkswagen Chattanooga employees while they were voting that the power and influence of German trade unions and works councils had limits. Management in a clinch had the upper hand.

The turnout for the representation election was 1,609 employees, which was 93 percent of those eligible to vote. (Roughly half of the workforce was eligible. Management, supervisors, and temporary employees supplied by an independent firm were not.) The UAW came up short once again in a close election: 776 employees supported the UAW becoming their exclusive bargaining agent; 833 opposed it. In other words, VW management's actions were enough to persuade roughly 15 percent of the eligible employees who had signed an authorization card to vote against unionization, which determined the outcome of the election. The margin, 48.2 percent for the UAW versus 51.8 percent against, was narrower than in 2014, when it was 46.8 percent versus 53.2 percent, but that was small consolation.

That evening a relieved Frank Fischer said, "Our employees have spoken. . . . We look forward to continuing our close cooperation with elected officials and business leaders in Tennessee."[382] UAW officials, in contrast, denounced VW's "brutal campaign of fear and disinformation."[383] "Our labor laws are broken," said Brian Rothenberg. "Workers should not have to endure threats and intimidation in order to obtain the right to collectively bargain. The law doesn't serve workers, it caters to clever lawyers who are able to manipulate the NLRB process." UAW organizing director Tracy Romero said,

> The Company ran a brutal campaign of fear and misinformation. Fear of the loss of the plant; fear of their participation in the union effort; fear through misinformation about the UAW; fear about current benefits in contract negotiations. Over a period of nine weeks—an unprecedented length of time due to legal gamesmanship—Volkswagen was able to break the will of enough workers to destroy their majority.[384]

UAW Region 8 director Mitchell Smith remarked on the narrow margin of defeat and suggested, "You'd try again. That's what I'd expect."[385]

Governor Bill Lee said he thought the workers "made the right decision. US representative Chuck Fleischmann said he was "very pleased by the vote," adding "I think it's time for the healing process, for those who voted against the union and those who voted for it to come together." US Senator Lamar Alexander did not get publicly involved in this representation election but after the vote mused, "I think this sends a signal across the Southeast that the UAW is probably going to have a difficult time organizing any of these plants." State representative Robin Smith said to VW employees, "You chose to put your company, its future first, not an outside labor union." In contrast, chair of the Tennessee Democratic Party Mary Mancini complained, "Those in powerful positions work to divide us."[386]

The anti-union lobbying groups expressed their satisfaction with the outcome as did the employee anti-union organization, Southern Momentum:

> We are happy for our families, for Volkswagen Chattanooga, and for our community. What started as just a handful of us grew into a force of hard-working employees determined to better educate voters about the decision before them. And now all of us have spoken. We will continue to advocate for the best interests of our families and for the future of Volkswagen Chattanooga and look forward to getting back to what we do best: working as one team to build quality cars.[387]

The CUF press release asserted that the result "sends a clear message to the UAW that its culture of corruption cannot be ignored."[388]

Workers' reactions varied depending on their side. Local 42's Facebook page post announcing the results read "We lost the election 776 yes to 833 no. We fought a brave fight against fear, intimidation, and high-priced lawyers. VW was able to stretch this out for 9 weeks to break our will. You stood strong in the face of the company's assault. Eventually, justice will prevail."[389]

The post received seventy-eight comments and forty-seven shares. A few were critical, but most expressed empathy and encouragement to continue. Local 42 recording secretary Billy Quigg expressed mixed emotions. "While I am hurt, it also strengthens me because I have seen such an outpouring of support from co-workers. I have seen a lot of people push and stand up to the company on a lot of issues. . . . You can't back down, you can never let it die out because there is always hope."[390]

Anti-union employee Brandi Gengler declared the results "wonderful; the badgering, division, intimidation, the house visits will be over." Comekia Mikes, who also voted no, described the plant as "very divided. We've got people who are angry—some about money, some about how lower management treats people."[391]

German employee representatives also weighed in on the results. The statement from IG Metall Wolfsburg accentuated the positive. "We all would have liked a different result, but given the unprecedented anti-union campaign that Chattanooga colleagues have been through in recent weeks, the result is worthy of honor. We have seen a fantastic campaign with numerous expressions of solidarity from Germany, but also from many other countries." The local newspaper in Wolfsburg, however, described the result as an "electoral debacle" that was a "slap in the face [*Ohrfeige*] for codetermination at VW."[392]

A little more than a month after the election, VW management announced that Frank Fischer would be returning to Germany, and Tom du Plessis, a South African national who had spent the previous five years working at various VW plants in China, became the plant's new CEO.[393] Volkswagen terminated the COE policy after the election, but plant management speaks with Local 42 president Steve Cochran on an informal basis.

The story of employment relations at VW's manufacturing operations in the United States is the most multifaceted of all the firms examined here because there were three representation elections at the Chattanooga plant (each of which is a case in this study). VW management's position changed more than any other foreign vehicle producer. It went from accepting card-check recognition in Westmoreland in 1978, to positive neutrality but insisting on a representation election in Chattanooga in 2013–2014, to negative neutrality in the 2015 skilled mechanics representation election, and then to engaging in a no-holds-barred union-avoidance campaign in the 2019 representation election.

Changes in VW management's position regarding unionization were neither inevitable nor the result of synoptical forethought. In 2014 it was unthinkable that VW management would use anti-union tactics, given the power of the works council network and the firm's commitment to corporate social responsibility and social partnership. Management's position started to change after the firm hired a union-avoidance law firm in 2016 to challenge the legality of a skilled trades micro unit. With time, local managers became increasingly comfortable working with Littler Mendelson and more deeply integrated into the Tennessee establishment, accepting many local preferences, including attitudes toward unions. Thus, by 2019, it was just a small step for management to choose to engage in a full-out anti-union campaign from right out of the now well-developed union-avoidance playbook.

Tracing the processes of these three recognition elections reveals four things. First, the 2014 recognition election showed that even when management takes a position of positive neutrality, a union can still lose a recognition election. When the state and local business and political elite judged VW management's position to be too accommodating of the UAW, they stepped in to fight unionization themselves. The massive subsidization of the plant's construction and expansions supercharged the scope and intensity of the establishment's interest in the plant.

Second, the 2014 unionization effort included an unprecedented degree of transnational cooperation between some employee representatives but repeated misunderstandings between others. Leaders from the UAW, IG Metall, and the VW works council network began holding meetings about organizing the Chattanooga plant in late 2009, which was well before the first car rolled off the assembly line. IG Metall leaders also facilitated the participation of VW's personnel director in the discussions. IG Metall invested significant time and resources to assist the UAW in the first organizing drive and provided as much support as UAW officials wanted. IG Metall leaders worked with the UAW within IndustriALL to pressure VW management to bargain with the skilled trades micro unit. The relationship between UAW officials and leaders of VW's works council network was not nearly as positive, however. Support of unionization from works council leaders was often late in coming and largely instrumental because the priority of the German works council officials was to establish a strong and autonomous works council at the Chattanooga plant, which included autonomy from the UAW. Many works council officials supported the UAW drives wholeheartedly, but the head of the works council network, Bernd Osterloh, often expressed reservations, which blunted the effectiveness of their efforts.

Transnational trade union cooperation did not prove to be the game changer that many on both sides of the Atlantic hoped it would be. Visitors and expressions of support from abroad did not change the votes of a sufficient number of employees to make a difference in the two wall-to-wall union recognition elections, and the prospect of obtaining a works council was too abstract and alien to have widespread appeal.

Third, following from the first two points, other actors besides employees, management, and union officials can affect the course and outcome of an organizing drive. The NLRA provides few tools for dealing with the intervention of outside actors in union recognition procedures because this was not a major issue in the 1930s when lawmakers wrote it. Outside interventions in these three cases resulted in greater uncertainty, melodrama, and hard feelings in a process intended to routinize and professionalize decisions regarding collective representation.

Fourth, the UAW leadership was neither frozen nor rigid in planning and executing organizing campaigns. Union officials innovated and changed strategies. For the first Chattanooga wall-to-wall campaign, they organized employee exchanges and jointly produced literature with IG Metall. They also coauthored a neutrality agreement with management that included details for creating a works council. When the first drive failed, they switched to organizing a micro unit in the plant and won a recognition election. When VW management impeded negotiations, the UAW leadership switched again, this time to a quick plant-based campaign to attempt to minimize the time that the Tennessee establishment and national anti-union organizations would have to wage counterattacks. The UAW leadership also dispensed with bargaining to organize and focused on problems in the plant rather than on international cooperation or abstract objectives like a works council. The UAW failed in Chattanooga because VW management and the Tennessee political and economic elite demonstrated an even greater willingness to change strategy and tactics, thereby outmaneuvering UAW officials and union supporters in the plant. Having something significant that the employer wanted—namely a works council—did not guarantee organizing success in these cases the way it did at DTNA when management wanted wage concessions.

The UAW made mistakes. The initial drive in Chattanooga relied heavily on a top-down strategy—bargaining to organize—that led union officials to pursue card check in vain, make establishing a works council a priority when few employees were interested, and commit prematurely to wage moderation. After the failure of the initial drive, the community organization engagement policy put Local 42 officers in a difficult position. If they spoke positively of the COE policy, it would weaken the case for unionization. Focusing on the COE policy's inadequacies, however, also risked undercutting the value of a works council in the eyes of employees. Local 42 leaders could have used the COE policy more aggressively between 2014 and 2019 to foreshadow to employees what a union could do, however.

In hindsight, the effort to organize a micro unit of skilled trades employees was a strategic error. The action was understandable. UAW support in the plant was strongest among the skilled trades employees, which made a victory likely in a recognition election limited to this group. Establishing a small unit within the plant would have broken the ice and resulted in dues-paying members for Local 42. It also would have given the UAW an opportunity to demonstrate what unions can do for employees. Given VW's professed commitment to corporate social responsibility, UAW officials could be forgiven for mistakenly thinking that management would ultimately recognize the unit. The successful recognition election instead precipitated the transformation of the attitudes of VW management regarding unionization because it led to the hiring of a union-avoidance law firm and ultimately adoption of the union-avoidance playbook. Local 42 leaders expended the bulk of their energy from 2015 to 2018 on the micro unit rather than on the plant as a whole, which meant that Local 42 leaders needed to pivot their focus hastily for the second wall-to-wall recognition election, which left little time to build deeper connections throughout the plant.

Although UAW leaders changed many aspects of their campaigns between 2014 and 2019, one element remained the same. They did little to forge bonds with sympathetic groups in civil society. This was also a characteristic of the UAW's successful efforts to organize DTNA and the failed drive at MBUSI. How much of a difference can engaging with civil society make? Chapter 4, which examines UAW's attempt to organize a Nissan plant in Canton, Mississippi, gives us an indication.

NISSAN NORTH AMERICA

From Conventional to Civil Rights–Centered Organizing

> **Worker rights have always been a civil rights issue. The struggle we had to abolish slavery was about worker rights. The struggles in the sixties was about the right of workers being able to organize. In fact, Dr. King was assassinated as he was organizing workers in Memphis who wanted the right to have a voice as sanitation workers.**

—Derrick Johnson, Mississippi NAACP president

Nissan Motor Company was the second Japanese-owned firm to build an automobile production plant in the United States and the first to do so in the South. It is the only Japanese-owned automobile producer ever to have union recognition elections at wholly owned plants in the United States. There have been three at Nissan plants: two in Smyrna, Tennessee, in 1989 and 2001, and one in Canton, Mississippi, in 2017. There was also an organizing attempt at the Smyrna plant in 1997 that was substantial enough to count as a case but did not culminate with an election. So, combined there are four cases of organizing at Nissan plants. The UAW's approach to organizing changed with successive cases. Union officials learned from previous mistakes and integrated new tactics and technologies. Nissan managers also innovated. They pioneered a number of measures that subsequently became standard tactics in the union-avoidance playbook, including taking a team approach that minimized distinctions between management and line employees, cross-training employees to do multiple jobs, paying wages that were slightly lower than union contracts but markedly higher than the area rate, offering a wider range of benefits to line employees, avoiding layoffs whenever possible, using in-plant monitors to broadcast pro-management and anti-union messages, hiring a law firm that specializes in union avoidance, and cultivating close community relations. These measures proved effective in keeping the share of employees willing to vote for union representation well below a majority. Since the strategies and tactics of labor and management evolved over time, it is most illuminating to trace the processes of the organizing attempts at Nissan chronologically.

Nissan Smyrna

Japanese automobile producers made their first substantial advances into the US market in the 1970s. The oil shocks of that decade increased demand for fuel-efficient vehicles, which was a specialty of Japanese firms, and reduced employment in the US automobile sector. In response, the heads of the Detroit automobile producers and the UAW pressured politicians for trade restrictions. In 1978, the Japanese and US governments agreed to a voluntary restraint agreement that capped the number of vehicles Japanese firms could export to the United States for several years.[1]

The trade restraint led Nissan management, which had a reputation for assertiveness, to decide to build a vehicle assembly plant in the United States. Nissan hired a US consulting firm to advise on several issues, including selecting the location for the plant. The consultants' assessment of VW's experience with a Pennsylvania plant led them to recommend investing in the South. Tennessee governor Lamar Alexander had already begun traveling to Japan in the late 1970s to promote investment in Tennessee. Once Alexander became aware of Nissan's intention, he assembled a task force of thirty to persuade Nissan management to invest in his state. Alexander also met with property owners and the entire leadership of Rutherford County to make available a site in Smyrna, a town of eight thousand about 15 miles southeast of Nashville. A team from Nissan spent a week in Tennessee in May 1978. Japanese manufacturers were already familiar with Tennessee. Sharp and Toshiba had their largest US electronics plants there. Alexander's task force stressed Tennessee's mild climate, central location, good highway and rail links, low taxes, and affordable cost of living.[2]

On October 30, 1980, Nissan management announced that the company had selected Smyrna. A group gathered in the small town to receive the announcement via telephone from Japan broke into loud cheers, and Mayor Sam Ridley reportedly shouted, "We're all gonna be rich!"[3]

Although twenty-four governors submitted site proposals to Nissan, the company's leadership was cautious regarding requests for incentives to avoid triggering a backlash against the foreign-owned firm, particularly given Japan's past as an adversary of the United States in World War II. Still, Tennessee politicians embraced the plant as a prestige project and were willing to subsidize it. Nissan received $33 million in incentives from state and local governments, including highway access and $7.3 million toward Nissan's job training program.[4]

Company leaders decided to start production with a compact pickup truck at the plant because trucks are relatively simple to build and the tariff on light trucks was 25 percent, which was ten times higher than the duty on automobiles. If successful, automobile production would soon follow.[5] Nissan broke ground on February 3, 1981, for the $660 million factory designed to produce two hundred thousand vehicles per year and employ 3,100 people. Nissan's Smyrna plant was the largest single Japanese investment in the United States at the time. The ceremony, which Governor Alexander attended, did not go well. Several hundred union activists, mostly from the construction trades, came to protest Nissan management's choice of a nonunion contractor. They waved signs reading "Quality projects with skilled UNION Workers" and "Go home, Japs" while a plane flew overhead with a banner that read "Boycott Datsun [i.e., the name at the time for Nissan vehicles sold outside of Japan]. Put America back to work." Some demonstrators threw rocks, damaging a truck. Nissan planned to use a snowplow to break ground. When the driver discovered that someone had slashed the tires, Marvin Runyon, the head of the Nissan plant, got in the truck and drove it himself. Runyon—a tall white-haired native Texan who rose to vice president for body and assembly in a thirty-seven-year career at Ford before moving to Nissan—said, "The demonstration so shocked the community . . . that they came down heavily on the union. The next day, the legislature passed a resolution condemning the building trades union. . . . [T]he union spent a lot of money saying how sorry they were. They ran full-page ads saying, 'Hey, we apologize. We really didn't mean it. Things got out of hand.'" Nonetheless, the wanton behavior tainted the attitude of many locals toward unions for years.[6]

After the rough start, plant construction, testing, and fine-tuning proceeded smoothly. On June 16, 1983, Marvin Runyon drove "Job 1"—a white pickup truck—off the assembly line at an elaborate ceremony, which the Tennessee governor also attended, that included a ride in the Goodyear blimp for 114 employees.[7] UAW leaders decided to issue a "philosophical and very friendly statement" for the occasion rather than stage a demonstration, given what had happened at the groundbreaking ceremony. They invited Nissan management to meet with the leaders of the UAW and the major domestic automobile producers "to be brought up to date on how our use of the collective bargaining process is strengthening the U.S. industry while preserving the rights of U.S. workers."[8]

UAW leaders welcomed Nissan building a plant in the United States rather than importing vehicles from Japan.[9] They were at first confident that they could organize Japanese-owned plants in the United States regardless of their location because of recent successes organizing GM plants in the South.[10]

GM built eleven new assembly and parts plants in the South during the 1970s, intending to establish a string of nonunion plants that would enhance the company's bargaining leverage over the UAW. Once union organizing began in some of the plants, GM management initially responded with anti-union leaflets and threatening meetings with the employees. In response, the UAW staged a "mini-strike" at northern plants that led the GM leadership to accept a neutrality agreement for the southern plants during the 1976 contract negotiations. When that agreement proved insufficient, UAW president Doug Fraser asked for a face-to-face meeting with GM chair Thomas A. Murphy in August 1978. Fraser warned Murphy that the company's continuing anti-union efforts would have repercussions at the bargaining table and threatened, "If you want war, you'll get war." After a month of private talks, GM negotiators agreed to a new hiring procedure that would give current union employees preference at the new plants. Fraser was pleased, announcing that "GM's statement and the procedures agreed upon should make it clear to workers at a nonunion GM facility that they are absolutely free to choose union representation without fear of reprisals."[11] After the agreement, UAW organizers quickly unionized GM's southern plants.

Organizing Nissan's Smyrna plant proved to be far more difficult than GM. There are two competing stories regarding Nissan's attitude toward unionization. Journalist David Gesanliter asserts that Nissan opposed the UAW from the start because the company's president, Takashi Ishihara, would not be able to dominate the UAW the way he did Nissan's enterprise union in Japan.[12] John Schnapp, a consultant who provides a more detailed account, tells a different story.[13] Schnapp was the partner in charge of Temple Barker & Sloan's automotive practice when Nissan hired the firm to help its planning team with the strategy for building a plant in the United States. Nissan's Japanese managers anticipated that the UAW would be like auto unions in Japan, that is, weak and accommodating to management,[14] until Schnapp's team and the head of Nissan US operations, Marvin Runyon, persuaded them otherwise.[15] Runyon went to great lengths to keep unions out of the Smyrna plant because he wished to avoid the "we-versus-them attitude" that he felt compromised productivity and quality.[16] He said, "In my experience, any time you have a third party in a relationship and that party is adversarial, then you have a real problem."[17] Although such language is commonplace now, at the time it was "almost unheard of in a business where organized labor was preeminent."[18] Nonetheless, Runyon objected to being called anti-union. "We're not anti anything," he asserted; Nissan was "just pro-employee."[19]

A big difference between Nissan and the other Japanese producers was the heavy reliance on US nationals to run the plant. Twelve Japanese were in Smyrna versus seven hundred in Marysville, Ohio, working for Honda.[20] Nonetheless, Runyan stressed that "we're transplanting Japanese techniques wherever we can, including morning exercises, company uniforms, cross-training in several jobs and a leaner management structure." Nissan management went to great lengths to make the factory physically appealing and minimize hierarchies. There were no time clocks to punch and no mandatory uniforms, and hourly employees had the title of "technician." Management instituted regular information meetings and an open-door policy that permitted any employee to bring suggestions or complaints directly to higher levels without having to go through a supervisor. Management also allowed any employee to shut down the line if quality problems arose. Employees received semiannual bonuses and a 3 percent bonus for learning a skill beyond their assigned duties and could lease a Nissan vehicle at a discount rate, which at the time was a benefit offered only to executives at US automakers. Management also adopted the Japanese practice of lifetime employment unless the survival of the plant was at stake. The plant had five layers of supervision from workplace groups to the plant chief executive, which was fewer than half of what was common in a typical US automobile assembly plant at the time. Managers had no executive dining room and no reserved parking places and at first wore light-blue uniforms just like the line employees, with the company logo on one side and the employee's first name on the other side. Runyon put great emphasis on ceremonies celebrating production milestones and other achievements to instill company loyalty. The firm also held Family Day and holiday festivities. The celebrations paid off. Nissan was named one of the best one hundred companies to work for in America in 1984 and 1987. Marvin Runyon's management innovations have become known as the one-team approach and have spread throughout the US automobile sector and beyond. Runyon still traveled to work in a chauffeur-driven limousine, however.[21]

Runyon embedded Nissan deeply in the community. Local newspapers "ran story after story lauding Nissan for donating seed money for this or that worthy cause."[22] Runyon collected a record amount of donations when he headed the Middle Tennessee United Way charities campaign in 1985.[23] His policies quickly proved effective for running a plant efficiently and minimizing the likelihood that employees would support unionization. Managers at other transplants readily adopted Runyon's model.

Eighty-five percent of Nissan employees were Tennesseans, which guaranteed that few of the line workers had experience in automobile production or familiarity with unions.[24] Runyan found the "homogeneity" of the plant's employees to be a positive attribute. "It doesn't matter what nationality they are; they're all Tennesseans. Here, people are the same, and that's like Japan." A willingness to go along with "the participative management we plan to use at the operation" was an important selection criterion for new hires.[25] The UAW vice president responsible for organizing and the Ford Department, Stephen Yokich, judged the intent of the hiring process differently. He said, "We know, for example, that Nissan screened the workers hired there very carefully so that pro-union people wouldn't be hired. They did it skillfully and perhaps just barely within the law, but we know they did it."[26]

The first batch of Nissan trainees were enthusiastic about the participatory approach Nissan management was using. Mike Harris said, "We've got a chance

now to express our ideas and we feel those ideas are looked at and discussed."
He added, "The idea is that we are a team-oriented organization. We should be
able to walk up to anyone—even Marvin Runyon—to express our ideas." Trainees voiced skepticism about unionization. One said, "We didn't invite them to
the party." Another asked, "What can a union do for us that Nissan can't?"[27]
Paint-shop robot technician Teresa Harding concluded, "As long as the company
treats us like they do now, I don't want the UAW digging into my paycheck.
I can use the money myself." Most of the employees were in their twenties and
were able to keep up physically with the arduous pace of automobile assembly.[28]

The Smyrna plant did have challenges. Containing costs was initially problematic. Runyon committed to paying "the prevailing wage of the auto industry."[29] In practice, the plant's wages were slightly lower than those specified in
union contracts. Still, Runyon's decision took wages off the table as an issue for
an organizing campaign, given that Nissan employees earned well above the typical middle Tennessee manufacturing wage and the local cost of living was relatively low. The decision did have a price, however. The plant's labor costs were
80 percent higher than those in Japan.[30] Management hoped to compensate by
using the latest manufacturing technologies and extensive automation. This
high-tech plant required greater training for employees, which generated additional up-front costs. The facility included a thirty thousand–square-foot training center.[31] Nissan management also spent $63 million on "pretraining" and
sent 375 US workers to Japan for up to four months to learn Japanese management and production practices.[32] Plant head Marvin Runyon estimated that the
plant would likely lose money during the first five years of operations.[33]

UAW president Doug Fraser predicted on a Sunday television news program
broadcast nationwide that the UAW would organize the Smyrna plant "because
the workers will want us there."[34] UAW spokesperson Peter Laarman later explained the union's motivation for organizing Nissan: "We feel we must have a
union there. A foreign-based auto manufacturer operating on a non-union basis would undercut our ability to negotiate with American manufacturers."[35]
Once Nissan began hiring in 1981, the UAW leadership named Jim Turner the
lead organizer and assigned three additional organizers to assist him. Turner
"was born in Dayton, Ohio, but as a boy had moved back and forth between Dayton and Crossville, Tennessee, where most of his relatives lived."[36] He became a
UAW officer in 1960 and organized several GM plants in the South. Turner
moved to Nashville in 1977 to become UAW national organizing coordinator
for nineteen states.[37] The bearded Turner exuded confidence. "We have no doubt
that employees, freely given their choice without discrimination, will join the
union. . . . Every other automotive assembly plant in America, including Volkswagen in Pennsylvania, is unionized. We see no reason why this one would be

any different, if they do not discriminate and live within the law." When asked about Runyon's opposition to unionization, Turner replied, "This is nothing new; we expected it because every Japanese plant that has been built in this country attempted to defeat unions."[38] Turner had one request nonetheless: "All we ask him to do is don't discriminate against people who have been in unions."[39] Nissan's hiring process did not change, however.

In the spring of 1983 shortly before the plant opened, UAW leaders added eight members to the existing four-person organizing team. The entire group served as a task force for the campaign.[40] When the plant opened, UAW spokesperson Peter Laarman was cautious in his assessment. "Nissan has not given us very fertile ground at all for starting a union in Smyrna. . . . That means it's going to take a little more effort from us to get organized there."[41] Jim Turner said that Tennessee's depressed economy and "fluffy" media coverage had made organizing doubly difficult.[42] In an internal memo, UAW associate general counsel Leonard Page stated that the union would not immediately start an organizing effort but would instead have a "watchdog presence" at the plant.[43] In August 1983, the union spent $3,284 on radio advertisements featuring Nashville-area UAW members. They were "intended to familiarize the community with the UAW in anticipation of a long organizing campaign."[44]

Although Peter Laarman said the UAW planned to "be visible in a way we think will be beneficial to the community,"[45] most of the UAW's efforts came from the top. UAW leaders worked with their counterparts in Japan. Confederation of Japan Automobile Workers Unions (JAW) president Ichiro Shioji declared at the UAW's 1983 convention that he would use "every means at my disposal" to help unionize the Smyrna plant but demurred when asked to be specific, responding, "If what I have in mind is reported, it would be stopped."[46] There were no protests or industrial actions in Japan regarding the Smyrna plant. Two years earlier, Shioji had offered to send a team of JAW members to Smyrna to urge employees to join the UAW, but the trip never materialized.[47] Owen Bieber, who became UAW president in May 1983, expressed hope that Japanese firms would end their opposition to unionization at US plants on a 1984 trip to Japan that included a meeting with Japanese prime minister Yasuhiro Nakasone.[48] Nissan management nonetheless continued to oppose unionization.

Management launched the Nissan News Network, which provided information about the company and auto industry trends on more than 120 monitors inside the plant. The Nissan News Network regularly ran negative stories about the UAW's efforts to promote federal domestic content legislation that would have required at least 70 percent of the value of the parts used to make a vehicle be made domestically for it to be classified as made in the USA. The trucks made in Smyrna fell short of that percentage because the plant imported engines from Japan. If the law had passed the Smyrna trucks would have been subject to the 25 percent tariff, and the plant would no longer be economically viable. Even though the legislation never became law, the UAW's advocacy for it, which included advertisements in area newspapers,[49] hurt the union's reputation locally.[50]

In May 1984, plant chief Marvin Runyon announced that Nissan would expand the Smyrna plant with a $150 million addition to produce Sentra automobiles. Tennessee governor Lamar Alexander was once again on hand when the first Sentra rolled off the assembly line on March 26, 1985. Alexander was also instrumental in persuading GM in 1985 to commit to building the experimental $3.5 billion Saturn plant in Spring Hill, Tennessee, which is near Smyrna about 15 miles south of Nashville.[51] Saturn differed from Nissan in that GM executives committed to a landmark collective bargaining pact with the UAW leadership that included a robust commitment to employee participation and an innovative compensation system that made line workers salaried employees and awarded them regular bonuses based on sales performance. The UAW leadership all but guaranteed that the workforce would vote to recognize the union by securing a provision that a majority of the employees at Saturn would be UAW members who had lost jobs at other GM plants. GM managers were slow in getting the plant into production because they decided to reinvent from scratch how they produced and marketed cars from design to sales. The company broke ground in 1986 and began to hire employees in 1988 before producing the first vehicle in 1990.[52]

Saturn's launch changed the environment for unionization in middle Tennessee. The launch introduced a union contract that in many respects was superior to Nissan's compensation package as well as more than three thousand union workers who could help to organize the Nissan plant.[53] On the other hand, the UAW experienced an embarrassing setback in 1985 when union leaders withdrew the election petition the night before the scheduled recognition election at Honda's plant in Marysville, Ohio, to avoid registering a big defeat.[54]

Organizing at Nissan continued. As the pace of production accelerated, management abandoned many of the Japanese participatory practices.[55] The plant first became profitable in 1986,[56] but soft sales and rapid productivity gains led to a decline in the size of the workforce. Management relied on attrition rather than layoffs to thin the staff. Shrinking employment left few opportunities for promotion. Many who had started on the night shift were still on it years later.[57] In mid-1986, the union began holding monthly meetings at the United Rubber Workers union hall in the neighboring town of LaVergne.[58] Turner reported to Yokich in late August that 190 workers had expressed a willingness to help in the drive but advised that it was premature to go public with the campaign.[59]

As the work pace intensified in the plant, "four or five" employees initially approached UAW representatives about organizing the plant in early 1987. Soon, the numbers quickly swelled to several hundred. An exposé that appeared in *The Progressive* magazine in May 1987 further fueled organizing. It reported on numerous problems at the Smyrna plant, including favoritism, sexual harassment, supervisor intimidation, and grueling work, which one employee likened to "eight-hour aerobics." The author, John Junkerman, asserted that Nissan management had abandoned innovative and participatory management practices in favor of speeding up the assembly line.[60] Other publications soon followed suit and painted a similar picture of Nissan.[61]

Stung by the accusations—which were the first bad press the Smyrna plant had ever received—Marvin Runyon wrote an incensed message that appeared in the plant's July 23 bulletin:

> It appears that the UAW has been recently trying to use the media to discredit our company with claims of unsafe working conditions, overwork, fear and intimidation.
>
> These stories, like the recent ones in the *Progressive* and the *Detroit Free Press*, are unfair, inaccurate, and typical of union efforts to create unnecessary employee concerns and uncertainty. This is the kind of environment that exists where unions are present. It is this type of activity which makes me feel so strongly that unionism would be detrimental to all of us.
>
> I'm extremely proud of all of you, the excellent products we build, and our open environment which is very different from the typical union workplace. I hope the confusion which the UAW is trying to create does not disrupt the positive and open atmosphere which we've worked so hard to build.[62]

Nissan management responded to the bad press by opening the shop floor to a reporter from a local newspaper with an editorial board sympathetic to Nissan to interview employees. None of the eleven interviewed expressed support for the union.[63]

The union added four full-time organizers from Tennessee to assist in what Turner described as "the first full, organized thrust effort," which a local newspaper described in a headline as an "all-out assault."[64] By August, support for the union had doubled when compared to the spring, according to Turner.[65] The union began to hold meetings twice a month; some had attracted more than one hundred employees. Still, organizers had little information about the workforce beyond the employees who had contacted them and their immediate associates. They had few addresses and no demographic information and were not even sure how many employees worked at the plant. Employee information was difficult to obtain because Nissan grouped workers into small teams and the uniforms only had first names on them. Smyrna was small, so most employees did not live near the plant. Some commuted from as far as one hundred miles away. Organizers attempted to expand their list of employees by sending fifty thousand flyers to union members in the region asking them to provide the names and addresses of Nissan workers whom they knew, but the effort produced little new information. Marvin Runyon suggested that the action was a sign of failure. "I think it indicates that our people are not going to the union." Runyon also criticized the effort as an infringement "on the privacy of our individuals."[66]

The UAW advanced the organizing drive a step further in November 1987 by opening an office in a former factory two miles from the plant. It could hold five hundred comfortably, but, Turner maintained, "we're not changing our approach to the organizing drive, we're just making it more convenient for the people who live down there. Our main strategy is still going to be personal contacts, one-on-one, and small meetings."[67] The organizing drive also suffered a blow that month when Turner learned that he had cancer of the bladder, colon, and liver. He decided to dedicate the remainder of his life to organizing the Nissan plant.[68]

Ronald Reagan appointed Marvin Runyon to head the Tennessee Valley Authority in December 1987. On January 1, 1988, Jerry Benefield—"a cigar-chewing Georgian with a love for horses and cowboy boots"—took the reins.[69] He was a barrel-chested forty-seven-year-old with aviator glasses who looked "a little like a county sheriff."[70] Runyon had recruited Benefield from Ford to be his deputy before the Smyrna plant had opened. Benefield maintained Runyon's approach to employee relations, including resolute opposition to unionization.

The UAW formally launched an organizing drive at the Smyrna plant on January 19, 1988. Supporters began distributing flyers during shift changes and breaks that made the case for unionization.[71] UAW president Owen Bieber participated in a rally of several hundred Nissan employees and UAW officials at the union's hall in Smyrna. Union proponents had put signs on the walls that had slogans for the campaign ahead, including "Job Safety," "No More Fear," "Put it in Writing," "End Sexual Harassment," and "Together We can speak for Ourselves." Jim Turner had a message about collecting authorization cards for union supporters: "The faster we do it, the better the chance we have of winning the election."[72] Bieber was the closing speaker. He stressed the historical importance of unions for getting fair treatment for workers; hit on the main issues of sexual harassment, unsafe working conditions, and compensation lower than the union rate; rejected the characterization of a union as a third party; and pointed out that the UAW had been working constructively with domestic automobile producers. Bieber urged employees "to make your own history here" and received a standing ovation at the end of his speech.[73]

Bieber acknowledged at a press conference in Nashville preceding the rally that organizing the Smyrna plant would not be "like falling off a log."[74] He was right. Nissan management engaged in a spirited campaign against unionization, in contrast to Honda and Toyota management who clearly did not support unionization at their plants but were much more circumspect in opposing it. Dan Minor, Honda's labor attorney, thought that Nissan was more aggressive because the plant president was American rather than Japanese.[75] Nissan management hired Ogletree, Deakins, Nash, Smoak, and Stewart of Greenville, South Carolina, a prominent union-avoidance law firm, to assist in crafting a strategy to keep out the UAW.

Perkins, a deputy in the UAW's organizing department, reported in mid-March to the department's head, Stephen Yokich, that "the enthusiasm among workers that was evident last year has vanished." Only 522 out of 2,400 production employees had signed union authorization cards. Union supporters said that employees were afraid to talk about unionization at work but also thought that "many workers would be receptive if we could talk to them away from work. Of course, our problem is we don't know where workers live."[76]

Organizing Black workers proved to be especially challenging. Nissan management stated that 17 percent of the production workers were African American, but UAW organizers did not know how many had signed cards. Perkins, who was Black, wrote that only one organizer was Black and that he was "not doing the kind of job that needs to be done among blacks."[77]

To reduce the information deficit, organizers spent six weeks in the spring of 1988 combing through phone books and other sources to assemble a fuller list of employees. They then sorted the employees into four categories: willing to serve on the in-plant voluntary organizing committee, card signer, on the fence, and anti-union. The improved employee list helped to advance the campaign. Organizers began to call employees and make house calls. In mid-May, UAW spokesperson Maxey Irwin indicated that the union had authorization cards from more than 30 percent of Nissan employees.[78] Difficulties remained, however. The closest UAW computer was in Nashville, which made keeping the list current problematic.[79]

UAW leadership gained the support of the JAW for the organizing drive. JAW president Teruhito Takumoto wrote a letter to Owen Bieber stating, "I strongly believe that at all automakers in the world, labor unions should be formed. . . . Especially in the U.S., workers at Japanese plants would benefit from belonging to the UAW due to the facts that the UAW has done an excellent job of serving its members." Organizers used the letter in the Nissan campaign. The JAW, however, was too weak to pressure Nissan management in Japan to change the company's position on unionization.[80]

Increased union activity provoked a response. Employees opposed to unionization began demonstrating outside of the plant in June.[81] Lead demonstrator George Patterson said, "We've got no president. It's just all our voices showing we don't want to vote the union in. . . . We've got a real good thing here we're trying to protect. We want to see the union go down the road for a while. We'd like to get back to our regular routine."[82] Yokich reported that organizers suspected that Nissan management was assisting the opposition because many held professionally printed signs that read "Nissan: Free and Proud of it" and "UAW—Go Back Home." Nissan management attempted to undermine card gathering by sending all 2,400 production employees authorization-card revocation forms and postage-paid preaddressed envelopes to send to the UAW.[83] The anti-union employees formed their own organization, which they initially named the United Nissan Workers, with a membership of 250.[84] The group held several meetings and rallies over subsequent months.[85]

An internal dispute that had been bubbling beneath the surface in the UAW at the national level for several years gained prominence in 1988, and Nissan management took full advantage of it. Increased foreign competition and the economic crises of the 1970s and early 1980s led Owen Bieber and his immediate lieutenants to make economic concessions and embrace greater cooperation with domestic producers to ensure the firms' economic survival. This policy, which became known as "jointness," had detractors at all levels of the union. In the mid-1980s associate director of the UAW's southwestern region, Jerry Tucker, launched a movement of local leaders and the rank and file skeptical of the union's accommodationist stance called New Directions. The youngest Reuther brother, Victor, embraced New Directions.[86] On May 4, 1988, Reuther, Tucker, and two other New Directions adherents made statements critical of the UAW leadership's cooperative approach in an interview on the *Today* show morning television program. Reuther went as far as saying that if he were a Nissan worker, he would not vote for the UAW to represent him. Nissan management played the segment to the Smyrna workforce repeatedly on the Nissan News Network and regularly ran a program at the start of each shift titled *The UAW—A House Divided*, which featured media reports on New Directions. Bieber described this as "disheartening."[87]

Nissan suffered a substantial slump in sales in 1988. The company parked thirty thousand unsold cars in cow pastures and an airfield near the plant. Observers suggested that layoffs were imminent. Nissan management, however, was able to avert layoffs by slowing down the assembly line and giving employees an extra week of training. Months later during the hot phase of the recognition election, Nissan management repeatedly reminded employees that the company had never laid off a worker, even during difficult times. UAW organizers tried to take credit for the company's policy; they claimed that the organizing drive forced Nissan management to retain workers when they otherwise would not have.[88]

Organizing continued to be difficult. In August, Yokich reported to Bieber that organizers had the names and addresses of 1,505 employees, which was just a little over 60 percent of the workforce eligible to vote in a recognition election, and 704 authorization cards, which was still barely above 30 percent. Campaign leadership was an issue. Jim Turner had told everyone that his cancer was in remission, but he was noticeably weaker. Turner blamed slow progress in gathering cards on employee fear of management reprisals and the "company-backed" anti-union committee.[89]

By January 1989—a year into the open campaign—the union had only 841 cards.[90] The organizing drive suffered serious setbacks that month. Worsening cancer forced Jim Turner to step down; he died in April.[91] Turner did not cultivate anyone locally to succeed him, which made the transition difficult. Jim Weaver, a veteran UAW organizer from Atlanta, filled in as the local lead organizer, and Yokich's deputy Ben Perkins took a more active role in strategic planning for the drive. Perkins conceded in internal correspondence that he would have trouble filling Turner's shoes because he lacked familiarity with both Tennessee and automobile assembly work. A second organizer, Ron Mason, also left in January after suffering a heart attack. Perkins noted that the organizers and in-plant supporters were starting to burn out.[92]

In January 1989, plant head Jerry Benefield had sent a letter to Jim Turner urging that the UAW bring the organizing drive to a close. Benefield asserted, "I think your union has had more than a fair chance to organize the employees at our Smyrna facility. There finally comes a time when you should put up or shut up. That time is here. Our people are entitled to be left alone." Turner's local replacement, Jim Weaver, penned a pointed response: "We don't take suggestions from hostile company executives about when to file a petition. . . . Our decisions are made by us in consultation with the workers active in the organizing drive."[93]

Frequently, union supporters in a plant are convinced that they have the votes to win a recognition election even if they do not have authorization cards from a majority of the employees. The plant did have union strongholds. For example, night-shift workers in the trim and chassis department made their own pro-union T-shirts.[94] Voluntary organizing committee members told Perkins that "some workers who had refused to sign cards had assured them that they would vote for the union." UAW officials, who had seen the union lose drives even when a majority of employees had signed cards, cautioned the committee members that it was premature to proceed to a recognition election. Perkins was particularly concerned that the union could suffer a big loss.[95]

On April 3, 1989, Benefield announced that Nissan would spend half a billion dollars to enlarge the plant by adding a new line to build a third vehicle. The $490 million expansion would double production capacity to 440,000 units and add two thousand jobs, starting in 1990. The announcement greatly helped Nissan management blunt the organizing drive because it took job security off the table as an issue. It also gave new hope to longtime night-shift employees that they would soon be able to move to the day shift and to employees aspiring to move into supervisory positions that there would shortly be many more opportunities for them.[96]

Union officials reasoned that they needed to move ahead with the election before the expansion, even if they did not have as many cards as they would have liked, because new hires are especially difficult to organize.[97] Later that month, Stephen Yokich told the 168 members of the voluntary organizing committee that if each of them got one additional employee to sign a card, the union would file a petition with the NLRB to hold an election.[98] The voluntary organizing committee did not even collect half that number, but the additional signatures meant that the UAW finally had cards from a majority of Smyrna employees, and the leadership agreed to move forward with an election.[99] A UAW victory that April in a hard-fought recognition election at a Mack Truck assembly plant in Winnsboro, South Carolina, buoyed UAW leaders' hope that success at Nissan was possible.[100]

On May 18, 1989, the UAW filed a petition at the Nashville NLRB office to hold a recognition election at the Smyrna plant.[101] That morning, 85 employees opposed to the union held a rally at the plant's main entrance.[102] After three days of wrangling in early June before NLRB representatives in Nashville over the eligibility of injured employees and 160 "lead technicians," lawyers representing Nissan and the UAW agreed to include both groups and to hold the vote from 1 to 4 p.m. on July 26 and from 10:30 p.m. on July 26 to 1:30 a.m. on July 27, which gave both day- and night-shift workers an opportunity to vote when they were already at the plant. The start date for voting was eleven days after employees returned from a two-week summer plant shutdown.[103]

Nissan's vice president for human resources Gail Neuman expressed confidence that the UAW would lose the recognition election because compensation at the Smyrna plant was comparable to those that the UAW had organized, and a majority of Nissan's employees did not want to pay union dues.[104] In June, management distributed "Keep 1 Team" buttons to employees.[105]

UAW leaders understood that unions often lose the first recognition election at plants with more than five hundred employees. It is common for an employer to make promises to stave off a union victory but then fail to keep them afterward. The union then wins on a second or third try. UAW leaders hoped that the union would at minimum have a close loss, which would tee up pursuing a second election.[106] Moreover, even a loss could still help the UAW beyond Nissan. Cornell University labor relations expert Harry Katz observed, "It would be a spectacular victory for the UAW, but even if they lose, the union is trying to raise the cost of union resistance."[107]

The leaders of both the UAW and Nissan understood that their reputations were on the line in this high-stakes union recognition election when the *New York Times* ran a front-page story in April reporting that an election was imminent.[108] Once the election date was set, UAW leaders increased the number of organizers in Smyrna from 10 to 30. They stepped up making house calls to employees, targeting 1,700 who were either on the fence or opposed to the union. Nissan management continued to run an information campaign critical of the UAW. The company continued to air slick anti-union videos on the ubiquitous monitors throughout the plant and began to hold meetings with small groups of workers to present the company's view regarding unionization. Nissan management erected two billboards on Nissan Drive with the message "Keep 1 Team." On the weekend before the vote, they added large red banners that read "Vote No" to the signs.[109]

Managers stressed that the Nissan plant had been successful because they had been one team working together. A union, they argued, would make the environment within the plant adversarial. A union, moreover, could not guarantee that a contract would include all the benefits workers currently had. The managers emphasized repeatedly that there had never been a single furlough or layoff at the plant, but with a UAW contract laid-off GM workers might be given a hiring preference for jobs at Nissan, which was the case at GM's Saturn plant that was about to open in Spring Hill, Tennessee. The sessions also showed lurid headlines and violent clashes from recent UAW strikes. Management put up posters in the plant with the message: "UAW Strikes: A Fact of Life."[110]

The anti-union employee committee, now called the Associates Alliance at Nissan, demonstrated at the plant gates waving anti-union signs and American flags. They distributed buttons and T-shirts that read "Nissan: Love it or leave it" and "I can speak for myself."[111] They also handed out flyers listing shutdowns and high injury rates at unionized automobile assembly plants punctuated with the sentence "Look what the UAW did for them."[112] Union proponents had T-shirts of their own with "Vote Yes for a Safer Workplace" and "Unite! The 13 colonies did it."[113] Division supplanted amiability in Smyrna. Union opponent Stanley Tribble said, "They sit at their own tables and we sit at ours. You don't eat with your enemies."[114]

UAW proponents made workplace safety their primary issue. They pointed out that the plant registered 151 injuries in 1988 that caused employees to miss at least seven days of work, which was up from 95 such injuries in the previous year, and said that fast line speeds and short paid break times compared to Ford were the causes.[115] As a part of the organizing drive, the UAW represented Nissan employees in workers' compensation cases and conducted seminars on health and safety, for which the union advertised in local newspapers.[116] Nissan management responded by using data from the National Safety Council to show that workdays lost and recordable injuries per 100 employees at the Smyrna plant were substantially lower than the automobile industry average: 3.8 workdays lost and 8.9 injuries at the Smyrna plan versus the industry average of 10.6 workdays lost and 25.8 injuries.

One reason why safety remained a central position throughout the campaign was Nissan management's refusal to honor the request of four employees on May 4 to see the company's Occupational Safety and Health Administration (OSHA) injury logs. OSHA requires companies to give employees access to "OSHA 200 logs" upon request.[117] Bill Collins, Tennessee Department of Labor general counsel, issued a letter on May 19 ordering Nissan to provide the records by June 19 or be subject to a fine. Initially management claimed that "patient confidentiality" was behind the decision not to make the logs available. George Patterson, an early member of the anti-union employee group, sued to block access to the OSHA 200 logs, asserting patient privacy. In mid-June Nissan attorneys responded to the letter from Collins with a new argument. They said these employees should not have access to the logs because they were "union agents" who had "regularly" acted on behalf of the UAW during the organizing drive. The letter stated, "We simply do not think that your agency should aid and abet a union in its campaign to organize workers or otherwise interfere in the voting process of an NLRB-conducted election."[118]

Two days later, Tennessee OSHA fined Nissan $5,000. In response, Nissan general counsel and vice president for human resources Gail Neuman issued a bulletin to employees that day stating "You should know that the company intends to vigorously contest the citation."[119] UAW spokesperson for the campaign Maxey Irwin asserted that management's refusal to release the logs confirmed their claims that the plant's safety record was poor.[120] Nissan management never released the accident logs. The incident generated several stories critical of the company, and Nissan management decided to stop talking to the media until after the recognition election.[121] Nonetheless, as historian Timothy Minchin concluded, "Overall, the UAW had identified a good issue, yet it was unable to turn it into a conclusive winner."[122]

As the recognition election drew closer, UAW proponents made a second issue prominent: compensation. They distributed flyers, put advertisements in local newspapers, and ran commercials on a local radio station claiming that compensation at Nissan was $7,900 less than at Ford.[123] Union organizers called the compensation difference "company dues," but "it was an argument that didn't take" because the average hourly wage was not that different ($15.06 at Ford versus $14.80 at Nissan), Nissan paid 37 percent more than the average manufacturing wage in the Nashville area, and the cost of living in Tennessee was low.[124]

The UAW ran a thirty-minute program on a Nashville television station critical of the plant's working conditions and the lack of protection without a union contract. On July 23, the union sent a letter from NAACP head Benjamin Hooks to African American employees urging them to vote for unionization. UAW officials circulated a letter from two top managers at a new Nissan plant in Great Britain, which they received from the British Amalgamated Engineering Union, that encouraged British employees to join a union, but it had little resonance in Smyrna.[125] UAW organizers stepped up making house calls. Their cars had mobile phones, which was relatively novel at the time. If an employee did not answer the door, they would call the person on the phone.[126] A week after the election, an editorial in a local paper argued that this "eleventh hour" action "backfired" because "the employees, most of whom were Southerners, found the high-pressure techniques offensive, particularly when the union reps knew so much about their work records."[127]

Despite the UAW's use of the media and mobile phones, observers describe the union as being "outgunned" by Nissan management's information campaign inside and outside of the plant. The company's $100 million annual payroll fueled economic growth in the region and made many businesses dependent on Nissan for their survival. The years that company leaders spent cultivating the local community through numerous ceremonies and charitable donations also paid off. Business owners, Church leaders, civic organizations, and local media outlets almost unanimously sided with Nissan in the recognition election. Three days before the election, a local newspaper ran a front-page article with the headline "UAW Win Could Hurt Local Economy."[128] In contrast, "community support for the UAW proved to be almost nonexistent."[129] US congressman from Tennessee Bart Gordon did not support the UAW in the drive despite being a Democratic Party member and having received endorsements from unions in the past. The UAW, moreover, never tried to develop leverage over Nissan through the firm's suppliers or customers.[130]

Nissan sent all employees the June–July issue of the plant newsletter *Nissan News*, replete with anti-union stories and stickers for employee homes that read "UAW Agents Respect My Privacy. Keep Away."[131] Nissan management celebrated the production of the one millionth vehicle at the Nissan Smyrna plant on July 19, just one week before voting was to begin in the union recognition election. Management included employees in the celebration and distributed T-shirts that read "1 Team Makes a Million," tying in the company's one-team anti-union slogan.[132]

The day before the election, Nissan management stopped production to hold a mandatory meeting for all line employees. Salaried and office employees lined the walls. The meeting opened with a "pro-Nissan" video that culminated with a request that employees "vote no." A speech from Jerry Benefield followed. Benefield implied that workers supporting the union were not proud of the plant's accomplishments, which provoked boos and chants of "Union! Union! Union!" from pro-union employees and a standing ovation for Benefield at the end from anti-union employees.[133]

On the day of the election, workers wore "Vote No" and "Vote Yes" T-shirts and buttons to express their preferences, but suspense and the desire not to ruffle feathers with others holding an opposing view made the mood in the plant and the town "quiet."[134] Reporters from the major US television networks and national newspapers and international correspondents from Germany, Japan, and the United Kingdom had all come to Smyrna to cover the story. The voter turnout was high: 97.9 percent. Both Nissan and UAW representatives said that they expected a close vote, but in the end it was not. The vote was 711 in favor of unionization and 1,622 against it. In other words, only 30.5 percent supported unionization.[135]

The "no" voters cheered and stomped their feet when the NLRB official announced the election results at 3:30 a.m. in the plant's media room, which was packed with employees and reporters from around the country and the world. Jerry Benefield appeared a short time later surrounded by anti-union employees waving US flags and chanting "team one, team one." An exuberant Benefield assessed the outcome. "The contest has been a long and hard one, and it's been disruptive, but our employees have finally won."[136] He continued, "The vast majority of our workers have demonstrated that this is a safe place to work and that wages are on par with other U.S. auto plants. I think our victory by better than two-to-one speaks for itself."[137] Regarding the union, he said, "I believe that this victory says to the UAW that in order to organize a work force today, you can't do it just because you have all the plants in the industry before. We believe it says to the UAW that there must be a reason, there must be an issue for employees to be willing to pay $30 a month to the UAW for their services."[138] The results left him "more convinced than ever before that the UAW will never organize Nissan."[139] Benfield urged "the winners to be humble, the vanquished to be good losers, and promised that there would be no retaliation against those who had been union sympathizers."[140]

The results "visibly upset" UAW officers.[141] In Smyrna, UAW deputy communications director Frank Joyce, who was noticeably angry in front of the bevy of television cameras, refused to comment immediately after the results were announced.[142] Back in Detroit, UAW communications director Peter Laarman called it a "bitter pill."[143] The union did release a prepared statement asserting that Nissan management "used every weapon in the union-buster's arsenal to defeat the UAW," including "smears and intimidation tactics." The statement also indicated that the UAW was not giving up. "The union drive in Smyrna is by no means at an end. All the election demonstrates is that when a company is determined to operate without a union and is willing to use threats and misrepresentation to an unlimited extent, that company can delay—if not escape—its day of reckoning. Acting together we can make a difference. As long as it takes, we will remain committed to helping you achieve the victory you need and deserve."[144] Officials promised to keep the UAW's Smyrna office open with three full-time staff to assist employees filing workers' compensation cases and to counsel on health and safety matters.[145]

Why did the employees at the Nissan Smyrna plant overwhelmingly reject unionization? Marvin Runyon intentionally made union opposition a key component of his one-team management model. Many subsequent decisions followed from that choice, including minimizing the distinctions between blue- and white-collar employees, offering a paternalistic "1 team" approach, using a hiring process designed to select employees unlikely to be interested in unionization, paying compensation slightly below the union rate in a low-cost region, offering popular benefits not found in union contracts, avoiding layoffs, creating the Nissan News Network to convey management's view ubiquitously to employees in the plant, and being active in the local community. Many employees said that the UAW had little to offer beyond what they were already getting. Some employees expressed fears that unionization would lead Nissan management to scale back investment plans, which would jeopardize their own dreams of moving into better positions in the company. UAW leaders made plant safety the paramount issue in the campaign because it was the only available weak point, but this was not enough to persuade even a third of the employees to vote for the union.

The broader impact of Nissan's victory at the Smyrna plant in the 1989 union recognition election was substantial. Nissan managers showed other automobile executives and politicians—particularly in the South—that it was possible to defeat the UAW. Subsequent transplant managers closely copied Nissan's tactics; which are still in widespread use to this day. Writing more than a decade later, *New York Times* reporter Keith Bradsher noted that "the 1989 defeat haunted the union ever since" because it made plain that the UAW was not invincible just when transplants had begun to proliferate.[146]

UAW leaders acknowledged the shortcomings of the Smyrna campaign. One was the failure to work with civil society organizations. Owen Bieber, in a speech at the convention of the Southern Christian Leadership Conference in September 1989, praised the organization's head, Joseph Lowery, as a key figure who

helped the UAW organize the Mack Truck factory in Winnsboro, South Carolina. Bieber proclaimed, "When we go back to Smyrna, Tennessee—and we're
going back—I want Reverend Lowery to go back with me."[147]

Another lesson was structural. In December 1988, eleven months after the
UAW formally launched the organizing drive in Smyrna, UAW associate general counsel Leonard Page sent a memo to Owen Bieber and Stephen Yokich
"with unsolicited advice on how to organize the remaining transplants (Nissan,
Honda, Isuzu and Toyota)." The memo had seven enumerated points:

1) Establish a *new* National Department attached to the President's office
   for organizing and serving the transplants. (Organizing the transplants,
   like conducting a war, is too important to be entrusted to the Regions).
2) Assign your *best* organizer to that new department with the exclusive
   job of organizing each transplant.
3) Consider new organizing approaches: Get a demographics book together
   on everything we currently know about each company; the community,
   the current workforce, past organizing efforts, etc. Invite outsiders or
   consultants to study the issues and make recommendations. Do some
   polling among workers at each location to see what's on their mind.
4) Establish an inter-department Team to work with the Organizing
   Coordinator (Legal, Public Relations, Research, Info Systems, etc.).
5) Make sure the rest of the union is aware of the efforts and gives the
   Team full support.
6) Require Monthly Reports from everyone on the Team as to what they
   have been doing and how they think things are going.
7) Let the companies know on the next UAW trip to Japan that *this time* we
   mean business.[148]

Eight days later Yokich sent a memo in reaction to Page's suggestions to his
and Bieber's deputies, Dick Shoemaker and Ben Perkins, who were copied on
Page's memo:

> When Owen and I reviewed the attached memo from Leonard, we im-
> mediately recognized that it is very probable that the Organizing De-
> partment is presently doing some of the things he is suggesting. When
> we have a chance, I'd like to discuss Leonard's suggestions with you in
> view of what the Department may be doing now that is either similar
> to or identical to what he's suggesting.
> When you have a chance, please give me a call regarding this matter.[149]

The UAW leadership restructured organizing largely along the lines Page proposed. The union announced the creation of the Transnational and Joint Ven-

tures Department under the UAW president to coordinate activities at the transplants.[150] The department was initially responsible for the eight thousand members at three plants: the GM-Toyota New United Motors Manufacturing Incorporated joint venture in Freemont, California; the Ford-Mazda joint venture in Flat Rock, Michigan; and the Chrysler-Mitsubishi Diamond Motors joint venture in Normal, Illinois.[151] The Transnational and Joint Ventures Department ultimately proved ineffectual because it received few resources and remained under the tight control of the UAW president, despite new more detailed recommendations from Page.[152]

UAW officials endeavored to obtain assistance in their next meeting with the president of the JAW, which took place in Detroit that same month. Many expressions of solidarity were exchanged, but no additional concrete actions emerged.[153]

In the second half of 1989, UAW officials tried to use unfair labor practice charges to advance the union's position in the Smyrna plant. In one instance, Nissan dismissed a union supporter for failing to report on his job application in 1983 that he had filed a worker's compensation claim.[154] In the second, an applicant alleged that Nissan failed to hire her because of union activity at her previous job.[155] The UAW had placed advertisements in local newspapers stating that "a charge has been filed by the UAW with the National Labor Relations Board charging that Nissan interviews applicants concerning their former union membership and then makes determination about that employee's employment based on the answers given." The ad asked individuals to call the UAW "if you or anyone you know has been asked about the union at your former employer or any questions concerning union membership."[156] The ad failed to uncover credible leads. The NLRB dismissed both claims owing to insufficient evidence in early 1990.[157] Interest in unionization was minimal at the Smyrna plant in the years immediately following the long organizing effort that culminated in the 1989 recognition election.

The UAW leadership did not react passively to the mounting set of problems besetting the union in the 1980s. Difficulties organizing transplants, concessions to domestic producers, intensified international economic competition, social change, the newfound popularity of neo-liberal economic policy, new technologies, increased anti-union attacks from business, greater sophistication in polling and political advertising, declining membership, and internal division prompted the union to create the Commission on the Future of the UAW at its 1986 convention. The task of the Commission was to present a report at the next UAW convention in 1989. The Commission was "not [to] supplant the regular governance structure in any way—but it will help us develop the information base we need to guide our specific actions and decisions."[158] Half of the Commission's members were top union officers. The other half were regional UAW officials. The Commission held day-long workshops in each of the union's 16 regions over the course of two years. The workshops had 1 participant per 1,000 members in a region so long as the total number did not exceed 100. The union's regional "directors were urged to invite participants who truly represented the diversity of backgrounds and viewpoints that exist within the union."[159]

Among the findings of the report were that members "are acutely aware how communication techniques have intensified throughout society . . . they want their union . . . to be part of this larger environment," and "We should expand our use of modern techniques such as polling, video and computers to identify issues in organizing campaigns and to help present a positive image of the union."[160]

The UAW leadership followed up on the report's recommendations in 1990 by soliciting proposals from public relations consulting firms to see if they could help improve the union's organizing campaigns at transplants. Several rounds of discussions culminated in early 1992 with a 15-page preliminary proposal from a corporate PR firm, Laird, Long & Sylvester. LLS recommended that the UAW conduct simultaneous community campaigns at the Honda plant in Ohio, the Nissan Smyrna plant, and Totoya's Georgetown, Kentucky, facility, and then move forward with the most promising one. Each community campaign would include 52 strategies (grouped into market research, PR, and sales and advertising) that would unfold in three phases. The proposal included a 30-page campaign "bible" to guide all actions and "rules of engagement" for interacting with national and local media. The campaign's theme was to be "The New UAW." It cast the union as "an upbeat, positive, American institution with significant experience, wisdom, and resources." The effort would emphasize "the 'American-ness' of the UAW" to draw a contrast between the union and the foreign-owned transplants. The report stressed, however, that the UAW should avoid explicitly xenophobic tactics. Sub-themes would "portray the benefits provided to American workers by the UAW throughout its long history. The purpose of this recommendation was to 'sell' transplant workers on the value of UAW services and to dispel any notion that the UAW is somehow alien, threatening, or unfair to its members."[161]

The report's authors argued that "a major identity problem for the UAW lies in its old-fashioned image as an adversarial organization" and asserted that "making the UAW understandable as a democratic and people-oriented organization is the first step toward creating a positive identity and eliminating the negative perceptions of transplant workers." This could be done by "communication programs designed to 'put a human face on the UAW'" through "videos showing UAW members and officers . . . describing the day-to-day benefits secured by the UAW" and "visits by UAW members and officers" to transplants. The union should create a series of videos explaining the UAW's structure, accomplishments, and opportunities for transplant workers. Each transplant campaign should have its own logo that incorporates the name of the company to reinforce the "localness" of the campaign.[162] The proposal called for extensive polling to tailor the message and assess its impact for the duration of the effort. UAW officials agreed to pay LLS $56,000 for a full proposal.[163] On April 10, 1992, LLS submitted a 123-page implementation plan to the UAW.[164] The elaborate proposal had an eye-watering $4.9 million budget, which led the union leadership to turn to a second consultancy—Greer, Margolis, Mitchell, Grunwald & Associates—to review the LLS proposal.

GMMG was more familiar with trade unions; it had worked with the UAW previously. GMMG identified the positive elements of the LLS proposal as the focus on community, emphasis on shaping media coverage, the recommendations regarding media and videos, and the development of a "bible" to establish rules of engagement. Negative elements included a failure to include a reason to vote for a union, spending too much on national promotion of the "new" UAW rather than focusing on target plants, spending too much money by targeting three plants at once instead of just one, and putting the cart before the horse by selecting campaign themes before doing opinion research.[165]

In January 1993, the renamed Greer, Margolis, Mitchell & Associates presented their own 31-one-page proposal with Lauer, Lalley & Associates, and the November Group polling firm to the UAW. The proposal asserted that the 1989 Nissan organizing drive failed because "young, rural Southerners . . . are happy to have their jobs and distrust unions." They argued that rural Southerners felt inferior to Northerners; the arrival of transplants therefore was a psychological boost that generated loyalty to the firms. The campaign would pitch union membership as the next step forward regarding status and respect by ending the second-class status of transplants through closing the compensation gap.[166] The budget for the entire proposal was $2 million.

The UAW leadership decided to go ahead with phase one of the proposal, which was a series of focus groups with employees from the Honda, Nissan, Subaru-Isuzu, and Toyota plants in the first half of 1994. All indications are that the focus groups were well done. Owen Bieber's chief aide and confidant Dick Shoemaker observed the sessions for Nissan and Toyota and took copious notes.[167] The results were disheartening for the UAW. The consultants' report concluded that "no transplant is ripe for organizing" and "traditional arguments about pay and benefits will not succeed." The focus groups revealed that most employees were happy with current pay and saw higher pay in Japan and the North as simply compensating for a higher cost of living. Contrary to the consultants' initial assumption, most of the participants did not feel that they had second-class status; they actually felt superior to employees at the three domestic automobile producers. The consultants concluded, "Given the results of the focus groups, one legitimate question is whether it makes sense to abandon efforts to organize transplants at all. . . . [By] ceasing organizing efforts, there might be some chance that management would allow wages to fall farther behind, and worker dissatisfaction would increase. In this new environment, the UAW might stand a better chance."[168]

UAW leaders rejected the conclusions of the report. Dick Shoemaker wrote in the right margin of the first page of his copy, "can't live with this." A post-it note in Shoemaker's handwriting on the first page of the report read, "Owen: I don't think we need these folks help at this time. We know what we have to do." A second post-it note in Bieber's handwriting read, "I agree. File." The UAW stopped using consultants to assist with organizing for many years.

Construction of the Smyrna plant's new assembly line took two and a half years. On June 11, 1992, the first Nissan Altima midsized sedan rolled off the assembly line. The company built it to compete with the Honda Accord and the Toyota Camry in the largest segment of the US car market. Harbour and Associates ranked Smyrna as the most efficient North American automobile assembly plant for five straight years starting in 1994 when measured by the number of hours needed to produce a vehicle.[169]

The plant's top ranking was one of the few bright lights for Nissan during the 1990s. "This company was hit with a big 'stupid stick,'" according to Jason Vines, spokesperson for Nissan North America. The bursting of the five-year Japanese asset-price bubble in 1991 led Nissan managers to retrench. They were slow to respond to rising demand for large pickup trucks and SUVs in the United States and failed to update the Altima after Honda and Toyota upgraded the Accord and the Camry. The company was only able to maintain sales by offering large rebates, which generated sizable losses. The Nissan management announced a three-year global restructuring plan in August 1992 but failed to implement large parts of it, deepening the firm's decline.[170]

Nissan's difficulties helped to revive discontent in Smyrna. In March 1994 Ben Perkins—now UAW organizing director—reported to Owen Bieber and his lieutenants after a discussion with mostly former members of the voluntary organizing committee that "in all my meetings with Nissan workers since our election, until this past week, they have constantly said the time was not right for a new campaign. For the first time, to a person, each one that I spoke with said now is the time to begin a campaign." Perkins summarized the reasons for the changed assessment:

> Older workers have seen an attitude change on the part of upper management. The Marv Runyon style of management, which relied in part on maintaining close contact between upper management and workers

on the line, has vanished. Jerry Benefield is rarely seen, not trusted, and ridiculed. His top assistant, Emil Hassan, is more or less a hatchet man, and disliked immensely by the workers.

The 401k Program is being switched to an investment program, and most workers are perplexed about which options they should choose. The company is not much help. . . .

The Stamping Plant is barely able to keep up. . . . During the ice storm, when the assembly plant was shut down and the workers were sent home and paid 80% of their normal take-home pay for those two days, the Stamping Plant was required to work. So, in the minds of the workers in Stamping, they worked for 20% of their pay since their brothers in the assembly operation had the time off. This is not viewed by them as being fair.[171]

Perkins continued with a long list of quality problems with the vehicles and Nissan management cutbacks on quality controls. The explanation at the plant for these developments was that "Nissan is money short, and they are cutting back in every conceivable way. . . . Pressure for productivity is probably greater than it ever has been and it's behind this sudden change in attitude of the older committeepeople at Nissan." Perkins closed by qualifying his assessment. "Not having worked in an auto car or truck plant, I don't know for sure how these problems stack up to normal assembly line problems."[172] The UAW leaders responded cautiously to the report, still smarting from the devastating 1989 loss. They decided to continue to monitor events and cultivate support but not to launch a new organizing drive at that time.

Nissan imported engines from Mexico for vehicles built in Smyrna, but they were of poor quality, which proved problematic. Smyrna was already Nissan's largest vehicle assembly plant in the world. The physical limitations of the plant and property made adding engine production there unfeasible. Nissan management decided instead to build a power train plant in Decherd, Tennessee, which was one hour south of Smyrna. The plant opened in May 1997.[173] The UAW has never launched an organizing drive at the Decherd plant.

Interest in unionization intensified at Nissan Smyrna in early 1997. A union meeting in March drew more than one thousand employees, causing a traffic jam.[174] The principal issues of contention were plant safety, poor treatment of injured employees, high-pressure working conditions, changes to retirement benefits, and compensation. GM's Saturn plant in nearby Spring Hill was a new source animating interest in organizing because it was organized and an easy reference point. The base wage was slightly lower at Saturn, but employees received a $10,000 bonus in 1996. A typical worker's bonus at Nissan was a few hundred dollars. The difference was particularly irksome to Nissan workers because of the Harbour and Associates ranking of Smyrna as North America's most efficient plant for several years running.[175]

The UAW leadership did not want a repeat of the long, fruitless organizing drive of the 1980s and retained some skepticism regarding plant employees' assessment of union strength. This time they took a different approach. In June 1997, lead organizer Chuck McDonald announced that the UAW would soon solicit authorization cards for several weeks. If two-thirds of the 4,900 line employees submitted cards, the union would file a petition for a recognition election.[176] The UAW added organizers and launched the campaign at the end of July with a series of meetings and leafleting at the plant.

Nissan human resources director Buck Kahl issued a statement in response. "We are disappointed that our employees will be subjected to the UAW pressure tactics, but as employees study the facts, they will make the decision best for them. We believe that will be the same decision they made in '89."[177] Nissan management made no further comments but continued to retain anti-union consultants and used the Nissan News Network to broadcast anti-union messages. Opponents produced T-shirts with anti-union slogans and signs depicting the UAW as a pacifier-waving crying baby. Local newspapers published a letter from Charlie Giffen, Smyrna's director of economic development, that argued against unionization.[178]

By early September organizers had collected cards from only 45 percent of the workforce, so the UAW ended the effort. Chuck McDonald expressed disappointment but pointed out that "we did this conditionally." Bucky Kahl commented, "Our employees evaluated all the facts and decided for themselves that UAW representation was not in their best interest. Now we can completely focus on that which we do best which is building high quality vehicles and we're excited about the launch of our new truck next week, the Frontier."[179] The UAW announced that it would be closing its small office in Smyrna and instead work out of the union's Region 8 office, which two years earlier had relocated to Lebanon, Tennessee, twenty-five miles north of the plant.[180]

Nissan's competitive woes worsened. The firm's global market share fell from 6.6 percent in 1988 to 4.6 percent in 1998. The company lost money in five out of six years between 1993 and 1998, accumulating $22 billion in external debt as well as $20 billion in liabilities owed to its Japanese keiretsu partners. In the United States, a fall in gasoline prices in 1998 led sales of the compact Sentra to fall by 50 percent. Altima sales continued to flag even after a $1,500 price cut, dropping by 38 percent. Management responded by instituting a four-and-a-half–day workweek in Smyrna from May to October and at the end of the year announced a plan to reduce production capacity worldwide by 15 percent. The

Smyrna plant slipped four rungs in one year in Harbour and Associates efficiency ranking for 1998, and an accident killed a worker in 1999.[181]

Takeover rumors circulated. Ultimately, the French automobile company Renault bought 36.8 percent of Nissan's stock for $5.4 billion in March 1999, and Carlos Ghosn—the Brazilian-born French national of Lebanese heritage who headed Renault—also became Nissan's chief operating officer. Ghosn had earned the nickname "le cost killer" in France because he had not hesitated to push through difficult changes to restore the French firm to profitability.[182] Ghosn took six months to reorganize top management and to produce a "Nissan revival plan" that prescribed plant closures and layoffs mainly in Japan, along with increased research and development and the launch of twenty-two new models in three years to improve Nissan's brand image. In March 2000, Jerry Benefield stepped down as CEO of the Smyrna plant at age sixty as part of a company-wide shake-up that included making Carlos Ghosn officially CEO of Nissan worldwide. Benefield's deputy, Dan Gaudette, succeeded him.[183] The revival plan succeeded quickly; Nissan's sales rose, and debt fell. Ghosn became a pop icon in Japan.[184]

The upheaval at Nissan reverberated throughout the company. Although the revival plan envisioned expanding production in Smyrna by 20 percent to five hundred thousand vehicles per year[185] and doubling the size of the Decherd engine plant,[186] the greater use of temporary employees, cuts to the pension program, rising health insurance costs, and continuing complaints about plant safety led more employees to consider unionization.[187] The UAW held informational meetings in Decherd and Smyrna in July and August 2000.[188] Roughly eight hundred turned out, and six hundred signed cards. UAW vice president for organizing Bob King had hoped for one thousand. Dave Curson, executive assistant to Stephen Yokich, relayed to Yokich in an email that "the turnout was large enough to have some hopes but small enough not to have great expectations. [King] is going to work at it for about one more week to get a better grasp on where they are at."[189] Workplace safety was again the most prominent issue.[190] By late October, however, it had become clear that the "drive to organize Nissan Motor Co.'s Middle Tennessee operations may not be picking up steam like organizers wanted."[191]

In the following year, UAW leaders and supporters decided to try a different approach. Previously, starting an organizing drive with a public campaign prompted Nissan management to launch a countercampaign. This time union organizers and supporters decided to pursue an under-the-radar effort with a smaller group of core supporters in the plant than was typical for an organizing drive. Once union officials judged that there was sufficient support, the first public act would be petitioning for a recognition election. The advantage of this approach, known as an ambush drive, is the element of surprise. It shortened the time Nissan managers had to organize and run an anti-union campaign.[192] The strategy depended on waging a more powerful "air war," as King put it, to substitute for a large number of adherents, which they did not have, who normally executed a traditional "land war" of leafletting, in-plant persuasion, and house calls. Specifically, UAW organizers made greater use of phone banks and a well-crafted website that included video clips of plant employees explaining why they favored unionization.[193]

On August 13, 2001, union supporters distributed flyers outside of the Smyrna factory to inform employees that UAW representatives and in-plant voluntary organizing committee members were about to file a petition for a recognition election and would conduct a series of meetings in the Grand Ballroom of Smyrna's Town Centre for workers with questions about unionization. (Organizers found insufficient interest in unionization at the Decherd plant to proceed there.) A steady stream of workers went to meet with union representatives. The next day, Nissan workers filed the petition. The theme was "It's about us; it's about our families and we deserve better."[194] Voluntary organizing committee member Mike Williams laid out the issues. "Nissan workers are worried about pensions, about how they are treated when they are injured on the job, about unfair treatment compared to Nissan workers in Japan and elsewhere and a lot of other things that we weren't concerned about years ago." Chet Konkle, another voluntary organizing committee member, added, "It's been more than a decade since Nissan workers had a chance to vote on union representation. We are confident that a majority now supports the UAW and we are ready to put that to the test."[195] The election was set for October 3.

The campaign initially gained some traction outside of the plant. The editorial board of the *Rutherford Courier*, a local newspaper, did not take a side but did back holding a recognition election. The board reasoned,

> For some, it will be their first opportunity to vote whether they should unionize. For others, it will be a chance to reconsider the way they voted the last time the United Auto Workers asked for their vote in 1989. Certainly employees at the plant were overwhelmingly satisfied with the day to day operations and management of the plant 12 years ago. But a lot has changed since then.[196]

The editorial then listed the principal issues at the plant—including pensions, workplace injuries, and superior treatment of Nissan's Japanese employees—describing them all as "legitimate concerns." It continued:

> A union could be the best way for the workers to maintain some assurance that they will not be forgotten or mistreated in the rush to revitalize Nissan's place in the auto market.

On the other hand, the numbers 12 years ago indicated that many workers were satisfied with the way things were and more wary about a union.

Either way, after 12 years, with more than 6,500 workers, they deserve a chance to decide for themselves.[197]

Other media outlets remained decidedly supportive of Nissan management, however.

Since management from the French auto firm Renault was running Nissan, UAW officials took a broader approach to generating international support than in the past, when they only tried to gain assistance from Japanese unions, but they still took a top-down approach. Back in October 2000, UAW director of governmental and international affairs Don Stillman had discussed getting letters of support from French unions and the JAW.[198]

A week into the drive the IMF, the global union federation for the metalworking sector to which the UAW belonged, publicized it on the organization's website.[199] A month later, the IMF's leadership contacted all its affiliates "urging them and their shopfloor members to send messages of solidarity to the United Auto Workers' union." IMF general secretary Marcello Malentacchi stressed, "There must be no interference by the company, either to threaten or otherwise discourage workers from joining the union." To underscore IMF support for the UAW, Malentacchi traveled to Smyrna in the days leading up to the election.[200] In late September, Malentacchi issued a statement correcting false assertions put out by Nissan management regarding the company's relations with unions in other countries. He expressed amazement regarding the false claim that "the socialist governments of Britain and France require large plants to have unions." He also pointed out that Nissan plants in France, Great Britain, Japan, Mexico, South Africa, Spain, and Taiwan all had union representation, which proved that "Nissan management can function quite effectively in a union environment."[201]

Nissan management attempted to lower the odds of a UAW victory by arguing before the NLRB that the Decherd and Smyrna plants should be considered a single unit for a union recognition election because the company's labor relations was centralized for the two plants. Ronald Hooks, regional NLRB director in Memphis, rejected Nissan management's argument, noting that the two plants were more than seventy miles apart and that each had an independent management structure responsible for day-to-day operations.[202] Nissan management appealed the decision but lost.[203]

The terrorist attack on September 11, 2001, dealt a huge setback to the organizing drive. Activities stopped for two weeks as the country tried to regain its bearings and come to grips with the consequences of the attack. Economic uncertainty rose, a melancholy mood with streaks of fear and anger overtook the nation, and reflexive patriotism swelled. Employee interest in departing from the status quo under such conditions dwindled.[204]

UAW leaders tried harder than in previous efforts to bring in domestic support from outside the union movement, but they did so only at the last moment and were not always successful. In September, UAW officials released a letter to Nissan employees from Gene Upshaw, executive director of the National Football League Players Association, and Frank Wycheck, tight end for the Tennessee Titans and the team's player representative, but the backing was oblique at best. The closing sentences read "We support the essential right of all working people to freely choose collective bargaining representation, without intimidation by management, and we wish you well in your upcoming election at the Nissan facility in Smyrna, Tennessee. Don't be afraid to win!"[205] Just a week before the election, Bob King asked Gordon Brehm, treasurer of the Interfaith Committee for Worker Justice in Little Rock, Arkansas, to help gather community support, particularly from the religious groups.[206]

Nissan management returned to the strategy of making no formal comments to media during a recognition election while engaging in an aggressive anti-union campaign inside the factory. Management incessantly ran anti-union videos featuring strikes and plant closings on the ubiquitous in-plant monitors, distributed pamphlets warning of detrimental effects of unionization, kept track of who supported the union, and held compulsory meetings for undecided employees. In one video message, plant CEO Dan Gaudette told employees not to talk to UAW supporters. Nissan again announced shortly before the election that the Smyrna plant would produce an additional vehicle and that employment at the plant would expand. This time, it was the full-size Maxima sedan. One local paper ran the headline "Maxima Impact" in large font. At the announcement, Nissan senior vice president of North American manufacturing Emil Hassan said that Smyrna's employees "have gained the vote of Nissan's top management."[207] When asked about unionization, Hassan replied, "We strongly believe that they will vote against it."[208] Bob King attempted to make the best of the announcement from the UAW's perspective, saying "I think it tells workers you don't have to worry about this plant. It's great news."[209] A local newspaper once again published a letter from a local director of economic development warning that "unionizing Nissan could hurt local jobs."[210]

On the day before the election, Bob King expressed optimism. "There's an energy in the plant that has not been there before. There's a buzz, a real talk of key issues. We're excited. . . . It's about trust, it's about integrity, and it's about how this corporation treats workers in that workplace."[211] Voluntary organizing committee member and sixteen-year Nissan employee Randy Gentry confidently proclaimed, "We will shock the world. I think we're going to win it."[212] Vic Wolaver, a twelve-year veteran of the night shift, was more cautious. "If they took a vote of people who have five years or more, it would be easy that the union would come in. People with five years or less, they're still intimidated."[213]

UAW officials and supporters under the leadership of Bob King did a better job in this organizing drive than the ill-fated attempt twelve years earlier. An editorial in a newspaper that had been consistently supportive of Nissan described the UAW's campaign as a "strong effort.... From the outside, the attempt at organizing the plant seemed stronger than the previous one a decade ago. More employee issues were presented and the campaign had less of a 'rah-rah, go-union-go' feel."[214]

On October 3, NLRB representatives finished counting the votes at 7:30 p.m. The turnout was high—96.7 percent of those eligible cast ballots—which initially buoyed the hopes of union adherents, but Nissan employees again overwhelmingly rejected unionization: 1,486 (32.3 percent) voted "yes," and 3,103 (67.7 percent) voted "no." The "yes" vote this time was only 1.9 percentage points higher than it had been twelve years earlier.[215]

Plant CEO Dan Gaudette announced the results to a group of about two hundred anti-union employees who chanted, "One team, one team."[216] His prepared statement said, "The majority of employees have made it clear that they have no interest in being represented by the UAW.... The contest has been a long and hard one and it's been disruptive, but our employees have made their choice clear. We hope now that the UAW will respect their wishes."[217] Off the cuff he added, "You're the ones who made this decision, and I think you made the right decision. Now it's time to get back to the business of building quality cars."[218]

The reality that "UAW supporters and officials made a strong effort, but still fell short," made this loss even more crushing.[219] The prepared statement from the UAW was long and unfocused. UAW president Stephen Yokich called the loss a "setback for Nissan workers":

> The fact remains that in the global economy, Nissan workers still need and deserve the seat at the decision-making table that only a union can provide. That's why Nissan workers and other workers can continue to count on the UAW's support in their efforts to unionize and build brighter futures for themselves and their families.
>
> Obviously we're disappointed that the UAW supporters at Nissan came up short in this election after working so hard and standing up to Nissan's intense anti-union campaign.... Yet, at the same time, we're proud of the courage and determination they displayed throughout.[220]

The statement also included several quotes from Bob King, which were a mix of thanks to supporters and accusations of Nissan management malfeasance:

> Our experience tells us that campaigns like this exert tremendous pressure on employers to maintain higher wages and better benefits for their workers than would otherwise be the case. Whether they know it or not, every Nissan technician owes a debt to the brave Nissan workers who campaign for the union. They are protecting every Nissan worker's standard of living.
>
> There can be no doubt that Nissan management's law breaking and campaign of fear and intimidation offers dramatic proof of the tremendous obstacles workers must overcome in the face of a hostile employer. . . . In this election and in far too many union elections, employers threaten workers with plant closings, moving to Mexico, loss of wages and benefits, and many other threats. Moreover, unlike political elections where all sides have comparable access to the voters, in union elections, the employer has unlimited workplace access to the workers while unions have no workplace access to workers.[221]

A subject heading in an email between two UAW organizers captured the reaction within the union far more succinctly: "Aarrrrrrrrrrrrrgh!"[222] Bob King was frank in media interviews regarding shortcomings. "I thought it was going to be a lot closer," he said.[223] "I won't make excuses. We clearly did not educate well enough."[224] "We tried to run a campaign about hope and positivity while they ran a campaign of hatred and fear. Unfortunately hatred and fear won out."[225] King conceded that Nissan management ran an effective campaign. "We thought we had a strong majority, and we thought the company's campaign moved 800 or 900 workers away from us and toward them."[226]

King cited three reasons for the loss: lack of access to company property, the company's negative campaign, and a "substantially smaller than normal" voluntary organizing committee, which meant there were few active supporters inside the plant. King said that "the issues were so great" that they thought they could wage a successful campaign without a full committee, but "that was a mistake on our part."[227] The union's much-touted air war proved inadequate.

On the evening of the loss Bob King said, "They won round two. . . . We'll be here for round three and four until we get justice and democracy for these workers."[228] An editorial in a local newspaper the next day provided what proved to be a more accurate prognostication: "One point is rather obvious. It will take a major—make that huge—change in the way Nissan treats its employees before unionization becomes a viable choice for the Smyrna automakers' rank-and-file workers."[229] The UAW never launched another organizing drive at the Smyrna plant.

Nissan Canton

The approach that the UAW leadership took to organize Nissan's second assembly plant—which opened in Canton, Mississippi, in 2003—differed substantially from the Smyrna drives. The core of the Canton campaign was to equate unionization with the struggle to achieve greater civil rights for African Americans. A campaign that depicted union organizing as a civil right fit both the workforce and the community. Eighty percent of the workforce in Nissan's Canton plant was African American, and Mississippi was a central battlefield of the civil rights struggle. The execution of this central plank of the organizing drive was successful. Union supporters built a strong external organization anchored in Black churches, civil rights organizations, and historically Black colleges and universities. UAW officials also succeeded in developing a second prong for the campaign, namely a network of foreign support to pressure Nissan management to change its behavior at the Canton plant.

The organizing drive nonetheless failed for six reasons: the weak labor market in Mississippi beyond the Nissan plant led many employees to be grateful for their jobs and reluctant to risk disrupting the status quo; massive state subsidies motivated the political elite in Mississippi to campaign actively against unionization, much like what unfolded at MBUSI and Volkswagen Chattanooga; Nissan management quickly put into place an aggressive anti-union campaign, drawing heavily from experience gained from combating organizing drives at the company's Smyrna plant; union supporters did not pursue a sustained and coordinated public relations campaign or a boycott to change Nissan management's behavior; union supporters failed to develop a workers organizing committee within the plant strong enough to provide basic information about the workforce or to demonstrate the utility of a nascent union; and although UAW officials spent considerable time building connections with employee representatives in Brazil, France, and Japan, none had institutional leverage vis-à-vis management comparable to their German counterparts. They were therefore unable to pressure Nissan management to take a more accommodating stance toward unionization.

Before turning to the UAW's campaign in Canton, it is important to understand why Nissan invested there and how the investment developed. Part of Carlos Ghosn's turnaround plan for Nissan was to build an additional factory in the United States because state governments provide substantial subsidies, which meant that the still cash-strapped firm would have to borrow far less to build a plant there than anywhere else in the world. In June 2000 a site-selection firm working for Nissan began contacting several state agencies, including the Mississippi Development Authority, about potential sites but did not disclose that Nissan was the client. In early August, Nissan management informed the Mississippi Development Authority that Nissan was behind the inquiry and that there were six southeastern states still under consideration.[230]

A "war between the states" to land major manufacturing plants had become commonplace at least since the early 1990s.[231] The State of Mississippi had participated in many of these contests but had always come up empty-handed. Newly elected governor Ronnie Musgrove, a Democrat, made securing this plant a priority. Musgrove first spoke with Nissan officials in July 2000. In August, the governor called a special session of the Mississippi legislature to pass a law to expand the state government's authority to offer incentives to attract major investments. The Mississippi Advantage Jobs Act created state income tax breaks for substantial development projects, increased the tax credit available for training individuals to become employees at such projects, and allowed for quarterly cash incentive payments to companies that fulfilled investment goals.[232]

In the third week of September 2000, Mississippi Development Authority director J. C. Burns and other state officials went to the Smyrna plant to talk with Nissan executives. A week later Burns, Musgrove, and Mississippi Republican US senator Trent Lott flew to Los Angeles to make Mississippi's pitch directly to Nissan CEO Carlos Ghosn. Ghosn spent forty-five minutes with the delegation, which the Mississippians took as a promising sign. In October Lott, who was also Senate majority leader at the time, added a provision to a federal spending bill to designate parts of Madison County, including the intended site for the plant, as a "renewal community," thus making businesses locating there eligible for federal tax breaks.[233]

In early October 2000, the Mississippi Development Authority learned that Nissan management had winnowed down the field to Alabama and Mississippi. In late October, Nissan notified Mississippi representatives that theirs was the "state of choice" for the new plant, but the state needed to enact additional measures to close the deal. On November 1, Governor Musgrove announced that he was calling in the Mississippi legislature for a one-day special session five days later to consider "an act to induce the location of a major capital economic development project proposed for Madison County." Musgrove did not specify the company because he had signed a confidentiality agreement, but speculation was widespread that the project was the Nissan plant.[234]

On the day of the special session, state senator Richard White, a Republican critic of Musgrove, quipped, "Look's like we've got a governor and a lobbyist all in one," because Musgrove personally worked with Mississippi lawmakers in the statehouse throughout the day to ensure the speedy passage of a satisfactory bill. Action was also required at the local level before Nissan management would commit to the project. On November 7 after some hesitation, Canton's city council (Canton's 2000 population was 12,900) agreed to a Nissan management requirement by voting that the city would not try to annex the Nissan site (which bordered Canton) for at least thirty years without the company's permission. Mississippi and Nissan officials completed the contract on the evening after the vote in Canton and on November 9 announced the company's decision to build the plant in Mississippi. Nissan management planned to start producing vehicles at the plant by mid-2003.[235]

The reaction in Mississippi to the news of the agreement to build a Nissan plant was exuberant. Banners on streetlights along major roads leading into Jackson, the state capital, proclaimed, "Nissan—Mississippi." A page-one headline in the Jackson *Clarion Ledger*, the newspaper of record in Mississippi, quoted a resident calling the decision "a blessing from God." Senator Trent Lott effused, "Finally, we get to say it—Nissan in Canton, Mississippi. Doesn't it sound good?"[236]

Nissan management chose Mississippi because the state and Madison County offered the company a generous initial incentives package that totaled $430.5 million for a plant that would produce 250,000 vehicles per year, employ three thousand, and had an initial price tag of $930 million. The state approved $295 million in bond authority to prepare the site, build access roads to the adjacent interstate highway, upgrade utilities, and subsidize worker training. The state also offered up to $20 million in tax incentives contingent on Nissan meeting investment targets. The Mississippi Department of Transportation chipped in $65 million worth of additional improvements to state roads. Madison County provided $23.5 million in bonds to improve county roads, $20 million in tax abatements over thirty years, and $2 million in school construction. The Madison County Development Authority received permission to borrow $5 million to construct a temporary headquarters and training center for Nissan. In addition, Mississippi State University agreed to build a $6 million extension center at the plant as well as provide $9 million to create the Center of Advanced Vehicular Systems in Starkville, which is two hours from the plant.[237] Many observers speculated that Mississippi's low unionization rate was also a factor in the decision, but Nissan CEO Carlos Ghosn dismissed this claim.[238]

In the spring of 2002 while the plant was still under construction, Nissan management decided to expand its capacity to be able to build five models rather than three, which increased its cost for the plant to $1.4 billion and raised projected employment at full operation to 5,300. The Mississippi state legislature approved $68 million in additional bond authority to support the expansion, which increased the state's total bond authority for the project to $363 million and total incentives to just shy of half a billion dollars.[239]

In late 2001, Nissan management began hiring employees to train them to work in the Canton plant. The facility began producing vehicles on May 27, 2003. On day one it had 2,000 employees. A year later, 5,340 worked there.[240] Nissan managers used the Runyon model for the Canton plant. They offered near union wages coupled with a generous benefit package. At Canton, Nissan paid production workers a base rate of $12.50 an hour to start and anticipated increasing pay to $21 an hour after two years. Skilled employees' hourly pay started at $19.55 and would reach $25.58 after two years. Pay at Ford and GM, in comparison, was $25 per hour for experienced production workers and $30 for skilled employees. (Ford and GM workers also paid monthly dues equal to two hours of wages.) For most production workers in Mississippi, Nissan's hourly wage was substantially higher than what they could find elsewhere in the state.[241]

Employee training sessions stressed that Nissan was committed to treating all employees "with dignity and respect."[242] Trainers stressed that Nissan was "non-union" even though the company dealt with unions in all of its plants except in the United States. Trainers said that unions only wanted dues money and that unionization resulted in plant closures.[243]

In April 2004, AFL-CIO national field representative Jim Evans said that the UAW was considering a unionization drive at the Nissan Canton. Gary Casteel, director of the UAW's southeastern region, tempered Evans's statement, commenting, "We have some places that we're looking at, but we haven't made any announcements."[244] The potential for union organizing in Mississippi did not look auspicious. The United Steelworkers of America had just lost union recognition elections at Tower Automotive and Yorozu Automotive, two Nissan suppliers.[245]

Nissan management set ambitious production goals for the Canton plant because the company had a lot of catching up to do. Nissan still had several holes in its model lineup. Auto companies typically launch at most one new model at a time from any plant. Within the space of a year, the Canton plant was producing four new models plus an existing model. Temporary employment agencies provided over one thousand employees, whom Nissan management called associates. Nissan called the four thousand full-time direct hires technicians, just like in Smyrna. The associates' pay and benefits were much lower than those of the technicians. Production quality at Canton was subpar at first. The J.D. Power 2004 Initial Quality Survey found 147 problems reported per 100 Nissan vehicles, which was substantially greater than the industry average of 119.[246] Nissan CEO Carlos Ghosn explained the poor quality by observing that "the root cause was a lack of experience. We'll be training a lot of new people we hired in Canton." Ghosn sent two hundred Japanese engineers to Canton to address the problem.[247]

UAW Region 8 director Gary Casteel reported that his union began to receive phone calls from Canton employees in November 2004. A top complaint was lack of respect stemming from Carlos Ghosn's explanation for the plant's quality problems, which some employees interpreted as blaming them. Employees also disliked the relatively low hourly starting wage rate for the unskilled. Casteel said that the UAW was only surveying employee complaints; the union had no plans at that moment to start an organizing campaign at the plant.[248] Nevertheless, Nissan management responded with an "anti-union surge" in late 2004. Shortly thereafter, Nissan management distributed internal memos to the plant human resource officers and supervisors enumerating "early warning signs" of unionization. Management required all employees to attend captive-audience meetings in groups of twenty to twenty-five to watch videos and listen to speeches critical of unions. Every meeting included a note taker, which led employees to keep silent to avoid being identified as sympathetic toward unionization. Nissan also installed television monitors in all break areas of the Canton plant. The company screened segments on a loop about Nissan sales, production quantity, consumer tips, health care advice, and seasonal features. Included in this fare were negative stories about Chrysler, Ford, GM, and the UAW.[249]

On March 14, 2005, UAW president Ron Gettelfinger, Bob King, and Gary Casteel went to Canton to gauge support for unionization. They met with a group of fifteen community leaders that included several ministers and a Catholic priest. The community leaders shared the complaints they had heard from Nissan employees about low starting salaries, difficult working conditions, and the firing of people for "speculative reasons" without a consistent and transparent process. Casteel explained to reporters, "We're not holding any mass meetings. We're trying to make sure that our message is on key." University of Mississippi journalism professor Joe Atkins, who had also been to the gathering, noted that the UAW leadership was laying the groundwork before proceeding with a unionization campaign because "they don't want to get into a situation like they did in Smyrna a few years back."[250] Eight days later, the UAW opened an office in a former church eight miles from the Canton plant and a five-minute drive from three of Nissan's parts suppliers in Gluckstadt. Casteel explained, "We've had enough response that warrants us to have a location in close proximity."[251] These actions did not move large numbers of Nissan Canton employees to support the union. By the end of 2006, 30 workers out of 4,000 (less than 1 percent) had joined the in-plant voluntary organizing committee of union supporters. This fell far short of the 10 percent mark, which the UAW uses as a benchmark when deciding whether to proceed with a recognition election. Similarly, only about 125 workers had attended recent union meetings. UAW officials estimated that union support in the plant was at 2 percent.[252]

In 2007, the UAW leaders tried again to stir interest in unionization. They organized an event at which three Nissan Canton employees talked about conditions in the plant. The employees recounted instances of dismissals for job-related injuries, intimidation, and anti-union propaganda. Workers from Nissan's Smyrna plant shared their experiences, which were similar. Religious leaders and community activists attended the gathering.[253]

In 2008 the UAW sent a female African American organizer, Sanchioni Butler, to take the lead in Mississippi.[254] UAW organizers worked with individual employees interested in organizing and local leaders, in particular the president of the Mississippi NAACP, Derrick Johnson. The UAW allowed other groups to use its office space, donated funds to charities and schools, sponsored fundraising banquets for local groups, and helped organize conferences and discussions on topics such as discrimination in the workplace.[255] The union did not, however, intensify the organizing effort.

When Bob King became head of the UAW in June 2010, he made organizing foreign-owned automobile assembly plants the signature goal of his presidency. King's strategy was to take a cooperative approach with the foreign-owned firms. He proposed a set of "Fair Election Principles" that included equal time for management and the UAW to make their case to the workers and no disparagement. King hoped to persuade management at the foreign-owned auto companies to agree to these principles.[256] The UAW leadership threatened to launch a global campaign to "rebrand" firms unwilling to accept these rules of engagement as human rights violators.[257]

King hired Richard Bensinger as acting organizing director. Bensinger had been the first organizing director of the AFL-CIO and was an advocate of an expansive approach to organizing drives, which involved community mobilization and public campaigns. The UAW also created the Global Organizing Institute based on the Organizing Institute training program that Bensinger had developed at the AFL-CIO in the early 1990s. The first group of interns included Brazilian, Chinese, German, Indian, Japanese, and South Korean nationals. They received training on effective techniques for speaking out against human rights violations and protesting at car dealerships and company headquarters. UAW secretary-treasurer Dennis Williams declared that the Global Organizing Institute had "the potential to be the largest, sustained consumer action by organized labor. We have the resources and the people to be successful in this mission."[258]

Bob King set a goal of unionizing at least one plant by the end of 2011. By year's end, however, the UAW had made little progress. Union officials gave two reasons for this. First, 2011 was an extraordinarily busy year for collective bargaining. The UAW negotiated new contracts with Caterpillar, Fiat Chrysler, Ford, GM, the State of Michigan, and several casinos, which left little time and energy to launch new efforts. Second, King explained that he was rethinking how to proceed. "Before, we said we are going to pick a target. Just in reflection . . . that sounds too adversarial. . . . We are shifting our strategy a little bit. We are not going to pick or announce a target at all. . . . We are not going to pick a fight." King and UAW secretary-treasurer Dennis Williams explained that they had spoken with management at several companies about ways to hold fair recognition elections. King set a new goal of organizing at least one foreign-owned plant during his tenure as UAW president, which would end in June 2014. "We have made a lot of progress, so I am very confident that we will be successful in organizing a number of them," King concluded.[259]

Despite a professed turn away from adversarialism, Bob King's comments about Nissan were not solely laudatory. He said that the UAW had received complaints that the company had violating civil and human rights. Some workers reported supervisors using racial epithets and favoring female workers based on appearance. Workers also complained about being assigned overtime with little or no notice as well as excessive line speeds and dangerous working conditions.[260] Nissan vice president David Reuter dismissed the allegations as "without merit." Company officials also disputed King's claim to have discussed unionization with managers at Nissan North America.[261] Mississippi governor-elect Phil Bryant, a Republican, stated at the end of 2011 that he would intercede if the UAW began an organizing drive at the Canton plant and asserted, "I just don't think that now is the time to try to unionize any of these organizations."[262]

The organizing effort at Canton would differ from those at the Mercedes and VW plants because Nissan was not like the German firms in three important respects. First, employee representation is much weaker in Japan than in Germany. The Japanese workplace is hierarchical and paternalistic. There are no equivalents of works councils or employee representatives on corporate boards. The JAW is much weaker and far more decentralized than Germany's powerful IG Metall. Nissan management had crushed a militant union in the 1950s.[263]

Second, Nissan is far more of a transnational company than either German automobile producer. By the mid-2000s, the French automaker Renault had acquired 44.4 percent of Nissan's outstanding stock. At the same time, Nissan bought a 15 percent stake in Renault through a purchase of nonvoting shares. The French government, in turn, has owned from 15 percent to almost 20 percent of Renault.[264] Nissan's partially public ownership has left the company potentially open to political pressure, but the nested structure makes it difficult to identify the location and salience of pressure points.

Third, approximately 80 percent of the workers at Nissan's Canton plant are African American, which is the mirror image of the Mercedes, VW, and Smyrna workforces, where 80 percent of the employees are white.[265] Using civil rights themes as part of an organizing campaign at the Canton plant held promise as a strategy to mobilize and unify most employees, whereas it risked distancing and dividing the workforce at the other locations. Moreover, the racial composition of the workforce at the Canton plant meant that anti-union diatribes by the white, conservative, Republican political leadership of the state would have less resonance than they had in Alabama or Tennessee. They could even backfire.

In late 2011, UAW leadership began to step up the organizing drive at Nissan Canton. Organizers quietly began to approach workers in their homes and meet with them in small groups. Employees' biggest complaints were about mandatory overtime and weekend shifts, speeding up the assembly line, and less vigilance to curb workplace accidents as well as lower wages and higher health care and pension contributions than at Nissan's Smyrna plant. Once Nissan managers discovered the home visits they retained the Littler Mendelson law firm, which specializes in union avoidance, and began to hold mandatory plant-wide roundtable meetings as well as small-group and one-on-one sessions that were critical of unionization in general and the UAW in particular.[266]

The intensification of the organizing effort included novel aspects. First, the UAW hired CRT/Tanaka, a public relations firm based in Richmond, Virginia, to assist the organizing effort.[267] Second, UAW officials began developing international support to a far greater degree than they had for the drives at the Smyrna plant. Union leaders sought help from Nissan's union in Japan, and UAW president Bob King took a Nissan Canton employee to Brazil to speak with trade unionists there. In April 2012, the UAW and the IndustriALL Global Union Federation, the successor organization to the IMF, asked the US State Department to mediate between the UAW and Nissan regarding alleged worker rights violations at the Canton plant. The State Department was willing to play this role, but Nissan management declined to participate. UAW officials said they were considering filing complaints about Nissan's actions at the Organisation for Economic Co-operation and Development (OECD) with the liaisons of the governments of France, Japan, and the Netherlands, where the Nissan-Renault alliance is incorporated.[268] Later that year, four prominent French trade union leaders with responsibilities for Renault plants sent a letter to Carlos Ghosn to express concern about the situation of employees at Nissan Canton.[269] Five days later Scott E. Becker, Nissan North America's senior vice president for administration and finance, responded with a defense of the company's policies and actions.[270] UAW staff met in London with officials from the United Kingdom's second-largest union, Unite. The British union officials "committed to providing assistance and advice to the UAW in securing [a] successful outcome in your campaign at Canton, Mississippi." Shortly thereafter, Bob King received a letter of support from Unite assistant general secretary Tony Burke.[271]

Third, the UAW began developing the civil rights component of the organizing drive. On May 1, 2012, the UAW moved its local office from Gluckstadt to directly across the street from the Nissan facility. A photograph of legendary UAW president Walter Reuther standing next to civil rights leader Dr. Martin Luther King Jr. at the 1963 March on Washington for Jobs and Freedom hung prominently on the wall.[272]

In a May 2012 interview, Bob King framed the organizing effort at the foreign-owned automobile assembly plants within his larger strategy for the UAW. "We can't be a meaningful union, we can't do the job our members at Ford, GM and Chrysler deserve if we don't organize the total industry."[273]

On June 3, 2012, UAW officials held a rally in Canton to formally announce that the union would attempt to organize the Nissan plant. The union estimated attendance at 250–300. Although organizing activity had already begun at the Mercedes and VW factories in Alabama and Chattanooga, this was the UAW's first formal announcement of an organizing drive at a foreign-owned automobile assembly plant since Bob King had become the union's president. UAW Region 8 director Gary Casteel pushed hard within the UAW for the formal announcement. He described Canton as "the perfect place" to take a stand and added, "We have tremendous worker support there. Nissan hired a heavily African American workforce. I think that's a plus because of the history and the battles fought in Mississippi against all odds. Being from Alabama, knowing how this works in the South. It is just one of those things, the heritage of Mississippi. They have had to fight for the things that they have achieved."[274]

Member of Congress Bennie Thompson, Mississippi NAACP president Derrick Johnson, and Rev. Isiac Jackson Jr., president of the General Missionary Baptist State Convention and pastor at Liberty Missionary Baptist Church, spoke at the June 3 announcement. They invoked civil rights themes as they pledged support for the organizing drive. Johnson pointed out that the average hourly wage was about $1.50 higher at Nissan's Smyrna plant, where a majority of the workforce is white, versus the Canton plant, where most workers are Black. The UAW put some of its best organizers in Canton. UAW officials said that unionization was about addressing these inequities and giving employees a voice in the workplace. Pro-union employees in the plant formed the Nissan Workers Committee for a Fair Election, which later became the Nissan Workers Organizing Committee (NWOC), the voluntary organizing committee for this drive.[275]

Union officials made no progress persuading Nissan management to agree to neutrality under Bob King's proposed fair election principles.[276] David Reuter, a Nissan spokesperson, provided the company's reaction to the UAW announcement and rally. "We don't believe that putting a third party between ourselves and our employees is going to make things better."[277] Reuter pointed to the captive-audience speeches as a response to the UAW's efforts: "We know there's been a lot of misinformation being communicated on the outside. We know the UAW has been attempting to engage our employees at their houses and in the local community, and we want to make sure our employees had our version of the facts as well."[278] Nissan chief executive Carlos Ghosn said, "We will naturally remain neutral on this. This being said, we still continue to think that direct management of the shop floor, direct contact with our people, is the best way to make a plant extremely productive and extremely efficient."[279] The local business community also reacted negatively to the UAW's announcement. An editorial in the *Mississippi Business Journal* opined that the publication supported the right of workers to form a union, "but that doesn't mean it will be a good thing for all of Mississippi if the United Autoworkers convinces folks to start a union at the Nissan auto plant in Canton."[280] Mississippi governor Phil Bryant expressed concern that "the automobile industry is very fragile" in Mississippi. "If the union involvement becomes active in the Southeastern automobile corridor, what does it do to industry? And I just don't see a positive outcome to that."[281]

The UAW leaders continued to stress civil and human rights as they advanced the Nissan campaign. "The civil rights experience was fought on that very ground," UAW Region 8 director Gary Casteel explained. "We've been saying that worker rights is the civil rights battle of the twenty-first century."[282] Gary Chaison, professor of industrial relations at Clark University, praised the UAW's approach. "Reinventing themselves as a civil rights movement—that's the right way to go."[283] Vanderbilt University sociologist Dan Cornfield observed, "When it comes to the civil rights movement in the South, there's a lot of history that has not been forgotten. It's possible that people in Mississippi could look at auto workers who don't have a voice on things like assembly line speed and their health care benefits and interpret that as workers not being treated with dignity."[284]

Pro-union Nissan Canton employees and UAW officials helped to facilitate the formation of the Student Justice Alliance, which was an organization modeled after the Student Nonviolent Coordinating Committee. The Student Justice Alliance started at Mississippi State University and Tougaloo College and worked with veterans from the 1960s civil rights struggle in the state to make the case for unionization at Nissan. The organization quickly grew to several hundred members as the founding students reached out to historically Black colleges and universities as well as universities with a labor relations program. The UAW sent some Global Organizing Institute interns to Jackson to work with the Student Justice Alliance on the Nissan Canton effort.[285]

In July 2012, the actor Danny Glover held a series of meetings with Canton employees. Glover has described himself as a lifelong union activist inspired by his father, who had been an engaged member of the American Postal Workers

Union in San Francisco. The actor had previously helped several other unions with their organizing drives, and he agreed to get involved in the Nissan Canton effort when Bob King asked him at a civil rights memorial presentation.[286] At a rally for Nissan Canton employees Glover said, "I'm here to be a part of what you're doing. . . . You are not alone. . . . I think of [former civil rights activist and field secretary of the Mississippi NAACP] Medgar Evers. He was only 37 years old when he died. Medgar Evers would be right out here supporting you."[287] UAW organizer Sanchioni Butler said that hundreds of workers had already signed authorization cards, which indicated progress, but this was still only a small percentage of the approximately 3,500 employees who worked directly for Nissan.[288] The equation of civil and labor rights may have persuaded some, but it had not moved a majority of the workforce.

Organizing at the Nissan plant proved to be challenging. Most of the employees did not live in the small town of Canton. They were scattered across the state; some lived as far as a hundred miles away. There was no place nearby where workers routinely gathered. At the end of a shift, most workers hurried to their cars and sped home. The thousand temporary associates at the Canton plant further fragmented the labor force. Since they did not work directly for Nissan, they could not be a part of a Nissan bargaining unit. Their presence in the plant also served as a constant reminder to permanent employees that the company could convert their jobs into temporary ones.[289]

In September 2012, Nissan management expanded the anti-union campaign to include engaging with temporary associates. By this time, the top wage for permanent employees had reached $23.22 per hour. The temporaries' base wage was only $12, even though many were doing the same work. Nissan management began holding roundtables with groups of twenty to twenty-five temporaries to present the same anti-union materials that management had been showing to the permanent employees since 2011. A Nissan human resources manager, a manager from the temporary agency, and a note taker were typically at the meeting, which served as a powerful disincentive to make critical comments.[290]

Supporters of unionization at Nissan Canton who were not employees formed a "community watchdog group" called the Mississippi Alliance for Fairness at Nissan (MAFFAN), chaired by Rev. Isiac Jackson Jr. "Labor rights are civil rights" was MAFFAN's principal slogan.[291] At a MAFFAN gathering in late October 2012, twenty Nissan employees talked about their experiences in the plant, including being forced to watch videos repeatedly about closings at plants organized by the UAW and increased scrutiny because they had expressed support for the union.[292] Jackson underscored that "Nissan attacks the entire community when it denies its workers, who are our family, our neighbors and our congregants, one of their most fundamental human rights. Nissan workers should not have to fear for their jobs because they want to form a union." Derrick Johnson, MAFFAN member and president of the Mississippi State Conference of the NAACP, stressed, "We are committed to standing beside Nissan workers until Nissan workers achieve a fair process."[293]

In mid-January 2013 Danny Glover and MAFFAN members, including students from Jackson State University and Tougaloo College, staged a protest outside of the North American International Auto Show in Detroit to support the right of Nissan Canton employees to vote in a union recognition election without employer interference.[294] "The right to work doesn't mean that you don't have the right to organize," Glover said. "They [Nissan] have unions in South Africa and Japan. We're only asking for the right to vote on a union and not face intimidation." The protesters distributed a press release that included a quote from Nissan Canton employee Michael Carter: "We need equal time to hear the union's side of whether we should have a union at Nissan." Meanwhile back in Canton, some anti-union employees were wearing T-shirts that read "Want a union? Move to Detroit."[295]

Approximately 200 union supporters held a rally at Tougaloo College in Jackson on January 29 that had the feeling of "an old-time revival meeting." "One Voice, One Dream, One Team, Nissan Workers United" read banners in Holmes Hall, and a men's choir sang "Oh Happy Day" and "Praise Him."[296] *The Ed Show*, hosted by Ed Schultz on the cable television channel MSNBC, covered part of the rally live and interviewed two Nissan Canton employees as well as Mississippi NAACP president and MAFFAN member Derrick Johnson. Johnson made a compelling case about the linkage between labor and civil rights on the show:

> Worker rights have always been a civil rights issue. The struggle we had to abolish slavery was about worker rights. The struggles in the sixties was about the right of workers being able to organize. In fact, Dr. King was assassinated as he was organizing workers in Memphis who wanted the right to have a voice as sanitation workers. So we see worker rights on the same playing field as voting rights, civil rights. It is about human dignity, and workers at Nissan should know when they go to work on Monday morning, they should be able to predict whether or not they go to work three hours that day or twelve hours that day, whether or not they're going to work seven days a week or five days a week. How can workers be expected to raise a family, have a quality of life if a company like Nissan don't respect them as human beings?[297]

Other speakers also hammered home the connection between civil rights and labor rights. Danny Glover pointed out that "Dr. King said the best anti-poverty program he knew was a union."[298] Mississippi's "fighting labor priest," Father

Jeremy Tobin, told the crowd, "Human rights are worker rights, and worker rights are human rights."[299]

Brazilian labor leaders João Cayres and Vagner Freitas attended the rally and pledged to support Nissan Canton workers. They observed that Nissan management works constructively with unions in many nations, including Brazil, Japan, and South Africa. Morris Mock, a Nissan Canton employee, accused a plant manager of saying that "they're going to move this factory away" if the employees voted in favor of union representation. Such a threat would violate federal labor law. Mock and other employees complained that Nissan management repeatedly made anti-union presentations and demanded that the company give UAW representatives equal time.[300] Nissan spokesperson David Reuter responded that the UAW had not filed a complaint with the NLRB and added, "The number of employees who are interested in unionizing is very small in comparison to the number who are telling us they're not interested in unionizing." Reuter asserted that this was because "if you are pro-union, you are anti-Nissan."[301]

Pro-union employees complained about the large number of temporary employees in the plant. They said that Nissan management intended to keep many of these employees as temps indefinitely and that management assigned temps to the day shift and easier jobs to reduce their attrition rate.[302] Nissan responded to these complaints by announcing the "Nissan Pathway Program" that created a process for some temps to become direct hires. Still, temps complained that they kept getting told "Nissan's going to hire you," but in practice only a minority of temps became direct employees.[303] Employees who did become permanent still received lower compensation than did "legacy" employees. MAFFAN members tried to mobilize temps under the slogan "Lead us not into Temp-nation" but made little headway.[304]

In the days that followed the January 29, 2013, rally, supporters of unionization at Canton stepped up the campaign, stressing the linkage of civil rights, human rights, and labor rights. In an interview with *Automotive News* Reverend Jackson said, "I was there when Dr. King was tear-gassed [in Memphis]. I was there. It's the same struggle. . . . If you want to understand the hook in this movement, money is not the issue. It's about rights—the right to choose."[305] UAW president Bob King, reacting forcefully to Nissan's anti-UAW videos, said, "They're threatening workers there that they're going to close the plant, and that's baloney." King accused Nissan North America management of violating labor standards established by the UNGC (which Nissan joined in 2004), the International Labor Organization, and the OECD.[306]

MAFFAN leaders announced that they would advocate for fair treatment of Nissan employees at auto shows and visit college campuses from February 7 to 18 in Chicago and from March 13 to 17 in Atlanta.[307] Nissan Canton employees

and MAFFAN leaders even went to Switzerland and held a tree-planting ceremony in front of the building hosting the Geneva Auto Show. While there, they
publicized their websites beneaththeshine.org and dobetternissan.org that made
the case for unionization.[308] In May 2013, a group of Nissan employees went to
protest in front of the New York International Auto Show. They also were guests
on a progressive radio program.[309] Later that year, a group that included Canton employees, ministers, Bob King, and Danny Glover went to South Africa.
They gained support for the Nissan Canton organizing drive from the National
Union of Metalworkers South Africa, which represents workers at the Nissan
plant there, and the Congress of South African Trade Unions, the confederation with which the National Union of Metalworkers South Africa is affiliated.[310]

On February 3, 2013, the former president of Brazil, Luiz Ignácio "Lula" da
Silva, spoke to 1,500 active and retired UAW members in Washington, D.C., at
the union's National Community Action Program legislative conference. Lula
had been president of a Brazilian metalworkers union before entering politics.
He gave a powerful speech, telling the audience that Brazilian workers were in
complete solidarity with American workers at Nissan Canton.[311] Lula followed
up in October with a letter to fellow Brazilian Carlos Ghosn and Nissan president and chief operating officer Toshiyuki Shiga.[312] Brazilian trade unionists had
also begun protesting Nissan management's actions at Nissan and Renault dealerships in their own country. In mid-March a delegation of Brazilian trade
union leaders, one of whom was also a member of the Brazilian parliament,
traveled to Canton. Member of Congress Bennie Thompson hosted the group at
the Rosemont Missionary Baptist Church. Church pastor Jimmie L. Edwards,
Bishop Ronnie Crudup, and MAFFAN head Isiac Jackson Jr. were there, as were
Mississippi state representative Jim Evans, Mississippi NAACP president Derrick Johnson, Bob King, and UAW senior adviser Richard Bensinger. The speakers again stressed the connection of civil rights, human rights, and labor rights.
King said,

> I am inspired by the Brazilians. They came here to organize, to estab-
> lish collective bargaining and to support the human rights of these
> workers. . . . There has not been a campaign that I am aware of anywhere
> in the United States that is led by the workers like the campaign in Can-
> ton, Mississippi. . . . This campaign to me is what I believe Mississippi
> is about and that is the heart of the civil rights movement. . . . We are
> going to win this because we are not going the traditional route to over-
> throw Nissan's abuse of workers here. Derek Johnson, MS-NAACP
> president has been in this from day one as well and speaks so eloquently
> about why it is important to have unions in America.[313]

Congress member Bennie Thompson also emphasized the connection in stark terms: "A month ago, Nissan came to my office in Washington for the first time in ten years and they brought black people with them. They were bringing people to tell me how good Nissan has been to them—just like the plantation. They are trying to counter everything you are saying, 'See how good we are! See how good we treat our slaves!'"[314] UAW representatives told a *Clarion Ledger* reporter in April 2013 that the union had authorization cards from more than 30 percent of eligible employees at Nissan Canton but was holding off from calling a recognition election because it did not think it was possible as things stood to have a fair vote.[315]

More letters of support for Canton workers arrived. A letter from Spanish trade union leaders who represented Nissan employees stated that Nissan's "tactics of intimidation run counter to the principles" of International Labor Organization Convention Number 87 and violated OECD guidelines. The letter urged Nissan management "to intervene so that workers in Canton can [be] treated in accordance with the values and principles that dictate Nissan management conduct in Japan and Europe."[316] The presidents of the JAW and the Federation of All Nissan and General Workers Union (Nissan Roren) declared their solidarity and pledged that they would "continuously negotiate with the management of Nissan HQ" to persuade them to order "local management . . . [to] maintain a neutral and fair position at Nissan's Canton plant."[317]

In the spring of 2013, significant numbers of local politicians expressed reluctance for the first time to accommodate Nissan's requests for additional subsidies. Nissan management asked the state legislature to authorize the Madison County Economic Development Authority to issue $100 million in taxable industrial development bonds. The money would permit the development authority to build and own a set of buildings to house Nissan suppliers, which would support an additional expansion of the Canton plant to accommodate the production of eight models. The request rankled Madison County political leaders because their jurisdiction had endured the biggest financial burden, but the Canton City Council had enacted a law at Nissan's request that prohibited Canton from expanding the boundary to include the plant. The resistance to Nissan management's latest subsidy request led the company to give the Canton Public School District a $500,000 education grant and to donate $100,000 to the Medgar and Myrlie Evers Institute.[318] Danny Glover did not speak at the 2013 annual Medgar Evers dinner for the first time in many years because the institute took Nissan money.[319] Nissan management also announced hourly increases starting in October—the first in seven years—ranging from 55 cents for production employees to $1.05 for lead technicians.[320]

MAFFAN leaders accentuated attention on Nissan's subsidies by releasing a report by the Good Jobs First research group, which the UAW had commissioned, at a news conference in the Mississippi capitol building in Jackson.[321] The report estimated that Nissan would receive $1.33 billion in state and local incentives during the first thirty years of the Canton plant's operation. This is over three times the official state figure. A good share of the difference results from the Good Jobs First report including a thirty-year estimate and payroll tax abatements for job creation as a part of the incentive package. The report also criticizes the state for counting temporary employees at the plant as direct employees when calculating employment targets and allowing payroll tax abatements despite wage rates falling short of targets specified in Nissan's agreement with the state.[322] Good Jobs First research director Phil Mattera said a principal finding of the report was that taxpayers are paying "premium amounts for jobs that in many cases are far from premium." Governor Phil Bryant denounced the report as "just another desperate attempt by big union bosses to scare Nissan's Canton employees."[323]

As the year progressed, the proponents of unionization continued to apply external pressure, with an emphasis on civil rights and international labor standards. In October 2013, the Mississippi NAACP released a forty-six-page report on the Nissan Canton organizing drive. The report listed Mississippi NAACP president Derrick Johnson and international labor law expert Lance Compa as authors, but Compa was the principal contributor. The UAW commissioned the report and paid for French and Japanese translations. The report spelled out international labor standards regarding freedom of association, Nissan's commitments regarding corporate social responsibility that include freedom of association, and numerous violations by Nissan of those standards and commitments. The final version took into account comments from a Nissan representative on an earlier draft. Johnson and Compa concluded that Nissan should come into compliance with international labor standards and company commitments and that the socially responsible investment community should encourage Nissan to adopt the recommendations of the report and "re-evaluate their portfolio holdings of Nissan stock" if Nissan managers do not change their behavior. They also recommended that the UNGC and the OECD review Nissan's record to consider the compatibility of the company's actions in Canton with the company's commitment to freedom of association under UNGC principle 3, International Labor Organization core labor standards, and the OECD guidelines for multinational enterprises.[324]

Derrick Johnson, MAFFAN chief Rev. Isiac Jackson Jr., and member of Congress Bennie Thompson released the report in Washington, D.C., at the National Press Club.[325] Nissan's official response to the final report was dismissive: "Allegations have been made by the union and a few employees working with the union that the plant management has 'intimidated' employees from joining the union. The Compa report repeats and is based entirely on these allegations. The allegations are absolutely not true and have been refuted by other employees."[326]

Two weeks after the release of the NAACP report, MAFFAN members and UAW director of international affairs Kristyne Peter traveled to France to garner support from French and other European employee representatives. They held a news conference at the Paris labor council (*bourse du travail*). Representatives from all four of the UAW's French partner union confederations were there (i.e., Confédération Générale du Travail, Confédération Française Démocratique du Travail, Confédération Française de l'Encadrement–Confédération Générale des Cadres and Force Ouvrière). They also went to Renault headquarters and asked to speak to the company's leaders but received no response.[327] Back in Canton, Cedric Gina, president of the National Union of Metalworkers of South Africa, visited the UAW office. He observed, "We think this is not supposed to be happening in a so-called First World country, a so-called bastion of democracy."[328]

From December 2013 to March 2014, MAFFAN and the UAW leadership ratcheted up the pressure on Nissan by generating a torrent of letters to Carlos Ghosn demanding that Nissan cease its anti-union activities. Twenty-six letters came from national unions, foreign unions, global union confederations, worker and environmental rights organizations, union organizations representing minorities, and church groups. Canton employees, MAFFAN members, students, and UAW officials also protested and held a news conference once again in January 2014 at the North American International Auto Show in Detroit. Protesters held a banner that read "Tell Nissan: Labor Rights are Civil Rights."[329] Mississippi NAACP president Derrick Johnson linked the Nissan Canton organizing drive to Freedom Summer from fifty years earlier.[330] The pro-union forces also announced support from two rappers: Sean Combs and Common.[331] Still, the letters, protests, and celebrity endorsements did not prompt Nissan management to change behavior.

Despite the formation of a broad pro-union coalition, considerable international outreach, and the framing of the organizing drive at Nissan Canton as a civil rights struggle, the organizing drive was having trouble attracting workers beyond about a third of the employees.[332] Rev. Isiac Jackson Jr. conceded that the union's opponents were "winning" but added that "they haven't won the war."[333] Union supporters attributed their lack of success to continued management intimidation. Union opponents pointed instead to high wages (the average hourly wage for permanent production workers had surpassed $20) and management's willingness to listen to employee complaints. The UAW's narrow loss in the union recognition election at Volkswagen Chattanooga in February 2014 was demoralizing for the pro-union forces in Canton, particularly because VW management had agreed to the kind of neutrality agreement that Canton employees had been struggling for years to obtain.

Political opposition to unionization in Mississippi intensified. Governor Phil Bryant declared that he did not want "unions involved in our businesses or our public sector." The Mississippi government enacted three laws that restricted worker rights to organize and demonstrate peacefully. Bryant also reiterated his explicit opposition to the organizing drive at Nissan Canton: "We will fight you every step of the way if you exercise your legal right to join a union and speak with a united voice."[334]

In April 2014, Nissan Canton workers protested again at the New York International Auto Show and were guests on a progressive radio program.[335] In the same month, Nissan management reached a settlement with Willard "Chip" Wells in an unfair labor practice case. Wells, a forty-three-year-old father of two who had served in both Afghanistan and Iraq, alleged that supervisors began treating him with hostility after media reports featured him as a pro-union employee. Specific events led Wells to file the charge. First, Nissan management accused Wells of distributing union authorization cards during worktime. Wells claimed he was doing so before his shift. Second, Wells alleged that he took unpaid medical leave in November 2013 because of pressure from a supervisor and that Nissan management did not allow him to return to work right after his physician cleared him. Wells did eventually return. The settlement required Nissan management to reiterate that the company abides by US labor laws and to remove from his personnel file any disciplinary action against Wells related to his organizing activities, but it did not include back pay. Spokesperson Justin Saia expressed Nissan's position: "Filing charges is a common tactic in an organizing campaign. These charges are unsubstantiated and there has been no finding of fault or admission of guilt."[336] Wells continued to push for back pay, and the UAW and MAFFAN supported him. In January 2015, the company agreed to a payment of $6,500. When asked why he succeeded, Wells said, "When they saw the pastors were not going to leave me hanging . . . and they started getting questions from me and the outside, (Nissan) said . . . 'We better go ahead and settle up.'"[337] Canton employees had lodged five other unfair labor practice cases since the organizing drive began in June 2012 that were either dismissed or withdrawn.

On April 28, 2014, the UAW leadership working with IndustriALL initiated an international process to advance the organizing drive. They asked the US Department of State to mediate between the union and Nissan management under the OECD guidelines for multinational enterprises. The guidelines require each country to maintain a national contact point (NCP) to serve as a facilitator for confidential mediation of disputes in areas that the guidelines cover, including industrial relations. The NCP for the United States is the State Department. Once a party submits a request, the NCP has three months to decide whether to offer mediation. All parties involved must agree for mediation to proceed. In previous cases, the State Department has relied on experienced mediators from the Federal Mediation and Conciliation Service to handle disputes. IndustriALL general secretary Jyrki Raina observed, "Nissan . . . works with unions in every part of the world, yet in the United States it acts very differently."[338] Bob King asserted, "Nissan is a global company that should abide by global standards that the United States and other countries have agreed on."[339] Spokesperson Justin Saia expressed Nissan management's position. "Nissan respects the labor laws of every country in which we operate. Allegations by the UAW that suggest otherwise are untrue and unfounded. . . . It would be premature to comment on mediation given that the State Department has not yet evaluated the submission, and the UAW already had compromised confidentiality provisions of the OECD guidelines."[340] Republican US senator from Mississippi Thad Cochran denounced the request for mediation, saying "the United States Department of State should concentrate on enhancing U.S. security interests and promoting peace around the world rather than interfering in domestic labor activities."[341]

Ultimately, the State Department did undertake an assessment of this "specific instance" of Nissan management's actions during the Canton organizing drive. Eight months later Melike Ann Yetken, the US NCP in the State Department, issued a twelve-page report. The report summarized the applicable portions of the OECD guidelines, made the case that this specific instance falls under the guidelines, and chronicled exchanges with Nissan, the UAW, IndustriALL, and other relevant parties. Yetken recommended mediation, but Nissan management declined to participate, for which Yetken expressed "regrets."[342]

Union proponents continued to apply pressure in 2014. Abroad, Bob King and a Nissan Canton employee, Calvin Moore, spoke to a crowd of 1.3 million at a May Day rally in Saõ Paulo, Brazil.[343] Moore had been an outspoken advocate for unionization, and Nissan fired him in March 2014 without cause. Moore said it was for engaging in union activities. Pressure from Brazil and at home resulted in his reinstatement in June with back pay.[344] On June 27, pro-union forces in Canton held a rally of 400 activists, ministers, students, and workers in front of the Nissan plant. Danny Glover delivered a petition at the front gate that stated, "Labor Rights are Civil Rights." Glover told the crowd, "We've got to organize to get what we want on the table. We need to organize to keep what we've got on the table. We're going to win this! We can't win it without you! We want a better America, a better Nissan! We're going to create another Nissan that respects human rights!" MAFFAN head Reverend Jackson declared to the crowd, "Nissan is exploiting the workforce of Mississippi with a plantation mentality." He then subverted the infamous quote by former Alabama governor George Wallace, shouting "Union today! Union tomorrow! Union forever!"[345]

Bob King completed his term as UAW president in June 2014. The UAW convention elected Secretary-Treasurer Dennis Williams to succeed him as president. UAW Region 8 director Gary Casteel was elected the new secretary-treasurer, which facilitated continuing the organizing effort at Nissan Canton. Casteel's former deputy, Ray Curry, became the new Region 8 director. Curry was the first African American to hold that position. The lead organizer for the foreign assembly plants, Richard Bensinger, was close to King but not to Williams. Bensinger left his position when King's term expired. The UAW officer in charge of organizing, Mark Haasis, took over strategic responsibilities for the campaign at Nissan Canton.

In mid-October 2014, IndustriALL general secretary Jyrki Raina headed a delegation of Brazilian, British, French, Japanese, South African, and Spanish leaders from metalworker unions to Canton to meet with Nissan employees. Raina said, "Our message to Nissan is that we are not going away until these Nissan workers win the right to a union, as [have] the 150,000 unionized [Nissan] workers elsewhere. And our message to Canton's Nissan workers is they are not alone in their fight; use our support and fight with our support to join the UAW."[346] In late October, a coalition of about one hundred church leaders held a prayer vigil outside the Canton plant and delivered a petition calling for a union recognition election at the plant.[347]

When the organizing drive at the Mercedes plant in Alabama stalled and union organizers at Volkswagen Chattanooga decided to concentrate on organizing a small unit of skilled mechanics, UAW secretary-treasurer Gary Casteel announced that the UAW would increase its efforts at Nissan Canton.[348] On June 10, 2015, over thirty union proponents held a prayer vigil by the front entrance of the Nissan plant. On October 7, Nissan Canton employee Robert Hathorn participated in two events at the White House Worker Voice Summit: a town hall–style meeting led by President Barack Obama and a panel headed by US labor secretary Thomas Perez. Hathorn emphasized that "labor rights are civil rights" and spoke out against the "'permatemp' culture" at Nissan Canton.[349] Hathorn wore a button that read "Nissan lead us not into Temp-Nation."[350] In June the following year, Hathorn spoke to the Democratic National Committee platform committee about the issue of temporary workers.[351]

An incident at the Canton plant in the fall of 2015 shook many employees. Thirty-seven-year-old Derrick Whiting collapsed during a late shift and sought assistance at the company medical unit. He was examined and sent back out to the assembly line. At the end of the shift, Whiting went to a hospital. He died hours later. Nissan management insisted that his death was "non-work related."[352]

On November 30, 2015, the UAW filed charges against Nissan Canton management for a restrictive uniform policy the company adopted in 2014 that authorized supervisors to send home employees wearing clothing with messages on them, be they pro- or anti-union. A week later, the regional director of the NLRB in New Orleans found sufficient reason to review the charge and set a hearing date of March 9, 2016. Nissan spokesperson Josh Clifton stated that the allegations were "untrue and unfounded." Nonetheless, Nissan issued a memorandum on December 1 that amended the uniform policy. It became voluntary.[353]

UAW officials filed additional charges of unfair labor practices against Nissan. The NLRB New Orleans regional director found sufficient reason to believe that Nissan managers "threatened employees with termination because of their union activities . . . , interrogated employees about their union support[,] . . . [and] threatened employees with plant closure if they choose the union as their representative."[354] UAW secretary-treasurer Gary Casteel drove home the UAW's characterization when he said that Nissan

> has been on the wrong side of the law for a long time. . . . [I]t's really kind of unexplainable why a company thinks they can come to the U.S. and treat workers worse than they do in other parts of the world. Why doesn't Nissan let these employees chose freely if they want to belong to a union, like they do globally? Here in the U.S. it's like we're some kind of third class citizens that we don't have the same rights like the rest of the world does with these labor laws.[355]

In the fall of 2015, union supporters increased international political pressure. They launched a "French campaign" to pressure the French government— as a major shareholder of Renault, a company that in turn owns a 43 percent share of Nissan and that Carlos Ghosn runs jointly with Nissan—to make Nissan management accept neutrality provisions for the unionization drive at the Nissan Canton plant. There was reason to believe that a pressure campaign might work. The French president, François Hollande, was a member of the French socialist party, and union supporters in the United States had already been interacting with French politicians and trade unionists sympathetic to their cause for several years. In September 2015 a delegation of union supporters, headed by Richard Bensinger in an advisory capacity to the UAW, went to Paris to meet with French trade union officials, politicians, Economy Minister Emmanuel Macron, and Labor Minister Myriam El Khomri.[356]

In February 2016 Nissan CEO Carlos Ghosn, testifying before the Finance Committee of the French National Assembly, said, "We had to verify that American regulations were completely respected. . . . To my knowledge, there is no anomaly at the Canton factory. Nissan has no tradition of not cooperating with unions."[357] In April, French National Assembly member and deputy chair of the assembly's Social Affairs Committee, Christian Hutin, sent Ghosn a letter charging that the Nissan CEO's testimony did not correspond with the facts. Hutin reported that he had seen an anti-union video that the company had shown in the Canton plant shortly after Ghosn's testimony in which a plant manager said

"We believe that it is not in the best interest of our employees, our customers or our community to have the UAW in there."[358]

A few days later, Hutin asked Ministers Macron and El Khombri on the floor of the French National Assembly during question time what the government could do to help Nissan employees. Minister El Khombri expressed sympathy but said that since Nissan owns the plant, "the French state has little room to maneuver."[359] Some thirty French parliamentarians headed by socialists Bruno Le Roux and Vincent Peillon and Greens Cécile Duflot and Noël Mamère sent a letter dated June 8 to Ghosn expressing the hope that "the social dialogue ceases to be hindered as soon as possible" at the Canton plant.[360] Ghosn never responded. On June 28 four Canton employees, Richard Bensinger, and approximately forty French trade unionists and political figures held a rally on the steps of Renault's Paris headquarters. They picked that date because Ghosn was scheduled to chair a meeting of the Renault group managing committee there. They planned to ask to see Ghosn, but he skipped the meeting, which Renault union official Fabien Gache branded as "not brave on his part."[361]

The intensification of international political pressure included Brazil because it was hosting the 2016 Summer Olympics. In February 2016, Nissan technician Morris Mock joined two hundred trade unionists outside of a meeting of the Olympics Organizing Committee in a demonstration coordinated by IndustriALL to demand neutrality in a recognition election for Nissan's Canton employees. IndustriALL assistant regional secretary for Latin America Marino Vani said to the demonstrators, "We cannot let the Olympic torch be carried by a company that maintains anti–trade union practices in its supply chain."[362] In April 2016, a delegation that included Nissan Canton employee Betty Jones, UAW lead organizer for Canton Sanchioni Butler, UAW Region 8 director Ray Curry, and Mississippi civil rights advocate Frank Figgers testified before the Brazilian Senate's Human Rights and Participatory Legislation Committee about circumstances at the Nissan Canton plant.[363] Nissan Canton employee Karen Camp traveled to Brazil to bring attention to the organizing drive. She said, "All we want in Mississippi is fairness, which is part of the Olympic spirit."[364] The Brazilian metalworkers union delivered a letter to the Olympic organizers charging that Nissan was violating Olympics sponsorship guidelines by violating employee rights in Canton and produced a radio story critical of Nissan's behavior in Canton in light of Nissan's sponsorship of the 2016 Olympic Games in Brazil.[365]

Back at home, a group of students, activists and union supporters protested again at the front gate of the Nissan Canton plant on April 2, 2016.[366] In May, the UAW filed a complaint with the NLRB alleging that Nissan was engaging in coercive and illegal tactics to thwart the unionization effort.[367] OSHA issued six

safety violations against the Nissan Canton plant between 2012 and 2016, fin-
ing the company $60,140.[368]

In July, OSHA cited the Nissan Canton plant for two violations involving slip
hazards.[369] OSHA officials tried to inspect the plant on August 8 after an employee lost three fingers in an accident. More than thirty employees asked representatives of the Nissan Workers Committee for a Fair Election to accompany
the inspector, but Nissan management refused. The OSHA inspector obtained
a warrant from a federal magistrate judge to permit employee representatives to
participate in the inspection. Nissan unsuccessfully attempted to quash the warrant. Nissan spokesperson Brian Brockman responded to inquiries about the
workplace safety violations with the assertion that "Nissan's Canton plant has a
safety record that is significantly better than the national average for automotive plants" and the assurance that "we also continue to work on determining
what can be done to prevent future occurrences."[370]

Nissan supporters in the business and political communities also became
more active in 2016. In March, an anti-union group of Canton employees called
Nissan Technicians for Truth and Jobs launched a Facebook page that included
negative stories about unions in general and the UAW in particular. The Facebook page also took language directly from a notice for Nissan Canton workers
from the NRWLDF regarding union recognition cards.[371]

In the first half of 2016, the Canton plant expanded employment by about
1,000 to 6,400. A high proportion of the new hires were temps. As a result, the
number of temps increased to about 2,700. Of the approximately 3,700 employees directly on Nissan's payroll, roughly 1,500 were former temps whose wage
rates and benefit packages were smaller than those of the permanent employees
whom Nissan hired from the start. Move Mississippi Forward, a business advocacy organization, commissioned the National Strategic Planning and Analysis
Research Center at Mississippi State University to study the impact of the Nissan plant on the Mississippi economy. The study found that the plant had directly and indirectly created 25,000 jobs and generated each year $2.6 billion in
disposable income and $300 million in state and local tax revenue.[372]

In July 2016, French National Assembly member Christian Hutin traveled to
Canton on a fact-finding trip. Nissan management at the Canton plant declined
to meet with Hutin or let him onto the plant premises. While in Canton, Hutin
characterized Mississippi as a "lawless place."[373] He said, "The situation in (Canton) is dire and sadly not new, with the rights of workers seriously being compromised. Every possible step is taken to prevent the personnel from organizing
a union inside the plant. Pressure, threats, harassment, routine propaganda . . .
every possible step is taken to prejudice the rights of workers in what is known

as a historic cradle of the civil rights movement in the United States of America."[374] "Workers' rights are in fact human rights," Hutin continued. "When I return to France, I will be informing the French Government and French president Hollande about anti-union practices in Canton." Mississippi NAACP president Derrick Johnson added, "We have bona fide civil rights concerns when it comes to Renault-Nissan and its poor treatment of workers in Canton. We cannot tolerate a disrespect for workers' rights in Mississippi in 2016. Our state has come too far over the years to allow these kinds of abuses to persist."[375]

Auto industry observers judged that "the UAW and its allies in Europe and South America have succeeded in making life uncomfortable for Nissan and its CEO Carlos Ghosn."[376] The pro-union forces continued to apply pressure. On October 12, 2016, American and French trade unionists, workers from the Nissan Canton plant, civil society representatives, a gospel choir, and Danny Glover marched from the Paris Auto Show to the French National Assembly to urge Nissan to accept neutrality for a union recognition vote at the Nissan Canton Plant. Glover told the crowd, "Workers rights are civil rights and our message is simple: enough is enough. Nissan must stop intimidating the workers and let them vote for a union without company interference." French National Assembly member Christian Hutin stressed, "France is the country of freedom and human rights, and we are asking Carlos Ghosn to act to change what is happening in Canton. The workers are not asking for a revolution, they are simply asking for fair treatment."[377]

On December 20, 2016, the UAW and IndustriALL representatives filed cases with the NCPs of France, Japan, and the Netherlands against Renault, Nissan, and the Renault-Nissan alliance under the OECD guidelines for multinational enterprises. They hoped that the simultaneous filings would lead the NCPs of the three countries to work together and pick up where the US NCP had left off in 2015. A press release quoted UAW secretary-treasurer Gary Casteel: "The Renault-Nissan Alliance's repeated failures to address the serious workers' rights and civil rights violations in Mississippi are deeply troubling to the UAW and the workers' allies, in the U.S. and around the world."[378]

The year 2017 was decisive for the Nissan Canton organizing drive. Union supporters expanded their efforts, and the NLRB ultimately held a recognition election at the plant in early August. The year began with the tentative use of the long-discussed tactic of protesting in front of Nissan dealerships. From January 26 to 28, workers, activists, students, and trade unionists protested, waving signs that read "Workers' rights are civil rights" and "Hey Nissan, Stop threatening your workers in Mississippi" in front of Nissan dealerships in Atlanta, Birmingham, Charlotte, Greensboro, Nashville, and New Orleans.[379] The dealership protests proved ineffectual compared to the United Farm Workers grape and lettuce boycotts from fifty years earlier and the Amalgamated Clothing and Textile Workers Union boycott of J. P. Stevens textile products of the 1970s because they were mostly onetime isolated undertakings with little effort to generate publicity beyond the local level. There was also no request for consumers or others to do anything that would have inflicted substantial economic pain on Nissan.

The UAW and union supporters did stage one event in 2017 intended to attract national attention. On March 4, they held the March on Mississippi. Advertising for the march included the slogan "Workers' Rights = Civil Rights." Danny Glover authored a 550-word opinion piece that appeared in *Newsweek* a week before the march,[380] and NBC News ran a 1,000-word article about the march featuring Glover.[381] The promotion efforts paid off. Organizers estimated that four thousand supporters went to Canton from several states, making it the largest protest in Mississippi since the 1960s civil rights movement. A dozen workers from Brazil also attended.[382]

The rally began at the Canton sportsplex with an hour of speeches. Orators included Danny Glover, NAACP national president Cornell William Brooks, Mississippi NAACP president Derrick Johnson, Sierra Club president Aaron Mair (whose father was a UAW member), local member of Congress Bennie Thompson, Ohio state senator Nina Turner, MAFFAN head Rev. Isiac Jackson Jr., UAW president Dennis Williams, and Nissan Canton employees. The closing speaker was Vermont senator Bernie Sanders. Most speakers hammered home the theme that workers' rights are civil rights.[383] Senator Sanders opined, "I am proud to join in fighting to give workers at Nissan's Canton[,] Mississippi, plant the justice, dignity and the right to join a union that they deserve. . . . What the workers at the Nissan plant in Mississippi are doing is a courageous and enormously important effort to improve their lives." Sanders continued, "So we say to Nissan, it's great that your CEO made $9 million. It's great that you made $6 billion in profit, but you know what? Share some of that wealth with your workers." The Vermont senator concluded, "The eyes of the country and the world are on you. Don't feel you are alone. You've got people all over this country—and many of my colleagues in the Senate are with you. We are with you in this struggle. Fight on and let's win this battle!"[384]

After the speeches, participants marched two miles to the Canton plant, where the event's leaders hand-delivered a letter addressed to Nissan North America chair José Muñoz to the front gate of the plant. The letter raised recent labor law and health and safety violations and made three demands. Nissan should: (1) "immediately cease intimidation and threats by Canton managers against Nissan employees who want a union. (2) Ensure a safe workplace in Canton. . . . (3) Meet with the representatives of MAFFAN and the UAW to discuss conditions for achieving neutrality and ensuring that Nissan employees in Canton can vote on a local union in a free and fair election."[385]

Nissan management responded by closing the plant on the day of the march and issuing a statement asserting that "the allegations made by the union are totally false." Management accused the UAW of engaging in a "campaign to pressure the company into recognizing a union, even without employee support." Nissan also began airing anti-union commercials on local television stations.[386] Sid Salter, chief communications director at Mississippi State University and an anti-union opinion writer for the *Clarion Ledger*, whose column many southern newspapers carry, challenged equating union rights with civil rights:

> The struggle for "civil rights" sounds far more noble and desirable than what is actually happening in Canton and across the landscape of foreign-owned automobile manufacturing plants in the South—which is a desperate struggle for survival by a weakened labor union that has endured a 75 percent membership decline since 1979. . . . This is a business fight over unionizing an automobile manufacturing plant, nothing more and nothing less.[387]

Nissan executive Scott Becker stated in a letter sent to the UAW on March 14 that "Nissan fully respects the rights of employees to unionize or not unionize, as they choose." Becker characterized accusations of Nissan intimidating pro-union employees as "categorically false" and asserted that "it would be inappropriate to have discussions with your union regarding employees at Nissan's manufacturing plant in Canton, Miss., without your union first having obtained the support of a majority of employees at the plant."[388]

The March on Mississippi was effective in both galvanizing those already committed to the organizing drive and attracting additional employees. Pro-union activists intensified their efforts. Organizer Jeff Moore said, "I think it opened the doors for us really. A lot of people were scared. . . . Every night, we just stand there at the turnstile and talk to people in the parking lot all night long. Sometimes we would leave the gate at 1 or 2 a.m. A lot of families have changed. It's a big sacrifice, but it's worth it." Within a month, UAW representatives reported that they had signed up 386 new members at the Canton plant, which was slightly more than 10 percent of the permanent employees eligible to vote.[389]

Promotion of the organizing campaign continued. On the first Saturday in April, one hundred people, including representatives from MAFFAN, the UAW, the Tennessee AFL-CIO Labor Council, Nashville Organized for Action and Hope, the A. Philip Randolph Institute, and several local Black pastors protested across the street from a Nissan dealership in Nashville that was nineteen miles south of Nissan North America headquarters in Franklin, Tennessee. The crowd sang "Nissan, respect your workers!" while holding signs that read "Union. Yes!"

and "Workers' rights are civil rights."[390] Again, however, this was a one-off local action.

The UAW lawyers continued to file unfair labor practice charges against Nissan and Kelley Services, one of the providers of temporary employers for the Canton plant. A March 31 filing, which the regional NRLB office found warranted review, claimed that a Kelley Services supervisor illegally threatened that the plant would close if the UAW won a recognition election, plant security guards harassed union supporters, and Nissan's policy banning unauthorized photos and recordings was illegal.[391] UAW lawyers filed an additional set of charges alleging additional counts of management harassment on June 26. Meanwhile, former US secretary of labor and newly elected chair of the Democratic National Committee Thomas Perez expressed strong support for the organizing drive at Canton.[392]

On July 10, 2017, members of the NWOC assisted by UAW officials traveled to the regional NLRB office in New Orleans to file a petition to hold a recognition election at the Nissan Canton plant. UAW officials never disclosed the number or percentage of employees who signed authorization cards, which differed from the Volkswagen Chattanooga organizing drive. Robert Hathorn, who was a member of the Nissan Workers Organizing Committee for two years, said, "We filed with not even half [of the employees having signed union recognition cards]."[393] Typically, union officials go ahead with a recognition election only after 60–65 percent of the employees have signed cards. Back in February and April, Casteel had indicated that he did not think it was time to move forward with a recognition election in Canton, given Nissan's alleged labor law violations, but in July he described the decision to move ahead as a "balancing act."[394]

The NLRB set two voting days: August 3 and 4. The petition proposed (and Nissan and the NLRB accepted) that the election only include the 3,700 employees whom Nissan had directly hired rather than all the plant's 6,400 production employees to avoid a protracted legal fight over whether employees supplied by temporary labor service firms should be included. Union proponents also made this decision because they were concerned that many temporary employees would be reluctant to support the UAW due to their precarious position. Union officials and supporters were hopeful that the 1,500 Pathway employees, who were permanent hires but still had a lower wage scale and fewer benefits, would be especially amenable to unionization because it offered them a way to eliminate their second-class status.[395]

The day after filing for a recognition election, union supporters held a rally in Canton. They cast themselves as underdogs but expressed confidence that they would win the election. Union supporter Nina Dumas said, "Nissan employees want fair wages for all workers, better benefits, and an end to unreasonable production quotas and unsafe conditions in Mississippi. The company doesn't respect our rights. It's time for a union in Canton."[396] Over three hundred Mississippi clergy backed the Canton organizing drive.[397] MAFFAN cochair Reverend Jackson declared, "This is a day that some said could never be in the state of Mississippi, but we discovered yesterday that we have gotten there."[398] "I've never seen a labor campaign of this size," said Frank Figgers, civil rights veteran and the other MAFFAN cochair. "This is a historic struggle about overcoming the effects of slavery in Mississippi."[399]

Nissan representatives responded to inquiries about the election filing with a more explicitly anti-union message: "Nissan Canton's success has been built upon the direct relationship we have with employees and given the UAW's history of layoffs and job closures, their presence could harm our plant's global competitiveness. . . . While it is ultimately up to our employees who will represent them, we do not believe that UAW representation is in the best interest of Nissan Canton and its workers."[400]

Beyond the company, an anti-union Facebook page titled #nouaw appeared that included numerous testimonials and comments from Canton employees opposed to unionization. Anti-union employees began to attack the UAW's charitable contributions to local civil rights and religious groups as buying the support of the African American community.[401] Mississippi Manufacturers Association president Jay Moon released a statement highly critical of the UAW: "Make no mistake—this campaign is not about hardworking Mississippians at Nissan—this is about a self-serving outsider campaign by a UAW desperate to survive."[402] The *Madison County Journal* ran an editorial with the headline "No to the UAW at Nissan" that described the recognition election as "a war of information, and in the UAW's instance, misinformation is key." The editorial stated that "the UAW accuses Nissan of intimidation and harassment but offers up no proof. On the other hand, we have reports of UAW runts running across the county bothering homeowners trying to peddle their lies." The editorial went on to attack the central argument of the organizing drive, that is, equating unionization with civil rights:

> The most disgusting piece of misinformation being perpetrated directly and indirectly by the UAW is that what we have here in Madison County is a civil rights issue. Trying to turn this into a race war and conjure up images of Mississippi Burning to fund their existence is nauseating. It's an affront to all the people who truly fought for civil rights in Mississippi and across this country.[403]

All over Canton, businesses put up signs that read "Our Team Our Future Vote No August 3–4."[404] Mississippi governor Phil Bryant again expressed his opposition to the UAW. On the day the union filed for a recognition election, Bryant commented, "Detroit is the perfect example of the damage the United Auto Workers can do to automotive manufacturing. . . . Mississippi is a right-to-work state because employees deserve the freedom to support their families without union interference."[405] Student labor activist Jaz Brisack reported that the Mississippi Department of Transportation used prison labor to remove pro-union signs from alongside a highway.[406]

Immediately after the filing of the petition for a recognition election, Nissan management launched a comprehensive campaign to secure a no vote. At no time did the Nissan management give UAW representatives or pro-union employees an opportunity to speak or to distribute information in the plant. On July 12, Nissan management forced all employees to watch a new anti-union video featuring plant vice president of manufacturing Steve March. March said that the UAW had a record of not delivering on promises made in recognition elections and asked the employees to keep the union out of the plant. Nissan also sent a letter from March to the homes of all employees with the same message.[407] Nissan management played the anti-union videos in a continuous loop on screens in employee break areas.

Nissan supervisors held one-on-one meetings and group roundtables with Canton employees. The principal message in these meetings was that plants in the United States that had UAW representation had a higher rate of closure than those that did not. "They're telling you you're gonna lose this, you're gonna lose that. You may go on strike, and if you go on strike, you'll be replaced by a replacement worker," said Michael Carter, a pro-union Canton employee.[408] Many employees were shaken after managers told them that current perks, such as vehicle leases at below-market rates without a credit check, could disappear if the union were to win the recognition election.[409]

Nissan management circulated posters and flyers in the plant with the theme "Our Team Our Future Vote No" and unveiled a website specifically created for the recognition election that included information about the vote, a "frequently asked questions" page, an "our voices" page featuring testimonials by anti-union employees, an "in the community" page with statements from opponents to unionization, and a resources page.[410] A week before the election, Nissan managers wore red T-shirts with the message "Our Team Our Future" on the front and "Vote No" on the back. In the days before the election, Nissan bought hundreds of television and radio advertising spots to broadcast anti-union messages to employees and their families.[411] Pro-union employees had two new T-shirts for the recognition election: one read "Pro-Nissan Pro-Union," and the other read "Nissan stop Modern-day Slavery."[412]

Union supporters in Canton expressed concern that Nissan management's campaign had eroded union support. Plant employee Shanta Butler said, "People who were for the union are now undecided."[413] Nissan employee Michael Carter reported that the management equated a vote for the UAW with "turning your back on the company." He said that such a claim was persuasive for many employees who had been earning $8 an hour in a previous job. "You give them $25, they think, 'I'm not going to do anything to jeopardize my $25.'"[414]

UAW officials knew the election was a long shot.[415] Two weeks before the vote, a former UAW organizer predicted that the union would lose two to one.[416] A year after the vote, Gary Casteel explained that union officials knew they were not going to win, but after more than a decade of effort and $70 million in expenditures, "we decided to call the question to bring an end to the spending and find out how many votes we had."[417]

At the time, UAW president Dennis Williams voiced cautious optimism. "A campaign can change from day to day and this will depend on employees in the plant."[418] "Do I feel like it will pass? Yeah, as of now. Any campaign you do; it's an ongoing evaluation. Do [the workers] have it in them to get over the fear?"[419] Williams observed that pressure from the local political establishment was present but less pronounced in Mississippi than it had been in Tennessee during the run-up to the 2014 election at Volkswagen Chattanooga.[420] One explanation for the difference was that VW management's cooperative relationship with the UAW appalled Tennessee business and political elites. They chose to fight the UAW because VW management would not. Since Nissan management pursued an aggressive campaign against the UAW, Mississippi business and political elites did not feel the same need as their counterparts in Tennessee to participate in the campaign.

In contrast to Williams, UAW secretary-treasurer Gary Casteel conveyed an air of resignation before the vote. "They [management] always say the same old things and they always do the same old things. . . . The reason they do them is because they work."[421] On other occasions before the vote, Casteel remained defensive but somewhat more upbeat. "Certainly, at one point, we think that there was enough workers there. What the impact of the employer's behavior is, is something we can't gauge on a daily basis. These workers are still wanting to fight. There are hundreds and hundreds and hundreds of them. . . . It's a substantial movement. We are certainly in a position to win an election, otherwise we would not have filed. We're not that foolhardy."[422] Casteel condemned the company's tactics. "Nissan has made it abundantly clear that it does not respect its Mississippi employees' rights to vote in a free and fair election. . . . In fact, the company is running one of the most aggressive anti-worker campaigns that we've seen in modern U.S. history."[423]

One story broke in late July that hurt the organizing effort. A federal prosecutor obtained an indictment of former Fiat Chrysler executives Alphons Iacobelli and Jerome Durden as well as Monica Morgan-Holiefield (the widow of a recently deceased UAW vice president) for a multimillion-dollar bribery and embezzlement scheme involving a training center for blue-collar employees.[424] Although the illegalities did not include anyone involved in the Canton organizing drive, Nissan management immediately added corruption to the list of criticisms of the UAW in a public statement: "The latest UAW corruption scandal in Detroit and the history of strikes, layoffs and plant closures at UAW-represented plants, along with the many false claims and promises made by the UAW during this campaign[,] are among the many reasons we do not believe that UAW representation is in the best interest of the employees at Nissan Canton."[425] Corporate labor attorney Gary Klotz commented on the potential impact of the charges. "If Nissan cannot use this indictment to win, it probably deserves to lose; if for no other reason, election campaign malpractice."[426] To contain the damage, the UAW leadership claimed that UAW officials involved in the scandal were "rogue individuals" whom the union disciplined and isolated even before the indictment.[427]

A second story broke at the same time as the UAW scandal that helped the union supporters' cause. NLRB regional director in New Orleans M. Kathleen McKinney filed new unfair labor practice charges based on UAW accusations alleging that Nissan threatened a loss of wages and benefits and plant closure in meetings with Canton employees.[428] The complaint also consolidated several past filings, some dating back years, that covered Kelly Services as well as Nissan.[429] Nissan spokesperson Brian Brockman responded, "Today, the UAW has launched another set of baseless allegations against Nissan Canton and threatened to issue more."[430]

On August 1, 2017, two days before voting was to begin, Nissan management issued a final statement:

> Nissan Canton workers enjoy pay and benefits that are among the best in Mississippi, a safe work environment, and a history of job security that exceeds UAW organized plants. We do not believe that UAW representation is in the best interest of Nissan Canton and the people who work here. However, it is ultimately up to the employees to decide. Nissan Canton's success has been built upon the direct relationship we have with each other. Given the UAW's history of strikes, layoffs, and plant closures, their presence could harm the plant's global competitiveness.[431]

There was also a final captive-audience speech. Nissan bused every employee on each shift to a large air-conditioned tent on the company's grounds where they listened to a succession of speeches from plant managers. Some struck a conciliatory tone. For example, Nissan vice president of Manufacturing Steve March conceded, "I want to tell you again, I heard you loud and clear. Taking care of business means I have to listen and support you more." Others stayed in attack mode. Senior vice president John Martin said, "Now the UAW isn't down here from Detroit to help you. The UAW is down here to help themselves. . . . The UAW needs you, but you don't need them." No manager took questions. Nissan launched an advertising blitz in local newspapers and on radio, television, and the streaming service Spotify, which made it hard for local residences to consume media without hearing a Nissan ad about the recognition election. UAW officials estimated that Nissan spent $12.5 million in 2017 to avoid unionization.[432]

In an interview with *Automotive News* on the day before voting began at Nissan Canton, Gary Casteel hedged his answer to a question about the likely outcome. He said he was confident that a majority of Canton workers were in favor of unionizing, but whether a majority of them would actually vote to do so was another question. Casteel responded to the claim that UAW leadership was desperately searching for new sources of dues money to stave off the demise of the union by pointing out that "our finances are the best they've been since we've been operating. It's not like [winning at Nissan] is pivotal in the sense of the survival of the UAW."[433] He accused Nissan management of spreading "outright lies" by casting doubt about the plant's future were the UAW to win. He also returned to the pending unfair labor practice charges and the OSHA violations. "These guys' rap sheet now reads like Al Capone. They just break law after law. Most companies of this size . . . have certain things they just don't do because it's unethical."[434] Casteel had complained a day earlier that the employee contact list, which the NLRB requires employers to share with union organizers during a recognition election, was riddled with errors, impairing the ability of the UAW to contact employees.[435]

External actors continued to weigh in on the Nissan Canton vote. Former US vice president Joe Biden expressed support for recognizing the UAW. Senator Bernie Sanders told UAW supporters in a videoconference on August 1 that Nissan should "start treating your workers with the respect and dignity that they deserve. . . . Give your workers the freedom to join a union, so that as a nation we can stop the race to the bottom."[436] On the other side, the Mississippi chapter of Americans for Prosperity—which is the political arm of the conservative Koch brothers, who subsidize many anti-union actions—sent twenty-five thousand mailers to Jackson area homes that read "Tell UAW, 'No Thanks'" and bought billboard, internet, and radio ads. Representatives of the Mississippi Chamber of Commerce and the National Association of Manufacturers also issued statements against union recognition at Nissan Canton.[437]

NLRB representatives counted the ballots on the evening of Friday, August 4. The turnout was high at 97 percent (3,551 out of 3,661). The vote was 1,307

(37 percent) in favor of recognizing the UAW as the Nissan Canton employees' exclusive bargaining agent and 2,244 (63 percent) against.[438] UAW president Dennis Williams released a prepared statement that praised union supporters and criticized Nissan management:

> The courageous workers of Nissan, who fought tirelessly for union representation alongside community and civil-rights leaders, should be proud of their efforts to be represented by the UAW. The result of the election was a setback for these workers, the UAW and working Americans everywhere, but in no way should it be considered a defeat.
>
> Perhaps recognizing they couldn't keep their workers from joining our union based on facts, Nissan and its anti-worker allies ran a vicious campaign against its own workforce that was comprised of intense scare tactics, misinformation and intimidation.[439]

UAW secretary-treasurer Gary Casteel issued a statement that was more harshly critical of Nissan management: "We're disappointed but not surprised by the outcome in Canton. Despite claiming for years to be neutral on the question of a union, Nissan waged one of the most illegal and unethical anti-union campaigns that I've seen in my lifetime. Clearly, Nissan will not honor workers' right to be free of coercion and intimidation without a binding court order."[440]

Nissan's management's official statement aimed to move beyond the organizing drive:

> With this vote, the voice of Nissan employees has been heard. They have rejected the UAW and chosen to self-represent, continuing the direct relationship they enjoy with the company. Our expectation is that the UAW will respect and abide by their decision and cease their efforts to divide our Nissan family. Now that the election is complete, Nissan will focus on bringing all employees together as one team, building great vehicles and writing our next chapter in Mississippi.[441]

Anti-union employees were ready to move on as well. The following post was on the Nissan Technicians for Truth and Jobs Facebook page the day after the vote:

IT'S TIME FOR UNITY—NOT A UNION!

> The last few weeks have been very hard and exhausting for us and all Nissan workers. We took on the task of pushing back against the UAW's false demonization of our plant for its own financial gain. In their corner they had a long list of influential local folks they had paid to push their agenda, celebrities, a sitting US Senator, college students getting class credit to help campaign, and local politicians doing press

conferences and recorded phone calls to us on the eve of the vote. Strangers came to our homes uninvited to coax us into voting for the UAW. The outside pressures were oppressive and intimidating.

But we had us. And you. And we won. And we did it in our "spare" time while still building world class cars right here in Canton, Mississippi.

Now emotions are running high and feelings and friendships have been damaged no doubt. But come start of the next shift we are all still ONE TEAM. Give your co-workers a kind word and a smile—even if one is not offered in return right now. It's going to take some time. But we must put this behind us and get back to the business of building good quality cars that people want to buy at a price they can afford. That is our REAL job security.[442]

The UAW leadership took steps to keep options open. Less than an hour before the voting ended, UAW lawyers filed seven new unfair labor practice charges against Nissan management. They included allegations that Nissan management denied UAW representatives equal access to the voters, provided the UAW with an inaccurate list of eligible voters, engaged in widespread surveillance of workers' union activities, maintained a rating system of workers "according to their perceived support for the UAW," brought about the firing of a temporary employee who was sympathetic to the union, threatened to withdraw benefits if workers voted for the union, and told employees that collective bargaining with the company would be futile.[443] Nissan management immediately challenged the unfair labor practice charges and questioned the motivation behind them. "Filing unfair labor practice charges is a common tactic used by unions in an organizing campaign. The UAW is again launching baseless and unsubstantiated allegations against Nissan Canton in a desperate, last-minute attempt to undermine the integrity of the secret ballot voting process."[444]

The election results were a body blow to the plant's core union supporters. "It hurts," said Phillip White. "We ran against a machine. We ran against a monster. We ran against all the lies."[445] Many struck a defiant tone. After hearing the results of the recognition election, UAW supporter Morris Mock told a gathering of like-minded employees, "It ain't over yet. Nissan, all you did was make us mad. We are gonna fight a little harder next time. We are gonna stand a little harder next time because next time we are never gonna give up." The crowd interrupted Morris with a chant of "six months," which would be earliest there could be a new election if the NLRB decided in favor of the UAW's unfair labor practice filings. Hazel Whiting, mother of Derrick Whiting, who died shortly after collapsing in the Canton factory, yelled, "Fight to win, fight to win, fight to win!" "It's the beginning of a war," said union proponent Robert Hathorn. "They lit a torch for us." Castes Foster also anticipated a rematch and explained why he thought the outcome would be different. "The company is gonna help us win this next campaign and they don't even realize it because they are not going to keep their word. Once a snake, always a snake."[446] Hathorn added, "[Nissan] is going to play this nice guy role for about 3 to 6 months . . . then everything will go back to normal. Then the same people who voted against us are gonna be the same ones leading the campaign more than we are."[447] Michael Carter pointed to the attitude of some employees to explain the loss. "They don't understand that they are the union. There is not a third party coming in there, the union is already in there, and that's what we gotta make them understand, that they are the union."[448] Since the loss, however, organizing has effectively ceased at the Nissan Canton plant.

What were the strengths and weaknesses of the Nissan Canton organizing drive? The strengths were the choice of the theme of the campaign—namely, that labor rights equal civil rights—and the development of supporting organizations outside of the plant to help advance the drive, in particular the Mississippi Alliance for Fairness at Nissan and the Student Justice Alliance. The theme placed the campaign within a narrative of successful struggle that had resonance with Mississippi, particularly among the African American community. The civil rights theme facilitated the attraction and retention of the support for over a decade of the NAACP state and national leaderships, over three hundred clergy, celebrities such as Danny Glover, and politicians such as Bernie Sanders. That said, the civil rights theme was persuasive to less than 40 percent of a workforce that was 80 percent African American. Other factors proved decisive for the majority.

The UAW leadership devoted significant time and resources to generate transnational support for the Canton organizing drive, far more than they spent during the two drives at the Smyrna plant. This time, the transnational effort generated considerably more pressure. The legislatures of Brazil and France pressed Nissan management, and Nissan and Renault CEO Carlos Ghosn was compelled to testify before a French parliamentary committee about Nissan's actions in Canton. The pressure did have limits. Supporters of the Canton organizing drive in the French National Assembly were unable to persuade French government officials to make Ghosn's tenure as Renault CEO contingent on ending anti-union actions in Canton or to use France's indirect stake in Nissan through minority ownership of Renault to try to change Nissan policy. Union supporters in Brazil were unable to sway the Brazilian government or even the Río de Janeiro Olympics organizing committee to change policy to put pressure on Nissan management. UAW officials frequently turned to the IndustriALL Global Union for resolutions and other forms of rhetorical support, but no one ever attempted to organize transnational actions beyond sporadic protests outside Nissan dealerships in Brazil. The UAW leadership used the OECD guidelines for multinational enterprises, but that mechanism failed to make a difference. Labor laws and practice in Japan and France also do not give employees nearly as much leverage vis-à-vis management as they do in Germany. Consequently, intensified international pressure proved insufficient to force Nissan management to drop the firm's anti-union position and practices at Nissan Canton.

While the massive subsidies that Nissan received to build the Canton plant did provide a predicate for Mississippi politicians—in particular Governor Phil Bryant—to weigh in on the organizing drive, political intervention did not play nearly as big a role in the Nissan Canton organizing drive as it did in the VW cases—especially the first one—because Nissan managers took a tough position on their own. They had already honed an aggressive strategy against unionization in previous organizing drives in the company's Smyrna, Tennessee, plant.

Unlike Freightliner and TBB in North Carolina, which are the only success-ful cases of organizing wholly owned foreign vehicle assembly plants in the US South to date, UAW leadership never had something that Nissan management desperately wanted but could not obtain without coming to an agreement with the union. Bargaining to organize was therefore never an option.

Four additional aspects stand out as explanations for why Nissan workers did not vote in favor of recognizing the UAW as their exclusive bargaining agent. First, a job at Nissan substantially improved the material lives of most Canton employees, and they were grateful to Nissan for it. Union organizer Bianca Cun-ningham recounted that many Nissan Canton workers said, "I lived in a mobile home with my wife and kids and now I work at Nissan and have a house and land and my life is better. They gave me a shot and now I will give them a shot to change."[449] Nissan had far higher compensation than Mississippi blue-collar workers could expect to receive anywhere else in the state. Many Nissan employ-ees were reluctant to do anything that potentially risked losing their jobs as a result, including expressing support for a union. Union supporters did raise the issue of a three-tier compensation system in the Canton plant (i.e., permanent direct hires, permanent pathway employees, and temporary employees) but never used it in as centerpiece of the organizing drive. The union campaign, for ex-ample, never prioritized current and potential pathway employees for support and did not attempt to engage the temporary employees.

Second, Nissan management's campaign against the union inside the plant once again proved effective. Union supporters acknowledged that the constant messaging associating the UAW with internal strife and plant closures, the one-on-one meetings with supervisors, and the roundtable group meetings and peer pressure—which Nissan management had refined in Smyrna—once again proved effective at the Canton plant in dissuading some employees from supporting the union. For example, Chip Wells, the longtime union supporter whom the UAW and MAFFAN helped get back his job and $6,500 in back pay from Nissan, came out publicly against the UAW days before the recognition election. Wells said that he switched because of pressure from anti-union coworkers, a decision he said he quickly came to regret after the recognition election.[450]

Third, union sympathizers did not follow through on some of the bigger and more unconventional ideas to advance unionization in Canton that would have applied much more public pressure on Nissan. For example, the initial discussions about protesting in front of Nissan dealerships envisioned a concerted nationwide effort, but it never materialized. No one proposed taking the idea a step further to a consumer boycott akin to those unions conducted in the 1960s and 1970s to organize farmworkers in California and J. P. Stevens textile employees in North Carolina. The UAW's message of "pro-union, pro-Nissan" did not leave room for more confrontational tactics.

Fourth, the workers' organizing committee within the plant was never strong enough to apply substantial inside leverage on company management. Union supporters invested much more time and effort into developing and sustaining MAFFAN, the Student Justice Alliance, and international ties than they did developing the NWOC. This imbalance had consequences. MAFFAN was the lead organization in most undertakings, such as protesting at auto shows, which crowded out opportunities for employees to take the initiative. Neither the Nissan Workers Committee for a Fair Election nor the NWOC attempted to act as the de facto shop-floor employee representative, as had been the case in other unionization drives, but instead simply talked about the benefits of unionization. As a result, undecided Nissan Canton employees never saw practical examples in the plant of the difference a union could make except for the successful effort in the fall of 2016—with the assistance of an OSHA inspector—to allow employee representatives to participate in a safety inspection in the aftermath of a serious accident.

When it came to the actual recognition election, the NWOC proved to be far too small and poorly organized to be effective. The NWOC had no presence in some departments and shifts. After the vote Jeremy Holmes, a Nissan Canton employee who was on the NWOC, said, "We couldn't cover everybody in the plant because the committee wasn't big enough and there were a lot of people on the committee that were not active like they were supposed to be. Probably only about half were doing the work that needed to get done."[451]

It is best practice in an organizing drive for organizers and organizing committee members to have at least one conversation with every eligible employee individually to assess the person's position on unionization. This did not happen in Canton. It was difficult to tell permanent from temporary employees because all wore the same clothing. So, union sympathizers never had a solid list of who was eligible to vote until Nissan provided one as required two weeks before the vote, and that list was incomplete and had errors. Consequently, when voting commenced, union sympathizers had not assessed the preference or noted the concerns of more than six hundred eligible employees. In contrast, Nissan management had for years sent its messages repeatedly through multiple media and had one-on-one conversations with all employees.[452]

Tracing the four organizing attempts at two Nissan plants enriches the overall investigation of the UAW's efforts to unionize transplants by expanding case variance. The time between the first and last organizing drives was the longest for any foreign-owned company continuously producing in the United States. Nissan is not a German-owned company, which helps to identify what is specifically German in the other cases.

The four Nissan cases reveal that shrewd managers can create an environment and policies that make unionization extremely difficult. Marvin Runyon was a principal author of the union-avoidance playbook that managers elsewhere have since followed. His contributions include: (1) offer employees compensation close to a union rate, including some benefits not commonly found in union contracts; (2) minimize hierarchy; (3) adopt an open-door policy that allows employees to bring their concerns directly to upper plant management; (4) avoid layoffs if at all possible; (5) hold frequent celebrations of corporate milestones; (6) deploy video monitors ubiquitously in the plant to communicate the company's message; (7) use small group meetings to convey the management's position during organizing drives; and (8) engage with the local community through recognition events and financial support.

The Nissan cases are additional examples of the difficulties of organizing in the United States in general and the South in particular. Careful process tracing shows that in instances when a union cannot reach a neutrality agreement with an employer, success in mobilizing civil society—either domestically or internationally—is insufficient to prevail in an organizing drive. Union proponents must establish a strong presence in the workplace. Persuading a majority of employees to support unionization is particularly challenging in the South. Jobs at vehicle plants are especially prized, given that average regional compensation is low and few comparable opportunities exist. Many employees hesitate to do anything that could lead to dismissal or even upset the status quo. Putting plants in small towns atomizes the labor force because few employees live close to one another, which makes building the connections and trust that facilitate organizing more difficult. Economic incentives that enhance the interest and influence of anti-union state and local political establishments in the question of unionization is evident in both Smyrna and Canton cases, but fierce management resistance resulted in state, local, and national elites playing a less prominent role in the Nissan cases than at VW's Chattanooga plant.

It is worth noting that union complacency is not an explanation for organizing failures at Nissan, particularly for the latter attempts. Each organizing effort was better than the previous attempt. To be sure, the first drive at the Smyrna plant in 1989 was conventional. Jim Turner, a regional UAW officer who came up from the ranks, relied largely on methods passed down through the union over the decades, which did not fare well against Marvin Runyon's one-team model. Union officials did attempt to generate some international pressure on Nissan management, but it was minimal and detached from the main campaign. The 1997 attempt at Smyrna, which set a short deadline for gathering authorization cards to induce employees to commit to the UAW and to minimize the time Nissan management had to counter the drive, was in many ways the opposite of the first effort, but it too came up short because management still had its defenses in place from the 1989 campaign. The 2001 Smyrna unionization drive was far more professional and one of the first to use a well-developed website including video testimonials from employees to compensate for management's refusal to allow UAW representatives in the plant, but the innovative approach once again failed to persuade more than one-third of the Smyrna workforce to support unionization.

The sophistication, technical capacity, and international component of UAW organizing efforts grew substantially in the years between the last recognition election in Smyrna and the 2017 election at Nissan's Canton, Mississippi, plant. As UAW president, Bob King added resources and a strategic framework to the effort, and Richard Bensinger provided the experience and guidance of a long-time activist. The participation of the actor Danny Glover, rappers, and Vermont senator Bernie Sanders brought greater public attention to the drive than previous efforts. International engagement and support were also far greater than in the past. The civil rights theme at the heart of the Canton campaign resonated well outside of the plant, both domestically and internationally. The Canton drive stands out as a rare instance when UAW officials engaged with civil society in a timely and sophisticated way. Nonetheless, all these innovations failed to persuade more than a third of Canton's eligible employees to support unionization.

The failure of the Canton campaign marked the end of the UAW's eight-year multiplant, multimillion-dollar effort to organize foreign-owned vehicle plants in the South.

CONCLUSION

It's incredible but it's true that I will sit in the office of a large chemical company somewhere in Germany and the guy will tell me with a straight face the trouble with American employers is that they are antiunion and they don't understand their social responsibilities. Five minutes later he's saying, "Now, when I go to the South, how do I operate on a nonunion basis?"

—Richard A. Beaumont, "Working in the South"

Few other unions [besides the UAW] have had the courage to risk so much so publicly in actually organizing the South—and for that, credit should be given.

—Chris Brooks, "Organizing Volkswagen: A Critical Assessment"

The purpose of the previous four chapters has been to chronicle and analyze in detail the UAW's organizing drives at foreign-owned vehicle-assembly plants in the southern United States. This chapter summarizes the case chapters, draws more general conclusions about the processes traced in the case chapters, assesses the performance of the UAW, discusses the significance of the emergence of the union-avoidance playbook, weighs the efficacy of the New Deal labor relations regime as it has evolved in recent decades for securing employee voice and representation, and compares the UAW experience to recent organizing efforts in other sectors.

Daimler Truck North America

The DTNA cases show that unions can organize foreign-owned vehicle plants in the South. The UAW organized four out of five production facilities in the Carolinas in two episodes that were a decade apart. The first episode had one case of organizing and the second episode had six (table I.1 has a list of all of the cases.)

Why was the UAW successful? Timing is an element. The UAW organized these plants before the union-avoidance playbook, massive subsidization to attract investment, and the intervention of the southern economic and political elite in unionization campaigns had become established tactics. DTNA, more-

over, did not hire a union-avoidance law firm, and outside lobbyists only intervened toward the end of the second episode, with minimal effect.

Transnational support played a role in both the first and second episodes of
organizing. The forceful intervention of Daimler-Benz general works council
chair Karl Feuerstein helped to dissuade management from hiring permanent
replacements during a contentious strike to achieve a first contract at the Mount
Holly plant, although the fact that it was an unfair labor practice strike also
helped take that aggressive option off the table. Nate Gooden's position on the
DaimlerChrysler supervisory board a decade later enabled the UAW to reach a
top-down bargaining-to-organize agreement with DTNA management that facilitated the unionization of three additional plants through neutrality agreements in exchange for concessions at the Mount Holly plant. The DTNA cases
demonstrate that transnational cooperation can make a difference, but it is not
sufficient to produce success. The UAW failed to organize DTNA's Gaffney, South
Carolina, plant because most of the young high-skilled workforce saw no need
to unionize at their high-end plant that had strong and stable demand.

Mercedes-Benz U.S. International

MBUSI was exasperating for UAW officials and employees interested in
unionizing the Alabama plant because two unions failed there, but failure was
not inevitable. A neutrality agreement to facilitate organizing the plant was in
the grasp of the UAW during Chrysler contract negotiations, but UAW president Stephen Yokich traded it away for other objectives. Daimler management
embraced a policy of negative neutrality toward unionization, which combines
a formal statement that unionization is a matter for employees to decide with
an expression of management's view that the employees would be better off without a union, plus a set of policies designed to dissuade employees from supporting a union. Daimler management drew heavily on the emerging union-avoidance
playbook while adding a new play to it: a heavy reliance on temporary employees supplied by an independent firm. This practice made it far easier to pay high
wages and to deliver job security to a core group of permanent employees, which
made unionization far less attractive to them. MBUSI is one of the first foreign-
owned vehicle plants to receive huge subsidies from state and local governments,
which made it a prestige project for state and local politicians. Most local politicians became actively engaged in opposing unionization as a result.

MBUSI demonstrates the limits of transnational employee cooperation and
international labor agreements. The relationship between the UAW and IG Metall
was the most developed at Daimler, although there were moments of discord.

During the years of the DaimlerChrysler merger, the UAW had a representative on the DaimlerChrysler supervisory board, which facilitated cooperation between UAW and IG Metall board members but did not result in union recognition in Alabama. Daimler's world employee council and general works council—particularly under the leadership of Michael Brecht—applied considerable pressure on management to recognize the UAW but did not prevail. The company's global framework agreement with IndustriALL, a corporate code of conduct that embraced labor-management cooperation in the abstract, and membership in the UNGC proved inadequate as tools to compel a recalcitrant management to recognize the union.

Volkswagen

A distinctive feature of the first organizing drive at Volkswagen Chattanooga was management accommodation. This accommodation was instrumental, to be sure. VW managers wanted a works council because the company's global works council network was the established conduit for employee voice within the firm; they accepted unionization once they realized that it was a prerequisite under US labor law to establishing a works council. Accommodation also had its limits. VW CEO Martin Winterkorn had confidentially "agreed on the front end" with US senator Bob Corker that the company "would have nothing to do with the UAW" as a part of a deal that included over $300 million in subsidies.[1] Even before the plant began production in 2011, IG Metall officials started to pressure management in Germany to recognize the UAW, which put VW management in a difficult position. VW's works council leadership immediately advocated for the creation of a works council in Chattanooga and, after some initial hesitation rooted in the structural rivalry between unions and works councils in Germany, supported unionization when they too realized that in the United States it was a prerequisite to creating a works council. Still, the works councilors' ultimate objective was to ensure that a works council would be the preeminent body representing employees in Chattanooga. That objective constantly generated tension with the UAW because US union officials envisioned a works council as subordinate to the union local.

VW management attempted to please all by tacitly supporting unionization to facilitate the creation of a works council but refusing to agree to card-check recognition. Management's "positive neutrality" included allowing UAW representatives exclusive access to the plant and an opportunity to speak to employees. VW management also signed an accord with UAW officials shortly before the first recognition election establishing a cooperative framework for labor relations and setting parameters for the creation of a works council. VW management's stance pleased none. UAW officials would have preferred to use a card-check procedure to decide recognition. Tennessee political officials started their own campaign against unionization because VW management would not. The local business community and anti-union organizations based in Washington, DC, joined them.

The UAW lost the first recognition election by a narrow margin. Failure demonstrated that management accommodation alone was insufficient for securing union recognition. External opponents to unionization filled the void with their own anti-union campaign. Union proponents largely neglected working with domestic civil society organizations to enhance their leverage. Transnational employee cooperation, while unprecedented in depth and scope for the US vehicle production sector, failed to tip the balance in favor of union recognition.

After the first recognition election, VW management again attempted to please all but satisfied none by issuing a policy on "community organization engagement" that established criteria for regular meetings with employee groups. The policy fell far short of full codetermination rights, however.

UAW officials and union supporters in the plant did not give up. They founded a "members only" local at Volkswagen Chattanooga without formal recognition as the employees' exclusive bargaining agent, which the union had not done since the passage of the NLRA in 1935. They also changed tack, opting for a second recognition election in early 2015 for a small unit of skilled trades employees within the plant. The skilled employees voted overwhelmingly in favor of the UAW, but management objected, arguing that only a wall-to-wall unit could serve as a prerequisite for establishing a plant-wide works council. Management challenged the choice of the unit in court and hired a union-avoidance law firm, which blocked proceeding to contract negotiations. Working with the law firm exposed VW management to the union-avoidance playbook. Employee representatives from several countries and the global union federation in the metalworking sector pressured VW management to recognize the skilled mechanics unit and ultimately suspended the global framework agreement with the company when management refused to do so. Transnational employee cooperation once again proved too weak to force management to change position.

In 2019, VW employees launched a new organizing drive for the whole plant. This time, union supporters and UAW officials attempted a quick ambush campaign in hopes of catching VW management unawares, but VW's lawyers used the pending case for the skilled trades unit to delay proceeding to a wall-to-wall recognition election. During the delay, management relied heavily on a union-avoidance law firm and the union-avoidance playbook to develop and deploy an overtly anti-union campaign. The UAW again received support from IG Metall, IndustriALL, and VW's works council, but transnational support was far less effective in an ambush campaign. VW management did not desist with the anti-union campaign. Management even prevented VW Global Works Council general secretary Johan Järvklo, who was also a member of VW's supervisory board, from entering the Chattanooga plant on the first day of the representation election. Once again, the UAW lost in a close election.

The most striking aspects here are the transformation of VW management's actions from tacit support of unionization to outright opposition—despite having the strongest set of agreements and commitments to social responsibility and employee rights in the automobile industry—and the inability of employee representatives to stop it despite considerable innovation in both tactics and strategy.

Nissan

The four Nissan cases are extraordinarily important for understanding why the UAW's organizing record at foreign-owned vehicle plants in the South has worsened in recent decades. Smyrna's founding plant manager, Marvin Runyon, is a principal author of the union-avoidance playbook. Runyon's one-team model—which leaves no role for unions—has become the norm today in foreign-owned vehicle plants throughout the southern United States. This model minimizes hierarchy, maintains an open-door policy for employees to meet with management, has no separate management dining halls or parking areas, avoids layoffs, provides more benefits (e.g., discount prices on car rentals), screens to hire only employees who are likely to be "team players," and offers wage rates just below those in a union contract but far higher than the local market rate. Runyon's objective was to give employees a degree of voice and compensation that would be sufficient to motivate them to do more than the bare minimum at work and thus conclude that there would be little added benefit to joining a union. Nissan Smyrna also pioneered the ubiquitous use of video monitors throughout plants to disseminate management's perspective on a range of topics, including unionization.

The one-team model was instrumental in limiting support for unionization to one-third of the employees in Nissan plants. Nissan managers also divided the workforces at their plants by hiring large numbers of temporary employees. Permanent jobs at Nissan were prized because the alternatives were mostly low-paying service-sector positions. Management persuaded many workers that unionization could put these scarce golden-ticket jobs at risk. Some employees even formed groups opposed to unionization with at least tacit support from management and the local business community, which has since become common at transplants whenever the UAW begins organizing activities. The rural location of the plant made organizing difficult because most workers had long commutes from a wide variety of locations.

Nissan did not initially receive huge subsidies to build the Smyrna plant, but it was nonetheless a prestige project for Tennessee governor Lamar Alexander and subsequent Tennessee politicians. The company did receive large state and local subsidies for subsequent expansion of the Smyrna facility and construction of plants in Decherd, Tennessee, and Canton, Mississippi. Politicians vested in recruiting these plants to their state subsequently intervened to oppose unionization efforts. They typically asserted that their actions were to preserve a favorable investment climate. Occasionally, some conceded publicly that they also opposed unionization so as to keep out an organization that would support progressive causes and Democratic Party candidates. Nissan management cultivated links to the local community through numerous plant celebrations and contributions to charities, schools, and other nonprofit organizations. Nissan's largesse made it difficult for the UAW to find support for organizing drives in the local community.

The organizing drive at Nissan Canton was the only effort where the UAW dedicated considerable time and resources to developing support from civil society. UAW officials and union supporters effectively mobilized civil rights leaders from Mississippi and beyond, brought in entertainment and political celebrities, and worked extensively with transnational employee representatives to put pressure on Nissan management, but this successful external mobilization fell short because union supporters did not develop a strong employee network within the plant.

Assessing the Performance of the United Auto Workers

The performance of the UAW in these organizing drives was mixed. Without question, UAW officials and supporters made errors in the unionization efforts at foreign-owned vehicle assembly plants. Stephen Yokich's decision to trade away management's preliminary acceptance of a neutrality agreement at MBUSI for other objectives in the 1999 Chrysler contract talks stands out as the most consequential. Bob King's excessive reliance on an "air war" of a website, video clips, and mobile phones over a "ground war" of in-plant organizing and house calls in the second representation election at Nissan Smyrna and Gary Casteel's unnecessary provocation of Senator Bob Corker, and the 2014 preelection agreement between the UAW and VW that committed the UAW to maintaining competitive wages are also noteworthy. That said, mistakes are to be expected in any organizing drive. Outcomes, however, are not simply a product of tallying the errors of each side. The industrial relations regime, the capacities of the institutional actors, and the talent of the individuals involved all have an impact on the outcome of any organizing effort.

Previous chapters frequently touch on the challenges for employees and unions when it comes to organizing that are specific to the US industrial relations regime. Numerous studies from a variety of disciplines discuss them as well.[2] Combined, these challenges make organizing in the United States a playing field tilted against employees and unions. As a result, employees can only prevail by making substantially fewer errors—and smaller ones—than employers. The slant of the playing field, moreover, has not remained stable. The sociopolitical environment for organizing has deteriorated substantially since the 1970s for a variety of reasons including globalization, economic fissuring, and the increased individualization of society, which makes the task harder and leaves less room for error.

The UAW cannot be accused of turning a blind eye to the expansion of automobile production in the South. The UAW is a much weaker organization in the twenty-first century than it had been in its heydays during the mid-twentieth century, and it has always been weakest in the South. Nonetheless, the union mounted a sustained effort to organize foreign-owned vehicle assembly plants there for over two decades. The UAW leadership devoted well over $100 million to organizing drives at foreign-owned transplants. Talented individuals invested considerable effort in these drives, especially Gary Casteel and Bob King. King made organizing southern transplants the UAW's principal mission when he was the union's president, describing it as an "all-in hand." No other union has come close to doing as much.

UAW officials did not take a one-size-fits-all approach to organizing in the South and did not mindlessly stick to the same strategy drive after drive. They were adaptive and creative, and they learned from mistakes. The UAW was among the first unions to use computers, mobile phones, a quality website, social media, and video clips in organizing drives. The union has been a pioneer in integrating international cooperation with foreign employee representatives into organizing drives. UAW officials were willing to experiment with novel and often controversial employment relations practices for the United States, such as a works council and members-only locals, to advance organizing drives. The UAW did multiyear drives and ambush drives as well as drives with fixed stop dates and no stop dates, depending on the circumstances. To be sure, UAW leaders exhibited a preference for top-down approaches (such as bargaining to organize), but they also pursued a campaign at the Nissan Canton plant with a civil rights theme that was centered on cooperation with grassroots civil society organizations. In brief, a shortage of attention, imagination, innovation, or resources does not explain the UAW's meager results in organizing efforts at foreign-owned vehicle plants in the South over the past two decades.

What does account for the failures? Besides the structural and systemic disadvantages discussed above, employers and local politicians opposed to unions were also innovative. Marvin Runyon's one-team employment practices and other features of the union-avoidance playbook have become the norm in the sector and have spread beyond the South, as the UAW's 2017 failed organizing drive at Fuyao Glass in Moraine, Ohio, illustrated.[3] (The Fuyao organizing drive is the subject of the 2020 Academy Award–winning documentary *American Factory*.) Political elites and lobbyists at local and national levels have learned how to use subsidies, political pressure, and public relations campaigns to make union organizing more difficult. High stakes organizing drives at transnational enterprises are no longer confined to the workplace. They unfold in the boardroom and the political sphere as well. An organizing drive must prevail in all three to succeed. Union opponents can thwart a drive simply by carrying the day in just one. In sum, the UAW's organizing drives have become less successful because advances on the anti-union side have proved more effective than the UAW's innovations, all within a larger environment that has become less conducive to unionization.

Repercussions for the US Labor Movement

Even after considering the UAW's successes at DTNA, the repercussions of the subsequent inability of the UAW to organize foreign-owned automobile assembly plants in the South are manifold. First, the failure to take compensation out of the competitive equation in automobile production in the United States lessens the UAW's bargaining power. Although managers are likely to maintain compensation at a near-union rate to fend off unionization, competitive pressures—which the 2014 neutrality agreement between the UAW and VW explicitly acknowledged—will continue to be substantial. As a result, the pressure on all auto producers to contain compensation, subcontract, squeeze suppliers, and operate without a union will persist. Second, union membership and density in the automotive sector will continue to decline because transplants have been adding employment while the domestic-based producers have not. The UAW will be a weaker organization as a result, despite successes in organizing employees outside of vehicle manufacturing. Third, the hegemony of the anti-union political elite in the southern United States will remain intact, which has implications beyond economic matters for everyone living in that region and beyond.

The unrelenting decline of unions since the mid-1950s has contributed to rising inequality, blue-collar malaise, and increasingly unchecked corporate power in the United States. Support has grown in recent years to address these ills by rebuilding worker power. In the past, many economists have been critical of unions, depicting them as groups of employees seeking rents for themselves at the expense of the economy as a whole,[4] but "in our post-2008, post-Piketty era, virtually every economist to the left of [director of the Trump administration's National Economic Council] Larry Kudlow is an evangelist for unions."[5] Support for strong unions even has adherents in some conservative intellectual circles.[6] What does the UAW's effort to organize foreign-owned vehicle assembly plants tell us about how to succeed at rebuilding worker power?

Some longtime observers of US labor relations have described our time of post-COVID labor shortages, a general dissatisfaction with the workplace status quo, and a surge among youth in the popularity of unions (which at times has a steampunk sensibility about it) as a "John L. Lewis moment,"[7] harking back to the glory days of the formation of the Congress of Industrial Organizations in the 1930s. They assert that large numbers of workers are ripe for organizing and claim that the main thing holding back a resurgence of the US labor movement is the bureaucratic cautiousness and frugality of today's union leaders. The analysis of the UAW's attempts to organize southern transplants in the preceding chapters makes it clear that things are not that simple. The relative power of workers will never improve without a substantial overhaul or even outright abandonment of the recognition election as the way to determine whether a union should represent a group of workers. This is ironic, since it was union leaders in the 1930s who pushed for representation elections as an alternative to recognition strikes, which were grueling confrontations that all too often turned violent. In the decades since, however, employers, law firms, and local political elites in many parts of the country have developed an increasingly sophisticated and effective playbook for keeping unions out of workplaces. Of the twelve organizing attempts under investigation in this study that went to the workers to decide, four used card-check recognition, and the UAW won all those. Eight had recognition elections. The UAW lost six and won two, and VW management refused to bargain and ultimately prevailed in preventing unionization in one of the two "wins." So, only two out of eight elections resulted in first contracts.

Most candidates for the 2020 Democratic Party presidential nomination—including Joe Biden—proposed comprehensive labor law reform and other measures to enhance worker power. Starting from a "clean slate," Sharon Block and Benjamin Sachs of the Harvard Law School's Labor and Worklife program drafted a plan for a new federal labor statute to boost worker power.[8] It is worth considering, however, whether it is ever possible, given the "privileged position of business" in a capitalist polity,[9] to construct a "juridico-discursive" regime of industrial relations that would not undercut collective mobilization as a counter-vailing force,[10] which is the wellspring of worker power. Dependence on the state as rule maker and referee unavoidably demobilizes workers, who become "practiced . . . docile bodies."[11] An alternative to a juridico-discursive "regime of truth" may be more effective at enhancing worker power.[12]

It is instructive to contrast the UAW cases with recent organizing efforts at Amazon and Starbucks, where union recognition elections have taken place at a handful of Amazon warehouses and hundreds of Starbucks coffee shops with some notable successes. First, Amazon and Starbucks are both service provid-ers rather than manufacturers. Consequently, they must have locations where they wish to provide their services, which includes cities with long union tradi-tions such as Buffalo and New York. Second, the services the two companies pro-vide also preclude managers from threatening offshoring to dissuade employees from organizing.

Third, although pay and benefits at Amazon and Starbucks exceed those at many unskilled service-sector jobs, they are lower than at most vehicle plants, and comparable employment opportunities are much more plentiful. Trying to organize is therefore less risky to workers' economic well-being, although long-time labor organizer Gene Bruskin attributed the loss in the union recognition election at the second Amazon warehouse in Staten Island to a portion of the workforce with limited alternatives who feared jeopardizing their jobs.[13]

Fourth, politicians have not used massive subsidies or political courtship to persuade Amazon or Starbucks to build warehouses or coffee shops in their ar-eas, and they are not considered prestige investments. Politicians are therefore not as vested in these workplaces as they are in foreign vehicle plants and are less worried that a union victory will upend their electoral prospects, so they have been less likely to get involved to thwart unionization.

It is worth noting that Amazon and Starbucks differ in several respects. These differences help explain why organizing at Starbucks took off and spread more quickly than at Amazon. Starbucks retail outlets typically employ twenty to forty people. Workers behind counters have opportunities to talk and get to know one another, which facilitates the mutual trust and solidarity needed to prevail in recognition elections and contract negotiations. Amazon, in contrast, employs hundreds to thousands at isolated workstations in factory-like warehouses that more closely resemble vehicle production, which makes communicating and forging bonds among employees a challenge. Amazon has placed many ware-houses in rural locations that have good access to interstate highways near cit-ies, much like the sites of the vehicle plants under investigation here, but Starbucks outlets must be convenient for a minimum number of customers to survive, which limits the possibilities for using a rural strategy to reduce the likelihood of unionization.

The strategy and tactics of organizing at Amazon and Starbucks differ in several respects from those the UAW used at foreign-owned vehicle plants. Employees rather than professional organizers have taken the lead in the unionization efforts. The Amazon Labor Union (ALU) is a start-up model replete with a GoFundMe webpage (https://www.gofundme.com/f/the-amazon-labor-union-solidarity -fund). As a result, Amazon managers could not use several plays from the union-avoidance playbook. They could neither characterize the organizers as outsiders nor depict the union as a distant third party that was simply interested in extracting dues money. ALU leaders have used unconventional tactics. They did not wait until they had authorization cards from well over a majority of employees before proceeding to a recognition election, shortening the length of organizing drives. They have also been savvy in their use of both social and traditional media. The ALU's start-up strategy has drawbacks. It relies on the skills of local employees, which can vary greatly from workplace to workplace. It also sacrifices the economies of scale and the defraying of risk that led unions to coalesce into national organizations in the latter half of the nineteenth century.[14] It is also worth noting the difference in scale between Amazon and Starbucks. To organize the same number of workers as in Amazon's Staten Island warehouse, Starbucks Workers United would have to organize 400 outlets.

Historically, union organizing has frequently come in waves. A century ago, common ethnicity and neighborhood were the media for transmitting waves.[15] Workers United, which is a platform that the Service Employees International Union created, has become a new means of transmission. It most closely resembles a franchise model of unionization. Workers United lowers the barriers to organizing once a core group of workers at a location begin to explore unionization. Starbucks Workers United, which was first established for organizing drives in Buffalo, has helped with logos, media strategy, website creation, and training. These measures have enhanced employees' resources and made them much less susceptible to captive-audience speeches and other plays from the union-avoidance playbook. Starbucks Workers United announces each time a shop asks for a recognition election and publicizes each victory, which generates new leads at additional stores that keep the wave going.

It is premature to declare a breakthrough for organized labor, despite recent victories in union recognition elections. Amazon and Starbucks management still have many plays left in the union-avoidance playbook and have not hesitated to use them. Starbucks management claims to embrace progressive values,[16] but in April 2022 CEO Howard Schultz said that firms such as Starbucks are being "assaulted" by unionization efforts, and he vowed to fight them.[17] Starbucks employees have alleged over two hundred instances of unfair labor practices.[18] Employees have also filed numerous unfair labor practice charges against Amazon.[19] Top Amazon managers have underscored the seriousness they place on fighting unionization by filing their own unfair labor practice charges against the ALU and firing the managers at the Staten Island warehouse who voted to recognize the ALU.[20]

It is also informative to look to countries where trade unions remain comparatively more influential than in the United States to see how they have done a better job retaining worker power. Canada uses card-check recognition rather than recognition elections and has a unionization rate that is three times that of the United States. This would be the most obvious reform. It was the centerpiece of the Employee Free Choice Act, which was first proposed in 2007 but never became law. It is included in the 2020 Protecting the Right to Organize Act. Resistance has been fierce to making card-check recognition standard practice, however. The US Chamber of Commerce asserts that reliance on card-check recognition would "undermine secret ballot elections [by] forcing workers to make their choice about unionizing in public and exposing them to threats and coercion from union agents."[21] This argument—and considerable lobbying pressure from multiple employers organizations—has proved effective.

An alternative would be to engage in collective bargaining or standard setting at the sectoral level. The current system of recognition for the purposes of collective bargaining at the workplace or the firm level is inherently divisive because it makes operating union-free an option, which puts a firm at a disadvantage if it were to become unionized but its competitors were not. Sectoral bargaining, in contrast, produces a contract that serves as a floor for compensation and working conditions for particular sectors (e.g., construction, health care, or metalworking) or occupations (e.g., electricians or truck drivers) for all at either a regional or national level. Employers may offer their employees more if they wish; they cannot offer them less than the sectoral contract. It is therefore impossible to operate as a nonunion firm.

Several proposals for labor law reform have emerged in recent years that include a shift to sectoral bargaining.[22] Most envision the federal government creating committees with business and labor representatives to undertake negotiations for individual sectors. Several European countries use forms of sectoral bargaining.[23] These practices have bolstered worker power even in places where union density has fallen considerably.

Sectoral bargaining would address many of the shortcomings in the current employment relations regime. It would increase coverage and make it impossible for firms to operate union-free since all firms would fall under a sectoral agreement. Increased coverage would help to reduce inequality, at least within sectors. Sectoral bargaining would also help to close racial and gender pay gaps by standardizing compensation and providing greater transparency.

Sectoral collective bargaining is not totally alien to the United States. Prevailing wage legislation, which exists principally in the construction sector, is one form.[24] During World War II, the National War Labor Board used tripartite panels to set wage standards at the national level for sectors vital to the war effort. The board was also responsible for wage stabilization and dispute settlement in other sectors, which it administered regionally.[25]

That said, the principal challenges to moving to sectoral bargaining are enacting it, operating it, and enforcing it. Business interests and prominent Republicans have already expressed their "screaming opposition" to sectoral bargaining.[26] Enacting sectoral bargaining would therefore take a veto-proof majority in the US Senate or an executive order, which would surely be challenged in court. Low union density means that US trade unions do not have sufficient power to push substantial labor law reform through Congress, but without substantial labor law reform unions have been unable to stanch density declines. Organized labor has been locked into this death spiral for over sixty years. It is unlikely that the impasse will be broken anytime soon. Even if labor law reform is enacted, sectoral bargaining would depend on cooperation from employers to serve on boards to develop standards and apply them. Such cooperation is by no means ensured. It is most likely, then, that employees and unions will have to live with the existing labor law for the foreseeable future and gain at best only modest reforms, such as stiffer penalties for labor law violations.

The UAW's efforts to organize foreign-owned vehicle assembly plants led to substantial advances in transnational cooperation between employee representatives. The depth of the cooperation between the UAW and IG Metall during the DaimlerChrysler merger and the presidency of Bob King is noteworthy, especially the joint brochures, employee exchanges, and leadership visits. UAW leaders also integrated the IndustriALL global union into its campaigns to an unprecedented degree.

Transnational trade union cooperation can make a difference, as the DTNA cases and the research of Marissa Brookes demonstrate,[27] but more often than not it still proved insufficient to change management's stance regarding unionization. This was particularly evident in the efforts to organize Volkswagen Chattanooga. UAW officials clearly would have preferred using a card-check procedure for the reasons discussed above, but VW management rejected it because of the commitment to the Tennessee political establishment that the company would not unilaterally recognize the UAW.

MBUSI and Volkswagen Chattanooga also demonstrated the limitations of global framework agreements and other international commitments that are not backed up by courts or strikes. When IndustriALL threatened and then suspended the VW global framework agreement over management's refusal to bargain, VW management did not change its position and subsequently waged a standard US-style anti-union campaign to thwart the UAW's second wall-to-wall organizing drive.

The UAW's campaigns to organize transplants certainly advanced transnational coordination among trade unions. They may be steps along the way toward creating effective and reliable transnational alliances among employee representatives, but we are not there yet.

Notes

INTRODUCTION

1. Stephen J. Silvia, *Holding the Shop Together: German Industrial Relations in the Postwar Era* (Ithaca, NY: Cornell University Press, 2013), 80–82.

2. Sarah Hamoudi, "State Competition for Foreign Direct Investment and Transnational Automotive Original Equipment Manufacturers in the U.S. South: Effects on Union Power" (master's thesis, Global Labour University, University of Kassel and Berlin School of Economics and Law, 2022), 101.

3. Ryan Nunn, Jimmy O'Donnell, and Jay Shambaugh, "The Shift in Private Sector Union Participation: Explanation and Effects," The Hamilton Project, Brookings Institution, August 2019, https://www.brookings.edu/wp-content/uploads/2019/08/UnionsEA_Web_8.19.pdf; Joseph Stiglitz, *The Price of Inequality: How Today's Divided Society Endangers Our Future* (New York: Norton, 2012); Kamala D. Harris and Martin J. Walsh, *White House Task Force on Organizing and Empowerment: Report to the President*, The White House, n.d. [released February 7, 2022], https://www.whitehouse.gov/wp-content/uploads/2022/02/White-House-Task-Force-on-Worker-Organizing-and-Empowerment-Report.pdf.

4. Michel Foucault, *The History of Sexuality*, vol. 1 (New York: Random House, 1978), 82.

5. The book treats DTNA and MBUSI as separate entities, even though a single transnational enterprise owned them both during the period under investigation, because management treated them as such. (The name of the enterprise changed from Daimler-Benz to DaimlerChrysler and then simply Daimler.) In 2022, management separated the subsidiaries into two completely independent entities: Daimler Truck, which owns DTNA, and Mercedes-Benz Cars & Vans, which owns MBUSI.

6. I do not consider organizing activity that does not advance beyond union interchange with a small share of plant employees to be a case. The book does not include as cases organizing efforts at joint ventures between a foreign and domestic firm (e.g., the GM-Toyota plant in Fremont, California) or wholly owned foreign plants that are not in the southeastern United States (e.g., VW in Westmoreland County, Pennsylvania, and Honda in Marysville, Ohio) because the relevant actors and interactions differ. Two borderline cases, which I do not include, are Toyota in Georgetown, Kentucky, and BMW in Spartanburg, South Carolina. In both instances, the UAW approached management in the years surrounding the opening of the plant, had some engagement with foreign employee representatives, and undertook some organizing activity but never attracted more than a small share of employees. For more on Toyota Georgetown, see Amy Bromsen, "Condescending Saviors: Union Substitution at Toyota Motor Manufacturing Kentucky (TMMK)" (PhD diss., Wayne State University, 2019), ProQuest 13811305. For more on BMW Spartanburg, see Stephen J. Silvia, "Organizing German Automobile Plants in the USA: An Assessment of the United Auto Workers' Efforts to Organize German-Owned Automobile Plants," Study 349, Hans Böckler Foundation, Düsseldorf, December 2016.

7. National Labor Relations Act (NLRA), section 9(b).

8. Andrew Bennett and Jeffery T. Checkel, "Process Tracing: From Philosophical Roots to Best Practices," in *Process Tracing: From Metaphor to Analytic Tool*, ed. Andrew Bennett and Jeffery T. Checkel (Cambridge: Cambridge University Press, 2014), 4.

9. David Collier, "Understanding Process Tracing," *PS: Political Science and Politics* 44, no. 4 (October 2011): 823.

10. "In the Matter of General Shoe Corporation and Boot and Shoe Workers Union, A. F. L.," case nos. 10-R-1958 and 10-C-093, National Labor Relations Board, April 16, 1948, https://apps.nlrb.gov/link/document.aspx/09031d4580079454.

11. Richard B. Freeman and Joel Rogers, *What Workers Want* (Ithaca, NY: Cornell University Press, 1999), 59; Thomas A. Kochan, "How American Workers View Labor Unions," *Monthly Labor Review* 102, no. 4 (April 1979): 23–31.

12. Thomas A. Kochan, Duanyi Yang, William T. Kimball, and Erin L. Kelly, "Worker Voice in America: Is There a Gap between What Workers Expect and What They Experience?," *Industrial and Labor Relations Review* 72, no. 1 (January 2019): 20.

13. "Union Members—2021," Bureau of Labor Statistics, January 20, 2022, https://www.bls.gov/news.release/pdf/union2.pdf; Barry T. Hirsch, "Sluggish Institutions in a Dynamic World: Can Unions and Industrial Competition Coexist?," *Journal of Economic Perspectives* 22, no. 1 (Winter 2008): 153–76; Barry T. Hirsch and David A. Macpherson, "Union Membership, Coverage, and Earnings from the CPS," Union Membership and Coverage Database, 2022, http://www.unionstats.com/.

14. See Richard B. Freeman and James L. Medoff, *What Do Unions Do?* (New York: Basic Books, 1984); Harry C. Katz, Thomas A. Kochan, and Alexander J. S. Colvin, *An Introduction to U.S. Collective Bargaining and Labor Relations*, 5th ed. (Ithaca, NY: Cornell University Press, 2017), 26–153.

15. Daniel K. Benjamin, "Voluntary Export Restraints on Automobiles," *PERC Reports* 17, no. 3 (Fall 1999), https://www.perc.org/1999/09/01/voluntary-export-restraints-on-automobiles/.

16. . *Ward's Automotive Yearbook* (Southfield, MI: Ward's Automotive, various years).

17. "Active members" means members who are employed or officially unemployed but not retirees and those no longer seeking work. The 1959 Labor Management Reporting and Disclosure Act requires unions to report these data annually to the US Department of Labor in LM-2 forms. That is this study's source for UAW membership data.

18. Author's calculation using US Department of Labor, "Form LM-2, LM-3, and LM-4 Financial Annual Report," LM-2 forms, https://www.documentcloud.org/documents/21111367-uaw-2020-lm2; Hirsch and Macpherson, "Union Membership."

19. David Welch, "GM Is Now Detroit's Smallest Auto-Making Employer," Bloomberg, August 29, 2019, https://www.bloomberg.com/news/articles/2019-08-29/once-giant-gm-is-now-detroit-s-smallest-auto-making-employer.

20. Hirsch and Macpherson, "Union Membership"; Ken Roberts, "Insult to Injury: Foreign Manufacturers Now Making More Cars in U.S. than U.S. Companies," *Forbes*, January 22, 2018; Tyler Durden, "Visualizing the De-Unionization of Auto Workers," ZeroHedge, February 25, 2014.

21. For example, Bromsen, "Condescending Saviors"; Steve Early, *Save Our Unions: Dispatches from a Movement in Distress* (New York: Monthly Review Press, 2013), 61–63, 223; Gregg Shotwell, *Autoworkers under the Gun: A Shop-Floor View of the End of the American Dream* (Chicago: Haymarket Books, 2011).

1. DAIMLER TRUCK NORTH AMERICA

1. To keep things simple, I use the name Daimler Truck North America throughout the chapter, even though Daimler management only began to use it in 2008 after the breakup of DaimlerChrysler. Daimler's biggest heavy vehicle line in North America has always been Freightliner Trucks. Starting in the late 1990s, Daimler management purchased Ford Trucks (renaming it Sterling), TBB, Detroit Diesel, and Western Star Trucks, and has managed all of these units as parts of DTNA.

2. These are not the only facilities the UAW has ever organized in the South. The union has organized assembly plants owned by domestic producers (e.g., GM in Spring Hill, Tennessee) and other parts plants. Foreign firms have also bought some plants that the UAW had already organized (e.g., AB Volvo bought the Mack Truck plant in Dublin, Virginia). Outside of the South, the UAW organized most of the auto assembly plants that were joint ventures between Japanese and US firms during the 1980s and 1990s (e.g., the Ford-Mazda plant in Flat Rock, Michigan), but the only other wholly foreign-owned vehicle assembly plant that the UAW successfully organized in the United States besides the DTNA factories in North Carolina was the VW plant in Westmoreland County, Pennsylvania.

3. Holm-Detlev Köhler, "From the Marriage in Heaven to the Divorce on Earth: The DaimlerChrysler Trajectory since the Merger," in *The Second Automobile Revolution: Trajectories of the World Carmakers in the 21st Century*, edited by Michel Freyssenet (London: Palgrave Macmillan, 2009), 316.

4. Motor Carrier Regulatory Reform and Modernization Act of 1980, Pub. L. No. 96–296, 94 Stat. 793, approved 1 July 1980.

5. R. J. Cole, "Daimler-Benz Set to Buy U.S. Truck-Making Unit," *New York Times*, March 6, 1981.

6. D. Olmos, "Layoff-Ridden Gaston County Bounces Back," *Charlotte Observer*, February 17, 1986.

7. "Freightliner Corporation," *Burlington Daily Times-News*, August 29, 1988.

8. D. Mildenberg and K. Nixon, "Demand Keeps on Truckin,'" *Charlotte Observer*, February 21, 1989; "Oshkosh Truck Moving Upstate," *Spartanburg Herald-Journal*, March 24, 1989.

9. J. F. French, "Gaston's Freightliner Corp. Goes Union in Close Vote," *Charlotte Observer*, April 7, 1990.

10. L. Hohmann, "Workers Accept Pay Terms," *Gaston Gazette*, December 21, 1991.

11. L. Hohmann, "Gaston: Never the Same," *Gaston Gazette*, December 22, 1991.

12. J. F. French, "Benefits Available in Freightliner Layoffs," *Charlotte Observer*, August 31, 1989.

13. French, "Gaston's Freightliner Corp. Goes Union in Close Vote."

14. J. F. French, "Survey Helps Freightliner Keep Its Wages High," *Charlotte Observer*, September 22, 1989.

15. J. F. French, "Freightliner Lays Off 114 Workers Indefinitely," *Charlotte Observer*, January 17, 1990.

16. French, "Gaston's Freightliner Corp. Goes Union in Close Vote."

17. J. F. French, "Freightliner Union Election to Be April 6," *Charlotte Observer*, March 7, 1990.

18. "In It for the Long Haul," *Solidarity*, March–April 2012.

19. J. F. French, "Freightliner Dismisses Personnel Manager," *Charlotte Observer*, March 30, 1990.

20. J. F. French, "More Cutbacks at Freightliner," *Charlotte Observer*, March 29, 1990.

21. A. D. Helms, "After Union Win, Freightliner Workers Seek Healing," *Charlotte Observer*, April 8, 1990.

22. C. Herndon, "Narrow Win Seen as Isolated," *Charlotte Observer*, April 7, 1990.

23. Kate Bronfenbrenner, "No Holds Barred: The Intensification of Employer Opposition to Organizing," Briefing Paper no. 235 (Washington, DC: Economic Policy Institute, 2009), 22.

24. G. Robertson, "Unions Blame Setback on Economy," *Charlotte Observer*, October 13, 1991.

25. C. Wilson, "Freightliner Orders Layoffs, Cutbacks," *Charlotte Observer*, August 10, 1990.

26. C. Wilson, "Slow Contract Talks Upset Union," *Charlotte Observer*, November 23, 1990.

27. J. F. French Parker, "NLRB: Actions Unfair," *Charlotte Observer*, April 5 and 13, 1991.

28. C. Wilson, "Freightliner Union Calls for Strike," *Charlotte Observer*, April 14, 1991.

29. C. Wilson, "Freightliner, Union Still Talking," *Charlotte Observer*, May 30, 1991.

30. L. Hohmann, "Freightliner 'Strike Notice," in Effect Today," *Charlotte Observer*, December 4, 1991.

31. Inter-Office Communication, John Christensen to Don Stillman, December 5, 1991, Owen Bieber Accession 1270/Series I, Box 4.23, United Auto Workers Collections, Walter P. Reuther Library Archives, Wayne State University, Detroit, Michigan (hereafter UAWC).

32. Correspondence from Jack G. Jerry to Scott Evitt, 15 October 1991, Owen Bieber Accession 1270/Series I, Box 4.23, UAWC.

33. B. Hallman, "Is Freightliner Really Thinking Shutdown?," *Gaston Gazette*, October 27, 1991.

34. L. Hohmann, "Union Sets Freightliner Deadline," *Gaston Gazette*, November 22, 1991.

35. N. Moore and L. Hohmann, "Union, Management Stay into the Night as Strike Looms," *Gaston Gazette*, November 23, 1991.

36. L. Hohmann, "Union Rejects Freightliner Offer," *Gaston Gazette*, November 27, 1991.

37. Inter-Office Communication, John Christensen to Don Stillman, December 5, 1991, Owen Bieber Accession 1270/Series I, Box 4.23, UAWC.

38. Correspondence from Franz Steinkühler to Owen Bieber, May 17, 1991, Owen Bieber Accession 1270/Series II, Box 26.74, UAWC.

39. M. Schechter, "BMW Marks 25th Year as 'Game Changer' in SC," *Greenville News*, June 22, 2017.

40. Inter-Office Communication, John Christensen to Don Stillman, 5 December 1991, Owen Bieber Accession 1270/Series I, Box 4.23, UAWC, emphasis in the original.

41. L. Hohmann, "All's Quiet on the Freightliner Front," *Gaston Gazette*, December 3, 1991.

42. *NLRB v. Mackay Radio & Telegraph Co.*, 304 U.S. 333, 1938.

43. *NLRB v. Thayer Co.*, 213 F.2d 748, lst Cir. 1954.

44. Hohmann, "All's Quiet on the Freightliner Front."

45. L. Hohmann, "Freightliner 'Strike Notice' in Effect Today," *Gaston Gazette*, December 4, 1991.

46. C. Wilson, "Union Threatens Freightliner with Strike," *Charlotte Observer*, December 4, 1991.

47. N. Moore and L. Hohmann, "Union Walkout Divides Friends—and Even Families," *Gaston Gazette*, December 5, 1991.

48. C. Wilson and J. Day, "800 Gaston Workers on Strike," *Charlotte Observer*, December 5, 1991.

49. L. Hohmann, "Mt Holly Plant Still Running as Negotiators Fail to Meet," *Gaston Gazette*, December 5, 1991.

50. Wilson, "800 Gaston Workers on Strike"; L. Hohmann, "Third Shift to Close during Strike," *Gaston Gazette*, December 6, 1991.

51. L. Hohmann, "Gaston: Never the Same," *Gaston Gazette*, December 22, 1991; John A. Salmond, *Gastonia 1929: The Story of the Loray Mill Strike* (Chapel Hill: University of North Carolina Press, 1995).

52. L. Hohmann, "Truck: Keep Rolling," *Gaston Gazette*, December 7, 1991.

53. C. Wilson and S. Jeffries, "Textile Workers Question Need for Strike," *Charlotte Observer*, December 5, 1991.

54. J. DePriest, "Freightliner Supervisor Charged with Hitting 2 Strikers with Car," *Gaston Gazette*, December 8, 1991.

55. N. Moore, "Deadline Looms as Plant, Strikers Face Unity Test," *Gaston Gazette*, December 8, 1991; L. Hohmann, "Freightliner, Union Set Talks," *Gaston Gazette*, December 10, 1991.

56. C. Glickman, "Strikers, Freightliner to Meet," *Charlotte Observer*, December 10, 1991.

57. L. Hohmann, "Strike Talks Fizzle," *Gaston Gazette*, December 14, 1991.

58. L. Hohmann, "Freightliner: Truck Production Up," *Gaston Gazette*, December 17, 1991.

59. L. Hohmann, "It's a Deal," *Gaston Gazette*, December 20, 1991.

60. C. Wilson, "Freightliner, Strikers Have a Tentative Pact," *Charlotte Observer*, December 20, 1991.

61. C. Wilson, "It Was Something to Fight for," *Charlotte Observer*, January 2, 1992.

62. Hohmann, "Workers Accept Pay Terms"; "Freightliner, UAW End Dispute," *Monthly Labor Review*, March 1992, 40.

63. Wilson, "Freightliner, Strikers Have a Tentative Pact."

64. "Freightliner Workers Returning to Jobs," *Greensboro News and Record*, December 20, 1991.

65. L. Hohmann, "Workers Accept Terms," *Gaston Gazette*, December 21, 1991.

66. For example, W. Harbin, "Job Security on the Line," *Gaston Gazette*, June 13, 1993; T. C. Shoats, "Union Members Build Quality Trucks for Freightliner," *Gaston Gazette*, June 29, 1993.

67. "Freightliner Executive to Take over as President," *Gaston Gazette*, March 10, 1992.

68. M. S. Leyfeld, "Freightliner Led 1992 Truck Sales," *Charlotte Observer*, January 16, 1993.

69. L. Hohmann, "Freightliner Tries to Eliminate Risk in Buying Trucks," *Gaston Gazette*, July 9, 1992.

70. L. Hohmann, "On a Roll," *Gaston Gazette*, September 29, 1992.

71. S. Leer, "Freightliner Moves to Buy Division," *Gaston Gazette*, March 2, 1995; P. Krouse, "Bus Maker Sold to Daimler," *Greensboro News and Record*, October 6, 1998.

72. DaimlerChrysler. *Annual Report* (2000), https://www.daimler.com/documents/investors/berichte/geschaeftsberichte/daimlerchrysler/daimler-ir-annualreport-2000.pdf, 19–21; Good Jobs First, "Subsidy Tracker Parent Company Summary: Daimler," 2001, http://subsidytracker.goodjobsfirst.org/parent/daimler.

73. B. Jensen, "Workers Favor Strike," *Charlotte Observer*, December 12, 1994.

74. F. Protzman, "German Labor Leader in Insider Stock Scandal," *New York Times*, May 21, 1993; "Mit Blaulicht," *Spiegel*, May 30, 1993.

75. "Angst vor der Explosion," *Spiegel*, November 21, 1993.

76. "UAW Ready to Strike Freightliner," *Wilson Daily Times*, December 16, 1994.

77. Inter-Office Communication, John Collings to Dick Shoemaker, February 16, 1995, Stephen Yokich Accession, UAWC.

78. B. Jensen, "Workers Won't Strike," *Charlotte Observer*, December 19, 1994.

79. J. Lowell, "State of the Union," *Wards Auto*, June 1, 1995.

80. M. E. Zielinski, "Freightliner Families Worried, Not Surprised, at Layoffs," *Charlotte Observer*, September 20, 1996.

81. P. L. Moore and D. Boraks, "Freightliner Confirms Plant in Cleveland," *Charlotte Observer*, May 9, 1996.

82. A. Y. Williams, "Freightliner Hiring 120 at Parts Plant," *Charlotte Observer*, September 11, 1997.

83. "Heavy Trucks to Get New Name," *Greensboro News and Record*, November 30, 1997.

84. A. Y. Williams, "UAW at Truck Plant OKs 3-Year Contract," *Charlotte Observer*, December 22, 1997.

85. E. L. Andrews and L. M. Holson, "Daimler-Benz Will Acquire Chrysler in $36 Billion Deal That Will Reshape Industry," *New York Times*, May 8, 1998.

86. Stephen J. Silvia, *Holding the Shop Together: German Industrial Relations in the Postwar Era* (Ithaca, NY: Cornell University Press, 2013), 53.

87. James A. Piazza, *Going Global: Unions and Globalization in the United States, Sweden, and Germany* (Lanham, MD: Lexington Books, 2002), 127.

88. K. Jackson, "UAW Concedes Defeat at Transplants—for Now," *Automotive News*, April 27, 1998.

89. S. M. Hopkins and A. Y. Williams, "Freightliner to Hire 1,095 in the Carolinas," *Charlotte Observer*, March 12, 1998.

90. J. Schlosser, "Thomas Built Joins List of Triad Takeovers,' *Greensboro News and Record*, October 6, 1998.

91. S. E. White, "Trucking Firm Shares the Wealth," *Charlotte Observer*, April 4, 1999.

92. J. Muller and A. Bernstein, "Hey, Thanks for the Bargaining Chip," *Business Week*, May 17, 1999.

93. J. Ball, "UAW, Daimler Discuss Organizing Two Plants," *Wall Street Journal*, May 27, 1999.

94. Interview, Bob King, Ann Arbor, MI, January 8, 2020.

95. Muller and Bernstein, "Hey, Thanks for the Bargaining Chip."

96. Report on UAW/DaimlerChrysler Council, Las Vegas, NV, February 17–19, 2000, Stephen Yokich Accession, UAWC.

97. S. Soendker, "Interview. Freightliner CEO James Hebe," *Land Line*, November 2000; "DaimlerChrysler to Lay Off 3,745 at Truck Unit," *New York Times*, August 15, 2000.

98. S. E. White, "Truck Workers Prep for Layoffs," *Charlotte Observer*, October 20, 2000; S. E. White and T. Reed, "Freightliner, Union to Talk Till Midnight," *Charlotte Observer*, December 15, 2000.

99. United Nations, "United Nations Global Compact," https://www.unglobalcom pact.org/.

100. S. E. White, "Union Rallies Supporters," *Charlotte Observer*, September 26, 2000; I. Spencer, "Freightliner Talks May Portend Future of N.C. Labor," *Charlotte Observer*, October 15, 2000.

101. S. E. White, "Lockout at Truck Plant Possible," *Charlotte Observer*, November 4, 2000.

102. E. L. Andrews, "Daimler Will Soon Replace President of a Struggling Chrysler," *New York Times*, November 15, 2000.

103. "Truck Maker Threatens to Move Plant to Mexico," *Wilson Daily Times*, December 11, 2000.

104. S. E. White, "Meeting Fires Up Freightliner Workers," *Charlotte Observer*, December 12, 2000.

105. S. E. White, "Freightliner, Workers Agree on New Contract," *Charlotte Observer*, December 18, 2000.

106. T. J. Monigan, "UAW Ratifies Deal with Freightliner," *Gaston Gazette*, December 18, 2000.

107. K. Bradsher, "DaimlerChrysler Weighs Steps to End Losses," *New York Times*, February 24, 2001.

108. D. Lang, "Freightliner's Hebe Has Plan for Truck Industry," *Transport Topics*, March 22, 2001.

109. J. B. White, "James Hebe Steps Down as Head of DaimlerChrysler Truck," *Wall Street Journal*, May 25, 2001.

110. T. J. Monigan, "Freightliner Laying Off 475," *Gaston Gazette*, June 28, 2001; T. J. Monigan, "Freightliner to Lay Off 123 at Gastonia Plant," *Gaston Gazette*, August 9, 2001.

111. "Freightliner to Keep Portland Headquarters but Shut Parts Plants," *Portland Business Journal*, October 12, 2001; G. Keenan, "Truck Maker to Close Assembly Plant," *Toronto Globe and Mail*, October 12, 2001.

112. "Freightliner Says Portland Plant Will Close If Concessions Not Met," Northwest Labor Press, October 5, 2001, https://nwlaborpress.org/2001/10-5-01Freightliner.html.

113. "Freightliner Wins Wage Cuts before Announcing Closure," Northwest Labor Press, October 19, 2001, https://nwlaborpress.org/2001/10-19-01Freightliner.html.

114. T. J. Monigan, "Freightliner Workers Anticipate Union Vote," *Gaston Gazette*, March 15, 2002; T. J. Monigan, "Challenges Put Hold on Freightliner Union Vote," *Gaston Gazette*, March 21, 2002; T. J. Monigan, "UAW Raises 300 Objections on Freightliner Union Vote," *Gaston Gazette*, March 28, 2002; "Once Doors Were Slammed in Their Faces: Now Freightliner Workers Have the Power of Their Own Union," *UAW Region 8 Review*, Spring 2003.

115. P. Nowell, "UAW Accuses Freightliner Executives," *Plainview Daily Herald*, March 19, 2002.

116. T. J. Monigan, "Freightliner Union Vote Gets Sept. 23 Hearing," *Shelby Star*, July 26, 2002.

117. Interview, Bob King, Washington, DC, February 9, 2019.

118. J. Muller, "Can the UAW Stay in the Game?," *Business Week*, June 10, 2002.

119. Correspondence from Stephen Yokich to Hilmar Köpper, no date; letter, correspondence from Stephen Yokich to Klaus Zwickel, May 15, 2002; Stephen Yokich Accession, UAWC.

120. Torsten Niechoj, "DaimlerChrysler Establishes World Employee Committee," Eurofound, Dublin, September 27, 2002, https://www.eurofound.europa.eu/publications/article/2002/daimlerchrysler-establishes-world-employee-committee.

121. DaimlerChrysler and World Employee Committee, "Social Responsibility Principles of Daimler Chrysler," Auburn Hills, Michigan, September 2002, https://www.industriall-union.org/sites/default/files/uploads/documents/GFAs/Daimler/daimler-gfa-english.pdf.

122. Dorothee Benz, "Organizing to Survive, Bargaining to Organize: Unions Start Using More of Their Potential Power," *Journal of Labor and Society* 6, no. 1 (July 2002): 97.

123. S. E. White, "Union Struggle Won't Go to Court," *Charlotte Observer*, January 8, 2003; "In It for the Long Haul."

124. National Right to Work Legal Defense Foundation, "Employees Considering Appeal of Cryptic Ruling Dismissing Federal Racketeering Suit against Freightliner and UAW Union," November 10, 2006, https://www.nrtw.org/news/employees-considering-appeal-of-cryptic-ruling-dismissing-federal-racketeering-suit-against-freightliner-and-uaw-union/.

125. Freightliner LLC and United Auto Workers, "Tentative Agreement by and between Freightliner LLC and UAW for the Purpose of Establishing a Card Check Procedure," final signature on December 16, 2002, https://www.nrtw.org/neutrality/freightliner/Freightliner_Tentative_CA.pdf.

126. Freightliner LLC and United Auto Workers, "Agreement on Preconditions to a Card Check Procedure between Freightliner LLC and the UAW," final signature on December 16, 2002, https://www.nrtw.org/20050228freightliner.pdf.

127. Correspondence from Scott W. Evitt to David McAllister, August 20, 2002, https://www.nrtw.org/20050215freightliner.pdf.

128. S. E. White, "Union Gathers Support," *Charlotte Observer*, January 24, 2003; S. E. White, "Freightliner Affirms Workers Chose Union," *Charlotte Observer*, January 30, 2003.

129. Ron Gettelfinger, Draft Remarks, UAW-DaimlerChrysler joint conference, Detroit, March 10, 2003; Ron Gettelfinger Accession, UAWC.

130. "Gaston Source," *Charlotte Observer*, May 11, 2003.

131. S. E. White, "M2 Truck Assembly Line Rolls South," *Charlotte Observer*, April 9, 2003; S. E. White, "Freightliner, Union Agree to 3-Year Deal," *Charlotte Observer*, June 21, 2003; Freightliner LLC and United Auto Workers, "Freightliner Corporation and International Union, United Automobile and Agricultural Implement Workers of America (UAW) Local 5285," 2003, https://ecommons.cornell.edu/bitstream/handle/1813/81150 /4205Abbyy.pdf?sequence=1&isAllowed=y.

132. S. E. White, "Freightliner Workers Approve Contracts," *Charlotte Observer*, December 22, 2003; Freightliner LLC and United Auto Workers, "Freightliner Corporation and International Union, United Automobile and Agricultural Implement Workers of America (UAW) Local 3520," 2003, https://ecommons.cornell.edu/bitstream/handle/1813 /81151/4215Abbyy.pdf?sequence=1&isAllowed=y.

133. D. Becker, "Union Effort to Begin at Plant," *Greensboro News and Record*, February 12, 2003; D. Becker, "Unionizers Complain of Interference," *Greensboro News and Record*, March 5, 2003; D. Becker, "Union Advocates Rally Thomas Built Workers," *Greensboro News and Record*, March 15, 2003.

134. "Business Briefs," *Greensboro News and Record*, February 24, 2004; D. Becker, "Plant Begins Vote on UAW," *Greensboro News and Record*, March 3, 2004; D. Becker, "Thomas Built Workers Unionize," *Greensboro News and Record*, March 19, 2004.

135. E. Swenson, "Thomas Built Workers Complete Vote on Unionizing," *Greensboro News and Record*, March 18, 2004.

136. Becker, "Thomas Built Workers Unionize."

137. E. Swenson and J. C. Hayes, "Worker Contesting Unionizing Process," *Greensboro News and Record*, April 14, 2004.

138. E. Gersten, "DC Unit Suspends Talks with UAW at Bus Plant," *Detroit News*, July 1, 2004.

139. S. Schultz, "Freightliner Proposes Settlement of Union Issue," *Greensboro News and Record*, March 3, 2005; S. Schultz, "Anti-Union Group Drops Objection," *Greensboro News and Record*, March 10, 2005; S. Schultz, "Union Election Dispute Settled," *Greensboro News and Record*, March 21, 2005.

140. "Anti-Union Group Drops Objection, Clearing Way for Vote at Thomas Built," *Greensboro News and Record*, March 10, 2005.

141. J. Vandiver, "Thomas Built Vote Approves Union," *Greensboro News and Record*, June 29, 2005.

142. "Thomas Built Bus Workers Vote for UAW," *UAW Region 8 News*, June 30, 2005.

143. J. Vandiver, "Thomas Built Vote Heartens Unions," *Greensboro News and Record*, June 30, 2005.

144. J. Vandiver, "Workers Challenge Unionization Vote," *Greensboro News and Record*, July 6, 2005; S. Schultz, "Board Tosses Out Challenge to Thomas Built Union," *Greensboro News and Record*, July 11, 2005; J. Vandiver, "Union Election Appealed against Thomas Built," *Greensboro News and Record*, July 20, 2005.

145. "UAW Members Reach Tentative Agreement with Thomas Built Bus," *UAW News*, October 8, 2005.

146. "UAW Members Ratify First Contract at Thomas Built Bus," *UAW Region 8 News*, Spring/Summer 2006.

147. Interview, Gary Casteel, Cambridge, MA, September 7, 2018.

148. T. J. Monigan, "Freightliner Cuts 2,700 Jobs," *Gaston Gazette*, October 13, 2001.

149. C. Winston, "2 Sue Freightliner to Fight Union," GoUpstate, August 12, 2003, https://www.goupstate.com/story/news/2003/08/12/2-sue-freightliner-to-fight-union /29679185007/.

150. National Labor Relations Board, "Charge against Labor Organization: International Union, United Automobile & Agricultural Implement Workers Union of American [UAW], AFL-CIO," August 11, 2003.

151. C. Winston, "2 Sue Freightliner to Fight Union." GoUpstate.com, August 12, 2003, https://www.goupstate.com/story/news/2003/08/12/2-sue-freightliner-to-fight-union /29679185007/.

152. L. Hilliard, "Settlement Reached over Freightliner Pay Raises," *Gaffney Ledger*, August 15, 2005.

2. MERCEDES-BENZ U.S. INTERNATIONAL

1. The company in these cases has had three names during the years under investigation. From 1926 to 1998, its name was Daimler-Benz. From May 1998 to May 2007, it was DaimlerChrysler. Thereafter, it became Daimler AG, or just Daimler for short. In this chapter, I use the name consistent with the time under discussion. If a discussion covers a period that extends beyond more than one name of the company, I use the name of the company when the period ends. Despite the name changes, it is important to recognize that there is legal and management continuity throughout.

2. Email from Gary Casteel, May 18, 2017.

3. Henning Oeltjenbruns, Martin Lawaczeck, and Uwe Bracht, "How to Assure Quality Work in Automotive Greenfield Projects—Project Experiences from the New Assembly Plant of Mercedes-Benz, Tuscaloosa, Alabama," unpublished manuscript, Lubbock, TX, June 23, 1999.

4. K. Wozniak, "Mercedes-Benz Sales Data & Trends for the U.S. Automotive Market," Carsalesbase, n.d., http://carsalesbase.com/us-car-sales-data/mercedes-benz/.

5. D. Woodruff and J. Templeman, "Why Mercedes Is Alabama Bound," *Business Week*, October 11, 1993.

6. "Key Dates in Mercedes-Benz Site Selection," *Greensboro News and Record*, September 29, 1993.

7. R. Brooks, "Big Incentives Won Alabama a Piece of the Auto Industry," *Wall Street Journal*, April 3, 2002.

8. Pronita Gupta, "The Art of the Deal," *Southern Exposure* 26, nos. 2 and 3 (Summer/Fall 1998), 30–31.

9. A. R. Myerson, "Alabama Paying Dearly to Have Mercedes Plant," *Greensboro News and Record*, September 7, 1996; D. W. Nauss, "Mercedes to Build Plant in Alabama," *Los Angeles Times*, September 30, 1993; E. S. Browning and H. Cooper, "States' Bidding War over Mercedes Plant Made for Costly Chase," *Wall Street Journal*, November 24, 1993.

10. Inter-Office Communication from Don Stillman to Owen Bieber, April 14, 1993; draft letter, Owen Bieber to Werner Niefer, April 15, 1993, Stephen Yokich Accession, United Auto Workers Collections, Walter P. Reuther Library Archives, Wayne State University, Detroit, Michigan (hereafter UAWC).

11. Correspondence from Bob Lent, Bob King, Ruben Burks, and Jack Laskowski to Herbert Gzik, May 4, 1993, Stephen Yokich Accession, UAWC.

12. "Key Dates in Mercedes-Benz Site Selection."

13. Correspondence from Owen Bieber et al. to Helmut Werner, September 27, 1993, Owen Bieber Accession 1270, Series I, box 5.62, UAWC.

14. Nauss, "Mercedes to Build Plant in Alabama."

15. The origin of the Allied Industrial Workers of America dates back to the split in the US labor movement in the 1930s. The leadership of the American Federation of Labor trade union confederation created a rival union to the UAW in 1935 when the UAW joined the competing confederation that eventually became the Congress of Industrial Organizations. Confusingly, the rival also used the name "United Auto Workers." The UAW-AFL was an irritant but never a serious challenge to the UAW-CIO. When the American Federation of Labor and the Congress of Industrial Organizations merged in 1955, the leadership of the UAW-AFL changed the organization's name to the Allied Industrial Workers of America. Given this history, UAW leaders remained wary of the Allied Industrial Workers of America even into the 1990s. The Allied Industrial Workers of America merged with the United Paperworkers International Union in 1994. John Barnard, *American Vanguard: The United Auto Workers during the Reuther Years, 1935–1970* (Detroit: Wayne State University Press, 2004).

16. Inter-Office Communication, Stan Marshall to Owen Bieber, September 30, 1993, Owen Bieber Accession 1270, Series I, box 5.62, UAWC.

17. Correspondence from Andreas Renschler to Owen Bieber, November 2, 1993, Owen Bieber Accession 1270, Series I, box 5.62, UAWC.

18. Correspondence from Franz Steinkühler to Owen Bieber, May 17, 1991, Owen Bieber Accession 1270, Series II, box 26.58, UAWC.

19. "Labor Group Blasts BMW over Union," GoUpstate.com, July 29, 1992, https://www.goupstate.com/story/news/1992/07/29/labor-group-blasts-bmw-over-union/29547916007/.

20. "BMW Details Plants," *Aiken Standard*, July 23, 1992.

21. UAW Translation of an IG Metall press release from July 28, 1992, Owen Bieber Accession 1270, Series I, box 1.23, UAWC.

22. For example, correspondence from Don Stillman to Dick Shoemaker, February 15, 1994, Stephen P. Yokich Accession, UAWC.

23. Correspondence from Klaus Zwickel to Owen Bieber, June 9, 1994, Owen Bieber Accession 1270, Series II, box 31.36, UAWC.

24. Correspondence from Klaus Zwickel to Owen Bieber, June 9, 1994, Owen Bieber Accession 1270, Series II, box 31.36, UAWC.

25. Correspondence from Klaus Zwickel to Owen Bieber, June 9, 1994, Owen Bieber Accession 1270, Series II, box 31.36, UAWC, incorporating UAW executive administrative assistant to the president Dick Shoemaker's handwritten edits.

26. Memorandum from Owen Bieber to Stan Marshall and Dick Shoemaker, June 9, 1994, Owen Bieber Accession 1270, Series II, box 31.36, UAWC.

27. Correspondence from Owen Bieber to Bobby Lee Thompson, August 4, 1994, Owen Bieber Accession 1270, Series I, box 5.62, UAWC.

28. Nauss, "Mercedes to Build Plant in Alabama."

29. Memorandum from Bobby Lee Thompson to Ted Letson, August 11, 1994, Owen Bieber Accession 1270, Series I, box 5.62, UAWC.

30. Brooks, "Big Incentives Won Alabama a Piece of the Auto Industry."

31. Inter-Office Communication from Ben Perkins to Stan Marshall, December 9, 1994, Stephen P. Yokich Accession, UAWC.

32. Inter-Office Communication from Ben Perkins to Owen Bieber, May 9, 1995; Inter-Office Communication, Larry Stevens to Don Stillman, May 22, 1995, Stephen P. Yokich Accession, UAWC.

33. Inter-Office Communication from Dave Smith to Bobby Lee Thompson, March 1, 1995, Ron Gettelfinger Accession, UAWC.

34. T. Pratt, "Merger Gives UAW Inroad to Vance Plant," *Birmingham News*, May 8, 1998.

35. Inter-Office Communication from Bob King to Steve Yokich, August 11, 1995; memorandum, Richard Bensinger to Organizing Institute Task Force, June 29, 1995, Stephen P. Yokich Accession, UAWC.

36. L. Aguilar, "Passion, Pragmatism Drive UAW's King," *Detroit News*, June 11, 2010; D. Durbin, "United Auto Workers Elect Bob King as President," Associated Press, June 16, 2010; N. Bunkley, "Next Chief Is Nominated for a Troubled Auto Union," *New York Times*, December 16, 2009; N. Bunkley, "New Autoworkers Leader Hopes to Revitalize Union," *New York Times*, June 17, 2010.

37. United Auto Workers, *Media Fact Book 2007* (Detroit: UAW, 2007), 58.

38. D. Linquist, "UAW Convention Official Sees a Pivotal Year Ahead for Union," *San Diego Union-Tribune*, June 5, 1986.

39. M. Massing, "Detroit's Strange Bedfellows," *New York Times*, February 7, 1988.

40. J. Lippert, "The UAW Campaign: Top Job Is a Given," *Detroit Free Press*, September 15, 1994.

41. "UAW Creates New Post," *Newsday*, November 14, 1997.

42. J. McCracken, "UAW Wins Major Pact," *Detroit Free Press*, August 14, 2003; B. Wieland, "Neutrality Pacts Hit Nerve for Workers," *Lansing State Journal*, May 16, 2004; C. Woodyard, "UAW Sees Growth Past Blue Collar," *USA Today*, June 16, 2006.

43. K. Jackson, "UAW Concedes Defeat at Transplants—For Now," *Automotive News*, April 27, 1998.

44. E. L. Andrews and L. M. Holson, "Daimler-Benz Will Acquire Chrysler in $36 Billion Deal That Will Reshape Industry," *New York Times*, May 8, 1998.

45. J. McElroy, "Disappointment and Disillusionment at DCX," *AutoWorld*, January 2001.

46. Michael D. Watkins, "Why DaimlerChrysler Never Got into Gear," *Harvard Business Review*, May 18, 2007.

47. Stephen J. Silvia, *Holding the Shop Together: German Industrial Relations in the Postwar Era* (Ithaca, NY: Cornell University Press, 2013), chap. 2.

48. Kim Moody, *An Injury to All: The Decline of American Unionism* (London: Verso, 1988), 153–54.

49. F. Swoboda, "Chrysler Deal Ties 2 Unions," *Washington Post*, May 8, 1998.

50. M. Woodhead, "Daimler's Cultures Collide," *Sunday Times*, September 20, 1998.

51. Bill Vlasic and Bradley A. Stertz, *Taken for a Ride: How Daimler-Benz Drove Off with Chrysler* (New York: Wiley, 2000), 241.

52. T. Schulten, "Industrial Relations Aspects of the Daimler-Chrysler Merger," Eurofound, May 27, 1998, https://www.eurofound.europa.eu/mt/publications/article/1998/industrial-relations-aspects-of-the-daimler-chrysler-merger.

53. James A. Piazza, *Going Global: Unions and Globalization in the United States, Sweden, and Germany* (Lanham, MD: Lexington Books, 2002), 127.

54. Swoboda "Chrysler Deal Ties 2 Unions."

55. Pratt, "Merger Gives UAW Inroad to Vance Plant."

56. J. Muller and A. Bernstein, "Hey, Thanks for the Bargaining Chip," *Business Week*, May 17, 1999; R. Meredith, "A Union March on Alabama," *New York Times*, June 29, 1999.

57. T. Pratt, "ZF, Pressac Reject Union," *Birmingham News*, January 15, 1999; A. Bernstein, J. Muller, and K. Naughton, "The UAW's Next Battleground," *Business Week*, July 26, 1999.

58. "NLRB Backs UAW in Claim That Supplier Tried to Thwart Drive," *Wall Street Journal*, February 17, 2000.

59. J. Park, "UAW Targets Vance," *Birmingham Business Journal*, May 23, 1999; J. Lippert, "UAW's Yokich Criticizes Vance," *Birmingham News*, April 28, 1999; Bernstein et al., "The UAW's Next Battleground."

60. Muller and Bernstein, "Hey, Thanks for the Bargaining Chip."

61. J. Ball and F. Warner, "UAW to Seek Car Firms' Tacit Accord in Bid to Organize Supplier Factories," *Wall Street Journal*, May 13, 1999.

62. Ball and Warner, "UAW to Seek Car Firms' Tacit Accord."

63. T. Pratt, "Doing It the Honda Way," *Birmingham News*, May 28, 1999.

64. Meredith, "A Union March on Alabama."

65. Meredith, "A Union March on Alabama."

66. T. Pratt, "Will Vance Unionize?," *Birmingham News*, July 30, 1999; J. Underwood, "EDPA Move on Organizing is Surprising," *Birmingham News*, September 5, 1999.

67. T. Pratt, "Will Vance Unionize?"

68. Bernstein et al., "The UAW's Next Battleground."

69. T. Pratt, "Will Vance Unionize?"

70. J. Lippert, "Daimler Looks Like UAW Target," *Birmingham News*, August 20, 1999; S. Franklin, "Union, Daimler Plow Forward," *Chicago Tribune*, September 15, 1999.

71. Lehr Middlebrooks Price & Proctor, "To Our Clients and Friends," *Employment Law Bulletin* 7, no. 8 (September 1999), 1.

72. J. Underwood and M. Tomberlin, "Consultant Hired to Fight UAW Drive at Mercedes," *Birmingham News*, September 2, 1999.

73. J. Underwood, "EDPA Move on Organizing Is Surprising," *Birmingham News*, September 5, 1999.

74. T. Pratt, "Union-Buster Still in Vance," *Birmingham News*, September 13, 1999.

75. B. Corbett, "UAW Looks for Membership AdVANCEment," *Wards Auto World*, July 1999.

76. "For Now, New Labor Agreement Won't Affect Mercedes Workers," *Birmingham News*, September 17, 1999; interview, Bob King, Ann Arbor, MI, January 8, 2020.

77. T. Pratt, "Vance Workers Ask Off UAW List," *Birmingham News*, October 15, 1999.

78. J. Ball, "Alabama Mercedes Plant Workers Have Sour Greeting for Organizers," *Wall Street Journal*, January 31, 2000.

79. Ball, "Alabama Mercedes Plant Workers Have Sour Greeting."

80. Ball, "Alabama Mercedes Plant Workers Have Sour Greeting"; T. Pratt, "UAW Revs Up Vance Activity," *Birmingham News*, November 4, 1999.

81. D. Waid, "Letters, Faxes and E-Mail," *Birmingham News*, November 16, 1999.

82. Ball, "Alabama Mercedes Plant Workers Have Sour Greeting."

83. "NLRB Backs UAW in Claim That Supplier Tried to Thwart Drive," *Wall Street Journal*, February 17, 2000.

84. T. Pratt, "Union Backs Off at Vance," *Birmingham News*, February 18, 2000.

85. R. Meredith, "Eaton to Retire from DaimlerChrysler," *New York Times*, January 27, 2000.

86. Report on UAW/DaimlerChrysler Council, Las Vegas, NV, February 17–19, 2000, Stephen Yokich Accession, UAWC.

87. Transmittal Slip from Gerald Lararowitz to Stephen P. Yokich, March 31, 2000, Stephen Yokich Accession, UAWC.

88. T. Pratt, "UAW Chief Heading to Vance," *Birmingham News*, March 26, 2000.

89. J. Gallagher, "'Good and Honorable Man' Felled by Stroke," *Detroit Free Press*, August 17, 2002.

90. A global union federation is an international organization to which national unions in an individual sector belong. The name for global union federations in the twentieth century was international trade secretariats.

91. President's Office Transmittal Slip from Stephen P. Yokich to Nate Gooden, March 15 and 20, 2000; from Yokich to Officers, March 15, 2000; from Yokich to Don Stillman, March 27, 2000; from Yokich to Regina Gabriel, March 23, 2000, Stephen Yokich Accession, UAWC.

92. K. Bradsher, "DaimlerChrysler to Expand Production in Alabama," *New York Times*, August 28, 2000.

93. M. Tomberlin, "Don't Import Union Workers for Mercedes Jobs, Riley Says," *Birmingham News*, September 19, 2003.

94. Correspondence from Eric Klemm to members of the Labor Committee, November 10, 2000; correspondence from Hartmut Schick to Stephen Yokich, November 17, 2000, Stephen Yokich Accession, UAWC.

95. McElroy, "Disappointment and Disillusionment at DCX."

96. D. Howes, "How Chrysler Lost American Leaders," *Detroit News*, November 15, 2000.

97. President's Office Transmittal Slip, December 5, 2000, Stephen Yokich Accession, UAWC.

98. T. Pratt, "UAW May Yet Gain Foothold," *Birmingham News*, November 29, 2000.

99. Fax from John Franciosi to Stephen Yokich, January 2, 2001, Stephen Yokich Accession, UAWC.

100. B. Cusak, "USA: Chrysler Contracts Will Be Fully Enforced—UAW," *Just Auto*, January 30, 2001, https://www.just-auto.com/news/usa-chrysler-contracts-will-be-fully-enforced-uaw/.

101. J. Muller, "Can the UAW Stay in the Game?," *Business Week*, June 10, 2002.

102. L. Chappell, "The UAW Knocks, but Few Workers Answer," *Automotive News*, April 8, 2002.

103. "Yokich: Chrysler Safe from Sale," *Ward's Auto World*, May 2001.

104. J. Gallagher, "'Good and Honorable Man' Felled By Stroke," *Detroit News*, August 17, 2002.

105. Muller, "Can the UAW Stay in the Game?"

106. Correspondence from Stephen Yokich to Hilmar Köpper, no date; letter, Stephen Yokich to Klaus Zwickel, May 15, 2002; Stephen Yokich Accession, UAWC.

107. Torsten Niechoj, "DaimlerChrysler Establishes World Employee Committee," Eurofound, September 27, 2002, https://www.eurofound.europa.eu/publications/article/2002/daimlerchrysler-establishes-world-employee-committee.

108. United Nations, "United Nations Global Compact," https://www.unglobalcompact.org/.

109. DaimlerChrysler and World Employee Committee, "Social Responsibility Principles of Daimler Chrysler," IndustriALL, September 2002, https://www.industriall-union.org/sites/default/files/uploads/documents/GFAs/Daimler/daimler-gfa-english.pdf.

110. Pronita Gupta, "The Art of the Deal."

111. J. Underwood, "Union Keeps Pushing for Mercedes," *Birmingham News*, August 31, 2003.

112. J. Underwood, "UAW Hopes for Prize in Alabama," *Birmingham News*, July 20, 2003.

113. J. Underwood, "UAW Sees Likelihood of Flag in Vance," *Birmingham News*, September 21, 2003.

114. M. Tomberlin, "Don't Import Union Workers for Mercedes Jobs, Riley Says," *Birmingham News*, September 19, 2003.

115. Tomberlin, "Don't Import Union Workers for Mercedes Jobs"; J. Underwood, "UAW Sees Likelihood of Flag in Vance," *Birmingham News*, September 21, 2003.

116. M. Landler, "Shake-Up at DaimlerChrysler," *New York Times*, July 29, 2005.

117. M. Tomberlin, "2006 CEO of the Year," *Birmingham News*, April 2, 2006.

118. David Welch, "Twilight of the UAW," *Business Week*, April 10, 2006.

119. Ian Greer and Marco Hauptmeier, "Political Entrepreneurs and Co-Managers: Labour Transnationalism at Four Multinational Auto Companies," *British Journal of Industrial Relations* 46, no. 1 (March 2008): 82.

120. Bernd Kupilas, "Countdown in Alabama," *Mitbestimmung*, November 2011.

121. Ron Gettelfinger, notes, February 13, 2006, Ron Gettelfinger Accession, UAWC.

122. IG Metall and UAW, "Joint Statement," February 13, 2006, Ron Gettelfinger Accession, UAWC.

123. "US-Autogewerkschaft entsendet ihren Chef in Daimler-Aufsichtsrat," *Handelsblatt*, July 3, 2016; "IG-Metall-Freund im Aufsichtsrat," *Manager Magazin*, June 19, 2006.

124. B. Clanton and B. Hoffman, "UAW Appoints New Guard," *Detroit News*, June 16, 2006.

125. "Alabama Auto Union Drive," *Washington Times*, March 26, 2006.

126. "M. Tomberlin, "New Attempt Is Being Made to Unionize Vance Factory," *Birmingham News*, March 31, 2006.

127. "Organizing Drive Gears Up at Alabama Mercedes Plant," International Association of Machinists, Press release, March 16, 2006.

128. "Effort to Unionize Mercedes Renewed," *Tuscaloosa News*, April 1, 2006.

129. R. L. Williams, "Machinist Union Eyes Vance Mercedes Plant," *Birmingham News*, March 18, 2006.

130. "Machinists Organizing at Mercedes-Benz Alabama," International Association of Machinists, Press release, March 21, 2006.

131. L. Chappell, "Mercedes Union Bid Attacked on Two Fronts," *Automotive News*, April 17, 2006.

132. Tomberlin, "New Attempt Is Being Made to Unionize Vance Factory."

133. A. Bernstein, "The UAW's Southern Discomfort," *Business Week*, April 17, 2006.

134. International Association of Machinists, "Charge against Employer, Mercedes-Benz US International," May 25, 2006; "NLRB Issues Charge against Mercedes-Benz," International Association of Machinists, Press release, August 31, 2006.

135. R. L. Williams, "NLRB Rules Pro-Unionists Intimidated," *Birmingham News*, September 6, 2006.

136. M. Hawk, "Mercedes, Union Reach Settlement," *Tuscaloosa News*, November 8, 2006.

137. R. L. Williams, "Union May Renew Mercedes Push," *Birmingham News*, 9 August 2007; R. L. Williams, "Unions Again Eye Auto Plants," *Birmingham News*, September 1, 2007; R. L. Williams, "Union Begins Effort to Organize," *Birmingham News*, September 5, 2007; R. L. Williams, "Union Membership Grows," *Birmingham News*, January 31, 2008.

138. "Daimler May Face Tough Sell," *Tuscaloosa News*, March 15, 2007.

139. N. Roubini, "The Impact of Chrysler's Bankruptcy," *Forbes*, May 7, 2009.

140. Ron Gettelfinger, officers meeting notes, Dearborn, MI, January 16, 2008, Ron Gettelfinger Accession, UAWC.

141. Ron Gettelfinger, officers meeting notes, Detroit, June 24, 2008, Ron Gettelfinger Accession, UAWC.

142. Correspondence from Marcello Malentacchi to Ron Gettelfinger, September 30, 2008, Ron Gettelfinger Accession, UAWC.

143. J. Puzzanghera, "Senate GOP Took a Swipe at Unions," *Los Angeles Times*, December 13, 2008.

144. J. Bresnahan, "Shelby Threatens Filibuster over Auto Bailout Deal," Politico, December 7, 2008.

145. M. Maynard, "U.A.W. at Center of Dispute over Bailout," *New York Times*, December 19, 2008.

146. Letter, Berthold Huber to Ron Gettelfinger, April 4, 2008, Ron Gettelfinger Accession, UAWC.

147. Notes, Ron Gettelfinger, July 28, 2009, Ron Gettelfinger Accession, UAWC.

148. Ron Gettelfinger, notes, November 23, 2009, Frankfurt, Ron Gettelfinger Accession, UAWC.

149. Interview, Bob King, Ann Arbor, Michigan, January 8, 2020.

150. "Mercedes-Benz Considers Moving Model to Vance Plant, Sparking Protests in Germany," Advance Local, December 1, 2009, https://www.al.com/live/2009/12/mercedes-benz_considers_moving.html.

151. D. Durbin and T. Krisher, "UAW to Nominate King as Next President," Associated Press, December 11, 2009; L. Aguilar, "UAW Dissident Will Seek Union Presidency," *Detroit News*, June 10, 2010; B. Snavely, "UAW's Bob King Expected to Give Union Spark," *Detroit News*, June 17, 2010; N. Bunkley, "Next Chief Is Nominated for a Troubled Auto Union," *New York Times*, December 16, 2009.

152. N. Bunkley, "New Autoworkers Leader Hopes to Revitalize Union," *New York Times*, June 16, 2010.

153. J. Slaughter, "UAW Says It Will Go 'All In' to Organize Foreign-Owned Auto Plants," *Labor Notes*, February 2011; M. Dolan, "UAW Sets Strategy on Foreign Car Plants," *Wall Street Journal*, January 3, 2011.

154. Bob King, "A UAW for the 21st Century," UAW president Bob King's speech to the Center for Automotive Research Conference, Ann Arbor, Michigan, August 2, 2010.

155. Dolan, "UAW Sets Strategy on Foreign Car Plants."

156. UAW International Executive Board, "UAW Principles for Fair Union Elections," Detroit, January 3, 2011.

157. Dolan, "UAW Sets Strategy on Foreign Car Plants."

158. D. Moberg, "UAW Plans for Negotiations, Organizing, Rebuilding Power," *In These Times*, March 24, 2011.

159. Slaughter, "UAW Says It Will Go 'All In' to Organize Foreign-Owned Auto Plants."

160. Timothy J. Minchin, "Look at Detroit: The United Auto Workers and the Battle to Organize Volkswagen in Chattanooga." *Labor History* 60, no. 5 (2019): 483.

161. N. Bunkley, "U.A.W. to Renew Organizing Efforts at Foreign-Owned Plants," *New York Times*, January 13, 2011.

162. D. Howe, "UAW Outlines New Strategy for Foreign Auto Plants." *Detroit News*, January 4, 2011.

163. Dolan, "UAW Sets Strategy on Foreign Car Plants."

164. B. Woodall, B. Klayman, and J. Schwartz, "Special Report: The UAW's Last Stand," Reuters, December 29, 2011.

165. IG Metall, "UAW startet Kampagne bei deutschen Herstellern," February 3, 2011, https://www.igmetall.de/politik-und-gesellschaft/internationales/uaw-startet-kampagne-bei-deutschen-herstellern; "UAW to Target German Auto Plants," IHS Global Insight Daily Analysis, December 30, 2011.

166. H. Hagood, "Last Chance UAW," *Birmingham News*, March 6, 2011.

167. Woodall et al., "Special Report: The UAW's Last Stand."

168. Helmut Lense, "Der Süden bleibt gewerkschaftsfrei," *Brennpunkt*, November 2011.

169. DaimlerChrysler and World Employee Committee, "Principles of Social Responsibility at Daimler," Stuttgart, Germany, February 2012, http://www.industriall-union .org/sites/default/files/uploads/documents/GFAs/Daimler/principles_of_social _responsibility_at_daimler.pdf.

170. P. Rupinski, "Experts: Union Defeat in Chattanooga Could Further Spur Efforts in Tuscaloosa County," *Tuscaloosa News*, February 23, 2014.

171. Lense, "Der Süden bleibt gewerkschaftsfrei."

172. P. Rupinski, "Cottondale Faurecia Workers Vote to Join Union," *Tuscaloosa News*, June 20, 2012; P. Rupinski, "Workers at Cottondale Plant Vote to Unionize," *Tuscaloosa News*, November 16, 2012.

173. "Daimler: Unionizing Vance Will Be Hard Sell," *Tuscaloosa News*, May 3, 2013.

174. "Global Daimler Unions Support MBUSI Workers Organizing in Alabama!," June 2013, https://vimeo.com/70978049.

175. D. Kent Azok, "Bentley: Alabama's Mercedes-Benz Plant Doesn't Need a Union," Advance Local, June 30, 2013, https://www.al.com/business/2013/06/bentley_alabamas _mercedes-benz.html; M. Dolan, "Daimler's German Labor Squeeze," *Wall Street Journal*, May 2, 2013.

176. D. Kent Azok, "A Prime Time to Organize?," Advance Local, August 23, 2013, https://www.al.com/business/2013/07/a_prime_time_to_organize_a_loo.html.

177. For example, "Editorial: Is a Labor Union Really Needed at MBUSI?," *Tuscaloosa News*, April 21, 2013.

178. Azok, "Bentley: Alabama's Mercedes-Benz Plant Doesn't Need a Union"; Azok "A Prime Time to Organize?"; D. Kent Azok, "Division over Union," 28 July 2013, https:// www.al.com/business/2013/07/division_over_union_uaw_push_t.html.

179. D. Kent Azok, "German Labor Union Playing Key Role in UAW's Latest Campaign at Alabama's Mercedes Plant," Advance Local, August 23, 2013, https://www.al .com/business/2013/08/post_63.html; "Outside Agitators," *Financial Times*, October 29, 2013.

180. "Daimler: No Need for German-Style Works Council in U.S.," Reuters, September 10, 2013; N. Boudette, "German Worries Help Auto Union Effort in U.S. Globalization, Europe's Slump Brings Once Wary Unions Together," *Wall Street Journal*, November 7, 2013.

181. Azok, "German Labor Union Playing Key Role in UAW's Latest Campaign at Alabama's Mercedes Plant"; D. Kent Azok, "Anti-Union Billboards Put up Near Alabama's Mercedes-Benz Auto Plant," Advance Local, August 30, 2013, https://www.al.com /business/2013/08/anti-union_billboards_put_up_n.html.

182. "Outside Agitators."

183. P. Rupinski, "Pro-Union Workers at Mercedes-Benz Airs Complaints," *Tuscaloosa News*, April 7, 2014.

184. "FOX 6 News Reporting on NLRB Complaint against Mercedes for Interfering with Workers' Union Campaign," January 26, 2014, https://vimeo.com/85461219.

185. D. Kent Azok, "Mercedes Accused of Interfering with Union Campaign at Alabama Plant," Advance Local, October 10, 2013, https://www.al.com/business/2013/10 /mercedes_accused_of_interferin.html; D. Kent Azok, "Mercedes-Benz Employees Accuse Automaker of Harassment and Intimidation in Union Campaign at Alabama Plant," Advance Local, January 27, 2014, https://www.al.com/business/2014/01/mercedes _employees_accuse_auto.html; D. Kent Azok, "Harassment Accusations Fly at Carmaker," *Birmingham News*, January 31, 2014.

186. D. Kent Azok, "Can UAW Survive Losing Alabama?," *Birmingham News*, February 19, 2014.

187. P. Rupinski, "Shelby Says Health Care Law Is on Minds of Alabama Workers," *Tuscaloosa News*, February 21, 2014.

188. Rupinski, "Shelby Says Health Care Law Is on Minds of Alabama Workers."

189. D. Kent Azok, "Pro-Union Employees at Alabama's Mercedes-Benz Plant Ask United Auto Workers Union to Halt Campaign," Advance Local, May 30, 2014, https://www.al.com/business/2014/05/pro-union_employees_at_alabama.html; "Disunity Strikes Mercedes Campaign," *Birmingham News*, June 4, 2014; B. Woodall, "UAW to Unveil New Plan to Organize Mercedes-Benz Alabama Plant," Reuters, June 5, 2014.

190. Minchin, "Look at Detroit," 495.

191. United Auto Workers, "Department Reports," 36th Constitutional Convention, Detroit, Michigan, June 2–5, 2014, 97.

192. M. Ramsay, "UAW to Form Local at Mercedes-Benz Factory in Alabama," *Wall Street Journal*, July 10, 2014.

193. "Daimler World Works Council Elects New Leadership," IndustriALL press release, July 27, 2014.

194. K. Burke, "Mercedes-Benz Violated Alabama Workers' Organizing Rights, Judge Rules," *Automotive News*, July 29, 2014; UAW, "UAW, Workers Condemn Response from Mercedes in NLRB Ruling," News from the UAW, July 31, 2014.

195. "Mercedes Expands Work at Alabama Plant," *New York Times*, September 5, 2014.

196. D. Shepherdson, "Daimler Neutral on UAW Effort to Organize Plant," *Detroit News*, September 5, 2014.

197. IG Metall, "IG Metall fordert Mitbestimmung bei Mercedes in den USA," Pressemitteilung, no. 28/2014, October 4, 2014; IG Metall, "Interessenvetretung in Tuscaloosa," IG Metall @ Daimler, October 4, 2014.

198. UAW, "Mitarbeiter von Mercedes-Benz in Alabama gründen Gewerkschaft," News from the UAW, October 3, 2014.

199. "Gewerkschaftsbüro für Daimler-Beschäftigte in Tuscaloosa eröffnet," October 16, 2014, https://www.youtube.com/watch?v=aZyczkx9ZcI.

200. D. Kent Azok, "United Auto Workers Union Ramps Up Efforts to Organize Alabama's Mercedes-Benz Plant, Backed by German Labor Leaders," Advance Local, 5 October 2014, https://www.al.com/business/2014/10/united_auto_workers_and_german.html.

201. "Mercedes Workers Sign with UAW," *Birmingham News*, October 5, 2014.

202. P. Rupinski, "UAW to Represent Workers at Mercedes Plant in Vance," *Tuscaloosa News*, October 3, 2014; "UAW to Form Local to Represent Mercedes Workers," Reuters, October 3, 2014.

203. S. Dethrage, "Mercedes Employees, Union Leaders Announce New UAW Local at Alabama Plant," Advance Local, October 3, 2014, https://www.al.com/news/tuscaloosa/2014/10/employees_of_mercedes_benz_pla.html.

204. Azok, "United Auto Workers Union Ramps up Efforts."

205. B. Snavely, "UAW Forms Official Chapter in Tuscaloosa, Ala," *Detroit Free Press*, October 3, 2014.

206. J. Irwin, "Mercedes Workers Can Distribute Union Literature at Ala. Plant," *Automotive News*, October 4, 2016; J. Szczesny, "UAW Aims to Open Door to South at Mercedes in Alabama," Wards Auto, March 11, 2015; "Mercedes-Benz U.S. International, Inc. (MBUSI)," Case number 10-CA-112406, Date filed 09/03/2013, https://www.nlrb.gov/case/10-CA-112406.

207. Joel Cutcher-Gershenfeld, Dan Brooks, and Martin Mulloy, "The Decline and Resurgence of the U.S. Auto Industry," Economic Policy Institute, Briefing Paper #399, May 6, 2015.

208. United Auto Workers, *Special Convention on Collective Bargaining* (Detroit: UAW, March 24–25, 2015), 12–13.

209. IG Metall, "Interessenvetretung in Tuscaloosa," IG Metall @ Daimler, May 25, 2015.

210. N. Naughton, "Top UAW Official Will Not Seek Re-election," *Detroit News*, April 17, 2018.

211. UAW Local 112, "UAW Secretary-Treasurer Ray Curry and Chairman of General Works Council Michael Brecht visit Local 112 Plant," Local 112 News, September 12, 2018.

3. VOLKSWAGEN

1. Timothy J. Minchin, "Look at Detroit: The United Auto Workers and the Battle to Organize Volkswagen in Chattanooga," *Labor History* 60, no. 5 (2019): 482.

2. VW management later renamed the subsidiary Volkswagen Group of America.

3. A. J. Jacobs, *The New Domestic Automakers in the United States and Canada: History, Impacts, and Prospects* (Lanham, MD: Lexington Books, 2016), 51–52; Volkswagen AG, "Internationalisation and Mass Production in the Era of Germany's Economic Miracle," n.d., https://www.volkswagenag.com/en/group/history/chronicle/1950-1960.html.

4. "U.S. Rabbit All Set to Hop," *Time*, April 10, 1978.

5. J. O'Dell, "New VW 'Bug' Off to Fast Start," *Los Angeles Times*, February 26, 1998; "VW's New Drive," *Time*, August 6, 1979.

6. Stefan Rüb, "World Works Councils and Other Forms of Global Employee Representation in Transnational Undertakings," Arbeitspapier 55, Hans Böckler Stiftung, Düsseldorf, 2002.

7. P. Kemezis, "Germans Approve VW Output in US," *New York Times*, April 24, 1976.

8. T. Moran, "VW Production Tripped Up in U.S.," *Automotive News*, October 17, 2005.

9. Rabbit was the name Volkswagen used in North America for the model that the company called Golf in its other markets until the 1984 model year, when VW adopted the Golf name in North America too.

10. W. Wylie, "Westmoreland Rabbit on Parade," *Pittsburgh Press*, April 10, 1978; "U.S. Rabbit All Set to Hop."

11. Briam began his working life as a reporter for *Welt der Arbeit*, which was the newspaper of the German Trade Union Federation. "Zum Abschuss frei," *Spiegel*, April 10, 1978.

12. B. Klayman, "VW, UAW Look to Avoid Pennsylvania Missteps in Tennessee Plant," Reuters, October 21, 2013.

13. Moran, "VW Production Tripped Up in U.S."

14. T. Hundley, "Tough Lessons Taught in VW Plant's Closing," *Chicago Tribune*, July 14, 1988.

15. J. Holusha, "Volkswagen to Shut U.S. Plant," *New York Times*, November 21, 1987.

16. "VW's New Drive."

17. J. Moody, "The Whys of the Area VW Contract Walkout," *Pittsburgh Post-Gazette*, October 13, 1978.

18. Klayman, "VW, UAW Look to Avoid Pennsylvania Missteps in Tennessee Plant."

19. "No Money, No Bunny, Hunny," *Mother Jones*, January 1979; L. Wilson, "VW Laying Off 4,000 Due to W.Va. Strike," *Pittsburgh Post-Gazette*, January 4, 1980; "Discrimination Suit Is Settled," *New York Times*, April 19, 1989.

20. C. Bahn, "A Bad Rap against Volkswagen," letters to the editor, *Pittsburgh Post-Gazette*, April 30, 1988.

21. Correspondence from Donn J. Viola to Owen Bieber, November 22, 1985, Owen Bieber Accession 1270/Series II, box 21.74, United Auto Workers Collections, Walter P. Reuther Library Archives, Wayne State University, Detroit, Michigan (hereafter UAWC).

22. B. Hartford, "Driving the '79 VW Rabbit," *Popular Mechanics*, November 1978.

23. R. Gazarik, "VW: Flop in New Stanton, Boom in Tennessee," Triblive.com, July 16, 2013.

24. J. O'Toole, B. Paris, and M. Roth, "Recession, Race Issues Sour VW Dream," *Pittsburgh Post-Gazette*, January 14, 1983.

25. C. Alvarez, "1974–2003 Volkswagen Golf Review," *Top Gear*, October 25, 2006.

26. Owen Bieber, Report, IMF Executive Committee and Central Committee Meeting, Zürich, Switzerland, June 7–10, 1983, Owen Bieber Accession 1270/Series I, box 20.3, UAWC.

27. Klayman, "VW, UAW Look to Avoid Pennsylvania Missteps in Tennessee Plant."

28. Holusha, "Volkswagen to Shut U.S. Plant."

29. David Kiley, *Getting the Bugs Out: The Rise, Fall, and Comeback of Volkswagen in America* (New York: Wiley, 2002), 134.

30. Moran, "VW Production Tripped Up in U.S."

31. Owen Bieber, Report, IMF Executive Committee and Central Committee Meeting, Zürich, Switzerland, June 7–10, 1983, Owen Bieber Accession 1270/Series I, box 20.3, UAWC.

32. Hundley, "Tough Lessons Taught in VW Plant's Closing"; Holusha, "Volkswagen to Shut U.S. Plant."

33. Bahn, "A Bad Rap against Volkswagen."

34. Gazarik, "VW: Flop in New Stanton, Boom in Tennessee."

35. Holusha, "Volkswagen to Shut U.S. Plant."

36. Bahn, "A Bad Rap against Volkswagen."

37. Klayman, "VW, UAW Look to Avoid Pennsylvania Missteps in Tennessee Plant."

38. K. Wozniak, "Volkswagen Sales Data & Trends for the U.S. Automotive Market," Carsalesbase, n.d., https://carsalesbase.com/us-volkswagen/.

39. W. Boston, "VW Quiet on Efforts to Mend Rift," *Wall Street Journal*, April 16, 2015.

40. Mark C. Schneider, *Volkswagen: Eine deutsche Geschichte* (Berlin: Berlin Verlag, 2016).

41. T. Schulten, "Volkswagen Sets Up a World Group Council," Eurofound, June 27, 1998.

42. Volkswagen AG, Volkswagen Group Global Works Council and International Metalworkers' Federation, "Declaration on Social Rights and Industrial Relationships at Volkswagen," Bratislava, June 6, 2002, http://www.industriall-union.org/sites/default/files/uploads/documents/GFAs/Volkswagen/vweng.pdf.

43. United Nations, "United Nations Global Compact," https://www.unglobalcompact.org/.

44. Volkswagen Group Executive Management, Volkswagen European Group Works Council and Volkswagen Group Global Works Council, "Charter on Labour Relations within the Volkswagen Group," Zwickau, Germany, October 29, 2009, https://ec.europa.eu/employment_social/empl_portal/transnational_agreements/Volkswagen_LabourRelationsCharter_EN.pdf.

45. Volker Telljohann, "The Implementation of the Global Labor Relations Charter at Volkswagen," in *Transnational Company Agreements: A Stepping Stone toward a Real Internationalisation of Industrial Relations?*, edited by S. Leonardi (Rome: Ediesse, 2012), 107–8.

46. Stephen J. Silvia, *Holding the Shop Together: German Industrial Relations in the Postwar Era* (Ithaca, NY: Cornell University Press, 2013), chap. 2.

47. J. Muller, "How Volkswagen Will Rule the World," *Forbes*, April 17, 2013; Volkswagen Aktiengesellschaft, *Driving Ideas: Geschäftsbericht 2008* (Wolfsburg: Volkswagen, 2008).

48. D. Schäfer and B. Simon, "Volkswagen Faces Tough Job to Crack the US," *Financial Times*, September 16, 2010.

49. "VW entscheidet sich für US-Werk," *Handelsblatt*, May 12, 2008.

50. D. Schäfer and B. Simon, "VW Takes on Toyota with New US Plant," *Financial Times*, July 14, 2008.

51. M. Pare, "Volkswagen Chattanooga Is Getting a New CEO," *Times Free Press*, May 24, 2019.

52. "Volkswagen baut seine erste US-Fabrik seit 20 Jahren," *Welt*, July 16, 2008.

53. C. Buttorff, "State Officials, VW Detail Incentive Package," *Nashville Post*, August 29, 2008.

54. Correspondence from Lamar Alexander and Bob Corker to Martin Winterkorn, September 19, 2013.

55. Chattanooga Chamber Foundation, "Application for Foreign-Trade Zone Temporary/Interim Manufacturing Authority and Manufacturing/Processing Authority for Foreign-Trade Zone no. 134 in Chattanooga, Tennessee for Volkswagen Group of America Chattanooga Operations LLC," July 10, 2009.

56. Douglas S. Meyer, letter to Foreign Trade Zones Board Executive Secretary Andrew McGilvray, Foreign Trade Zones Board, US Department of Commerce, August 17, 2009, 2–6; "UAW Opposition Halts Application for VW Foreign-Trade Zone," *Chattanoogan*, August 20, 2009.

57. Michael Fichter and Horst Mund, "Transnationale Gewerkschaftsarbeit entlang globaler Wertschöpfungsketten," in *Wissenschaft und Arbeitswelt—Eine Kooperation im Wandel*, edited by Ludger Pries, Hans-Jürgen Urban, and Manfred Wannöffel, 209–44 (Baden-Baden: Nomos edition sigma, 2015).

58. Ron Gettelfinger meeting notes, Frankfurt/Main, Germany, November 23, 2009, Ron Gettelfinger Accession, UAWC.

59. Ron Gettelfinger meeting notes, Frankfurt/Main, Germany, November 23, 2009.

60. G. Nelson, "4 Key Decisions Shaped UAW Vote's Course," *Automotive News*, February 22, 2014.

61. See Joel Cutcher-Gershenfeld, Dan Brooks, and Martin Mulloy, *Inside the Ford-UAW Transformation: Pivotal Events in Valuing Work and Delivering Results* (Cambridge, MA: MIT Press, 2015).

62. Ron Gettelfinger meeting notes, Frankfurt/Main, Germany, November 23, 2009.

63. J. Reed and C. Bryant, "Carmaking," *Financial Times*, August 9, 2011.

64. "Volkswagen Academy Opens Doors," Local 3 News, June 4, 2020, https://www.wrcbtv.com/story/12595517/volkswagen-academy-opens-doors.

65. "UAW to Target German Auto Plants," IHS Global Insight Daily Analysis, December 30, 2011.

66. A. Wilson and G. Nelson, "An Ultimatum for VW Chattanooga?," *Automotive News*, June 24, 2013.

67. M. Pare, "VW Labor Exec Won't Promote UAW in City," *Times Free Press*, August 19, 2011.

68. Pare, "VW Labor Exec Won't Promote UAW in City."

69. A. Cremer and J. Schwartz, "VW Labor to Outline UAW Stance to US Plant Workers," Reuters, May 24, 2012.

70. Nelson, "4 Key Decisions Shaped UAW Vote's Course."

71. Sanford M. Jacoby, "Current Prospects for Employee Representation in the U.S.: Old Wine in New Bottles?," *Journal of Labor Research* 16, no. 3 (Summer 1995): 388–98.

72. Dennis M. Devaney, "Much Ado about Section 8(a)(2): The NLRB and Workplace Cooperation after Electromation and DuPont," *Stetson Law Review* 23, no. 1 (1993): 39–52.

73. Nelson, "4 Key Decisions Shaped UAW Vote's Course."

74. Silvia, *Holding the Shop Together*, 2.

75. C. Morrison, "New Human Resource Leader at Volkswagen Talks Production, Unions," nooga.com, March 4, 2013.

76. Industriegewerkschaft Metall and United Auto Workers, *Co-determining the Future: A New Labor Model* (Detroit: UAW, 2013).

77. C. Brooks, "Why the UAW Lost Another Election in Tennessee," *Nation*, June 19, 2019.

78. G. Nelson, "VW, UAW Discuss Setting up Chattanooga Labor Board," *Automotive News*, March 15, 2013.

79. M. Pare, "VW Chattanooga Opens Door to Unionization," *Times Free Press*, March 20, 2013.

80. Pare, "VW Chattanooga Opens Door to Unionization."

81. B. Klayman and B. Woodall, "Exclusive: German Union Chief to VW Tennessee Workers—Join UAW," Reuters, March 20, 2013.

82. M. Pare, "Volkswagen Layoffs in Chattanooga Marked by Surprise, Regret," *Times Free Press*, April 19, 2013.

83. "UAW Chums It Up with VW," *Tennessean*, April 6, 2013.

84. M. Pare, "UAW President Upbeat over Volkswagen Plant Prospects," *Times Free Press*, May 16, 2013.

85. "UAW Chums It Up with VW."

86. C. Morrison, "Union Debate Is a Community Issue, Some Say," nooga.com, July 18, 2013.

87. M. Pare, "UAW Slammed at Forum on Labor Organization Efforts at Chattanooga's Volkswagen Factory," *Times Free Press*, July 19, 2013; M. Elk, "VW Isn't Fighting Unionization," *In These Times*, November 13, 2013.

88. G. Nelson, "UAW's King: Germany Has 'a Great System,'" *Automotive News*, June 24, 2013.

89. Nelson, "4 Key VW Decisions Shaped UAW Vote's Course."

90. Nelson, "UAW's King."

91. Nelson, "UAW's King."

92. Pare, "UAW Slammed at Forum on Labor Organization Efforts at Chattanooga's Volkswagen Factory."

93. Interview, Gary Casteel, Cambridge, MA, September 7, 2018.

94. Nelson, "4 Key Decisions Shaped UAW Vote's Course."

95. "VW Incentive Documents," https://www.documentcloud.org/documents/1096921 -ecd-vw-document.html#document/p151/a155373.

96. P. Williams, "Haslam Offers No Apologies for $300M Volkswagen Offer," *Tennessean*, April 2, 2014.

97. "UAW Statement on VW Works Council in Chattanooga," United Auto Workers, September 6, 2013, https://uaw.org/uaw-statement-on-vw-works-council-in-chattanooga/.

98. "VW Incentive Documents."

99. N. Boudette, "UAW Edges toward Organizing VW Plant in South," *Wall Street Journal*, September 13, 2013.

100. E. Schelzig, "Corker Calls VW Talks with UAW 'Incomprehensible,'" Associated Press, September 11, 2013.

101. B. Woodall and B. Klayman, "US VW Executives 'Forced' by German Boss to Sign UAW Letter: Senator Corker," Reuters, September 11, 2013.

102. B. Klayman, "UAW Pushes VW to Recognise Union as Rep for Tennessee Workers," Reuters, September 12, 2013.

103. M. Randle, "UAW Hopes to Get Recognition at Chattanooga VW Plant without Vote," The Randle Report, September 13, 2013.

104. Klayman, "UAW Pushes VW to Recognise Union as Rep for Tennessee Workers."

105. Correspondence from Lamar Alexander and Bob Corker to Martin Winterkorn, September 19, 2013.

106. Klayman, "UAW Pushes VW to Recognise Union as Rep for Tennessee Workers"; M. Pare, "Chattanooga Workers to File Federal Charges against UAW, Group Says," Times Free Press, September 25, 2013.

107. N. Bunkley, "UAW Uses Multifront Push to Organize Imports," Automotive News, October 21, 2013.

108. Boudette, "UAW Edges toward Organizing VW Plant in South."

109. Pare, "Chattanooga Workers to File Federal Charges against UAW"; M. Pare, "Anti-UAW Petitions Handed Over to VW Chattanooga Managers," Times Free Press, October 5, 2013.

110. A. Cremer, "VW Labor Chief Backs UAW Union Bid for U.S. Works Council," Reuters, October 7, 2013.

111. J. Slaughter, "Autoworkers Try a New Angle at Volkswagen," Labor Notes, October 28, 2013.

112. C. Morrison, "Documents Reveal Past Meetings between Volkswagen, Government Officials," nooga.com, December 23, 2013.

113. Morrison, "Documents Reveal Past Meetings."

114. E. Schelzig, "U.S. Union Vote Won't Affect VW Plans," Associated Press, November 15, 2013.

115. "VW's Union Battle Sets Stage for Regional Fight," Nashville Business Journal, November 22, 2013.

116. L DePillis, "The Strange Case of the Anti-Union Union at Volkswagen's Plant in Tennessee," Washington Post, November 19, 2014.

117. J. Schwartz, "German Union's Boss Warns VW about Avoiding Unions," Reuters, November 13, 2013.

118. C. Woodyard and J. Healey, "U.S. Volkswagen Group CEO Leaves," USA Today, December 13, 2013.

119. Correspondence from Berthold Huber to Volkswagen Chattanooga employees, December 18, 2013.

120. Volkswagen Group of America and United Auto Workers, "Agreement for a Representation Election," Chattanooga, TN, January 27, 2014. Page citations appear in the subsequent text.

121. S. Early, "VW to UAW: So Long Partner?," CounterPunch, February 19, 2014.

122. E. Nawaguna and B. Woodall, "Volkswagen Tennessee Workers to Vote on UAW February 12–14," Reuters, February 3, 2014.

123. Correspondence from Mike Burton to Frank Fischer, February 3, 2014.

124. B. Woodall, "Second Group Files to Keep UAW from Reversing VW Plant Vote," Reuters, February 28, 2014.

125. Correspondence from Bill Haslam to Frank Fischer, February 4, 2014, https://www.documentcloud.org/documents/1096921-ecd-vw-document.html#document/p7.

126. N. Boudette, "Rivals Gear Up ahead of Volkswagen Vote," Wall Street Journal, February 4, 2014.

127. M. Pare, "Drama High in Union Vote at Chattanooga VW Plant," Times Free Press, February 6, 2014.

128. "Haslam Warns about UAW Impact in Chattanooga," *Knoxville News Sentinel*, February 7, 2014.

129. M. Pare, "Tennessee Gov. Haslam Repeats VW Union Criticism," *Times Free Press*, February 7, 2014.

130. M. Pare, "Pro-, Anti-UAW Activity Gears Up ahead of VW Election," *Times Free Press*, February 9, 2014.

131. S. Greenhouse, "Outsiders, Not Auto Plant, Battle U.A.W. in Tennessee," *New York Times*, January 29, 2014.

132. Nawaguna and Woodall, "Volkswagen Tennessee Workers to Vote on UAW February 12–14."

133. Greenhouse, "Outsiders, Not Auto Plant, Battle U.A.W. in Tennessee."

134. Greenhouse, "Outsiders, Not Auto Plant, Battle U.A.W. in Tennessee."

135. "Pyongyang, Tennessee," editorial, *Wall Street Journal*, January 28, 2014.

136. "Tennessee Anti-Union Billboard Has Spelling Mistake," Talking Union, https://talkingunion.wordpress.com/2014/02/10/22301/.

137. S. Greenhouse, "Labor Regroups in South after VW Vote," *New York Times*, February 16, 2014.

138. "Labor Watchdog Posts Billboards in Tennessee to Reach VW Workers," *Washington Free Beacon*, February 4, 2014.

139. Pare, "Drama High in Union Vote at Chattanooga VW Plant."

140. J. Logan, "Corker Must Come Clean on the Volkswagen Union Election," The Hill, April 5, 2014.

141. B. Woodall, "U.S. Senator Drops Bombshell during VW plant Union Vote," Reuters, February 13, 2014.

142. M. Elk, "Emails Show Sen. Corker's Chief of Staff Coordinated with Network of Anti-UAW Union Busters," *In These Times*, April 1, 2014.

143. "Volkswagen Workers Call for an End to Outside Interference," Talking Union Blog, February 10, 2014.

144. The Volkswagen Global Works Council is also called the Volkswagen World Group Council. Some use elements from each of these names in quotations in this chapter. I use the term Global Works Council because it is the simplest and because it communicates that it is part of VW's works council network. I leave alternative appellations in quotations as is. The important thing to remember is that it is the only worldwide body of VW workplace representatives.

145. M. Pare, "Pro-, Anti-UAW Activity Gears Up ahead of VW Election," *Times Free Press*, February 9, 2014.

146. M. Pare, "Anti-UAW Group Hits Neutrality Pact at Chattanooga Volkswagen Plant," *Times Free Press*, February 10, 2014.

147. Pare, "Anti-UAW Group Hits Neutrality Pact at Chattanooga Volkswagen Plant."

148. M. Elk, "After Historic UAW Defeat at Tennessee Volkswagen Plant, Theories Abound," *In These Times*, February 15, 2014.

149. "Tenn. Lawmakers: VW Incentives Threatened by UAW," *Washington Examiner*, February 10, 2014.

150. H. Webb, "Bo Watson Says VW May Lose State Help If the UAW Is Voted in at Chattanooga Plant," *Chattanoogan*, February 10, 2014.

151. L. DePillis, "All Eyes on Chattanooga," *Washington Post*, February 14, 2014.

152. C. Isadore, "Union Vote at VW Plant Sparks a Backlash," *CNNMoney*, February 12, 2014.

153. G. Nelson, "UAW Vote at VW Plant Has High Stakes for Industry, Labor," *Automotive News*, February 10, 2014; E. Schelzig, "Tenn. Lawmakers: VW Incentives Threatened by UAW," *Associated Press*, February 10, 2014.

154. UAW, "Volkswagen Workers Call for an End to Outside Interference," February 9, 2014, https://uaw.org/volkswagen-workers-call-for-an-end-to-outside-interference/.

155. Nelson, "UAW Vote at VW Plant Has High Stakes for Industry, Labor."

156. "UAW Statement on Corker Press Conference," News from the UAW, February 11, 2014.

157. B. Woodall, "U.S. Senator Drops Bombshell during VW Plant Union Vote," Reuters, February 13, 2014.

158. L. DePillis, "All Eyes on Chattanooga," *Washington Post*, February 14, 2014.

159. C. Morrison, "Corker Reiterates Statement Linking UAW Vote and SUV," nooga .com, February 14, 2014.

160. R. Cowan and B. Woodall, "Obama Weighs In on Contentious Union Vote at Volkswagen Plant," Reuters, February 14, 2014.

161. Cowan and Woodall, "Obama Weighs In."

162. C. Brooks, "Volkswagen Workers Celebrate Election Win, but Question Union's Partnership Strategy," *Labor Notes*, December 2015.

163. C. Morrison, "UAW Loses Representation Vote at Volkswagen Chattanooga," nooga.com, February 15, 2014.

164. "UAW Regroups after Stinging VW Setback," *Automotive News*, February 16, 2014.

165. B. Snavely, "UAW May Challenge Volkswagen Vote Results," *Detroit Free Press*, February 15, 2014.

166. "UAW Regroups after Stinging VW Setback."

167. N. Boudette, "Corker 'Thrilled' UAW Vote Failed in Chattanooga," *Wall Street Journal*, February 14, 2014.

168. Morrison, "UAW Loses Representation Vote at Volkswagen Chattanooga."

169. American Federation of Labor–Congress of Industrial Organizations, *At What Cost? Workers Report Concerns about Volkswagen's New Manufacturing Jobs in Tennessee* (Washington, DC: AFL-CIO, 2017), 10.

170. Snavely, "UAW May Challenge Volkswagen Vote Results."

171. B. Parker and J. Richard, "Interview: Corruption and Collaboration in the UAW," *Labor Notes*, February 2018.

172. Kate Bronfenbrenner and Tom Juravich, "It Takes More Than House Calls: Organizing to Win with a Comprehensive Union-Building Strategy," in *Organizing to Win: New Research on Union Strategies*, edited by K. Bronfenbrenner, S. Friedman, R. W. Hurd, R. A. Oswald, and R. L Seeber (Ithaca, NY: ILR Press, 1998), 20.

173. Chris Brooks, "Organizing Volkswagen: A Critical Assessment," *Journal of Labor and Society* 19 (September 2016): 410.

174. Interviews with Volkswagen Chattanooga employees, July 28–30, 2015; AFL-CIO, *At What Cost?*, 5–8.

175. Brooks, "Volkswagen Workers Celebrate Election Win, but Question Union's Partnership Strategy."

176. Elk, "After Historic UAW Defeat at Tennessee Volkswagen Plant, Theories Abound."

177. Interview, Bob King, Ann Arbor, MI, January 8, 2020.

178. L. DePillis, "Auto Union Loses Historic Election at Volkswagen Plant in Tennessee," *Washington Post*, February 15, 2014.

179. "Industry Labor Cost," *Automotive News*, March 24, 2015.

180. C. Brooks, "Volkswagen in Tennessee: Productivity's Price," *Labor Notes*, February 2018.

181. Brooks, "Organizing Volkswagen," 409.

182. Minchin, "Look at Detroit,"482.

183. For example, A. Sher, "UAW, Opponents Used Vastly Different Strategies," *Times Free Press*, February 16, 2014.

184. P. Williams, "Haslam, Corker Subpoenaed by UAW Lawyers," News Channel 5, April 9, 2014, https://www.newschannel5.com/news/newschannel-5-investigates/tennessees-secret-deals/haslam-corker-subpoenaed-by-uaw-lawyers.

185. P. Williams, "Congress Opens Inquiry into Haslam Administration's $300M Offer," News Channel 5, April 16, 2014, https://www.newschannel5.com/news/newschannel-5-investigates/tennessees-secret-deals/congress-opens-inquiry-into-haslam-administrations-300m-offer.

186. B. Hoffmann, "Tennessee Sen. Bob Corker to Snub UAW Subpoena," Newsmax, April 17, 2014, http://www.newsmax.com/US/UAW-Volkswagen-Bob-Corker/2014/04/17/id/566218/.

187. A. Becker and B. Woodall, "UAW Suddenly Retreats from Fight at Tennessee," Reuters, April 21, 2014; Gary Casteel letter to Volkswagen Chattanooga employees, April 21, 2014.

188. "Statement: Gary Casteel, June 21, 2016," Politico, June 21, 2016, http://static.politico.com/9e/89/d87738b746629ad6a5286b6fce10/uaw-documents-on-chattanooga.pdf.

189. "Statement: Gary Casteel, June 21, 2016."

190. G. Chambers Williams III, "Despite Roadblocks, UAW Finds a New Path in the South," *Tennessean*, July 10, 2014.

191. "UAW Continues Union Fight in Chattanooga," *Tennessean*, July 11, 2014.

192. Correspondence from Gary Casteel to Volkswagen Chattanooga employees, July 23, 2014.

193. T. Devaney, "Volkswagen Employees Say UAW Violating 'No-Fly Zone,'" The Hill, August 1, 2014.

194. Interviews with Volkswagen Chattanooga employees, August 19, 2015.

195. M. Pare, "UAW Congratulates Volkswagen and Employees on New Product Line in Chattanooga," *Times Free Press*, July 14, 2014.

196. M. Pare, "Chattanooga VW Workers Seek Their Own Union," *Times Free Press*, August 27, 2014.

197. American Council of Employees, "ACE Announces Leadership Transition," August 14, 2015.

198. Correspondence from Mike Cantrell to UAW Local 42 members, November 11, 2014.

199. Volkswagen Chattanooga, "Policy #: HR-C20. Community Organization Engagement," November 12, 2014, 1–4. Page citations appear in the subsequent text.

200. B. Snavely, "Volkswagen Opens the Door to the UAW in Chattanooga," *Detroit Free Press*, November 12, 2014.

201. Gary Casteel, "UAW Statement on Volkswagen Policy," United Auto Workers, November 21, 2014, https://uaw.org/uaw-statement-on-volkswagen-policy/.

202. Brooks, "Volkswagen Workers Celebrate Election Win, but Question Union's Partnership Strategy."

203. S. Greenhouse, "VW to Allow Labor Groups to Represent Workers at Chattanooga Plant," *New York Times*, November 12, 2014.

204. Snavely, "Volkswagen Opens the Door to the UAW in Chattanooga."

205. IG Metall, press release, November 13, 2014.

206. G. Klotz, "How the UAW May Finally Make History in Chattanooga," Salon, December 14, 2014.

207. M. Pare, "Labor Group Critical of UAW Seeks Recognition at VW's Chattanooga Plant," *Times Free Press*, February 4, 2015.

208. B. Snavely, "UAW Chief Has Faith in Southern Strategy," *Detroit Free Press*, December 16, 2014.

209. ACE, News release, February 16, 2015.

210. "UAW Unveils Works Council Proposal for Volkswagen Plant," Associated Press, May 7, 2015; D. Barkholz and R. Beene, "UAW Pushes to Form Works Council at VW Chattanooga Plant," *Automotive News*, May 7, 2015

211. M. Clothier, "VW Denies UAW Request to Be Sole Representative in Tennessee," *Bloomberg Business*, May 7, 2015.

212. C. Morrison, "UAW Eyeing 'Multiple Paths' to Collective Bargaining at VW," nooga.com, August 4, 2015.

213. C. Morrison, "UAW Files Petition to Organize VW's Maintenance Workers," nooga.com, October 23, 2015.

214. UAW Local 42, "UAW Local 42 Seeks NLRB Election for Volkswagen Maintenance Employees," News release, October 23, 2015.

215. For the 2009 to 2015 model years, VW secretly installed software on its cars with diesel motors that allowed them to sense the parameters of an emissions test. In test mode, the software made the cars' exhaust compliant with US and California emissions standards, but when driving normally, the cars significantly exceeded standards for nitrogen-oxide emissions. The scandal broke in September 2015 when the Environmental Protection Agency issued a notice of VW's violation of the Clean Air Act. The US government subsequently reached a set of settlements with Volkswagen that requires the firm to spend $10 billion on a car buyback program for consumers and $4.7 billion in additional fines. C. Atiyeh, "Everything You Need to Know about the VW Diesel-Emissions Scandal," *Car and Driver*, May 4, 2019.

216. Correspondence from Christian Koch and Sebastian Patta to Volkswagen Chattanooga employees, October 23, 2015.

217. M. Pare, "Volkswagen Letter to Workers Calls UAW Petition Timing 'Unfortunate,'" *Times Free Press*, October 31, 2015.

218. M. Pare, "UAW Seeks New Vote at Volkswagen's Chattanooga Plant," *Times Free Press*, October 24, 2015.

219. C. Morrison, "Volkswagen Files Petition to Stop UAW Organization of Maintenance Employees," nooga.com, November 3, 2015.

220. Silvia, *Holding the Shop Together*, 107–10.

221. M. Pare, "Vote to Proceed Despite VW's Plan to Appeal Union Election at Chattanooga Plant," *Times Free Press*, December 1, 2015.

222. M. Pare, "UAW Unworried about Blowback over German Union Cooperation," *Times Free Press*, November 19, 2015.

223. M. Pare, "Today's VW Vote on Representation Meets Resistance from the Company," *Times Free Press*, December 3, 2015.

224. AFL–CIO, *At What Cost?*, 11.

225. J. Szczesny, "UAW Gains Foothold in VW's Chattanooga Plant," *Detroit Bureau*, December 7, 2015.

226. B. Woodall, "UAW Wins Historic Victory in U.S. South with Vote at VW Plant," Reuters, December 4, 2015.

227. "United Auto Workers Win Vote at VW's Tennessee Plant," *Detroit Free Press*, December 4, 2015.

228. M. Pare, "UAW Local 42 Files Charge against VW over Chattanooga Plant," *Times Free Press*, December 21, 2015.

229. M. Pare, "Business Groups Support VW Appeal of UAW Vote in Chattanooga," *Times Free Press*, January 9, 2016.

230. "UAW Union Hopes for 'Reset' on Volkswagen Labor Relations," Associated Press, January 23, 2016.

231. "UAW Adds to Unfair Labor Practices Allegations at Volkswagen," Associated Press, February 9, 2016.

232. American Federation of Labor–Congress of Industrial Organizations, "AFL-CIO Executive Council Statement on Volkswagen," February 23, 2016, https://uaw.org /afl-cio-executive-council-statement-on-volkswagen/.

233. C. Morrison, "NLRB Denies VW Request to Reconsider Small Bargaining Unit," nooga.com, April 13, 2016.

234. J. Szczesny, "CrossBlue in Crosshairs as VW-UAW Clash Escalates," *Wards Auto*, May 12, 2016.

235. Szczesny, "CrossBlue in Crosshairs."

236. M. Pare, "Hillary Clinton Tweets in Support of UAW at VW Chattanooga," *Times Free Press*, May 6, 2016.

237. W. Boston, "VW and UAW to Meet for Talks on Car Maker's Chattanooga Plant," *Wall Street Journal*, May 1, 2016.

238. C. Morrison, "VW, UAW Plan Meeting in Attempt to Reconcile Differences," nooga.com, May 3, 2016; M. Pare, "VW to Meet with UAW over Labor Stalemate at Chattanooga Plant," *Times Free Press*, May 2, 2016.

239. W. Boston, "No Progress for VW, Auto Workers' Union in Resolving U.S. Labor Dispute," *Wall Street Journal*, June 9, 2016.

240. Boston, "No Progress for VW, Auto Workers' Union."

241. IndustriALL, "Resolution on Volkswagen to Respect Worker Rights in Chattanooga, Tennessee, USA," IndustriALL Executive Committee Meeting, Frankfurt/ Main, Germany, May 25–26, 2016.

242. "News from the Associated Press," Associated Press, June 21, 2016; "Statement: Gary Casteel, June 21, 2016."

243. A. Cremer, "Volkswagen Will Not Help UAW Union Organize Tennessee Plant: HR Chief," Reuters, June 22, 2016.

244. Correspondence from Dan Kildee et al. to Christian Koch and Sebastian Patta, July 9, 2016.

245. Correspondence from Dan Geanacopoulos to Daniel T. Kildee, September 1, 2016.

246. M. Pare, "Volkswagen Files Lawsuit to Block UAW Vote," *Times Free Press*, September 1, 2016.

247. UAW, "Statement in Response to Volkswagen Appeal of NLRB Order," September 1, 2016, https://uaw.org/statement-response-volkswagen-appeal-nlrb-order/.

248. N. Doll and P. Vetter, "Schade, dass VW so ängstlich ist," *Welt*, September 11, 2016.

249. M. Pare, "Rival Group to United Auto Workers at Volkswagen Plant Fails to Meet Minimum Membership Threshold," *Times Free Press*, September 23, 2016.

250. IndustriALL, "Holding Volkswagen Accountable," Second Global Congress, Rio de Janeiro, Brazil, October 3–7, 2016, https://www.industriall-union.org/sites/default/files /uploads/documents/2016/Brazil/industriall_congress_resolution_re_vw_english.pdf.

251. UAW Local 42, "Steve Cochran's Report from Wolfsburg," http://local42.org /2016/12/steve-cochrans-report-from-wolfsburg/, December 22, 2016.

252. National Right to Work Legal Defense Foundation, "Worker Files Brief against Coercive Union Boss Gerrymandering Scheme," February 3, 2017, http://www.ntrw.org /news/worker-files-brief-against-coercive-union-boss-gerrymandering-scheme020217.

253. C. Morrison, "VW Employee Files Brief to Appeal NLRB Decision on UAW Micro-Unit," nooga.com, February 6, 2017.

254. IndustriALL, "Volkswagen's Empty Promises! Union-Busting in Chattanooga," http://admin.industriall-union.org/sites/default/files/uploads/documents/2017/SWITZERLAND/tell_vw_to_stop_union_busting.pdf.

255. IndustriALL, "Joint Statement from IndustriALL Global Union Meeting of Unions at Volkswagen in Chattanooga, Tennessee, USA, April 12–13, 2017, http://www.industriall-union.org/sites/default/files/uploads/documents/2017/USA/joint_statement_from_industriall_global_union_meeting_of_unions_at_volks.pdf.

256. IndustriALL, "Global Support for Workers at VW Chattanooga Plant," April 13, 2017, http://www.industriall-union.org/global-support-for-workers-at-vw-chattanooga-plant.

257. AFL–CIO, *At What Cost?*

258. "Workers at Volkswagen's Plant in Chattanooga Discuss Their Situation," YouTube, April 26, 2017, https://www.youtube.com/watch?time_continue=12&v=YleFBefx36s&feature=emb_logo.

259. "Volkswagen: Stop Union Busting," Sum of Us, n.d., https://actions.sumofus.org/a/volkswagen?sp_ref=296650187.99.180473.f.574433.2&referrer_id=19958001&source=fb.

260. K. Laing, "UAW Accuses VW of Stalling on Tenn. Labor Negotiations," *Times Free Press*, April 27, 2017.

261. IndustriALL, "UAW Tells Shareholders That Volkswagen Must Stop Union Busting," May 11, 2017, http://www.industriall-union.org/uaw-tells-shareholders-that-volkswagen-must-stop-union-busting.

262. M. Pare, "Union Puts Pressure on Volkswagen's Chattanooga Plant," *Times Free Press*, May 10, 2017.

263. For example, "Streit um Betriebsräte bei VW," *Berliner Morgenpost*, May 10, 2017.

264. M. Pare, "National Labor Relations Board Files Complaint against VW Chattanooga," *Times Free Press*, May 12, 2017.

265. M. Pare, "Corker Seeks Reversal on NLRB's Approval of Micro-Unions," *Times Free Press*, May 26, 2017.

266. N. Naughton, "Former UAW President Pleads Guilty to Embezzlement," *Wall Street Journal*, June 3, 2020.

267. "UAW Scandal Timeline," *Automotive News*, n.d., https://www.autonews.com/static/section/content01.html.

268. C. Morrison, "VW Chattanooga Gets New Head of Local Operations," nooga.com, June 17, 2017.

269. UAW Local 42, "Maintenance Employees Have Their Day in Court," https://local42.org/2017/11/maintenance-employees-have-their-day-in-court, November 10, 2017.

270. "Labor Ruling Could Impact Chattanooga's Volkswagen Plant," *Times Free Press*, December 19, 2017.

271. M. Pare, "Volkswagen, Labor Union Clash over Request Involving Chattanooga Plant," *Times Free Press*, December 22, 2017.

272. N. Carey, "UAW Head Does Not See More Charges in U.S. Training Center Probe," Reuters, December 20, 2017.

273. M. Pare, "Court Sends VW Chattanooga Case Back to Labor Board," *Times Free Press*, December 27, 2017.

274. R. Greszler, "Why VW Workers Have More to Lose Than Gain from Unionizing," *Daily Signal*, May 13, 2019.

275. "IndustriALL Global Union Executive Committee Resolves," IndustriALL Global Union Executive Committee, n.d., http://www.industriall-union.org/sites/default /files/uploads/documents/2019/GERMANY/industriall_global_union_executive _committee_resolution_on_vw.pdf.

276. Correspondence from Valter Sanches to Herbert Diess and Gunnar Kilian, IndustriALL, December 4, 2018, http://www.industriall-union.org/sites/default/files /uploads/documents/2019/GERMANY/resolution_des_industriall_zur_anerkennung _der_wahl_im_bereich_der_facharbeiter_im_werk_in_chattanooga.docx.pdf.

277. IndutriALL, "IndustriALL Mounts Pressure on Volkswagen to Engage with US Union," December 11, 2018, http://www.indutriall-union.org/industriall-mounts -pressure-on-volkswagen-to-engage-with-us-union.

278. IndustriAll, Gunnar Kilian reply to Valter Sanches, January 15, 2019, http:// www.industriall-union.org/sites/default/files/uploads/documents/2019/GERMANY /02_de_schreiben_industriall_antwort_killian.pdf.

279. IndustriAll, Valter Sanches response to Gunnar Kilian, January 21, 2019, http:// www.industriall-union.org/sites/default/files/uploads/documents/2019/GERMANY /industriall_letter_to_vw.pdf.

280. M. Pare, "Chattanooga Will Be Home to Volkswagen's First Electric Vehicle Manufacturing Facility in North America," *Times Free Press*, January 14, 2019.

281. Volkswagen Chattanooga, "JumpStart," December 14, 2018. Personal time off is a personnel practice that collects vacation, sick days, personal days, and any other type of paid time off into a single pool of bankable hours for each employee.

282. M. Pare, "VW Chattanooga Plant Workers Meet with Management about Time Off during 3-day Shutdown," *Times Free Press*, December 14, 2018; M. Elk, "Volkswagen Workers Talk Wildcat Strike," *Payday Report*, June 15, 2019.

283. UAW Local 42, Flyer, Facebook, December 14, 2018, https://www.facebook.com /UAWlocal42/photos/a.447010295440332/1205959039545450/?type=3&theater.

284. C. Brooks, "Why the UAW Lost Again in Chattanooga," *Labor Notes*, June 14, 2019.

285. "Director of UAW Organizing, Tracy Romero, Speaks about the Benchmarks to Win a Union Contract at Volkswagen," Facebook, February 12, 2019, https://www .facebook.com/UAWlocal42/videos/702693190132346/.

286. UAW Local 42, "It's Time to Put Chattanooga Workers First," Facebook, n.d., https://www.facebook.com/pg/UAWlocal42/videos/.

287. "Volkswagen Chattanooga Raises Minimum Wage to $16," News Channel 9, March 20, 2019, https://newschannel9.com/news/local/vw-chattanooga-raises-minimum -wage-to-16.

288. Brooks, "Why the UAW Lost Again in Chattanooga."

289. UAW local 42, "This Is It," April 9, 2019, https://facebook.com/UAWlocal42 /videos/388754185043491.

290. C. Brooks, "Third Time's the Charm?," *Labor Notes*, April 11, 2019.

291. UAW Local 42, "Why in Chattanooga Do We Have to Make Suggestions, Not Sit Down and Bargain Like Every Other VW Plant?," April 9, 2019, https://www .facebook.com/UAWlocal42/posts/1281493671991986.

292. "It's Time! UAW Local 42—Volkswagen, Chattanooga TN Authorization Card!," The Action Network, n.d., https://actionnetwork.org/forms/its-time-uaw-local-42-volkswa gen-chattanooga-tn-authorization-card.

293. M. Pare, "Chattanooga Volkswagen Workers File Petition to Join United Auto Workers," *Times Free Press*, April 9, 2019.

294. T. Evanoff, "UAW Making New Push at VW Chattanooga," *Memphis Commercial Appeal*, April 9, 2019.

295. UAW Local 42, "It's Time to Put Chattanooga Workers First."

296. M. Pare, "United Auto Workers Officials Want No 'Outside Interference' in Proposed Union Election at Volkswagen's Chattanooga Plant," *Times Free Press*, April 10, 2019.

297. M. Pare, "Chattanooga Volkswagen Workers File Petition to Join United Auto Workers," *Times Free Press*, April 9, 2019.

298. Pare, "Chattanooga Volkswagen Workers File Petition."

299. C. Brooks, "Tennessee Gov. Bill Lee's Office Is Working with Volkswagen to Crush a Union Drive," The Intercept, May 30, 2019, https://theintercept.com/2019/05/30 /volkswagen-anti-union-tennessee-governor-bill-lee/.

300. C. Opfer and J. Diaz, "Punching In," *Bloomberg Law Daily Labor Report*, April 15, 2019.

301. Myron Roomkin and Hervey Juris, "Unions in the Traditional Sectors: Mid-Life Passage of the Labor Movement," in *Proceedings of the Industrial Relations Research Association, 28–29 December 1977,* edited by Barbara D. Dennis (Madison, WI: Industrial Relations Research Association, 1978): 212–22.

302. M. Pare, "Volkswagen, United Auto Workers Tangle over Chattanooga Plant Election Questions before New Vote," *Times Free Press*, April 16, 2019.

303. M. Pare, "Blackburn Says Union Effort at Volkswagen Chattanooga Harms Workers," *Times Free Press*, April 18, 2019.

304. C. Brooks, "Volkswagen Jump-Starts Anti-Union Campaign," *Labor Notes*, April 24, 2019.

305. M. Elk, "Volkswagen Launches 'Passive-Aggressive' Anti-Union Campaign," *Payday Report*, April 22, 2019.

306. B. McMorris, "UAW Scandal Hits Chattanooga," *Washington Free Beacon*, April 17, 2019.

307. M. Pare, "Blackburn Says Union Effort at Volkswagen Chattanooga Harms Workers," *Times Free Press*, April 18, 2019.

308. Pare, "Blackburn Says Union Effort at Volkswagen Chattanooga Harms Workers."

309. D. Carroll, "Governor Lee's Surprise Visit to Volkswagen Stirs Union Vote Talk, UAW Responds," Local 3 News, April 30, 2019, https://www.wrcbtv.com/story/40393742 /governor-lees-surprise-visit-to-volkswagen-stirs-union-vote-talk-uaw-responds.

310. M. Pare, "Tennessee Gov. Bill Lee Makes a Visit to Chattanooga Volkswagen Plant," *Times Free Press*, April 29, 2019.

311. C. Brooks, "Tennessee Governor Leads Anti-Union Captive Audience Meeting at VW," *Labor Notes*, April 29, 2019.

312. Brooks, "Tennessee Governor Leads Anti-Union Captive Audience Meeting."

313. UAW Local 42, "GOVERNOR LEE VISITS OUR PLANT!," April 29, 2019, https://www.facebook.com/UAWlocal42/photos/a.445141975627164/129534204 3940482/

314. M. Pare, "Anti-United Auto Workers Group Forms Ahead of Possible Chattanooga Volkswagen Plant Election," *Times Free Press*, April 30, 2019.

315. T. Evanoff, "Pro-Union? Anti-Union? Chattanooga Hears It All on Eve of UAW Election," *Memphis Commercial Appeal*, June 5, 2019.

316. C. Brooks, "Trump Labor Board Postpones VW Vote while Company Manufactures Climate of Fear," *Labor Notes*, May 3, 2019.

317. Republican appointees John F. Ring and Marvin E. Kaplan were in the majority. Democratic appointee Lauren McFerran dissented. William Emanuel recused himself because he previously worked for Littler Mendelson. The fifth seat was vacant.

318. "Volkswagen Group of America Chattanooga Operations, LLC," National Labor Relations Board, n.d., https://www.nlrb.gov/case/10-RC-239234.

319. UAW Local 42, "It's Time to put Chattanooga Workers First!," May 8, 2019, https://fb.watch/eM30ZCapTB/.

320. M. Pare, "United Auto Workers Renew Call for Volkswagen Chattanooga Plant Union Vote," *Times Free Press*, May 6, 2019.

321. Southern Momentum, "Press Releases," May 3, 2019.

322. United Auto Workers, "Statement on Behalf of Chattanooga Volkswagen Workers," News from the UAW, May 6, 2019.

323. Southern Momentum, "Press Releases," May 6, 2019.

324. B. Rolfe, "VW Doesn't Need UAW Presence," *Times Free Press*, May 6, 2019.

325. T. Evanoff, "VW Chattanooga Workers Say Union Vote Is Near," *Memphis Commercial Appeal*, May 9, 2019.

326. D. Flessner, "UAW Trying to Organize Volkswagen Chattanooga Plant amid Battle for New Union Election," *Times Free Press*, May 17, 2019.

327. T. Evanoff, "NLRB Puts VW Chattanooga Vote on Hold," *Memphis Commercial Appeal*, May 22, 2019.

328. "Rep. Fleischmann Weighs In on VW Union Vote," Local 3 News, May 10, 2019, https://wrcbtv.com/story/40455631/rep-fleischmann-weighs-in-on-vw-union-vote.

329. Center for VW Facts, Facebook, https://www.facebook.com/vwfacts/.

330. Center for VW Facts, "For Immediate Release," May 13, 2019.

331. D. Flessner, "UAW Trying to Organize Volkswagen Chattanooga Plant amid Battle for New Union Election," *Times Free Press*, May 17, 2019.

332. For example, Brooks, "Organizing Volkswagen."

333. "Let Us Vote!," Facebook, May 22, 2019, https://www.facebook.com/watch/?v =1083024975240407.

334. M. Pare, "Labor Rally Supports Volkswagen Chattanooga Vote, but UAW Watchdog Cites Union's 'Culture of Corruption,'" *Times Free Press*, May 20, 2019.

335. Brooks, "Why the UAW Lost Another Election in Tennessee"; Letters and C. Brooks Response, *Labor Notes*, August 2019.

336. D. Shepardson, "U.S. Senators Urge Volkswagen to End Delay in Tennessee Union Vote," Reuters, May 21, 2019.

337. Southern Momentum, "Press Releases," May 22, 2019.

338. National Labor Relations Board, Case 10-RC-239234, May 22, 2019.

339. National Labor Relations Board, Case 10-RC-239234.

340. "Update: NLRB Rules Against UAW Petition in Split Decision," Local 3 News, December 1, 2021, https://wrcbtv.com/story/40277048/update-nlrb-rules-against-uaw -petition.

341. "Union Files for New Vote at Volkswagen's Tennessee Plant," *Oakridger*, May 23, 2019.

342. M. Pare, "Labor Board Dismisses United Auto Workers Vote," *Times Free Press*, May 22, 2019.

343. VWGOA, "Info," vwelectioninfo.com, Chattanooga, TN, June 17, 2019..

344. VWGOA, "Home," vwelectioninfo.com, Chattanooga, TN, June 17, 2019.

345. VWGOA, "Working at Volkswagen," vwelectioninfo.com, Chattanooga, TN, June 17, 2019.

346. VWGOA, "About the UAW," vwelectioninfo.com, Chattanooga, TN, June 17, 2019.

347. VWGOA, "Decertification," vwelectioninfo.com, Chattanooga, TN, June 17, 2019.

348. VWGOA, "Negotiations," vwelectioninfo.com, Chattanooga, TN, June 17, 2019.

349. VWGOA, "Works Councils," vwelectioninfo.com, Chattanooga, TN, June 17, 2019.

350. Pare, "Volkswagen Chattanooga Is Getting a New CEO."

351. C. Brooks, "A Tumultuous Week for Chattanooga Volkswagen Workers," *Labor Notes*, May 24, 2019.

352. UAW Local 42, "A Sincere 'Welcome Back to Chattanooga' to Frank Fischer," Facebook, May 28, 2019, https://www.facebook.com/UAWlocal42/photos/a.447010295 440332/1317081421766544/?type=3&theater.

353. C. Brooks, "As VW Election Nears, CEO Stokes Fears Over Plant Closing from 1988," *Labor Notes*, May 31, 2019.

354. M. Elk, "VW Threating to Close Chattanooga Plant If UAW Wins," *Payday Report*, June 7, 2019; Elk, "Volkswagen Workers Talk Wildcat Strike."

355. Brooks, "Why the UAW Lost Again in Chattanooga Tennessee"; Letters and C. Brooks Response, *Labor Notes*, August 2019.

356. UAW Local 42, "It's Time to Put Chattanooga Workers First."

357. "We Are Chattanooga Volkswagen Workers," YouTube, June 10, 2019, https://www.youtube.com/watch?v=HCSdbXrqq2g&feature=youtu.be.

358. "Stephen Voted No in 2014. Here's What Changed His Mind," Facebook, June 12, 2019, https://www.facebook.com/UAWlocal42/videos/450170012440606/.

359. C. Butler, "Volkswagen Chattanooga Employee Releases Testimonial Against the UAW," *Tennessee Star*, May 30, 2019.

360. M. Pare, "Ad Campaigns Heat Up as Union Vote Nears at Volkswagen's Chattanooga Plant," *Times Free Press*, May 31, 2019.

361. C. Butler, "Southern Momentum Puts Out Additional Ads to Oppose at Volkswagen Chattanooga," *Tennessee Star*, June 2, 2019.

362. A. Wallender, "Volkswagen Union Tensions Trigger Battle of the Airwaves," *Bloomberg Law Daily Labor Report*, June 6, 2019.

363. Jerry B. Merrill, "Facebook Is Data-Mining Chattanoogans' Activity to Suss Out Which Ones Are 'Interested in United Auto Workers,'" Twitter, June 16, 2019, https://twitter.com/jeremybmerrill/status/1136717053501595649.

364. J. Dukes, "Gov. Bill Lee Weighs In on UAW Vote during Visit to Chattanooga," Local 3 News, May 30, 2019, https://www.wrcbtv.com/story/40568292/gov-bill-lee-weighs-in-on-uaw-vote-during-visit-to-chattanooga.

365. M. Pare, "Hamilton County Legislators Say UAW Jeopardizes Volkswagen Chattanooga's Future Growth," *Times Free Press*, June 7, 2019.

366. UAW Local 42, UAW Local 42 Facebook, "Andy Berke, Mayor of Chattanooga," June 6, 2019, https://www.facebook.com/search/top?q=uaw%20local%2042%20berke.

367. "County Mayor Jim Coppinger Urges VW Workers to Reject UAW," The Chattanoogan, June 20, 2019, https://chattanoogan.com/2019/6/10/391762/County-Mayor-Jim-Coppinger-Urges-W V.aspx.

368. Correspondence from Jörg Hofmann to VW Chattanooga employees, Frankfurt/Main, Germany, June 4, 2019.

369. Correspondence from Bernd Osterloh and Johan Järvklo to Volkswagen Chattanooga employees, Wolfsburg, Germany, June 6, 2019.

370. Tracy Romano, telephone interview, July 16, 2019.

371. "Message of Support from Germany to Chattanooga VW Workers," TN Holler, June 12, 2019, https://tnholler.com/2019/06/message-of-support-from-germany-to-chattanooga-vw-workers/.

372. "UAW Loses Election at VW Chattanooga by Narrow Margin," IndustriALL, June 18, 2019, www.industriall-union.org/uaw-loses-election-at-vw-chattanooga-by-29-votes.

373. UAW Local 42, "It's Time to Put Chattanooga Workers First."

374. C. Brooks, "Volkswagen Declares War against Works Council and German Union," *Labor Notes*, June 12, 2019.

375. Brooks, "Volkswagen Declares War against Works Council and German Union"; Elk, "Volkswagen Workers Talk Wildcat Strike."

376. Elk, "Volkswagen Workers Talk Wildcat Strike."

377. UAW Local 42, "CEO Fischer Is in a Tough Spot," Facebook, June 10, 2019, https://www.facebook.com/UAWlocal42/photos/a.447010295440332/132725163074 9523/?type=3&theater.

378. UAW Local 42, "This Election Isn't about Union Facts or 'Southern Momentum' or VW Facts or Politicians or Outside Lawyers," Facebook, June 10, 2019, https://www .facebook.com/UAWlocal42/photos/a.447010295440332/1327251650749521/?type =3&theater.

379. Bernd Osterloh, "Wahlen in Chattanooga haben begonnen," IG Metall, June 12, 2019, https://www.igmetall-wob/meldung/wahlen-in-chattanooga-haben-begonnen/.

380. Osterloh, "Wahlen in Chattanooga haben begonnen."

381. Jörg Hofmann, "Die IG Metall unterstützt die Bemühungen der Gewerkschaft United Auto Workers UAW," Press statement, June 12, 2019, https://www.igmetall.de /presse/pressemitteilungen/die-ig-metall-unterstuetzt-die-interessenvertretung?print =true.

382. M. Pare, "Union Loses again at Volkswagen," *Times Free Press*, June 14, 2019.

383. C. Atiyeh, "Volkswagen's Chattanooga Workers Vote for Second Time Not to Join UAW," *Car and Driver*, June 15, 2019.

384. "UAW Calls for Comprehensive Labor Law Changes after VW Organizing Campaign," News from the UAW, June 14, 2019.

385. M. Pare, "Future at Volkswagen Eyed Amid Union Loss," *Times Free Press*, June 15, 2019.

386. "Gov. Lee, Top Republicans Celebrate Failed UAW Bid to Unionize Volkswagen," *Times Free Press*, June 15, 2019.

387. "Southern Momentum's 'Excited' about Volkswagen's Union Vote Outcome," *Times Free Press*, June 15, 2019.

388. Pare, "Future at Volkswagen Eyed amid Union Loss."

389. UAW Local 42, "We Lost the Election 776 Yes to 833 No," Facebook, June 15, 2019, https://m.facebook.com/UAWlocal42/posts/1331069390367747.

390. Elk, "Volkswagen Workers Talk Wildcat Strike."

391. Pare, "Future at Volkswagen Eyed amid Union Loss."

392. "Wahldebakel ist eine Ohrfeige für die VW-Mitbestimmung," *Wolfsburger Nachrichten*, June 17, 2019.

393. M. Pare, "Volkswagen Names New Chattanooga CEO," *Times Free Press*, July 18, 2019.

4. NISSAN NORTH AMERICA

1. Daniel K. Benjamin, "Voluntary Export Restraints on Automobiles," *PERC Reports* 17, no. 3 (Fall 1999), https://www.perc.org/1999/09/01/voluntary-export-restraints-on -automobiles/.

2. David Gelsanliter, *Jump Start: Japan Comes to the Heartland* (New York: Farrar, Straus & Giroux, 1990), 48–49.

3. V. Gibson, "Nissan Coming to Rutherford," *Daily News-Journal*, October 30, 1980; Greg Tucker, "Banker with Japanese Ties Key to Nissan Decision," January 25, 2015, http://rutherfordtnhistory.org/remembering-rutherford-banker-with-japanese-ties -key-to-nissan-decision/.

4. Gelsanliter, *Jump Start*, 45, 48; V. Gibson, "UAW Agrees with Runyon on Profit," *Tennessean*, December 22, 1981.

5. C. Dole, "Here Come the Made-in-US Minitrucks," *Christian Science Monitor*, June 5, 1981.

6. Gelsanliter, *Jump Start*, 57.

7. J. Tenpenny, "Nissan Impacts Area, Nation," *Daily News-Journal*, June 16, 1983.

8. J. Tenpenny, "UAW Push NOT Set for Job 1," *Daily News-Journal*, June 15, 1983; J. Tenpenny, "UAW Promises to Organize Nissan," *Daily News-Journal*, June 16, 1983.

9. Owen Bieber, Report: International Metalworkers Federation Executive Committee and Central Committee Meeting, Zurich, Switzerland, June 7–10, 1983, Owen Bieber Accession 1270, Series II, box 20.3, United Auto Workers Collections, Walter P. Reuther Library Archives, Wayne State University, Detroit, Michigan (hereafter UAWC).

10. J. Tenpenny, "Nissan Job 1," *Daily News-Journal*, June 12, 1983.

11. F. Swoboda, "GM Agrees to Let UAW Organize Plants in South," *New York Times*, September 12, 1978; M. Sorge, "UAW's Top Problems," *Automotive News*, May 9, 1983; L. Windham, "VW Workers Not the First Southern Auto Workers to Face Choice on Union," *Facing South*, February 12, 2014.

12. Gelsanliter, *Jump Start*, 46–48.

13. "Cross Country," *Wall Street Journal*, February 22, 2014.

14. Robert E. Cole, "Japanese Unions," remarks by Prof. Robert E. Cole at UAW Production Workers' Conference, Detroit, February 18, 1982.

15. "Cross Country."

16. "Japan's U.S. Plants Go Union," *Business Week*, October 5, 1981.

17. J. Holusha, "In Tennessee, the U.S. and Japan Mesh," *New York Times*, June 16, 1983.

18. W. Brown, "The UAW's Tennessee Test," *Washington Post*, July 27, 1989.

19. "Nissan's U.S. Plant to Build New Car," *New York Times*, April 4, 1984.

20. E. Baxter, "Nissan Expansions Killed Union," *Tennessean*, December 8, 1989.

21. S. Lohr, "Nissan Uses Japan's Ways in Tennessee," *New York Times*, April 4, 1983; D. Vise, "The Japanese Style Is Catching on in Tennessee," *Washington Post*, July 25, 1982.

22. Gelsanliter, *Jump Start*, 59–60.

23. E. Gregory, "Corporate, Civic Roles Earn Respect," *Tennessean*, September 12, 1987.

24. K. Sawyer, "Nissan's Tennessee Plant Cool to Labor Organizers," *Washington Post*, June 19, 1983.

25. Lohr, "Nissan Uses Japan's Ways in Tennessee."

26. Stephen P. Yokich, "Country Report," Japan Institute of Labour, Tokyo, April 17, 1984, 8, Stephen P. Yokich Accession, UAWC.

27. L. Human, "Japan Trip," *Tennessean*, October 6, 1981.

28. R. Evans and R. Novak, "Smyrna's Nissan Plant Has Non-Union 'Utopia,'" *Tennessean*, September 28, 1983.

29. V. Gibson, "UAW Agrees with Runyon on Profit," *Daily News-Journal*, December 22, 1981.

30. "Labor Costs at Smyrna Plant Offset Tariff Savings," *Tennessean*, July 12, 1983.

31. Human, "Japan Trip."

32. G. Miles, "Nissan Says High Labor Costs Threaten Its US Truck Plant," *Christian Science Monitor*, May 27, 1983.

33. "Nissan May Lose 1st 5 Years in Smyrna," *Tennessean*, December 22, 1981.

34. "UAW Head Predicts a Nissan Union," *Daily News-Journal*, September 6, 1982.

35. D. Jarrard, "UAW Says Nissan Union a Must," *Tennessean*, June 14, 1983.

36. Gelsanliter, *Jump Start*, 66.

37. "Services This Morning for UAW National Organizer Jim Turner," *Tennessean*, April 25, 1989.

38. A. Cason, "UAW Plans to Start Organizing When Nissan Begins Hiring," *Tennessean*, September 12, 1981.

39. "Nissan Non-Union Talk No Surprise," *Daily News-Journal*, September 13, 1981.

40. "Plans for Stepping Up Nissan Unionizing Set," *Tennessean*, March 23, 1983.

41. Jarrard, "UAW Says Nissan Union a Must."

42. "Nissan Awards U.S. Contracts," *Daily News-Journal*, October 2, 1983.

43. Inter-Office Communication, Leonard Page to Dick Martin et al., June 6, 1983, Owen Bieber Accession 1270, Series IX, box 155.111, UAWC.

44. Inter-Office Communication, Stephen Yokich to Ray Majerus, August 24, 1983, Owen Bieber Accession 1270, Series IX, box 155.111, UAWC.

45. J. Tenpenny, "UAW Push Not Set for Job 1," *Daily News-Journal*, June 15, 1983.

46. J. Holusha, "In Tennessee, the U.S. and Japan Mesh," *New York Times*, June 16, 1983.

47. Human, "Japan Trip."

48. "UAW Boss Bieber Upholds Export Cut," *Japan Times*, April 26, 1984.

49. For example, "If Nissan's Good for Nashville, Why Not Toyotas from Tennessee, Too?," *Daily News-Journal*, August 8, 1982.

50. M. Tucker, "Additional Hearings Scheduled on Domestic Content Bill," *Rutherford Courier*, April 21, 1983; E. Gregory, "Nissan Managers Use U.S. Style," *Tennessean*, July 8, 1984.

51. J. Pratt, "Saturn Landed," *Tennessean*, July 27, 1985.

52. D. Sherman, "Saturn Timeline: 1982–2009," October 1, 2009, *Automobile*, https://www.automobilemag.com/news/saturn-timeline-1982-to-2009/.

53. Pratt, "Saturn Landed"; R. Hilman, "UAW Achieves Foot-in-Door with Saturn Pact," *Tennessean*, July 30, 1985.

54. G. Patterson, "UAW Is Calling for Union Vote at Nissan Plant," *Wall Street Journal*, May 22, 1989.

55. T. Hundley, "UAW May Be on Line at Nissan's Plant," *Chicago Tribune*, May 14, 1989.

56. E. Baxter, "CEO: Smyrna Plant in It 'for the Long Run,'" *Tennessean*, January 10, 1990.

57. Gelsanliter, *Jump Start*, 66.

58. E. Nelson, "UAW Begins Campaign at Nissan," *Tennessean*, January 19, 1988.

59. Memorandum, Jim Turner to Stephen Yokich, August 24, 1986, Owen Bieber Accession 1270, Series IX, box 155.111, UAWC.

60. John Junkerman, "Nissan, Tennessee," *The Progressive*, June 1987.

61. For example, "Union a Thorn in Nissan's Crown," *Chicago Sun-Times*, May 18, 1987; "Nissan Denies Magazine's Report That Tenn. Crews Are Overworked," *Detroit Free Press*, May 8, 1987; R. Hilman, "Overwork, Intimidation Claimed at Nissan," *Tennessean*, May 7, 1987.

62. D. Whittle, "UAW Plans All-out Nissan Assault," *Daily News-Journal*, August 2, 1987.

63. Whittle, "UAW Plans All-out Nissan Assault."

64. Whittle, "UAW Plans All-out Nissan Assault."

65. R. Hilman, "Auto Union Beefs Up Staff at Nissan Plant," *Tennessean*, August 6, 1987.

66. "AFL-CIO Aiding UAW Unionization Efforts at Nissan," *Daily News-Journal*, October 17, 1987.

67. "AFL-CIO Aiding UAW Unionization Efforts at Nissan."

68. Gelsanliter, *Jump Start*, 68.

69. L. Chappell, "Jerry Benefield," *Automotive News*, May 19, 2008.

70. Gelsanliter, *Jump Start*, 109.

71. D. Whittle, "UAW President to Meet Nissan Workers at Rally," *Tennessean*, January 19, 1988.

72. Gelsanliter, *Jump Start*, 111–12.

73. J. Schlessinger, "UAW Starts Nissan Organizing Drive," *Wall Street Journal*, January 20, 1988; "Draft Remarks of Owen Bieber, Nissan Rally, Smyrna, Tennessee, January 19, 1988," Owen Bieber Accession 1270, Series I, box 11.71, UAWC.

74. E. Nelson, "UAW Refuses to Set Deadline for Plan to Organize Nissan," *Tennessean*, January 20, 1988.

75. Gelsanliter, *Jump Start*, 205–6.

76. Inter-Office Communication, Ben Perkins to Stephen Yokich, March 16, 1988, Owen Bieber Accession 1270, Series IX, box 155.113, UAWC.

77. Inter-Office Communication, Ben Perkins to Stephen Yokich, March 16, 1988, Owen Bieber Accession 1270, Series IX, box 155.113, UAWC.

78. T. Spigolon, "Auto Union Predicting Nissan Win," *Daily News-Journal*, May 15, 1988.

79. Inter-Office Communication, Stephen Yokich to Owen Bieber et al., June 16, 1988, Owen Bieber Accession 1270, Series IX, box 155.113, UAWC.

80. Correspondence, Teruhito Tokumoto to Owen Bieber, April 30, 1988, Ron Gettelfinger Accession, UAWC.

81. D. Whittle, "Nissan Picketers Oppose Union," *Daily News-Journal*, June 9, 1988.

82. "Nissan Employee Group Working against UAW," *Chicago Tribune*, June 26, 1988.

83. Inter-Office Communication, Stephen Yokich to Owen Bieber et al., June 16, 1988, Owen Bieber Accession 1270, Series IX, box 155.113, UAWC.

84. D. Whittle, "Anti-Union Rally Attracts 200," *Daily News-Journal*, June 10, 1988.

85. Whittle, "Anti-Union Rally Attracts 200"; R. Hilman, "UAW to Represent Nissan by Saturn Opening: Organizer," *Tennessean*, July 17, 1988; "Nissan Workers Vow to Fight Union Try," *Tennessean*, July 23, 1988.

86. M. Massing, "Detroit's Strange Bedfellows," *New York Times*, February 7, 1988; J. Holusha, "Union Rebel," *New York Times*, October 23, 1988.

87. Inter-Office Communication, Stephen Yokich to Owen Bieber, June 16, 1988, Owen Bieber Accession 1270, Series IX, box 155.113, UAWC; Owen Bieber to Stephen Yokich, June 17, 1988, Owen Bieber Accession 1270, Series IX, box 155.113, UAWC.

88. Gelsanliter, *Jump Start*, 115; D. Levin, "Showdown for Nissan," *New York Times*, July 26, 1989.

89. Gelsanliter, *Jump Start*, 119.

90. Inter-Office Communication, Stephen Yokich to Owen Bieber, August 15, 1988, Owen Bieber Accession 1270, Series IX, box 155.113, UAWC.

91. "Services This Morning for UAW National Organizer Jim Turner," *Tennessean*, April 25, 1989.

92. Inter-Office Communication, Ben Perkins to Stephen Yokich, January 24, 1989, Owen Bieber Accession 1270, Series IX, box 155.115, UAWC.

93. Correspondence, Jerry L. Benefield to James M. Turner, January 3, 1989; Correspondence, Jim Weaver to Nissan Employees, January 18, 1989, Owen Bieber Accession 1270, Series IX, box 155.115, UAWC.

94. Gelsanliter, *Jump Start*, 196.

95. Inter-Office Communication, Ben Perkins to Stephen Yokich, January 24, 1989, Owen Bieber Accession 1270, Series IX, box 155.115, UAWC.

96. E. Baxter, "Nissan Expansions Killed Union," *Tennessean*, December 8, 1989.

97. E. Baxter, "Nissan Workers Now in the Driver's Seat," *Tennessean*, May 21, 1989.

98. E. Baxter, "UAW Seeks 168 Signature Cards at Nissan," *Tennessean*, April 27, 1989.

99. Minutes, UAW International Executive Board, May 30–June 1, 1989, UAW International Executive Board Accession 1270, 54, box 11, UAWC.

100. E. Groat, "Union Victorious at Mack Trucks Plant," Associated Press, April 28, 1989.

101. E. Baxter, "Change Would Be Certain If Nissan Went Union," *Tennessean*, May 19, 1989.

102. S. Stockard, "Anti-UAW Foes Rally," *Daily News-Journal*, May 18, 1989.

103. S. Stockard, "Eligible Nissan Voters Issue in Union Election," *Daily News-Journal*, June 1, 1989; E. Baxter, "Nissan, Union Agree to July 26–27 Vote," *Tennessean*, June 7, 1989.

104. S. Stockard, "Nissan Expects UAW Vote to Fail," *Daily News-Journal*, May 19, 1989.

105. "UAW, Nissan Accusing Each Other of Delay," *Daily News-Journal*, June 3, 1989.

106. Gelsanliter, *Jump Start*, 196.

107. K. Crowe, "Stakes High in UAW-Nissan Conflict," *Newsday*, July 23, 1989.

108. P. Applebome, "Union and Nissan Near a Showdown," *New York Times*, April 28, 1989.

109. S. Stockard, "Wages, Benefits OK: UAW Foes," *Daily News-Journal*, July 25, 1989.

110. Gelsanliter, *Jump Start*, 202; J. Risen, "Discontent Spurs UAW Chances in Key Nissan Vote," *Los Angeles Times*, July 22, 1989.

111. Hundley, "UAW May Be on Line at Nissan's Plant."

112. Gelsanliter, *Jump Start*, 200.

113. G. Patterson, "Labor Showdown," *Wall Street Journal*, July 25, 1989.

114. Patterson, "Labor Showdown."

115. Patterson, "Labor Showdown"; Levin, "Showdown for Nissan."

116. "Workers' Health and Safety Awareness Weekend," *Daily News-Journal*, July 10, 1989; L. Moore, "Some Boo, Chant during Nissan 'Performance,' Workers Report," *Tennessean*, July 26, 1989.

117. E. Baxter, "Change Would Be Certain If Nissan Went Union," *Tennessean*, May 19, 1989; E. Baxter, "Labor Department Tells Nissan to Open Injury Logs to Workers," *Tennessean*, May 24, 1989.

118. E. Baxter, "State, Nissan Locked in Job-Injury Records Battle," *Tennessean*, June 21, 1989.

119. E. Baxter, "State Fines Nissan for Not Releasing Worker Injury Log," *Tennessean*, June 23, 1989.

120. "Nissan Records Refusal Confirms Claims: UAW," *Daily News-Journal*, June 22, 1989.

121. Gelsanliter, *Jump Start*, 198–199.

122. Timothy J. Minchin, "Showdown at Nissan: The 1989 Campaign to Organize Nissan in Smyrna, Tennessee, and the Rise of the Transplant Sector," *Labor History* 58, no. 3 (2017): 406.

123. E. Baxter, "Pro-Union Flier at Nissan Touts Ford Wages," *Tennessean*, July 18, 1989; E. Baxter, "Union Election at Nissan Has World's Attention," *Tennessean*, July 24, 1989.

124. Gelsanliter, *Jump Start*, 204; S. Stockard, "Wages, Benefits OK: UAW Foes," *Daily News-Journal*, July 25, 1989; Patterson, "Labor Showdown."

125. Inter-Office Communication, Don Stillman to Ben Perkins, July 21, 1989, Owen Bieber Accession 1270, Series IX, box 155.116, UAWC.

126. M. West, "Whole World Watching," *Rutherford Courier*, July 27, 1989.

127. "Where UAW Organizers Turn Next in Smyrna?," *Rutherford Courier*, August 3, 1989.

128. S. Stockard, "UAW Win Could Hurt Local Economy: Officials," *Daily News-Journal*, July 23, 1989.

129. Gelsanliter, *Jump Start*, 209.

130. Minchin, "Showdown at Nissan," 409.

131. Gelsanliter, *Jump Start*, 203.

132. J. Zimanek, "Nissan Makes a Million," *Daily News-Journal*, July 19, 1989; Crowe, "Stakes High in UAW-Nissan Conflict."

133. S. Stockard, "UAW Backers Claim Nissan 'Setup,'" *Daily News-Journal*, July 26, 1989; Moore, "Some Boo, Chant during Nissan 'Performance,' Workers Report."

134. L. Moore, "Nissan Waits for UAW Vote Tally," *Tennessean*, July 27, 1989.

135. L. Moore, "Nissan Wins," *Tennessean*, July 28, 1989.

136. D. Levin, "Nissan Workers in Tennessee Spurn Union's Bid," *New York Times*, July 28, 1989.

137. "American Nissan Workers Vote to Reject Union," *Deseret News*, July 27, 1989.

138. Moore, "Nissan Wins."

139. J. Risen, "UAW Rejected at Nissan Plant in Major Defeat," *Los Angeles Times*, July 28, 1989.

140. Gelsanliter, *Jump Start*, 205.

141. Risen, "UAW Rejected at Nissan Plant in Major Defeat."

142. "Where UAW Organizers Turn Next in Smyrna?"

143. Levin, "Nissan Workers in Tennessee Spurn Union's Bid."

144. D. Whittle and J. Pochel, "Margin No Surprise to Officials," *Daily News-Journal*, July 27, 1989; D. Landis, "UAW Loses Nissan Election," *USA Today*, July 28, 1989.

145. L. Moore, "UAW May Have to Rethink Tactics," *Tennessean*, July 30, 1989.

146. K. Bradsher, "United Auto Workers Make Bold, New Bid to Unionize Nissan Plant," *New York Times*, August 14, 2001.

147. "UAW Leader Vows to Return to Nissan," *Newsday*, August 18, 1989.

148. Inter-Office Communication, Leonard Page to Owen Bieber and Stephen P. Yokich, December 8, 1988, Stephen P. Yokich Accession, UAWC.

149. Inter-Office Communication, Stephen P. Yokich to Ben Perkins and Dick Shoemaker, December 16, 1988, Stephen P. Yokich Accession, UAWC.

150. "New UAW Division," *New York Times*, September 7, 1989.

151. George Ruben, "Bargaining in 1989: Old Problems, New Issues." *Monthly Labor Review* 113, no. 1 (January 1990): 24.

152. Inter-Office Communication, Leonard Page to Dick Shoemaker, October 30, 1989, Stephen P. Yokich Accession, UAWC.

153. Memorandum, John Christensen to Peter Laarman and Owen Bieber, August 18, 1989, Owen Bieber Accession 1270, Series II, box 24.22, UAWC.

154. S. Stockard, "Worker Says UAW Support Netted Firing," *Daily News-Journal*, August 23, 1989.

155. E. Baxter, "Nissan's Plums Require Sacrifice," *Tennessean*, December 24, 1989.

156. "Nissan Applicant," *Daily News-Record*, November 30, 1989.

157. S. Stockard, "Appeals Planned to Overturn Alleged Nissan Union Firing," *Daily News-Record*, March 8, 1990.

158. United Auto Workers, *A Strong Union for a Changing World: The Report of the Commission on the Future of the UAW* (Detroit: UAW, 1989), 8–9.

159. United Auto Workers, *A Strong Union for a Changing World*, 11.

160. United Auto Workers, *A Strong Union for a Changing World*, 23, 34.

161. Laird, Long, and Sylvester, "Proposed UAW Transplant Marketing Strategy," February 1992, Stephen P. Yokich Accession, UAWC, 2–4.

162. Laird, Long, and Sylvester, "Proposed UAW Transplant Marketing Strategy," February 1992, Stephen P. Yokich Accession, UAWC, 7–8.

163. Transmittal Slip, Ben Perkins to Stan Marshall and Dick Shoemaker, March 16, 1992, Stephen P. Yokich Accession, UAWC, 7–8.

164. Laird, Long, and Sylvester, "UAW Transplant Marketing Project. Implementation Plan," April 10, 1992, Stephen P. Yokich Accession, UAWC.

165. Memorandum, Greer, Margolis, Mitchell, Grunwald & Associates to Ben Perkins, November 13, 1992, Stephen P. Yokich Accession, UAWC.

166. Greer, Margolis, Mitchell, Grunwald & Associates; Lauer, Lalley & Associates, Inc.; and the November Group, Inc., "Organizing the Transplants: A Proposal Presented to the International Union, UAW," January 14, 1993, Stephen P. Yokich Accession, UAWC, 5.

167. Dick Shoemaker, "Focus Group," April 14, 1994, and "Toyota Focus Group," April 21, 1994, Stephen P. Yokich Accession, UAWC.

168. Greer, Margolis, Mitchell, Grunwald & Associates; Lauer, Lalley & Associates, Inc.; and the November Group, Inc., "Transplant Recommendations," February 17, 1995, Stephen P. Yokich Accession, UAWC, 1.

169. D. Winter, "1999 Harbour Report," *Wards Auto*, July 1, 1999.

170. D. Nauss and M. Magnier, "Nissan Is Struggling to Shift Out of Reverse," *Los Angeles Times*, January 31, 1999.

171. Inter-Office Communication, Ben Perkins to Owen Bieber, Stan Marshall, and Dick Shoemaker, March 7, 1994, Stephen P. Yokich Accession, UAWC.

172. Inter-Office Communication, Ben Perkins to Owen Bieber, Stan Marshall and Dick Shoemaker, March 7, 1994, Stephen P. Yokich Accession, UAWC.

173. M. Davis, "At 4,000,000 Cars, Nissan's Smyrna Plant Just Wants More," *Tennessean*, December 9, 1997.

174. "Union Organization?," *Daily News-Journal*, March 14, 1997; L. Marchesoni, "Workers at Nissan Meet with UAW," *Daily News-Journal*, June 21, 1997.

175. M. Davis, "At 4,000,000 Cars, Nissan's Smyrna Plant Just Wants More," *Tennessean*, August 9, 1997.

176. "UAW Casts Its Net at Japanese Carmaker's Workers," *Chicago Tribune*, June 19, 1997.

177. "UAW Petitions Nissan Workers," *Daily News-Journal*, July 31, 1997.

178. C. Giffen, "Unionization Wrong Move for Smyrna Plant," letter, *Daily News-Journal*, August 4, 1997; C. Giffen, "Giffen Encourages Nissan Workers to Review Impact of Unionization," letter, *Rutherford Courier*, August 7, 1997; M. Davis, "UAW Tries Again to Unionize Nissan," *Tennessean*, July 29, 1997.

179. "UAW Ending Nissan Effort," *Daily News-Journal*, September 5, 1997.

180. M. Davis, "Nissan Union Drive Fails to Take Off," *Tennessean*, September 5, 1997.

181. B. Akre, "Nissan Lowering Price on Altima in Price War," *Daily News-Journal*, June 20, 1997; G. Fann, "Nissan Resumes Full Production," *Tennessean*, October 7, 1998; "Nissan Considers Production Cuts, Shutting Plants," *Tennessean*, December 19, 1998; K. Carlson, "Nissan Worker Dies in Accident at Plant," *Tennessean*, October 31, 1999; Winter, "1999 Harbour Report."

182. Nauss and Magnier, "Nissan Is Struggling to Shift Out of Reverse."

183. B. Carey, "Benefield Retires amid Nissan Shakeup," *Nashville Post*, March 16, 2000.

184. M. Magnier, "Sputtering Nissan Shifts Gears," *Los Angeles Times*, December 24, 2000.

185. "Nissan Plans to Expand Plants," *New York Times*, July 21, 2000.

186. Bush Bernard, "Job Security Key to Vote," *Tennessean*, August 15, 2001.

187. K. Bradsher, "Union Moves to Hold Vote at Nissan Plant in Tennessee," *New York Times*, August 15, 2001.

188. T. Sells, "UAW Makes Pitch to Nissan Workers," *Rutherford Courier*, August 23, 2000.

189. Communication, Dave Curson to Stephen Yokich, August 2, 2000, Stephen P. Yokich Accession, UAWC.

190. M. Davis, "UAW Takes Steps to Gauge Interest," *Tennessean*, August 26, 2000.

191. M. Davis, "Midstate Nissan Plants Resisting Union Efforts," *Tennessean*, October 25, 2000.

192. J. Callow, "Union Making Another Push to Organize in Smyrna," *Daily News-Journal*, August 16, 2001.

193. "www.uawnissan.org," pages downloaded on October 2, 2001, Ron Gettelfinger Accession, UAWC.

194. T. Sells, "UAW Makes Its Pitch," *Daily News-Journal*, August 17, 2001.

195. J. Callow, "UAW Files Nissan Vote," *Daily News-Journal*, August 15, 2001.

196. "Nissan Workers Deserve Chance to Vote on Union," *Rutherford Courier*, August 16, 2001.

197. "Nissan Workers Deserve Chance to Vote on Union."

198. Inter-Office Communication, Don Stillman to Stephen Yokich, October 5, 2000, Stephen Yokich Accession, UAWC.

199. IndustriALL, "UAW Makes Bid to Organize Nissan Workers," August 21, 2001, www.industriall-union.org/archive/imf/uaw-makes-bid-to-organise-nissanworkers.

200. IndustriALL, "Nissan Workers to Vote in Tennessee," September 23, 2001, www .industriall-union.org/archive/imf/nissan-workers-to-vote-in-tennessee.

201. IndustriALL, "Nissan USA Interferes in Union Campaign," September 30, 2001, www.industriall-union.org/archive/imf/nissan-usa-interferes-in-union-campaign.

202. J. Dixon, "Ruling Aids UAW's Nissan Drive," *Times Free Press*, September 8, 2001.

203. A. Common Hayes, "Nissan Workers Vote on Union Oct. 3," *Tennessean*, September 27, 2001.

204. "One Point Very Obvious about Nissan/UAW Vote," editorial, *Daily News-Journal*, October 5, 2001; J. Ball, "Vote at Nissan Plant in Smyrna, Tenn., Is Key Union Test," *Wall Street Journal*, September 28, 2001.

205. "www.uawnissan.org," pages downloaded on October 2, 2001, Ron Gettelfinger Accession, UAWC.

206. A. Common Hayes, "Nissan Workers Vote on Union Oct. 3," *Rutherford Courier*, September 27, 2001.

207. B. Bernard, "Nissan, Union Confident Heading into Vote," *Tennessean*, September 28, 2001.

208. B. Bernard, "Nissan Workers Vote on Union," *Tennessean*, October 3, 2001.

209. Bernard, "Nissan, Union Confident Heading into Vote."

210. R. Brewer, "Unionizing Nissan Could Hurt Local Jobs," letter, *Daily News-Journal*, September 30, 2001.

211. J. Gallagher, "Depleted UAW Sees Big Win on Horizon," *Detroit Free Press*, October 2, 2001.

212. Bernard, "Nissan Workers Vote on Union."

213. Gallagher, "Depleted UAW Sees Big Win on Horizon."

214. "One Point Very Obvious about Nissan/UAW Vote."

215. B. Bernard, "Nissan Workers Soundly Reject Union," *Tennessean*, October 4, 2001.

216. Bernard, "Nissan Workers Soundly Reject Union."

217. "Nissan Employees Reject UAW Representation," HRN Guide, October 3, 2001, www.hrmguide.net/usa/relations/nissan_representation.htm.

218. J. Miller, "Nissan Workers Reject UAW," *Detroit News*, October 4, 2001.

219. "One Point Very Obvious about Nissan/UAW Vote."

220. "UAW Comments on Nissan Vote," News from the UAW, October 3, 2001.

221. "UAW Comments on Nissan Vote."

222. Email, Hedy Hilburn to Judy Harden, October 8, 2001, Ron Gettelfinger Accession, UAWC.

223. D. Hakim, "Big Loss at Nissan Seems to Undercut U.A.W. Objectives," *New York Times*, October 5, 2001.

224. Bernard, "Nissan Workers Soundly Reject Union."

225. T. Sells, "Union Rejected," *Daily News-Journal*, October 4, 2001.

226. R. Moore, "Nissan Workers Vote 2 to 1 against UAW at Smyrna Plant," *Nashville Business Journal*, October 4, 2001.

227. Moore, "Nissan Workers Vote 2 to 1 against UAW at Smyrna Plant."

228. Sells, "Union Rejected."

229. "One Point Very Obvious about Nissan/UAW Vote."

230. A. Lindsay, "Resident: 'It's a Blessing from God,'" *Clarion Ledger*, November 10, 2000; M. Burnham, "Starting Construction 'Like Birth of New Life,'" *Clarion Ledger*, April 7, 2001.

231. Pronita Gupta, "The Art of the Deal," *Southern Exposure* 26, nos. 2 and 3 (Summer/Fall 1998): 30.

232. R. Schoenberger, "Mississippi Chosen for Auto Plant, Lawmaker Says," *Clarion Ledger*, October 26, 2000.

233. R. Schoenberger, "Nissan Ushers in New Industry," *Clarion Ledger*, November 10, 2000.

234. E. Wagster, "Musgrove Calls 'Super Project' Session," *Clarion Ledger*, November 2, 2000; M. Burnham, "Starting Construction 'Like Birth of New Life,'" *Clarion Ledger*, April 7, 2001.

235. E. Wagster, "Musgrove Takes Active Role in Luring Nissan," *Clarion Ledger*, November 7, 2000; Schoenberger, "Nissan Ushers in New Industry."

236. Schoenberger, "Nissan Ushers in New Industry"; J. Lyne, "Nissan Driving $950 Million, 4,000-Employee Plant to Mississippi Delta," *Site Selection*, November 13, 2000.

237. S. Metz, "Madison County to Issue Bonds for Roads, Building Training Site," *Clarion Ledger*, November 10, 2000; H. Smith, "New Plant Top Issue for Board," *Clarion Ledger*, December 30, 2000.

238. R. Schoenberger, "Gamblin' Ghosn: Putting Plant in Canton Was 'a Winning Bet'," *Clarion Ledger*, June 7, 2003; "editorial," *Mississippi Press*, June 8, 2003.

239. R. Schoenberger, "Driving toward Profits," *Clarion Ledger*, June 23, 2002.

240. S. Waller, "Nissan Mississippi," *Clarion Ledger*, May 28, 2003; J. Valcourt, "A Year of Triumphs, Troubles," *Clarion Ledger*, May 30, 2004.

241. J. Valcourt, "Downside: Dues, Slide in Number," *Clarion Ledger*, April 20, 2004; J. Valcourt, "Union Cites Contact from Nissan Workers," *Clarion Ledger*, December 4, 2004.

242. J. Valcourt, "Southern Auto Plants," *Clarion Ledger*, February 22, 2004.

243. Derrick Johnson and Lance Compa, "Choosing Rights: Nissan in Canton, Mississippi, and Workers' Freedom of Association under International Human Rights Standards," Mississippi State Conference, National Association for the Advancement of Colored People, Jackson, MS, October 8, 2013, 23.

244. J. Valcourt, "Unions Not Abandoning South," *Clarion Ledger*, April 20, 2004.

245. J. Valcourt, "Paving a New Road," *Clarion Ledger*, May 30, 2004.

246. Valcourt, "A Year of Triumphs, Troubles."

247. Y. Yamaguchi, "Ghosn: Mea Culpa on Nissan Quality," *Automotive News*, September 13, 2004.

248. J. Valcourt, "Union Cites Contact from Nissan Workers," *Clarion Ledger*, December 14, 2004.

249. Johnson and Compa, "Choosing Rights," 23–28.

250. J. Valcourt, "Union Leaders Hear Nissan Complaints," *Clarion Ledger*, March 15, 2005.

251. J. Valcourt, "UAW Opens Site Near Nissan," *Clarion Ledger*, March 23, 2005.

252. Ron Gettelfinger, untitled notes from meeting, February 9, 2007, Ron Gettelfinger Accession, UAWC.

253. T. Burns, "Battle to Unionize Nissan," *Jackson Free Press*, July 18, 2012.

254. S. Anderson, "Solidarity for Black Workers at Nissan," Inequality.org, https://inequality.org/great-divide/stand-black-workers-nissan/.

255. N. Chandler, "UAW Continues Effort to Become Part of the Community," *Clarion Ledger*, May 25, 2008; G. Petty, "Minorities, Immigrants Focus of 3-Day Forum," *Clarion Ledger*, December 3, 2009.

256. Burns, "Battle to Unionize Nissan."

257. D. Moberg, "UAW Plans for Negotiations, Organizing, Rebuilding Power," *In These Times*, March 24, 2011.

258. Moberg, "UAW Plans for Negotiations, Organizing, Rebuilding Power"; "UAW Establishes Global Organizing Institute to Aid in Transplant Organization," *Left Lane*, March 23, 2011.

259. B. Snavely, "UAW Shifts Unionizing Strategy," *Detroit Free Press*, December 8, 2011.

260. United Auto Workers, "When an Election is Neither Free nor Fair: Nissan and the 2017 Union Election in Mississippi," A UAW Briefing Paper, 25 October 2017, https://uaw.org/wp-content/uploads/2017/09/Nissan-Report-3.pdf.

261. B. Hoffman, "Nissan Emerges as Likely UAW Organizing Focus," *Detroit News*, December 8, 2011.

262. B. Woodall, "UAW Targets Nissan Miss. Plant in Organizing Push," Reuters, June 8, 2012.

263. John Price, *Japan Works: Power and Paradox in Postwar Industrial Relations* (Ithaca, NY: Cornell University Press, 1997), 107–10.

264. "Renault," Wikipedia, n.d., https://en.wikipedia.org/wiki/Renault.

265. J. Atkins, "UAW Targets Mississippi Nissan Plant for Its Southern Campaign," *Facing South*, June 25, 2012.

266. B. Hoffman and C. Tierney, "UAW Steps Up Organizing Effort at Nissan," *Detroit News*, June 12, 2012.

267. Atkins, "UAW Targets Mississippi Nissan Plant for Its Southern Campaign."

268. Y. Nakao, "Nissan Rejects U.S. Government Offer to Mediate Mississippi Row," Reuters, November 6, 2012.

269. Correspondence from Fred Dijoux, Laurent Smolnik, Fabian Gâche, and Dominique Chauvin to Carlos Ghosn, December 5, 2012, https://dobetternissan.org/global-support-for-nissan-canton-workers/.

270. Correspondence from Scott E. Becker to Dijoux et al., December 10, 2012, https://www.facebook.com/uaw.union/posts/10154844641821413.

271. Correspondence from Tony Burke to Bob King, December 19, 2012, https://dobetternissan.org/global-support-for-nissan-canton-workers/.

272. Burns, "Battle to Unionize Nissan."

273. B. Woodall, "UAW Sets Sights to Organize Nissan Plant in U.S. South," Reuters, June 8, 2012.

274. Burns, "Battle to Unionize Nissan."

275. J. Amy, "UAW Tries to Organize Nissan Plant in Mississippi," Associated Press, June 4, 2012; Hoffman and Tierney, "UAW Steps Up Organizing Effort at Nissan"; Burns, "Battle to Unionize Nissan"; J. Slaughter, "Nissan Workers Seek Fair Shake in Mississippi Plant," *Labor Notes*, August 2, 2012; S. Greenhouse, "At a Nissan Plant in Mississippi, a Battle to Shape the U.A.W.'s Future," *New York Times*, October 7, 2013; Woodall, "UAW Sets Sights to Organize Nissan Plant in U.S. South."

276. B. Woodall, "UAW Invokes Civil Rights at Nissan's Mississippi Plant," Reuters, July 31, 2012.

277. Amy, "UAW Tries to Organize Nissan Plant in Mississippi."

278. Woodall, "UAW Sets Sights to Organize Nissan Plant in U.S. South."

279. Woodall, "UAW Invokes Civil Rights at Nissan's Mississippi Plant."

280. "UAW Foothold in Mississippi Would Be Bad for Business," editorial, *Mississippi Business Journal*, June 8, 2012.

281. Atkins, "UAW Targets Mississippi Nissan Plant for Its Southern Campaign."

282. Woodall, "UAW Invokes Civil Rights at Nissan's Mississippi Plant."

283. Woodall, "UAW Sets Sights to Organize Nissan Plant in U.S. South."

284. L. Chappell, "UAW Takes a Civil Rights Tone at Nissan," *Automotive News*, February 11, 2013.

285. B. Fletcher, "Black Students Take on Nissan," *The Progressive*, June 1, 2013.

286. L. Chappell, "Danny Glover's New Role," *Automotive News*, April 8, 2013.

287. Burns, "Battle to Unionize Nissan."

288. Atkins, "UAW Targets Mississippi Nissan Plant for Its Southern Campaign."

289. A. Sutton, "United Auto Workers (UAW) Sounds the Alarm about Contract Workers," *Jackson Advocate*, August 9, 2012; Woodall, "UAW Invokes Civil Rights at Nissan's Mississippi Plant."

290. Johnson and Compa, "Choosing Rights," 34–35.

291. Greenhouse, "At a Nissan Plant in Mississippi, a Battle to Shape the U.A.W.'s Future."

292. J. Aktins, "A Right to Choose at Nissan," *Jackson Free Press*, October 31, 2012.

293. A. Thomas-Tisdale, "Nissan Workers Ready for UAW to Show Them the Upside of Collective Bargaining," *Jackson Advocate*, November 11, 2012.

294. "Actor Danny Glover, Nissan Workers Protest for Union Consideration," *Detroit News*, January 12, 2013.

295. J. Ayres, "Group Pushing Union Vote at Nissan Plant," *Clarion Ledger*, January 15, 2013.

296. J. Atkins, "Does UAW Rally at Mississippi College Signal Revival of Labor in the South?" *Facing South*, January 31, 2013.

297. *The Ed Show*, MSNBC, January 29, 2013, https://archive.org/details/MSNBCW _20130130_010000_The_Ed_Show.

298. "Union Backers Say Nissan Threatens Plant Closure," *Jackson Free Press*, January 30, 2013.

299. J. Atkins, "What's Needed for Labor Success in the South: Some Holiness Fire!," *Facing South*, March 4, 2013.

300. "Union Backers Say Nissan Threatens Plant Closure."

301. *The Ed Show*, MSNBC, January 29, 2013.

302. Greenhouse, "At a Nissan Plant in Mississippi, a Battle to Shape the U.A.W.'s Future."

303. J. Ayres, "Local Pro-Union Group, Actor Push for a Vote at Nissan," *Clarion Ledger*, January 30, 2013; S. Jaffe, "Forever Temp?," *In These Times*, January 6, 2014.

304. L. DePillis, "This Is What a Job in the U.S.'s New Manufacturing Industry Looks Like," *Washington Post*, March 9, 2014.

305. Chappell, "UAW Takes a Civil Rights Tone at Nissan."

306. V. Beriwal, "UAW Steps Up Organizing Efforts at Nissan," IHS Global Insight, February 13, 2013.

307. Ayres, "Local Pro-Union Group, Actor Push for Vote at Nissan."

308. IndustriALL, "US Nissan Workers at Geneva Motor Show," press release, March 7, 2013.

309. "Organizing Mississippi Nissan Workers," Building Bridges Radio, May 21, 2013.

310. S. Warburton, "South Africa: UAW and Danny Glover Gain NUMSA Support for Nissan Union Campaign," Just Auto, May 30, 2013, https://www.just-auto.com/news/south -africa-uaw-and-danny-glover-gain-numsa-support-for-nissan-union-campaign/.

311. "Brazil's Lula Excites the Crowd at Opening of 2013 UAW National Community Action Program Conference," Laborweb Preview, February 4, 2013.

312. Correspondence from Luiz Inácio da Silva to Carlos Ghosn and Toshiyuki Shiga, October 4, 2013.

313. A. Ma'at, "Mississippi Alliance for Fairness at Nissan Welcomes Brazilian Trade Union Leader," The Mississippi Link, March 21, 2013.

314. Ma'at, "Mississippi Alliance for Fairness at Nissan Welcomes Brazilian Trade Union Leader."

315. J. Ayres, "Nissan Job Creation Lags," *Clarion Ledger*, May 18, 2013.

316. Correspondence from Javier Urbana and Manuel Garcia Salgado to Ignacio Tor-res Zambrana and Ruth Pina, April 24, 2013, https://dobetternissan.org/global-suppo rt-for-nissan-canton-workers/.

317. Correspondence from Yasunobu Aihara and Akira Takakura to Bob King, June 19, 2013, https://dobetternissan.org/global-support-for-nissan-canton-workers/.

318. "Lawmakers Mull $100 Million in Bonds for Nissan," *Jackson Free Press*, March 27, 2013; J. Atkins, "Smiling in Heaven," *Jackson Free Press*, May 8, 2013.

319. J. Atkins, "Nudging Nissan," *Jackson Free Press*, August 7, 2013.

320. J. Ayres, "Public Support, Climate Topic of Ongoing Debate," *Clarion Ledger*, April 7, 2013.

321. Good Jobs First, "A Good Deal for Mississippi? A Report on Taxpayer Assis-tance to Nissan in Canton, Mississippi," Washington, DC, issued May 2013, updated June 2013, https://www.goodjobsfirst.org/sites/default/files/docs/pdf/nissan_report .pdf.

322. L. Chappell, "UAW Study Chides Nissan for Tax Breaks at Miss. Plant," *Auto-motive News*, May 17, 2013.

323. Ayres, "Nissan Job Creation Lags"; P. Mattera, "How Taxpayers Subsidize Union Avoidance by Wal-mart and Nissan," *Facing South*, June 10, 2013.

324. Johnson and Compa, "Choosing Rights," 2013.

325. J. Atkins, "Nissan Is Violating International Labor Standards at Mississippi Plant, Report Says," *Facing South*, October 11, 2013.

326. S. Warburton, "France: MAFAN Mulls Japan Visit to Press Nissan Mississippi Cause," Just Auto, October 25, 2013, https://www.just-auto.com/news/france-mafan -mulls-japan-visit-to-press-nissan-mississippi-cause/.

327. Warburton, "France: MAFAN Mulls Japan Visit to Press Nissan Mississippi Cause."

328. J. Atkins, "Southern Right-Wingers Wage War against Labor," *Facing South*, October 21, 2013.

329. T. Warren, "Protests over Mississippi Plant Follow Nissan to Detroit," *New York Times*, January 15, 2014.

330. J. Ayres, "Nissan Group Takes Message to Detroit," *Clarion Ledger*, January 14, 2014.

331. "Celebrities Endorse Union Push at Canton Nissan Plant," *Clarion Ledger*, March 22, 2014; "Common Performs in Support of Nissan Workers," UAW News, March 24, 2014.

332. Ayres, "Nissan Group Takes Message to Detroit."

333. D. Paletta, "UAW Faces another Southern Setback," *Wall Street Journal*, March 14, 2014.

334. J. Atkins, "When You're Down and Out," *Jackson Free Press*, May 14, 2014.

335. "United Automobile Workers Sets Its Sight on Mississippi Nissan," Building Bridges Radio, April 29, 2014.

336. "Nissan Settles Worker's Labor Practice Charge," *Jackson Free Press*, April 4, 2014.

337. J. Atkins, "A Union Presence," *Jackson Free Press*, January 28, 2015.

338. IndustriALL, "UAW and IndustriALL Alert OECD to Rights Abuses at Nissan USA," press release, April 29, 2014.

339. B. Snavely, "UAW Seeks Mediation to Settle Dispute with Nissan in Mississippi," *Detroit Free Press*, April 29, 2014.

340. B. Woodall, "UAW Seeks U.S. State Department Help in Mississippi Spat with Nissan," Reuters, April 28, 2014.

341. "Cochran: State Department Should Stay Out of Nissan Labor Issues," *Mississippi Business Journal*, May 2, 2014.

342. United States National Contact Point for OECD Guidelines for MNEs, "Final Statement," Washington, DC, January 30, 2015, https://2009-2017.state.gov/documents/organization/237185.pdf.

343. "Do better together," https://twitter.com/dobetternissan?lang=en.

344. Atkins, "A Union Presence."

345. J. Atkins, "Hundreds Rally for a Union Election at Mississippi Nissan Plant during Freedom Summer Gathering," *Facing South*, July 7, 2014.

346. "Leader of 50-Million Member Labor Federation Blasts Nissan in Mississippi," *People's World*, October 14, 2014.

347. J. Ayres, "Clergy Group Supports Pro-Union Nissan Workers," *Clarion Register*, October 28, 2014.

348. J. Stoll, "UAW to Ramp Up Efforts to Unionize Mississippi Nissan Plant," *Wall Street Journal*, March 24, 2015.

349. "Canton Nissan Worker Attends White House Summit on Worker Voice," *MS News Now*, October 7, 2015.

350. "Nissan Leading U.S. into 'Temp-Nation,'" *Solidarity*, December 7, 2015.

351. "Video: Nissan Worker Robert Hathorn Speaks to DNC Platform Committee," UAW News, June 10, 2016.

352. Michelle Chen, "Mississippi Autoworkers Mobilize," *Dissent* 64, no. 3 (Summer 2017): 36.

353. Nissan North America and Kelley Service and United Auto Workers, National Labor Relations Board Region 15 Cases 15-CA-145043, 15-CA-150431, and 15-CA-145053, November 30, 2015; J. Amy, "Nissan Charged with Violating Labor Laws in Mississippi," Associated Press, December 5, 2015.

354. "Mississippi Yearning," *Solidarity*, March–April 2017.

355. S. Fowler, "Union Files Complaint against Nissan," *Clarion Ledger*, December 9, 2015.

356. C. Maillard, "La croisade des salaries américains de Nissan pour leurs droits syndicaux," *l'usine nouvelle*, November 12, 2015, https://www.cfdt.fr/portail/actualites/inter national/europe/la-cfdt-renault-soutient-la-creation-d-un-syndicat-dans-le-mississippi -srvl_333485.

357. F. Bergé, "Pourquoi les syndicats américains de Nissan s'invitent chez Renault," *BFM Business*, June 27, 2016.

358. G. Casteel, "Renault-Nissan Mistreats Workers in Mississippi," *Detroit News*, November 22, 2016; J. Atkins, "A French Government Official Weighs In on Nissan," *Jackson Free Press*, May 4, 2016.

359. "Politique anti-syndicale chez Nissan Canton (USA): Christian Hutin interpelle le Gouvernement," Mouvement républicain et citoyen, April 27, 2016, https://www .mrc-france.org/Politique-anti-syndicale-chez-Nissan-Canton-USA-Christian-Hutin -interpelle-le-Gouvernement_a966.html?print=1.

360. "Renault-Nissan interpellé sur des 'pratiques antisyndicales' aux Etats-Unis," *Le Parisien*, June 27, 2016.

361. "Du Mississippi à Paris, pour revendiquer leurs droits," *l'Humanité*, June 29, 2016.

362. Chen, "Mississippi Autoworkers Mobilize," 38.

363. "Situação dos trabalhadores da Nissan serà tema audiencia em comissão," jusbrasil.com.br, April 11, 2016.

364. Casteel, "Renault-Nissan Mistreats Workers in Mississippi."

365. "Protesto contra a Nissan na passagem da Tocha Olímpica," Sindicato dos Metalúrgicos, July 25, 2016, http://metalurgicos.org.br/noticias/noticias-do-sindicato/pro testo-contra-nissan-na-passagem-da-tocha-olimpica/.

366. J. Atkins, "Students and Activists to Protest Nissan's Anti-Union Policies," Alternet, March 26, 2016, https://www.alternet.org/2016/03/students-and-activists-protest -nissans-anti-union-policies/.

367. J. Szczesny, "UAW Ramps Up Pressure to Organize Mississippi Plant," *Wards Auto*, August 10, 2016.

368. A. Wolfe, "Union Effort Intensifies at Nissan," *Clarion Ledger*, February 25, 2017; R. Nave, "Nissan Canton Fined for Safety Violations," *Mississippi Today*, February 21, 2017.

369. R. Reily, "French Official Visits Mississippi to Push for Unionizing," *Manufacturing News*, July 26, 2016.

370. R. Nave, "Nissan Canton Fined for Safety Violations," *Mississippi Today*, February 21, 2017.

371. Nissan Technicians for Truth and Jobs, Facebook, https://facebook.com /NissanTechsforTruth; http://www.nrtw.org/en/print/4547.

372. J. Pender, "Study: Nissan Continues to Pay Off for Mississippi," *Clarion Ledger*, June 23, 2016; "Move Mississippi Forward Press Conference 6/24/16," Mississippi Economic Council, https://msmec.com/move-mississippi-forward-press-conference-6-24-16/.

373. "Nissan Snubs UAW Pressure in Mississippi," *Japan Times*, July 27, 2016.

374. Szczesny, "UAW Ramps Up Pressure to Organize Mississippi Plant."

375. J. Irwin, "UAW Blasts Renault-Nissan for Denying French Lawmaker a Meeting," *Automotive News*, July 27, 2016.

376. Szczesny, "UAW Ramps Up Pressure to Organize Mississippi Plant."

377. IndustriALL, "Workers at Nissan US Fight for the Right to Organize," press release, October 13, 2016; "L'acteur de l'arme fatale manifeste à Paris avec les salaries de Nissan," *ouest france*, October 12, 2016.

378. IndustriALL, "Trade Unions File OECD Case against Renault-Nissan Alliance in Three Countries," press release, December 20, 2016; R. Nave, "Union Complaints about

Nissan's Mississippi Plant Filed in Three Countries," *Mississippi Today*, December 27, 2016.

379. M. Kanell, "Nissan Rejects Charges by Union-Led Protests in Marietta," *Atlanta Journal Constitution*, January 27, 2017; L. Alfs, "70 in Nashville Protest Canton Nissan Plant's Work Conditions," *Tennessean*, January 26, 2017.

380. D. Glover, "Nissan Workers in the South Need a Union," *Newsweek*, March 3, 2017.

381. "March on Mississippi: Danny Glover, Bernie Sanders Are Taking on Nissan," NBC News, March 4, 2017, https://www.nbcnews.com/news/nbcblk/march-mississippi -danny-glover-bernie-sanders-are-taking-nissan-n728776.

382. A. Dreher, "Workers, Advocates and Politicians March for Unionization at Nissan," *Jackson Free Press*, March 6, 2017.

383. J. Davis, "March on Mississippi Held to Support Nissan Workers in Canton, Mississippi," *UAW Region 8 News*, March 6, 2017.

384. "Mississippi Yearning."

385. MAFFAN letter to José Muñoz, *The Ed Show*, MSNBC, January 29, 2013, https:// archive.org/details/MSNBCW_20130130_010000_The_Ed_Show.

386. M. Elk, "Pro-Union Rally in Mississippi Unites Workers with Community: 'We Are Ready,'" *The Guardian*, March 5, 2017.

387. S. Salter, "Nissan March Just a Grab for UAW Relevance," *Clarion Ledger*, March 5, 2017.

388. "Nissan Declines Talks with Union after Mississippi Rally," *Jackson Free Press*, March 24, 2017.

389. M. Elk, "Mississippi Nissan Workers Hope for Historic Win in 14-Year Fight to Unionize," *The Guardian*, July 24, 2017.

390. J. Garrison, "Unions Lead Protest Outside Nissan Dealership in Nashville," *Tennessean*, April 1, 2017.

391. "Nissan Faces More Labor Law Charges at Mississippi Plant," Associated Press, April 10, 2017.

392. M. Elk, "In Louisville, Perez & Bernie Call on Southern Democrats to Embrace Organized Labor," *Payday Report*, April 19, 2017.

393. C. Brooks, "Why Did Nissan Workers Vote No?," *Labor Notes*, August 11, 2017.

394. "UAW Wins Important Round in Fight to Unionize," *Atlanta Black Star*, July 11, 2017; B. Snavely, "UAW Aiming to Unionize Tesla, VW, Nissan Plants," *Detroit Free Press*, February 16, 2017.

395. J. Amy, "Former Contract Workers Key in Mississippi Nissan Union Vote," Associated Press, July 25, 2017; N. Scheiber and B. Vlasic, "U.A.W. Says Nissan Workers Seek a Union Vote in Mississippi," *New York Times*, July 11, 2017.

396. "Nissan Employees Move Forward with Union Organizing Drive," UAW News, July 11, 2017; "Nissan Union Vote Set for Aug. 3–4 in Mississippi," UAW News, July 17, 2017.

397. M. Elk, "UAW Confident in Nissan Union Votes," *Payday Report*, July 21, 2017.

398. J. Amy, "UAW Files for Vote by Workers at Nissan Plant in Mississippi," Associated Press, July 11, 2017.

399. Elk, "Mississippi Nissan Workers Hope for Historic Win in 14-Year Fight to Unionize."

400. J. Diaz, "Can Nissan Organizers Ever Pass Finish Line in Mississippi?" Bloomberg BNA News, July 11, 2017.

401. N. Scheiber, "Nissan Workers in Mississippi Reject Union Bid by U.A.W.," *New York Times*, August 5, 2017.

402. J. Amy, "UAW Nissan Vote," Associated Press, July 16, 2017.

403. "No to the UAW at Nissan," editorial, *Madison County Journal*, July 19, 2017.

404. M. Elk, "'Nissan, You Made Us Mad,'" *The Guardian*, August 5, 2017.

405. "UAW Petitions for Union Vote at Nissan's Mississippi Plant," CBS News, July 11, 2017, http://cbsnews.com/news/uaw-union-vote-nissan-mississippi-plant/.

406. J. Atkins, "Voices: Anti-Union Intimidation Won the Day at Nissan, but Not the War," *Facing South*, August 11, 2017.

407. United Auto Workers, "When an Election is Neither Free nor Fair," 4.

408. D. Jamieson, "Nissan Launches Anti-Union Blitz ahead of Pivotal UAW Election," Huffington Post, July 30, 2017.

409. J. Miller, "Nissan Union Loss Underscores Labor's Big Dilemma," *American Prospect*, August 8, 2017.

410. Nissan, "Our Team. Our Future," https://nissanourfuture.com/about-us/.

411. Jamieson, "Nissan Launches Anti-Union Blitz ahead of Pivotal UAW Election."

412. A. Wolfe, "Nissan Workers Soundly Reject UAW Representation in Mississippi," *Detroit Free Press*, 4 August 2017; M. Grevatt, "Mississippi Union Organizers at Nissan Vow to Fight on," Southern Workers Assembly, August 9, 2017, http://southernworker .org/2017/08/mississippi-union-organizers-at-nissan-vow-to-fight-on/.

413. "Union Battle," Fox Business, July 21, 2017.

414. Jamieson, "Nissan Launches Anti-Union Blitz ahead of Pivotal UAW Election."

415. B. Snavely, "Trouble Ahead for the UAW after Wide Margin of Defeat at Nissan in Mississippi," *Detroit Free Press*, August 7, 2017.

416. J. Allen, "Making Sense of UAW's Devastating Loss in Mississippi," *In These Times*, August 7, 2017.

417. Interview, Gary Casteel, Cambridge, MA, September 7, 2018.

418. Elk, "UAW Confident in Nissan Union Votes."

419. B. Snavely, "UAW President Hopeful about Campaign to Unionize Nissan Plant," *Detroit Free Press*, July 20, 2017.

420. J. Szczesny, "UAW President Accuses Nissan of Intimidating Workers," *Wards Auto*, July 21, 2017.

421. "Union Battle," *Fox Business*, July 21, 2017.

422. A. Wolfe, "Inside the Fight over Unionizing Nissan," *Clarion Ledger*, August 1, 2017.

423. Elk, "UAW Confident in Nissan Union Votes."

424. "Ex-Fiat Chrysler Executive Charged in Union Official Payoff," *Times Free Press*, July 26, 2017.

425. B. Snavely, "UAW Faces Big Hurdles in Nissan Unionization Vote," *Detroit Free Press*, August 1, 2017.

426. Snavely, "UAW Faces Big Hurdles in Nissan Unionization Vote."

427. J. Irwin, "Union Vote Gets Ugly amid Allegations of Nissan Obstruction, UAW Corruption," *Automotive News*, August 2, 2017.

428. Nissan North America and Kelley Service and United Auto Workers, National Labor Relations Board Region 15 Cases 15-CA-145043, 15-CA-150431, and 15-CA-145053, November 30, 2015, 15-CA-145043, 15-CA-150431, 15-CA-175295, 15-CA-190791, and 15-CA-194155 against Nissan North America, Inc., 15-CA-145053 and 15-CA175297 against Kelly Services, July 28, 2017.

429. C. Isadore, "Nissan Charged with Unfair Labor Practices ahead of Union Vote," CNNMoney, July 31, 2017.

430. J. Diaz, "Can Nissan Organizers Ever Pass Finish Line in Mississippi," Bloomberg BNA News, July 31, 2017.

431. T. Evanoff, "Union Vote at Nissan Canton Plant to Begin Aug. 3," *Commercial Appeal*, August 1, 2017.

432. N. Scheiber, "Racially Charged Nissan Vote Is a Test for U.A.W. in the South," *New York Times*, August 2, 2017; United Auto Workers, "When an Election is Neither Free nor Fair."

433. Irwin, "Union Vote Gets Ugly amid Allegations of Nissan Obstruction, UAW Corruption."

434. Irwin, "Union Vote Gets Ugly amid Allegations of Nissan Obstruction, UAW Corruption."

435. Wolfe, "Inside the Fight over Unionizing Nissan."

436. C. Jackson, "The Nissan Battle Is Heating Up," MS News Now, July 25, 2017; "Nissan Workers in Mississippi Vote on Whether to Unionize," *Jackson Free Press*, August 4, 2017.

437. "Nissan Workers in Mississippi Vote on Whether to Unionize," *Jackson Free Press*, August 4, 2017.

438. Wolfe, "Nissan Workers Soundly Reject UAW Representation in Mississippi."

439. "Statement from UAW President Dennis Williams on Today's Nissan Vote," UAW News, August 4, 2017.

440. "Nissan Threats, Intimidation Tilt Outcome of Union Election in Mississippi," UAW News, August 4, 2017.

441. K. Laing, "UAW Defeated in Bid to Organize Nissan Workers in South," *Detroit News*, August 4, 2017.

442. Nissan Techs for Truth, "It's Time for Unity–Not Union," Facebook, August 5, 2017, https://www.facebook.com/NissanTechsforTruth.

443. "Nissan Threats, Intimidation Tilt Outcome of Union Election in Mississippi"; H. Kanu, "Nissan Faces New Set of UAW Complaints Filed as Polls Closed," Bloomberg BNA News, August 7, 2017.

444. Wolfe, "Nissan Workers Soundly Reject UAW Representation in Mississippi."

445. "UAW Defiant in Mississippi as Union Opponents Celebrate," *Jackson Free Press*, August 7, 2014.

446. Elk, "'Nissan, You Made Us Mad.'"

447. M. Elk, "Nissan Workers Plan to Push Back Following Loss," *Payday Report*, August 8, 2017.

448. Elk, "Nissan Workers Plan to Push Back Following Loss."

449. Brooks, "Why Did Nissan Workers Vote No?

450. Brooks, "Why Did Nissan Workers Vote No?"

451. Brooks, "Why Did Nissan Workers Vote No?"

452. Brooks, "Why Did Nissan Workers Vote No?"

CONCLUSION

1. N. Boudette, "UAW Edges toward Organizing VW Plant in South," *Wall Street Journal*, September 13, 2013.

2. For example, Kate Bronfenbrenner and Tom Juravich, "It Takes More Than House Calls: Organizing to Win with a Comprehensive Union-Building Strategy," in *Organizing to Win: New Research on Union Strategies*, edited by K. Bronfenbrenner et al. (Ithaca, NY: ILR Press, 1998), 19–36; Samuel Estreicher, "Improving the Administration of the National Labor Relations Act without Statutory Change," *Florida International University Law Review* 5, no. 2 (2010): 361–84; Thomas Geoghegan, *Only One Thing Can Save Us: Why America Needs a New Kind of Labor Movement* (New York: New Press, 2014); Steven Greenhouse, *Beaten Down, Worked Up: The Past, Present, and Future of American Labor* (New York: Knopf, 2019); Jane McAlevey, *A Collective Bargain: Unions, Organizing, and the Fight for Democracy* (New York: HarperCollins, 2020).

3. T. Gnau, "Workers at Fuyao Reject UAW," *Dayton Daily News*, November 11, 2017.

4. Mancur Olson, *The Logic of Collective Action: Public Goods and the Theory of Groups* (Cambridge, MA: Harvard University Press, 1965).

5. Eric Levitz, "Unions Have Won the War of Ideas. Will That Win Them Power?," *New York Magazine*, September 4, 2019.

6. For example, Oren Cass, *The Once and Future Worker: A Vision for the Renewal of Work in America* (New York: Encounter Books, 2018); E. Jacobs, "A Q&A with Michael Strain," WorkRise, November 20, 2020, https://www.workrisenetwork.org/working -knowledge/qa-michael-strain.

7. Steven Greenhouse and Harold Meyerson, "Labor's John L. Lewis Moment," *American Prospect*, June 9, 2022.

8. Sharon Block and Benjamin Sachs, *Clean Slate for Worker Power: Building a Just Economy and Democracy* (Cambridge, MA: Labor and Worklife Program, Harvard Law School, 2019).

9. Charles E. Lindblom, *Politics and Markets: The World's Political-Economic Systems* (New York: Basic Books, 1977).

10. Michel Foucault, *The History of Sexuality*, Vol. 1 (New York: Random House, 1978), 82.

11. Michel Foucault, *Discipline and Punish: The Birth of the Prison* (New York: Random House, 1978), 138.

12. Michel Foucault, "Four. 30 January 1980," in *On the Government of the Living: Lectures at the Collège de France, 1979–1980*, edited by Michel Senellart (Basingstoke, UK: Palgrave Macmillan, 2014), 82.

13. N. Scheiber, "A Union Blitzed Starbucks. At Amazon, It's a Slog," *New York Times*, May 12, 2022.

14. Lloyd Ulman, *The Rise of the National Trade Union*, 2nd ed. (Cambridge, MA: Harvard University Press, 1955).

15. Alice Kessler-Harris, "Organizing the Unorganizable: Three Jewish Women and Their Unions," *Labor History* 17, no. 1 (Winter 1976): 5–23.

16. Starbucks, "Expect More Than Coffee," https://www.starbucks.com/careers /working-at-starbucks/culture-and-values/.

17. P. Blest, "Starbucks CEO Howard Schultz Says Companies Are Being 'Assaulted' by Unions," Vice, April 5, 2022, https://www.vice.com/en/article/akv9kp/starbucks -union-howard-schultz.

18. K. Rogers, "Starbucks Hit with Sweeping Labor Complaint Including over 200 Alleged Violations," CNBC, May 6, 2022, https://www.cnbc.com/2022/05/06/starbucks -accused-of-more-than-200-labor-violations-in-nlrb-complaint.html.

19. W. Thornton, "Union: Amazon Interfering in Second Bessemer Election," Advance Local, February 22, 2022, https://www.al.com/business/2022/02/union-amazon-interfering -in-second-bessemer-election.html; J. Love and D. Weissner, "Amazon Accused of Violating U.S. Labor Law after Union Supporters' Arrests," Reuters, February 24, 2022.

20. K. Weise and N. Scheiber, "Amazon Abruptly Fires Senior Managers Tied to Unionized Warehouse," *New York Times*, May 6, 2022.

21. United States Chamber of Commerce, "Stop the PRO Act," https://www .uschamber.com/stop-the-pro-act.

22. For example, Block and Sachs, *Clean Slate for Worker Power*; David Rolf, *A Roadmap to Rebuilding Worker Power* (New York: Century Foundation, 2018), 37–44.

23. For example, Miguel Ángel García Calavia and Michael Rigby, "The Extension of Collective Agreements in France, Portugal and Spain," *Transfer* 26, no. 4 (2020): 399–414; Stephen J. Silvia, *Holding the Shop Together: German Industrial Relations in the Postwar Era* (Ithaca, NY: Cornell University Press, 2013), 18–31.

24. Nooshin Mahalia, "Prevailing Wages and Government Contracting Costs: A Review of the Research," EPI Briefing Paper #215, Economic Policy Institute, Washington, DC, 2008.

25. Joseph Shister, "The National War Labor Board: Its Significance," *Journal of Political Economy* 53, no. 1 (March 1945): 37–56.

26. H. Nolan, "The Case for Sectoral Bargaining Is Now Stronger Than Ever," *In These Times*, May 21, 2020.

27. Marissa Brookes, *The New Politics of Transnational Labor: Why Some Alliances Succeed* (Ithaca, NY: Cornell University Press, 2019).

Bibliography

American Federation of Labor–Congress of Industrial Organizations. "AFL-CIO Executive Council Statement on Volkswagen." February 23, 2016. https://uaw.org/afl-cio-executive-council-statement-on-volkswagen/.

American Federation of Labor–Congress of Industrial Organizations. *At What Cost? Workers Report Concerns about Volkswagen's New Manufacturing Jobs in Tennessee.* Washington, DC: AFL-CIO, 2017.

Applebome, Peter. *Dixie Rising: How the South Is Shaping American Values, Politics, and Culture.* New York: Random House, 1996.

Barnard, John. *American Vanguard: The United Auto Workers during the Reuther Years, 1935–1970.* Detroit: Wayne State University Press, 2004.

Beaumont, Richard A. "Working in the South." In *Southern Business: The Decade Ahead*, edited by David A. Shannon and Rand V. Araskog, 56–71. Indianapolis: Bobbs-Merrill, 1981.

Benjamin, Daniel K. "Voluntary Export Restraints on Automobiles." *PERC Reports* 17, no. 3 (Fall 1999). https://www.perc.org/1999/09/01/voluntary-export-restraints-on-automobiles/.

Bennett, Andrew, and Jeffery T. Checkel. "Process Tracing: From Philosophical Roots to Best Practices." In *Process Tracing: From Metaphor to Analytic Tool*, edited by Andrew Bennett and Jeffery T. Checkel, 3–37. Cambridge: Cambridge University Press, 2014.

Benz, Dorothee. "Organizing to Survive, Bargaining to Organize: Unions Start Using More of Their Potential Power." *Journal of Labor and Society* 6, no. 1 (July 2002): 95–107.

Block, Sharon, and Benjamin Sachs. *Clean Slate for Worker Power: Building a Just Economy and Democracy.* Cambridge, MA: Labor and Worklife Program, Harvard Law School, 2019.

Bromsen, Amy. "Condescending Saviors: Union Substitution at Toyota Motor Manufacturing Kentucky (TMMK)." PhD diss., Wayne State University, 2019, ProQuest 13811305.

Bronfenbrenner, Kate. "No Holds Barred: The Intensification of Employer Opposition to Organizing." Briefing Paper no. 235. Washington, DC: Economic Policy Institute, 2009.

Bronfenbrenner, Kate, and Tom Juravich. "It Takes More Than House Calls: Organizing to Win with a Comprehensive Union-Building Strategy." In *Organizing to Win: New Research on Union Strategies*, edited by K. Bronfenbrenner, S. Friedman, R. W. Hurd, R. A. Oswald, and R. L Seeber, 19–36. Ithaca, NY: ILR Press, 1998.

Brookes, Marissa. *The New Politics of Transnational Labor: Why Some Alliances Succeed.* Ithaca, NY: Cornell University Press, 2019.

Brooks, Chris. "Organizing Volkswagen: A Critical Assessment." *Journal of Labor and Society* 19 (September 2016): 395–417.

Cass, Oren. *The Once and Future Worker: A Vision for the Renewal of Work in America.* New York: Encounter Books, 2018.

Chen, Michelle. "Mississippi Autoworkers Mobilize." *Dissent* 64, no. 3 (Summer 2017): 32–38.

Cole, Robert E. "Japanese Unions." Remarks by Prof. Robert E. Cole at UAW Production Workers' Conference. Detroit, February 18, 1982.

Collier, David. "Understanding Process Tracing." *PS: Political Science and Politics* 44, no. 4 (October 2011): 823–30.

Cutcher-Gershenfeld, Joel, Dan Brooks, and Martin Mulloy. "The Decline and Resurgence of the U.S. Auto Industry." Economic Policy Institute, Briefing Paper #399, May 6, 2015.

Cutcher-Gershenfeld, Joel, Dan Brooks, and Martin Mulloy. *Inside the Ford-UAW Transformation: Pivotal Events in Valuing Work and Delivering Results.* Cambridge, MA: MIT Press, 2015.

DaimlerChrysler. *Annual Report 2000.* https://www.daimler.com/documents/investors /berichte/geschaeftsberichte/daimlerchrysler/daimler-ir-annualreport-2000.pdf.

DaimlerChrysler and World Employee Committee. "Principles of Social Responsibility at Daimler." Stuttgart, Germany, February 2012. http://www.industriall-union.org /sites/default/files/uploads/documents/GFAs/Daimler/principles_of_social _responsibility_at_daimler.pdf.

DaimlerChrysler and World Employee Committee. "Social Responsibility Principles of Daimler Chrysler." Auburn Hills, Michigan, September 2002. https://www .industriall-union.org/sites/default/files/uploads/documents/GFAs/Daimler /daimler-gfa-english.pdf.

Devaney, Dennis M. "Much Ado about Section 8(a)(2): The NLRB and Workplace Cooperation after Electromation and DuPont." *Stetson Law Review* 23, no. 1 (1993): 39–52.

Early, Steve. *Save Our Unions: Dispatches from a Movement in Distress.* New York: Monthly Review Press, 2013.

Estreicher, Samuel. "Improving the Administration of the National Labor Relations Act without Statutory Change." *Florida International University Law Review* 5, no. 2 (2010): 361–84.

Fichter, Michael, and Horst Mund. "Transnationale Gewerkschaftsarbeit entlang globaler Wertschöpfungsketten." In *Wissenschaft und Arbeitswelt—Eine Kooperation im Wandel,* edited by Ludger Pries, Hans-Jürgen Urban, and Manfred Wannöffel, 209–44. Baden-Baden: Nomos edition sigma, 2015.

Foucault, Michel. *Discipline and Punish: The Birth of the Prison.* New York: Random House, 1978.

Foucault, Michel. "Four. 30 January 1980." In *On the Government of the Living: Lectures at the Collège de France, 1979–1980,* edited by Michel Senellart, 72–92. Basingstoke, UK: Palgrave Macmillan, 2014.

Foucault, Michel. *The History of Sexuality,* Vol. 1. New York: Random House, 1978.

Freeman, Richard B., and James L. Medoff. *What Do Unions Do?* New York: Basic Books, 1984.

Freeman, Richard B., and Joel Rogers. *What Workers Want.* Ithaca, NY: Cornell University Press, 1999.

Freightliner LLC and United Auto Workers. "Agreement on Preconditions to a Card Check Procedure between Freightliner LLC and the UAW." Final signature December 16, 2002. https://www.nrtw.org/20050228freightliner.pdf.

Freightliner LLC and United Auto Workers. "Freightliner Corporation and International Union, United Automobile and Agricultural Implement Workers of America (UAW) Local 3520." 2003. https://ecommons.cornell.edu/bitstream/handle/1813 /81151/4215Abbyy.pdf?sequence=1&isAllowed=y.

Freightliner LLC and United Auto Workers. "Freightliner Corporation and International Union, United Automobile and Agricultural Implement Workers of America

(UAW) Local 5285." 2003, https://ecommons.cornell.edu/bitstream/handle/1813
/81150/4205Abbyy.pdf?sequence=1&isAllowed=y.

Freightliner LLC and United Auto Workers. "Tentative Agreement by and between
Freightliner LLC and UAW for the Purpose of Establishing a Card Check Procedure." Final signature December 16, 2002. https://www.nrtw.org/neutrality
/freightliner/Freightliner_Tentative_CA.pdf.

García Calavia, Miguel Ángel, and Michael Rigby. "The Extension of Collective Agreements in France, Portugal and Spain." *Transfer* 26, no. 4 (2020): 399–414.

Gelsanliter, David. *Jump Start: Japan Comes to the Heartland* (New York: Farrar, Straus
& Giroux, 1990).

Geoghegan, Thomas. *Only One Thing Can Save Us: Why America Needs a New Kind of
Labor Movement.* New York: New Press, 2014.

Good Jobs First. "A Good Deal for Mississippi? A Report on Taxpayer Assistance to Nissan in Canton, Mississippi." Washington, DC, issued May 2013, updated June 2013,
https://www.goodjobsfirst.org/sites/default/files/docs/pdf/nissan_report.pdf.

Good Jobs First. "Subsidy Tracker Parent Company Summary: Daimler." http://
subsidytracker.goodjobsfirst.org/parent/daimler.

Greenhouse, Steven. *Beaten Down, Worked Up: The Past, Present, and Future of American Labor.* New York: Knopf, 2019.

Greer, Ian, and Marco Hauptmeier. "Political Entrepreneurs and Co-Managers: Labour
Transnationalism at Four Multinational Auto Companies." *British Journal of Industrial Relations* 46, no. 1 (March 2008): 76–97.

Greer, Margolis, Mitchell & Associates, Inc., Lauer, Lalley & Associates, Inc., and the
November Group, Inc. "Organizing the Transplants: A Proposal Presented to the
International Union, UAW." Washington, DC, January 14, 1993.

Gupta, Pronita. "The Art of the Deal." *Southern Exposure* 26, nos. 2–3 (Summer/Fall
1998): 30–31.

Hamoudi, Sarah. "State Competition for Foreign Direct Investment and Transnational
Automotive Original Equipment Manufacturers in the U.S. South: Effects on
Union Power." Master's thesis, Global Labour University, University of Kassel
and Berlin School of Economics and Law, 2022.

Harris, Kamala D., and Martin J. Walsh. *White House Task Force on Organizing and Empowerment: Report to the President.* The White House, n.d. (released February 7,
2022). https://www.whitehouse.gov/wp-content/uploads/2022/02/White-House
-Task-Force-on-Worker-Organizing-and-Empowerment-Report.pdf.

Hirsch, Barry T. "Sluggish Institutions in a Dynamic World: Can Unions and Industrial
Competition Coexist?" *Journal of Economic Perspectives* 22, no. 1 (Winter 2008):
153–76.

Hirsch, Barry T., and David A. Macpherson. "Union Membership, Coverage, and Earnings from the CPS." Union Membership and Coverage Database, 2022. http://
www.unionstats.com/.

IndustriALL. "Resolution on Volkswagen to Respect Worker Rights in Chattanooga,
Tennessee, USA." IndustriALL Executive Committee Meeting. Frankfurt/Main,
Germany, May 25–26, 2016.

Industriegewerkschaft Metall and United Auto Workers. *Co-determining the Future:
A New Labor Model.* Detroit: UAW, 2013.

Jacobs, A. J. *The New Domestic Automakers in the United States and Canada: History,
Impacts, and Prospects.* Lanham, MD: Lexington Books, 2016.

Jacoby, Sanford M. "Current Prospects for Employee Representation in the U.S.: Old
Wine in New Bottles?" *Journal of Labor Research* 16, no. 3 (Summer 1995):
388–98.

Johnson, Derrick, and Lance Compa. "Choosing Rights: Nissan in Canton, Mississippi, and Workers' Freedom of Association under International Human Rights Standards." Mississippi State Conference, National Association for the Advancement of Colored People, Jackson, MS, October 8, 2013.

Katz, Harry C., Thomas A. Kochan, and Alexander J. S. Colvin. *An Introduction to U.S. Collective Bargaining and Labor Relations*, 5th ed. Ithaca, NY: Cornell University Press, 2017.

Kessler-Harris, Alice. "Organizing the Unorganizable: Three Jewish Women and Their Unions." *Labor History* 17, no. 1 (Winter 1976): 5–23.

Kiley, David. *Getting the Bugs Out: The Rise, Fall, and Comeback of Volkswagen in America*. New York: Wiley, 2002.

King, Bob. "A UAW for the 21st Century." UAW president Bob King's Speech to the Center for Automotive Research Conference, Ann Arbor, Michigan, August 2, 2010.

Kochan, Thomas A. "How American Workers View Labor Unions." *Monthly Labor Review* 102, no. 4 (April 1979): 23–31.

Kochan, Thomas A., Duanyi Yang, William T. Kimball, and Erin L. Kelly. "Worker Voice in America: Is There a Gap between What Workers Expect and What They Experience?" *Industrial and Labor Relations Review* 72, no. 1 (January 2019): 3–38.

Köhler, Holm-Detlev. "From the Marriage in Heaven to the Divorce on Earth: The DaimlerChrysler Trajectory since the Merger." In *The Second Automobile Revolution: Trajectories of the World Carmakers in the 21st Century*, edited by Michel Freyssenet, 309–31. London: Palgrave Macmillan, 2009.

Lindblom, Charles E. *Politics and Markets: The World's Political-Economic Systems*. New York: Basic Books, 1977.

Mahalia, Nooshin. "Prevailing Wages and Government Contracting Costs: A Review of the Research." EPI Briefing Paper #215. Washington, DC: Economic Policy Institute, 2008.

McAlevey, Jane. *A Collective Bargain: Unions, Organizing, and the Fight for Democracy*. New York: HarperCollins, 2020.

Minchin, Timothy J. "Look at Detroit: The United Auto Workers and the Battle to Organize Volkswagen in Chattanooga." *Labor History* 60, no. 5 (2019): 482–502.

Minchin, Timothy J. "Showdown at Nissan: The 1989 Campaign to Organize Nissan in Smyrna, Tennessee, and the Rise of the Transplant Sector." *Labor History* 58, no. 3 (2017): 396–422.

Moody, Kim. *An Injury to All: The Decline of American Unionism*. London: Verso, 1988.

National Right to Work Legal Defense Foundation. "Employees Considering Appeal of Cryptic Ruling Dismissing Federal Racketeering Suit against Freightliner and UAW Union." November 10, 2006. https://www.nrtw.org/news/employees-considering-appeal-of-cryptic-ruling-dismissing-federal-racketeering-suit-against-freightliner-and-uaw-union/.

Niechoj, Torsten. "DaimlerChrysler Establishes World Employee Committee." Eurofound, September 27, 2002. https://www.eurofound.europa.eu/publications/article/2002/daimlerchrysler-establishes-world-employee-committee.

Nunn, Ryan, Jimmy O'Donnell, and Jay Shambaugh. "The Shift in Private Sector Union Participation: Explanation and Effects." The Hamilton Project, The Brookings Institution, August 2019. https://www.brookings.edu/wp-content/uploads/2019/08/UnionsEA_Web_8.19.pdf.

Oeltjenbruns, Henning, Martin Lawaczeck, and Uwe Bracht. "How to Assure Quality Work in Automotive Greenfield Projects—Project Experiences from the New Assembly Plant of Mercedes-Benz, Tuscaloosa, Alabama." Unpublished manuscript, Lubbock, TX, June 23, 1999.

Olson, Mancur. *The Logic of Collective Action: Public Goods and the Theory of Groups.* Cambridge, MA: Harvard University Press, 1965.

Piazza, James A. *Going Global: Unions and Globalization in the United States, Sweden, and Germany.* Lanham, MD: Lexington Books, 2002.

Price, John. *Japan Works: Power and Paradox in Postwar Industrial Relations.* Ithaca, NY: Cornell University Press, 1997.

Rolf, David. *A Roadmap to Rebuilding Worker Power.* New York: Century Foundation, 2018.

Roomkin, Myron, and Hervey Juris. "Unions in the Traditional Sectors: Mid-Life Passage of the Labor Movement." In *Proceedings of the Industrial Relations Research Association, 28–29 December 1977,* edited by Barbara D. Dennis. Madison, 212–22. Madison, WI: Industrial Relations Research Association, 1978.

Rüb, Stefan. "World Works Councils and Other Forms of Global Employee Representation in Transnational Undertakings." Arbeitspapier 55. Hans Böckler Stiftung, Düsseldorf, 2002.

Ruben, George. "Bargaining in 1989: Old Problems, New Issues." *Monthly Labor Review* 113, no. 1 (January 1990): 19–29.

Salmond, John A. *Gastonia 1929: The Story of the Loray Mill Strike.* Chapel Hill: University of North Carolina Press, 1995.

Schneider, Mark C. *Volkswagen: Eine deutsche Geschichte.* Berlin: Berlin Verlag, 2016.

Shister, Joseph. "The National War Labor Board: Its Significance." *Journal of Political Economy* 53, no. 1 (March 1945): 37–56.

Shotwell, Gregg. *Autoworkers under the Gun: A Shop-Floor View of the End of the American Dream.* Chicago: Haymarket Books, 2011.

Silvia, Stephen J. *Holding the Shop Together: German Industrial Relations in the Postwar Era.* Ithaca, NY: Cornell University Press, 2013.

Silvia, Stephen J. "Organizing German Automobile Plants in the USA: An Assessment of the United Auto Workers' Efforts to Organize German-Owned Automobile Plants." Study 349. Hans Böckler Foundation, Düsseldorf, December 2016.

Silvia, Stephen J. "The United Auto Workers Attempts to Unionize Volkswagen, Chattanooga." *Industrial and Labor Relations Review* 71, no. 3 (May 2018): 600–24.

Stiglitz, Joseph. *The Price of Inequality: How Today's Divided Society Endangers Our Future.* New York: Norton, 2012.

Telljohann, Volker. "The Implementation of the Global Labor Relations Charter at Volkswagen." In *Transnational Company Agreements: A Stepping Stone toward a Real Internationalisation of Industrial Relations?,* edited by S. Leonardi, 105–22. Rome: Ediesse, 2012.

Ulman, Lloyd. *The Rise of the National Trade Union: The Development and Significance of Its Structure, Governing Institutions, and Economic Policies.* 2nd ed. Cambridge, MA: Harvard University Press, 1955.

United Auto Workers. *Media Fact Book 2007.* Detroit: UAW, 2007.

United Auto Workers. *Special Convention on Collective Bargaining.* Detroit: UAW, March 24–25, 2015.

United Auto Workers. *A Strong Union for a Changing World: The Report of the Commission on the Future of the UAW.* Detroit: UAW, 1989.

United Auto Workers. "When an Election Is Neither Free nor Fair: Nissan and the 2017 Union Election in Mississippi." September 2017. https://uaw.org/app/uploads /2017/09/WHEN-AN-ELECTION-IS-NEITHER-FREE-NOR-FAIR.pdf.

United Nations. "United Nations Global Compact." 2000. https://www.unglobalcompact .org/.

United States National Contact Point for OECD Guidelines for MNEs. "Final Statement." Washington, DC, January 30, 2015. https://2009-2017.state.gov/documents/organization/237185.pdf.

Vlasic, Bill, and Bradley A. Stertz. *Taken for a Ride: How Daimler-Benz Drove Off with Chrysler.* New York: Wiley, 2000.

Volkswagen Aktiengesellschaft. *Driving Ideas. Geschäftsbericht 2008.* Wolfsburg: Volkswagen, 2008.

Volkswagen Group of America. "HR-C20: Community Organization Engagement." Chattanooga, TN, November 2014.

Volkswagen Group of America and United Auto Workers. "Agreement for a Representation Election." Chattanooga, TN, January 27, 2014.

Index

Figures and tables are indicated by an italic *f* and *t* following the page number.

OECD (Organisation for Economic
Co-operation and Development), 214, 221–22,
224–25, 230, 242
Opel (GM European subsidiary), 69, 76
Organisation for Economic Co-operation and
Development (OECD), 214, 221–22, 224–25,
230, 242
organizing foreign-owned plants: Amazon
and Starbucks unionization contrasted
with, 255–57; card-check procedure and, 5,
254, 257; case studies of, 5–6, 5*t*; constraints
on, 2, 9; data for study of, 6–7; effectiveness
of, 1–7, 251–53; foreign managers and, 3–4;
IG Metall and, 2, 74–75, 258; methodology
for study of, 6–7, 261n6; NLRB and, 7–8;
organization of present volume on, 5;
overview of, 1–6, 5*t*, 251–59; political
intervention and, 3–4, 254–55; repercussions for labor movement of, 7–8, 253–59;
rise of transplants and, 8–12; transnational
cooperation and, 4, 258; UAW membership
and, 9–11, 9*t*; union density and, 8, 11–12,
11*f*, 253–54; union-avoidance playbook and,
3; unusual aspects of, 7–8
Organizing Institute (AFL-CIO), 52, 212
OSHA (Occupational Safety and Health
Administration), 190, 228–29, 238, 243
Oshkosh Custom Chassis plant, 26
Osterloh, Bernd, 98, 100–102, 109, 111–12, 137,
164–66, 168, 172

Page, Leonard, 181, 194–95
Patta, Frank, 102, 104, 111
Patta, Sebastian, 104, 108, 122, 130, 133, 137
Patterson, George, 186, 190
Patterson, Jim, 38
Patterson, Matt, 80, 106, 119, 127
Pawley, Dennis, 54
Payne, Sam, 123
Perez, Thomas, 138, 226, 233
Perkins, Ben, 51, 185, 187, 194, 198–99
personal time off (PTO), 145–46, 167–68
Peter, Kristyne, 223
Peters, Gary, 158
Pfeffer, Earl, 35
Piëch, Ferdinand, 132
Piedmont Associated Industries, 38
Pinto, Antonio, 142, 145, 148, 150, 154–55, 161
Plecas, Amanda, 145, 149, 152, 161, 167
Plessis, Tom du, 171
political intervention: AFL-CIO and, 64;
DTNA and, 13, 41, 87; Freightliner Mount
Holly and, 22, 25; MBUSI and, 50–51, 61,

64, 69, 80; Mercedes-Benz Vance and, 50–51;
Nissan Canton and, 207–10, 221–24, 226,
236, 238, 241–42, 251; organizing foreign-
owned plants and, 3–4, 254–55; union-
avoidance playbook and, 3; Volkswagen
Chattanooga and, 98, 100, 104–6, 108–10,
119–24, 152–59, 173
Porth, Wilfried, 76–77
Portland Freightliner plant, 14–18, 21–22, 24,
26, 34
Pressac, 55
Projections (consultancy), 120
Protecting the Right to Organize Act (2020),
257
PTO (personal time off), 145–46, 167–68

Quigg, Billy, 158, 170

Radabaugh, John, 150
Raina, Jyrki, 225–26
Ramsey, Claude, 111
Reagan, Ronald, 45, 184
recognition elections: Freightliner Mount
Holly and, 15–16, 25; Local 42 and, 132–34,
149–53, 156–57, 160–62, 166, 168, 170;
MBUSI and, 54, 57, 59, 77, 79, 85; Nissan
Canton and, 218, 226, 228, 230, 233–35,
240–41, 243; Nissan Smyrna and, 188–93,
195, 200–205, 245; NLRA and, 7–8, 127–28,
150, 167, 172; overview of, 5–6, 254; Volks-
wagen Chattanooga and, 80, 89, 109–14,
117–18, 122, 126–29, 132–50, 152, 155–63,
171–74, 248–49
Reed, David, 129, 133
Renault, 201, 203, 213–14, 220, 223, 227–28,
230, 241
Renschler, Andreas, 47, 79
Reuter, David, 213, 215, 219
Reuther, Walter, 215
Ridley, Sam, 176
right to work laws, 10, 56–57, 105, 147, 167,
218, 235
Riley, Bob, 63–64
Robinson, James, 135
Rolfe, Bob, 156–57
Romero, Tracy, 147, 169
Roseboro, Stanley, 18, 21, 24
Rothenberg, Brian, 147, 149, 152, 157, 159, 163,
169
Rothschild, Roxanne, 157
Rumpeltes, Denise, 79
Runyon, Marvin, 177–84, 193, 210, 244–45,
250, 253

Printed in the USA
CPSIA information can be obtained
at www.ICGtesting.com
LVHW070713150923
758208LV00003B/546